THE FSG BOOK OF

TWENTIETH-CENTURY

ITALIAN POETRY

THE FSG BOOK OF

TWENTIETH-CENTURY

ITALIAN POETRY

An Anthology

EDITED BY

GEOFFREY BROCK

FARRAR STRAUS GIROUX

NEW YORK

FOR RAVI KEATS AND MIRA FRANCESCA

AND FOR PADMA AND OUR PARENTS

AND WITH GRATEFUL THANKS TO

THE JOHN SIMON GUGGENHEIM MEMORIAL

FOUNDATION AND THE AMERICAN

ACADEMY IN ROME

Farrar, Straus and Giroux
18 West 18th Street, New York 10011

Introduction and selection copyright © 2012 by Geoffrey Brock
All rights reserved
Distributed in Canada by D&M Publishers, Inc.
Printed in the United States of America
First edition, 2012

Owing to limitations of space, permissions
acknowledgments appear on pages 655–672.

Library of Congress Cataloging-in-Publication Data
The FSG book of twentieth-century Italian poetry : an anthology /
edited by Geoffrey Brock. — 1st ed.
    p. cm.
ISBN 978-0-374-10538-9 (alk. paper)
    1. Italian poetry—20th century. I. Brock, Geoffrey, 1964–

PQ4214 .F74 2012
851'.91—dc23

2011036690

Designed by Quemadura

www.fsgbooks.com

1 3 5 7 9 10 8 6 4 2

CONTENTS

INTRODUCTION

GEOFFREY BROCK

Nearly eight centuries ago, believing people should be able to pray in their own tongue, Giovanni Francesco di Bernardone (better known today as Saint Francis) wrote his *Canticle of the Sun* not in Latin, the literary language of the day, but in the dialect of Umbria—and Italian poetry was born. Or else: Nearly eight centuries ago, Frederick of Sicily, the man Dante called the father of Italian poetry, began collecting in his Palermo court the poets (including Giacomo da Lentini, inventor of the sonnet) now known as the Sicilian School, and Italian poetry was born . . .

Other narratives, too, might be offered, but what's beyond dispute is that a lifetime before Dante epitomized the *dolce stil novo* ("sweet new style") and a century before Petrarch immortalized Laura, durable poetry was being written in the vernacular in and around the Italian peninsula. And in any telling, the troubadours—the singer-songwriters of medieval southern France—are a key part of the backstory. The courtly love lyrics of the Sicilian school were written in self-conscious imitation of the troubadours, and even Saint Francis, whose mother was from Provence and who wanted nothing more as a young man than to *be* a troubadour, was steeped in Provençal poetry. But while Saint Francis may plausibly be called the first Italian poet, he can't be said to have had much influence on the course of Italian poetry. It was the Sicilian poets (along with, again, the troubadours) who were the primary influences on the Tuscan School, which culminated in Dante and Petrarch. And it was Dante and Petrarch (along with Boccaccio—since great Italian writers seem to come in threes) whose towering achievements ultimately led the Tuscan dialect to replace Latin as the primary literary language of Italy.

The word *Italy* here is, of course, merely what Metternich called "a geographical expression"; it refers to that jumble of kingdoms and city-states into which the Italian peninsula was for so long carved. Italy as a unified nation would not be born until after the birth of the first several poets in this anthology.

One reason I like to think of Italian literature as beginning with the *Canticle of the Sun* is that metaphors of daylight have, at least since Petrarch, figured memorably in conceptions of it. Petrarch is widely credited with first describing the medieval period as a "dark" age, in contrast to the cultural brilliance of antiquity. If we think of the thirteenth and fourteenth centuries, then, as the dawn of Italian vernacular literature, and of the Renaissance—Machiavelli, Ariosto, Tasso—as midday, and so on (after something of a siesta) through the brightly lit Romantic afternoon of Foscolo, Manzoni, and Leopardi, then we can better understand how some Italians felt by the end of the nineteenth century: as if twilight had fallen. Italian had given birth to a literary tradition to rival that of any European language, but along with it had come a stultifying reverence toward its own eloquent past that bordered on fetishism—an attitude known as *passatismo*.

To be fair, the best Italian minds, for much of the nineteenth century, had been engaged with more pressing matters than poetry. After centuries of foreign rule, a resurgence of nationalist sentiment gradually coalesced into a movement—now known as the Risorgimento—to liberate and unify the Italian peninsula. The movement's origins can be traced back to the fall of Napoleon I and the Congress of Vienna, which redrew the map of Europe in 1815; its aims were not achieved until after Napoleon III withdrew the last of his troops from Rome in 1870. It's a period that overlaps closely with Italy's idiosyncratic brand of Romanticism, which because of the political backdrop was generally more nationalistic and less individualistic than its counterparts in other countries.

Once unification was achieved, however, and Italy the geographical expression had evolved into Italy the nation, poets could begin to sing again of matters other than *libertà*. And if nations need national poets ("If hours be years"), Italy had one at the ready in Giosuè Carducci, a classicist whose stately, backward-looking, marmoreal verse stands as a monument to *pas-*

satismo. For the latter third of the nineteenth century he was the de facto poet laureate of Italy, occupying the nation's most prestigious professorship, the very title of which—Professor of Italian Eloquence (later renamed "Professor of Italian Literature")—suggests one of the difficulties facing poets who might have wished to look forward toward a new day, rather than backward: Italian eloquence was seen as virtually synonymous with Italian literature. Yet many felt the paths up the Parnassian slopes had been worn into ruts, or that eloquence was fundamentally ill-suited to the harsh mechanical realities of the new millennium—or both.

Those who came after Carducci attempted to come to grips with what might be called "the eloquence problem" in various ways. The two other major poets of the fin-de-siècle triad—Giovanni Pascoli and Gabriele D'Annunzio—were a generation younger than Carducci, and their radically different approaches to the problem had serious implications for modern poetry. D'Annunzio saw no sunset or, if he did, didn't doubt his own ability to single-handedly turn back the sun. His poetry, steeped in myth and symbol, pursued Eloquence and Beauty and all the other capitalized virtues, and sometimes achieved them—he was indeed a prodigiously gifted stylist and rhetorician. Pascoli, on the other hand, took a humbler, more homespun approach. At his worst he was mawkish, but at his best his relatively plainspoken style provides what Joseph Cary, in his outstanding book *Three Modern Italian Poets*, calls "a rough antithesis or even antidote" to the grandeur, or grandiosity, of Carducci and D'Annunzio. Pascoli's world consisted of carefully observed "*piccole cose*," small things, which he named and described with a precision new to Italian poetry—not exactly "no ideas but in things," but (especially in his early work) a real step in that direction. The title of his first book, *Myricae*, is neatly emblematic of this aspect of his poetics: taken from a reference by Virgil to "humilesque myricae," humble tamarisks, it emphasizes the humble object, properly named. It also, of course, emphasizes Pascoli's old-fashioned classical erudition: he in fact composed a large body of poetry in Latin, and even wrote occasional pieces—such as the epigram that opens this anthology, a tribute to Carducci, his mentor—in ancient Greek.

Pascoli and D'Annunzio, then, can be seen as Janus figures, straddling the nineteenth and twentieth centuries. The extent of D'Annunzio's sway was enormous, if often negative; his influence on many poets can be best described by the ways in which they reacted *against* him. Pascoli, on the other hand, while not completely modern himself, can in certain respects be seen to point a way, especially in the fragmentary, image-driven, muted tones of his earlier work, toward modernity.

The early twentieth century was marked, even before World War I, by a radical break with the poetry of the past and an explosion of new styles as Italian poets tried to find their places in a world of motor cars and aeroplanes. In the first two decades there were the Crepuscularists and the Futurists; there were the poets who clustered around influential new journals such as the reform-minded *La Voce* and the avant-garde *Lacerba*; on a completely different cultural stratum, there were enormously popular dialect poets (usually omitted from anthologies of highfalutin verse) such as Salvatore Di Giacomo and Trilussa; and of course there were also solitary figures who did not belong to any camp, such as the *poète maudit* Dino Campana, who in 1914 self-published his only book, the dizzying, expressionistic classic *Canti orfici* (*Orphic Songs*), and then spent most of the rest of his life in a psychiatric hospital.

Crepuscularism has been called the first Italian literary movement of the new century, but it was less a movement than a pathology. The critic Giuseppe Antonio Borgese first used the term *crepuscular* to describe (and disparage) the work of a group of young poets—Sergio Corazzini, Corrado Govoni, and Guido Gozzano, among others—who seemed wholly resigned to the notion that theirs was a twilit age. Active in the first years of the century, they took Pascoli's humility and plain speech to often dull and sometimes bathetic extremes. Italian poetry, according to Borgese, was "growing dim . . . in a mild, protracted twilight," and Italian poets were mired in "the gloomy, murky melancholy of having nothing to say or do." Corazzini perhaps best embodies the negative qualities associated with Crepuscularism, while Gozzano, thanks to his saving wit and irony, is often so good that the label's negative connotations simply don't apply. Indeed, Gozzano's death from tuberculosis in 1916, at the age of thirty-two, deprived modern Italian poetry of one of its most promising voices.

If Crepuscularism soon went gentle into a good night of its own making, another *ism* was set to rage onto the scene. In 1909, Filippo Tommaso Marinetti published *The Futurist Manifesto*, a seismic event that can be understood only against the backdrop of the *passatismo* that fostered it. Marinetti's literary doctrines were, as Lawrence R. Smith observes in the introduction to his excellent anthology of post-1945 Italian poetry, "the most radical the world had ever seen." And though Futurism produced little of lasting literary value—indeed, the manifesto itself might be considered the movement's highest poetic achievement—it had a profound influence on every subsequent European and American avant-garde movement, in addition to serving as a much-needed shock to Italian poetry of the day. Marinetti's ideas (and his genius for propaganda) energized a group of talented young poets including Aldo Palazzeschi, Corrado Govoni, and Ardengo Soffici, all of whom, during the movement's brief heyday in the mid-teens, called themselves Futurists and participated in the poetic experimentation that shook the Italian tradition right down to its dusty plinth. But these poets, and indeed nearly all of Marinetti's early followers, soon left his side to seek their own paths, leaving the founder of Futurism only a few minor, if often amusing, acolytes (see the brief selections by Farfa, Fillia, and Pino Masnata). But Marinetti's work was already done: he had flung open the doors to the future, creating a world in which almost anything seemed possible—except going backward. And this, it seems to me, remains his best legacy.

The tradition of viewing Italian literature as shaped by a series of triads of major writers, though inevitably reductive, is a venerable and sometimes valuable one. The twentieth century, for example, might usefully be viewed in terms of two triads. The first—Carducci, Pascoli, D'Annunzio—casts its shadow over much of the first half of this anthology despite having ceased to be a creative force by the time of Marinetti's manifesto: Carducci had died in 1907, having just received a deathbed Nobel but having written virtually nothing in the new century; Pascoli died in 1912 after declining in his last years into the role, left vacant by Carducci, of national poet; and D'Annunzio, though still very much alive, had long since ceased to be a poet, reinventing himself as an action hero and proto-

Fascist. (In 1919, he infamously raised a private army, captured the disputed Austrian port of Fiume, and ruled it as an independent city-state—he called it a "dictatorship of art"—for nearly sixteen months, relying on tactics and rhetoric that profoundly influenced Mussolini.) Yet writers continued for decades to react in various ways against those three poets, even while being, in other ways, positively influenced by them. Smith explains that for many poets of that era the triad, despite major differences among them, stood almost monolithically for "artificial language and diction, and the heavy use of rhetoric and classical literary convention." The Crepuscularists and the Futurists had both, in their starkly different ways, defined themselves against these qualities, but it was the second triad of the century that would succeed in stripping away the stale language and rhetoric in ways that made them truly modern. By 1925, the year Mussolini adopted the title *Duce*, the three poets who were to leave the deepest impressions on the century—Umberto Saba, Giuseppe Ungaretti, and Eugenio Montale—had all revealed their distinctive geniuses, and the "mild protracted twilight" of the first decade was a dim memory.

Of the three, Saba was the eldest, the first to publish, and the last to have his achievement fully recognized. This latter fact may be partially due to his work's apparent simplicity (as deceptive as Frost's) and to the feeling that, compared with his fellow Modernists, he was the least "modern," particularly formally. Yet Saba's idiom—his tone, his diction, his intimate directness—was utterly new, and though he did have a classical sense of poetic form, his handling of it was unmistakably fresh. He rejected not only the pessimism of the Crepuscular poets but also the radicalism of the Futurists, feeling that their "uncontrollable desire to be original" resulted in mere novelty. The path to authentic originality led, he believed, through the forest of the self, and his was arguably more dense and difficult than most. Born Umberto Poli to a Jewish mother and a non-Jewish father who left before his son was born, Saba grew up among Jews but admits, "I never felt myself anything but an Italian among Italians." (This despite the fact that his native Trieste belonged to the Austro-Hungarian Empire, not Italy, until Saba was in his mid-thirties.) His sexual identity, too, was complex: homosexual love poems stand alongside love poems to his wife. Saba seems to have forged his vexed identity in his poems. His masterpiece, *The Song-book*—which has been called both a "lyrical autobiography" and a "psychological novel"—first appeared in 1921 and continued to evolve and expand (much like *Leaves of Grass*) over the next several decades, containing in the end more than four hundred poems.

Ungaretti had little in common with Saba. Born in Egypt and educated primarily in French, influenced by both Futurism and French Symbolism, he developed a radically pared-down style (stripping away traditional meters and punctuation, fracturing syntax) through which he sought to unify and reconcile, as Robert Dombrowski has observed, "the atemporality of being and events experienced within the flux of time." In 1919 he published his first major collection, *Allegria di naufragi* (*Joy of Ship-wrecks*), which includes many of the minimalist masterpieces, written when he was a soldier on the front, for which he remains best known. In the 1920s, Ungaretti (like many Italian intellectuals, though unlike Montale or Saba) was seduced by Mussolini's populist message and joined the Fascist party. He was motivated, however, as Luciano Rebay has demonstrated, by misplaced idealism rather than nationalism or racism, and indeed when the Racial Laws were passed, Ungaretti opposed them. (He and Montale were among the friends who harbored Saba after he fled Trieste in the wake of those laws.) And while Montale and Saba both gradually evolved over the course of their careers away from Italian metrical traditions, Ungaretti went in the opposite direction, turning after his avant-garde beginnings back to the hendecasyllable (the Italian counterpart of our iambic pentameter), which he came to regard as "the natural poetic measure of Italian speech."

Montale was the youngest of the three and the last to publish, but when his first collection, *Ossi di seppia* (*Cuttlefish Bones*), appeared, he was quickly recognized as a major voice. Like Ungaretti, Montale had served in the war, though in his case one would hardly guess from the poems. And compared with the formal radicalism of Ungaretti's early style, Montale's early work looks almost traditional. His subversions of tradition, however, if less obvious, were arguably equally influential: his rhythms and rhymes are often roughened around the edges, and his lexicon mixes low and high, eloquence and anti-eloquence—creating dissonances that get under the skin of his harmonies, resulting in what Jonathan Galassi has called "a nervous, astringent music." If this music is the typical score of a Montale poem, the corresponding scenery is often the "rocky and austere" Ligurian coastal landscape of his youth; he spent his summers until he was thirty in the Cinque Terre area, which despite its astonishing beauty (it is now an enormously popular tourist destination) figures in his poetry as a kind of wasteland. Set against such music and scenery, the typical dramas of Montale's poems are, as in Dante, both existential and passionate. Many of his poems feature an interlocutor, nearly always female, and though they were based on real-life women, they are, as Montale insisted, "Dantesque, Dantesque"—by which he meant that, like Beatrice (and unlike, say, the women in Saba's poems), they are more figurative than literal. After publishing only three full-length volumes in his first seventy-five years, all of them major monuments of Italian poetry, he published four in his final decade, in a fluid, almost diaristic style that differed markedly from his chiseled earlier work. In 1975, exactly fifty years after his debut, he received the Nobel Prize.

In short, by 1925—though no one knew it yet—a new triad was at work, one that would cast its shadow, in turn, over the rest of the century. Though all three of its members (even Saba, I would argue) were formally innovative in various ways, and though Ungaretti was positively revolutionary, none defined himself against the poetic *forms* of the past to the degree that, say, Pound and Williams did in the American tradition. Indeed, my sense is that the Modernist revolution was, for Italians (as it was, arguably, for the British and Irish), more tonal and rhetorical than formal. I don't want to overstate this difference, because it's clear that the various brands of Modernism sought to "make it new" in all those ways. But the contrast between Pound's and Montale's retrospective descriptions of their early intentions is telling: Pound's "first heave" was "to break the pentameter," while Montale (echoing Verlaine) wanted "to wring the neck of the eloquence of our old courtly language."

The tradition of Italian eloquence weighed far more heavily on Montale, and on most modern Italian poets, than did the hendecasyllable. Indeed, none of the three major Italian Modernists mentioned above had the sort of hostile relationship to received forms that Pound and Williams had, and all produced (like Eliot and Stevens) important work in both metrical and free verse. Two poets of a later generation, Allen Ginsberg and Pier Paolo Pasolini, also make for an interesting juxtaposition in this regard: committed leftists of roughly the same age whose celebrity would soon go far beyond the poetry world, they published their most important poems within a year of each other ("Howl" in 1956 and "Gramsci's Ashes" in 1957). While "Howl" was a masterpiece of manic free verse, "Gramsci's Ashes" was written in, of all things, terza rima—Dante's form.

The emphasis on triads is of a piece with the famous Italian penchant for taxonomy. Dana Gioia once joked that "Italy has more poetic schools than soccer teams," and Ninetta Jucker has noted that "the language itself can hardly refrain from adding an -*ism* to every concept." My own feeling is that these labels muddle as often as they illuminate and, on the whole, are probably more useful for understanding poetry criticism than poetry itself. Few poets, after all, and none of the best ones, wrote with the intent to be part of any school. Yet categorization and oversimplification may be unavoidable, even desirable, in an introduction to a complex subject, and in any case these labels have become such fixtures in conversations about Italian poetry that I would be remiss if I did not attempt to acquaint readers of this anthology with at least a handful of them.

Perhaps the single most vexed label of the century is Hermeticism, a term that, like Crepuscularism, was coined by a critic as a slight. The critic, Francesco Flora, was attempting to describe a new, intensely private mode of poetry practiced in the twenties and thirties—a period largely coextensive with Fascist rule—by Ungaretti, Montale, Salvatore Quasimodo, Mario Luzi, and others. Hermetic poetry can be seen as a strain of *poésie pure*, an oblique poetry of essences and of interiority, shorn (in varying degrees, depending on the poet) of elements such as narrative, rhetoric, punctuation, ornament, and syntax. It's usually hard to know what a Hermetic poem is "about," hard to talk about what it might "mean"—indeed, a Hermetic poem often makes questions such as "What is it about?" or "What does it mean?" seem beside the point, even naïve. A better question to ask of this sort of poem might be: What does it evoke?

It's not as though the kinds of obscurity associated with Italian Hermeticism were new to literature. The term itself, after all, derives from an ancient source, Hermes Trismegistus, a syncretic deity and the purported author of a collection of esoteric texts known as *The Hermetica*. And even the troubadours, those grandfathers of Italian poetry, had their *trobar clus*: an arcane, "closed" style that could be appreciated only by an elite coterie. It may be true that, over the course of the last century, Hermetic qualities gradually became so commonplace that to many European and American readers they now seem, for better or worse, part of the presumptive nature of poetry itself. Yet Hermeticism may be better understood simply as part of an ongoing dialectic, a perennially available mode that finds favor in some periods more than others and, in any given period, with some poets more than others.

But why this period? Why, in other words, did Italy's particular strain of Hermeticism thrive during the Ventennio—the twenty-year reign of Fascism? This question became central in the postwar period, when Italian poetry entered a period of intense politicization during which many poets and critics rejected the Hermetic mode as insufficiently responsive to the times. The Catholic critic Carlo Bo, who prior to the war had been an exponent of Hermeticism, later described the presence of Italian intellectuals during the Ventennio as an "absence," and argued that they were guilty of the "sin of omission." The Communist writer Fabrizio Onofri judged them more harshly, suggesting that the "Italian art, literature, and culture" of that period be "condemn[ed] entirely" on the grounds that they had done "nothing to oppose Fascism." And even Quasimodo, who in the 1930s had been the quintessential Hermetic poet (and one of the few to embrace the label), did an about-face, changing the way he wrote and urging others to do the same: the contemporary poet, he argued, should try "to locate himself in the real world, not some ideal one, so as not to get blindsided again while inwardly watching the setting of the Pleiades."

But these reactions, while eminently understandable in their historical context, are based on several tenuous assumptions: that art has an obliga-tion to be *engagé*, at least in times of crisis; that such engagement might ac-tually be effective; and even that such engagement is feasible at all. And, indeed, a defender of Hermeticism might point out that writers who were openly critical of the Fascist regime were likely to be, at best, muzzled through confinement (like Cesare Pavese and Carlo Levi) or, at worst, tor-tured to death (like Leone Ginzburg). Arguably, then, the only paths open to Italian writers of the period were either to write private poems or to write such obliquely political poems that their political content might not be noticed at all, except by the choir of cognoscenti.

A good example of a politically coded brand of Hermeticism might be Montale's exquisite cameo "To Liuba, Leaving," which he once called "the end of an unwritten poem," as if there had been more that he had been, whether for personal or political reasons, unable to say:

> No cricket guides you now,
> just your pet cat,
> bright domestic god of your scattered family.
> The house you carry in its cloak
> (a cage? a hatbox?)
> rides out the blind times as a light ark rides
> the waves—and is enough to save you.

Few readers, at a glance, would see this as a political poem—it requires several readings (more than Fascist censors would likely have bothered to give it) as well as a little reading between the lines. We might first notice the delicate simile through which the container's gentle up-and-down mo-tion, as Liuba walks away, is compared with that of an ark on an ocean. The specter of the Flood is certainly ominous, and if we know the poem was written in the late thirties, shortly after the anti-Jewish Racial Laws were passed, and that Liuba is often, though by no means exclusively, a Jewish name (and even if we have no idea that Montale's Jewish lover, Irma Brandeis, had just fled Italy in the wake of these laws, or that the name Liuba means "love"), we might begin to grasp the poem's unspoken drama:

a woman, likely Jewish, carrying a cat, or so it seems, in some sort of covered container, preparing possibly to board a train (as Montale later suggested) but in any case "leaving" someplace, perhaps her home (for which the little portable "house" is then both metonym and emblem of diminishment and displacement), perhaps even fleeing, like the other members of her "scattered family" (and the Italian word for "scattered"—*disperso*—is cognate with *diaspora*), the oppressive new laws governing the "blind times" of (by now it seems obvious) Fascism. Liuba, though she carries only one animal, becomes a modern-day Noah: a Jew trying to survive a Flood. Once we as readers catch the poem's scent, we quickly follow until we find ourselves, as if suddenly, in a sort of clearing, witnessing a scene that is both poignant and profoundly *political*.

And yet: as appealing as it may be to see Hermeticism as a kind of underground *resistenza*, and as apt as it may be in a few cases, most Hermetic poetry was simply not directly political in this way, and its obliquity was not shaped by fear of censors any more than Eliot's was. Indeed, Hermeticism might simply be seen as Italy's brand of Modernism, akin to the Eliotic strain in Anglophone poetry. And as is the case with Eliot's work, what seemed profoundly obscure in the 1930s doesn't necessarily seem so today. Hermeticism, in other words, no longer seems quite as Hermetic as it once did.

Whatever their individual politics, the primary concerns of most Hermetic poets (like most Modernists in general) were aesthetic and philosophical, even as Mussolini grabbed power and war broke out and Italy was devastated and humiliated by both the Germans and the Allies. But the choice *not* to use poetry as an overt political instrument—with the Fascists actively encouraging the politicization and the utilitarianism of art—made a strong, and arguably anti-Fascist, statement about what these poets believed was the appropriate relation between culture and politics. Even Montale, whose refusal to join the Fascist party cost him his job and whose work of the period is frequently darkened by the shadow of real-world events (to such an extent that he is in fact increasingly read as a political poet), would never have subordinated his poetry to his politics. He and the other so-called Hermetics—as well as non-Hermetic poets, including

Saba, who avoided overtly political poetry—saw themselves as safeguarding the purity of their art in the face of violent, corrupting political pressures. Ironically, after the war it was the anti-Fascist left, and particularly the Communists, who led the call for the politicization and utilitarianism of art, and in their view, writers who had refused to politicize their art during the Ventennio were, at best, ivory tower elitists, at worst collaborators.

Quasimodo's career might be seen as a microcosm of this broad cultural shift: in the 1930s he was the quintessential Hermeticist, known for the often inscrutable imagistic lyrics of his first two collections, *Acque e terre* (*Waters and Lands*, 1930) and *Oboe sommerso* (*Sunken Oboe*, 1932). But what he later saw as his failure, and the failure of prewar poetry in general, to effectively oppose Fascism led him, after the war, to commit his talents to the political struggles of his people. He was awarded the Nobel Prize in 1959, a choice widely thought to have been based as much on his politics as on his poetry.

The transformations of the Italian political landscape in the wake of World War II led to another splintering of the literary landscape. Of the various postwar trends, the earliest to manifest itself was Neorealism, which flourished in the forties and early fifties, primarily in the realms of film and fiction. Later came a loose confederation of diverse, mostly Milanese poets dubbed the *linea lombarda* (Lombard line), after an influential 1952 anthology of the same name. A few years after that came the Neo-avant-garde, whose origins are often dated to 1956, the year Luciano Anceschi (also the editor of *Linea Lombarda*) founded the journal *Il Verri*, and whose ideas dominated poetic discourse throughout the 1960s. Hermeticism and the qualities associated with it did not simply vanish after the war by any means, but the pendulum swung in the direction of less introspective, more outward-looking styles.

Neorealism defined itself against Hermeticism on one hand and Fascism on the other. In poetry, it was less a movement than the influential idea that poetry should pay more attention to the masses as both subjects and readers, and indeed should exalt their lives and the events (whether historical or quotidian) that shaped them. It was a populist, progressive, anti-elitist stance; its dangers were didacticism and paternalism. Cesare Pavese's verse, particularly his 1936 collection *Lavorare stanca* (*Work's Tiring*), appears in retrospect as an important precursor to Neorealism: against all contemporary trends, Pavese had written clear-sighted "poem-stories" about a range of characters, including prostitutes, hoboes, laborers, and drunks, who hadn't often appeared in the eloquent annals of Italian poetry. None of the poets gathered here was, strictly speaking, a Neorealist, but those influenced by the Neorealist idea included Pasolini, Rocco Scotellaro, Franco Fortini, Primo Levi, and Quasimodo.

Among the original *linea lombarda* poets were Vittorio Sereni, Luciano Erba, Giorgio Orelli, and Nelo Risi, but others, including the Sicilian Bartolo Cattafi, later came to be associated with the group. These poets, like those of the New York School, had strikingly different styles but shared, in addition to loose geographical connections, certain tendencies perhaps best described by Lawrence Smith: "Like the *crepuscolari* of the first part of the century, the *linea lombarda* poets reacted against both the heroic anger and heroic optimism of the realists, replacing those passions with their more modest voices of disillusionment. High emotion was the mode of the new realists; the mode of the *linea lombarda* was irony." While the term began as a description of a particular group of poets, it has broadened over the years to include both their ancestors and their descendants.

The Neo-avant-garde set itself against Hermeticism in particular and much contemporary culture in general. They shared with Neorealists a desire to shift the lens of poetry away from the "I" and toward the material realities of postwar life, but their strategies were starkly different. Though far from monolithic, the Neo-avant-garde shared a belief that politics and literature were inseparable and that the poetic culture of the day, including any notion that language could accurately represent reality, served the interests of dominant consumerist ideologies they opposed. They sought, then, as the Futurists had in their more scattershot way, to dismantle and radically remake poetic language. The movement's key text was the seminal 1961 anthology *I novissimi*, which featured generous selections from five younger poets: Alfredo Giuliani, Edoardo Sanguineti, Antonio Porta, Nanni Balestrini, and Elio Pagliarani. Though these five are sometimes seen as the nucleus of the Neo-avant-garde, the movement was far broader, including a range of writers and intellectuals who came to be known as Gruppo 63 (after a 1963 gathering in Palermo). In this group, if uncomfortably so, was Amelia Rosselli, who became one of the strangest, most original poets of the era.

And then a funny thing happened: after the political and social upheavals that began in the wake of World War II and culminated in the protests of 1968, after the Neorealism of the fifties and the Neo-avant-gardism of the sixties, Italian poetry seemed suddenly to fall into something like a taxonomic sleep—for which some of my readers might, by this point, be grateful. Robert Pogue Harrison and Susan Stewart have called Gruppo 63 "the last real 'movement' in Italy," and indeed the last three decades of the century are notable for the scarcity of *isms* and for the lack of anything resembling a dominant triad of poets. It's as if the name of that anthology *I novissimi*—those whom none can be newer than—marks the dead end of an entire history of nomenclature. Italian poetry itself, I should add, did not fall into any sort of sleep. It has simply become, to use Harrison and Stewart's word, a predominantly "monadic" enterprise, perhaps because it has grown increasingly untethered—for better or worse—from the larger cultural and political dynamics of the nation. As a result, the closer we come to the present day, the harder it is to generalize; like contemporary Anglophone poetry, there is profuse variety.

But despite this variety, trends can be observed. I'd like to mention two major developments in late-twentieth-century Italian poetry that were of a different order than those that had come before; both might be said to be sociological, even demographic, in nature. Whatever they were reacting against, virtually all of the century's movements or tendencies—those I've touched on and others I've scanted—had in common two things: that their leading exponents were almost exclusively men, and that these men, whatever regional dialect they grew up hearing around them, wrote primarily in standard Italian, the language that originated with the Tuscan dialect of Dante, Petrarch, and Boccaccio. The last quarter of the century, however, saw the proliferation of both women and dialect poets.

Women poets who managed to gain serious attention have been few and far between in Italian history. It's telling that even Gruppo 63, which challenged so many ingrained cultural norms, never seriously challenged the extraordinary male dominance of Italian poetry (and it's ironic that one of the few women associated with the group, Rosselli, may prove its most enduring voice). Consider that, until recently, the standard Italian anthologies of twentieth-century poetry were those edited by Sanguineti in 1969 and Pier Vincenzo Mengaldo in 1978. Each ran to more than a thousand pages, and each is in many ways magisterial; I treasure both. Yet the former included no women at all, the latter only Rosselli. Nor was the old-boys-club quality of these collections at all atypical. A remarkable feature, then, of late-twentieth-century Italian poetry was the relatively sudden influx of women poets (Vivian Lamarque, Patrizia Cavalli, Patrizia Valduga, Giulia Niccolai, and many others) who published with prestigious houses and gained substantial critical attention and readerships. Alda Merini is a special case: having debuted to some acclaim in the early fifties, she suffered a series of breakdowns and was institutionalized for most of the sixties. Thus, when she emerged from a twenty-year silence in 1980, it was almost as if a new poet had come onto the scene, and she quickly made up for the lost years: by the time of her death in 2009 she had become one of the most prolific and beloved poets in Italy.

Though not directly related, the rise of women coincided, more or less, with a revival of poetry written in regional dialects. (The term *dialect* is slippery and often misleading; I use it loosely here, for convenience, to mean any language native to Italy other than standard Italian.) Italy boasts a rich tradition of dialect poets, the sovereign of whom is the brilliant nineteenth-century satirist G. G. Belli, who wrote thousands of sonnets, often vulgar and/or anticlerical, in his native Romanesco, the dialect of Rome. (Because this genuinely populist tradition tended toward satire, sensuality, and sentimentality, it has often been regarded by the literati as inferior to high art.) In the early twentieth century this tradition still flourished; poets such as Trilussa in Rome, Delio Tessa in Milan, and Salvatore Di Giacomo in Naples were national celebrities and local heroes. The tradition never died, exactly, but it and the dialects themselves eventually eroded, particularly when televisions allowed standard Italian, Trojan-horse-style, to infiltrate the last bastion of dialects: the living room. Many poets, fearing the disappearance of the languages spoken in their childhood homes, began choosing to write primarily in their own regional dialects instead of standard literary Italian. Yet often their poetry was informed less by the old tradition of dialect poetry than by the highbrow tradition whose eloquent language they were abandoning: the ambitions of poets such as Franco Loi, who writes in the Milanese dialect, and Raffaello Baldini, who wrote in Romagnolo, are undeniably modern. Such poets probably won't save their dialects from extinction, but they are leaving some marvelous artifacts. And for the time being these poets also gain access to fresh storehouses of language, untroubled by the eloquence problem, undespoiled by eight centuries of tradition.

This anthology concludes, as it began, with poets born in mid-century, all of whom are still active and evolving—indeed, they ought to be considered mid-career. I will let their poems speak for themselves. In closing, though, I'll offer one final generalization, which I find worth repeating because it is both surprising and oddly logical. The old Italian eloquence, so tyrannical at the dawn of the twentieth century, took quite a beating, first from the poets themselves, many of whom had sought to wring its neck (and understandably so, given its stultifying effect in those times). More recently, the surviving descendants of that eloquence—by which I mean registers that are more formal than informal, more literary than colloquial, more written than spoken—have found themselves, as Harrison and Stewart argue in their introduction to *Contemporary Italian Poetry*, "under fierce assault, even threatened with disappearance, by the public dominance of journalism and media." Far from being tyrannical, then, eloquence at the end of the twentieth century was nearly a dead language, closer to extinction, arguably, than many of the endangered dialects that certain poets have been working to conserve. The tables have thus turned to such a degree that Harrison and Stewart can now plausibly argue that "if there is a common bond among this great proliferation of poets in Italy, it is perhaps a deeply rooted commitment" to that "courtly" language rejected by Montale and others at the start of the century. "There seems to be a need among Italian writers of poetry," they add, "to speak otherwise than in the idiom of the day" (this in sharp contrast, they note, to their American contemporaries, who "aspire to render their poems as colloquial and demotic and unillustrious as possible").

Such an argument raises many questions, of course. Will future scholars label the present period an era of "New Eloquence"? Does the language of contemporary media culture weigh as heavily on today's poets as the language of literary tradition did on the poets of a century ago? And if so, can today's poets manage this burden as inventively and variously as their precursors managed theirs? Such questions will no doubt be addressed by future anthologies.

TWO TUNNELS

A NOTE ON TRANSLATION

The most notorious and thoughtlessly repeated remark in English about translation is the chestnut attributed to Robert Frost: "Poetry is what is lost in translation." Though Frost's authority on the subject is dubious, his remark—like the Italian phrase *traduttore traditore* ("translator betrayer")—lends epigrammatic zing to the old notion that the translation of poetry is an impossible task. Arthur Schopenhauer, ever the pessimist, declared, "Poetry cannot be translated." The great Peruvian poet Cesar Vallejo said simply, "Everyone knows that poetry is untranslatable." And Roman Jakobson, the Russian linguist, argued, "Poetry is by definition untranslatable." These are just a few examples of this commonplace, chosen almost at random from a large storehouse. Philosophers, poets, and linguists, it seems, agree. So why this anthology?

The confusion, as it turns out, lies not, as Jakobson's formulation implies, with the definition of *poetry*, but rather with the definition of *translation*. It's a word many people (even many philosophers, poets, and linguists) fail to grasp. If we understand the verb *to translate* in a strict, literal sense—to transfer from one place to another—then, yes, the translation of poetry from one language to another is an impossible, even absurd notion. If a bishop is translated from Rome to Boston, he remains the same man, at least physically, in a new setting; but when a poem is translated from Italian into English, it acquires a new body entirely: all its original sounds are replaced with new ones. The original poetry, then—or at least whatever part of it inheres in its sounds—is indeed simply lost. And this loss is admittedly enormous. But it is the translator's task not to prevent that loss but to create an entirely new body of sounds that, while utterly distinct from the original body, is nonetheless muscular or beautiful or nimble enough to carry across the poem's most essential nonsonic cargo:

its tone, mood, imagery, story, logic, meaning, thought, sentiment, humor, motion—whatever (aside from its particular and necessarily local sounds) makes the poem what it is. To translate a poem, then, is to attempt a kind of reincarnation. And if the translator is a good enough poet in the new language and a good enough reader of the old one, then something very like the original spirit can in fact be breathed into the new body. Frost, in other words, was right, in the sense that poetry is lost in every translation. But in *good* translations, poetry is also found. And to understand that both statements may be simultaneously true is to grasp the nature, and the real possibility, of literary translation.

Fortunately, this is what translation, in a literary context, has always meant to the best translators: not a simple transposition, but a re-creation of the original. Etymologically, to *translate* is to make a *metaphor*: both words signify a carrying of something from one place to another. And if we see the act of translation as an instance of metaphor-making, as an art rather than a science, then the pointlessness of calling it "impossible" becomes plain. One can speak of good and bad metaphors, after all, but one cannot speak of the impossibility of metaphors.

One implication of these observations is that translators of poetry must also be poets—at least in their translations—which may in part explain why so many of the translators in this anthology are also poets in their own right. Translators must always be listening *as poets* to their own translations, even while listening *as translators* to the original. (And any notion of fidelity must therefore include an understanding of the kinds of liberties necessary to find poetry in the translation.) Whenever possible, I have preferred translations that seem to have found among the poetic resources of the English language nearly as much as they have lost in their border-crossing trip—translations that are, in other words, real poems in English. A happy side effect of the presence in these pages of so many Anglophone poets is that this anthology of twentieth-century Italian poetry may also be seen as a partial survey of the engagement of Anglophone poets with their twentieth-century Italian counterparts.

I am tempted to apologize here for both the incompleteness of this anthology and for its biases; that any anthology is by nature *partial* in both senses of that word ought, however, to go without saying. But I would like to offer some caveats: I have defined "Italian poetry" broadly, to include, for instance, non-Italian poets (such as Orelli and Pusterla, both Swiss) who write in Italian, and Italian poets who write in languages or dialects other than standard Italian; I have had to omit important and marvelous poets and poems, either because I lacked space or because I was unable to find or make sufficiently marvelous translations; I have occasionally included marvelous translations of admittedly minor originals (the most obvious examples being Ezra Pound's lovely versions of the obscure Italian poet Saturno Montanari, who appears in no Italian anthologies). Also, and perhaps most important, I have chosen in most cases to represent individual poets with multiple translators, a choice that places certain demands on you, dear reader: namely that you try to hear your way through the varied voices of different translators to the original voice that lies beyond them. While using a single translator for each poet might present a unified front, I believe that, as with stereo speakers, multiple perspectives may offer a fuller sense of the original sound.

And finally, as a sort of catchall caveat, I would like to echo the late poet and translator A. K. Ramanujan, who in his brilliant essay on translating Tamil poetry offers the following delightful parable for translators and readers of translations:

> A Chinese emperor ordered a tunnel to be bored through a great mountain. The engineers decided that the best and quickest way to do it would be to begin work on both sides of the mountain, after precise measurements. If the measurements were precise enough, the two tunnels would meet in the middle, making a single one. "But what happens if they don't meet?" asked the emperor. The counselors, in their wisdom, answered, "If they don't meet, we will have two tunnels instead of one."

Given the nature of mountains and the slipperiness of our instruments, I suspect two tunnels are in truth the best we can hope for. But wouldn't you *rather* have two?

THE FSG BOOK OF

TWENTIETH-CENTURY

ITALIAN POETRY

ΟΙΝΩΤΡΙΟΣ

Τῇδ᾽, ὦ ξεῖνε, φίλοις Οἰνώτριος ἕζετ᾽ ἀείδων,
 τρὶς δ᾽ ὅγε Πιερίδων μνήσατ᾽ ἰοπλοκάμων·
οἱ δὲ σιωπῶντες μελιηδέα οἶνον ἔπινον
 τερπόμενοί τ᾽ οἴνῳ, τερπόμενοί τε μέλει·
οἴνου τ᾽ ἦν γλυκεροῦ μεγάλη χάρις, ἡ δέ τ᾽ ἀμείνων·
 ἡ μὲν γὰρ βαιὴ γίγνεται, ἡ δ᾽ ἐς ἀεί.

1 8 9 0

NOVEMBRE

Gemmea l'aria, il sole cosí chiaro
che tu ricerchi gli albicocchi in fiore,
e del prunalbo l'odorino amaro
 senti nel cuore.

Ma secco è il pruno, e le stecchite piante
di nere trame segnano il sereno,
e vuoto il cielo, e cavo al piè sonante
 sembra il terreno.

Silenzio, intorno: solo, alle ventate,
odi lontano, da giardini ed orti,
di foglie un cader fragile. È l'estate,
 fredda, dei morti.

1 8 9 1

Giovanni Pascoli

1855–1912

OENOTRUS

Here, O Stranger, Oenotrus sat, singing to his friends.
    Thrice he invoked the violet-tressed Muses.
In silence his friends drank the honey-sweet wine,
    Enjoying the wine, enjoying the tune,
Grateful for the sweet wine, yet the tune was better—
    For wine runs out soon, but song is forever.

A. E. STALLINGS

NOVEMBER

Gemlike the air, the sun so bright above,
you look for blossoms on the apricot trees,
recall the bitter whitethorn scent you love
        and sniff the breeze.

But the whitethorn's withered, the brittle boughs
hatch their black schemes against the empty blue,
and earth rings hollow now beneath the blows
        of every shoe.

Around you, silence, but for sighs that spill
in upon every gust, from grove and wood:
frail settlements of leaves. This is the chill
        summer of the dead.

GEOFFREY BROCK

SAPIENZA

Salì pensoso la romita altura
ove ha il suo nido l'aquila e il torrente,
e centro della lontananza oscura
        sta, sapïente.

Oh! scruta intorno gl'ignorati abissi:
più ti va lungi l'occhio del pensiero,
più presso viene quello che tu fissi:
        ombra e mistero.

1 8 9 2

ULTIMO SOGNO

Da un immoto fragor di carrïaggi
ferrei, moventi verso l'infinito
tra schiocchi acuti e fremiti selvaggi . . .
un silenzio improvviso. Ero guarito.

Era spirato il nembo del mio male
in un alito. Un muovere di ciglia;
e vidi la mia madre al capezzale:
io la guardava senza meraviglia.

Libero! . . . inerte sì, forse, quand'io
le mani al petto sciogliere volessi:
ma non volevo. Udivasi un fruscio
sottile, assiduo, quasi di cipressi;

quasi d'un fiume che cercasse il mare
inesistente, in un immenso piano:
io ne seguiva il vano sussurrare,
sempre lo stesso, sempre più lontano.

1 8 9 4

WISDOM

Climb with your thoughts up the lonely height
where the eagle and the waterfall leave their nests,
and stand as the center of a blur of distance,
    clutching your wisdom.

O examine 'round you the unvisited depths:
the farther out the eye of thought can go,
the closer comes the thing you're staring into:
    mystery, shadow.

ALISTAIR ELLIOT

LAST DREAM

Out of a motionless infernal
shudder and clang of steel on steel
as wagons moved toward the eternal,
a sudden silence: I was healed.

The storm cloud of my sickness fled
on a breath. A flickering of eyes,
and I saw my mother by my bed
and gazed at her without surprise.

Free! Helpless, yes, to move the hands
clasped on my chest—but I had no
desire to move. The rustling sounds
(like cypress trees, like streams that flow

across vast prairies seeking seas
that don't exist) were thin, insistent:
I followed after those vain sighs,
ever the same, ever more distant.

GEOFFREY BROCK

ALLORA!

Allora . . . in un tempo assai lunge . . .
felice fui molto; non ora:
ma quanta dolcezza mi giunge
da tanta dolcezza d'allora!

Quell'anno! . . . per anni che poi
fuggirono, che fuggiranno;
non puoi, mio pensiero, non puoi
portare con te, che quell'anno!

Un giorno fu quello, ch'è senza
compagno, ch'è senza ritorno:
la vita fu van parvenza
sì prima sì dopo quel giorno!

Un punto! . . . così passeggero,
che in vero passò non raggiunto;
ma bello così, che molto ero
felice felice, quel punto!

1897

NELLA NEBBIA

E guardai nella valle: era sparito
tutto! sommerso! Era un gran mare piano,
grigio, senz'onde, senza lidi, unito.

E c'era appena, qua e là, lo strano
vocìo di gridi piccoli e selvaggi:
uccelli spersi per quel mondo vano.

BACK THEN!

Back then, in those now-distant times,
I was the happiest of men—
no longer. Yet what sweetness comes
still from that sweetness then!

That year! Of all the years now gone,
and all that, soon, shall disappear,
my thoughts shall carry with them none—
none, I say—but that year!

A day is what it was, its brilliance
peerless, and then it slipped away,
rendering life but a vain semblance
before and since that day!

A moment . . . one that passed me by
before I'd ever really known it.
But that's fine: I was happy, I
was happy, in that moment!

GEOFFREY BROCK

IN THE FOG

And I stared toward the valley: it was gone—
wholly submerged! A vast flat sea remained,
gray, with no waves, no beaches; all was one.

And here and there I noticed, when I strained,
the alien clamoring of small, wild voices:
birds that had lost their way in that vain land.

Giovanni Pascoli 7

E alto, in cielo, scheletri di faggi,
come sospesi, e sogni di rovine
e di silenzïosi eremitaggi.

Ed un cane uggiolava senza fine,
né seppi donde, forse a certe péste
che sentii, né lontane né vicine;

eco di péste né tarde né preste,
alterne, eterne. E io laggiù guardai:
nulla ancora e nessuno, occhi, vedeste.

Chiesero i sogni di rovine: «Mai
non giungerà?» Gli scheletri di piante
chiesero: «E tu chi sei, che sempre vai?»

Io, forse, un'ombra vidi, un'ombra errante
con sopra il capo un largo fascio. Vidi,
e più non vidi, nello stesso istante.

Sentii soltanto gl'inquïeti gridi
d'uccelli spersi, l'uggiolar del cane,
e, per il mar senz'onde e senza lidi,

le péste né vicine né lontane.

1900

NEBBIA

Nascondi le cose lontane,
tu nebbia impalpabile e scialba,
tu fumo che ancora rampolli,
su l'alba,
da' lampi notturni e da' crolli
d'aeree frane!

And high above, the skeletons of beeches,
as if suspended, and the reveries
of ruins and of the hermit's hidden reaches.

And a dog kept yelping, as if it could hear,
wherever it was, a sound I also heard,
of footsteps, neither far away nor near—

echoing footsteps, neither slow nor quick,
alternating, eternal. Down I stared,
but I saw nothing, no one, looking back.

The reveries of ruins asked: "Will no
one come?" The skeletons of trees inquired:
"And who are you, forever on the go?"

I may have seen a shadow then, an errant
shadow, bearing a bundle on its head.
I saw—and no more saw, in the same instant.

All I could hear were the uneasy screeches
of the lost birds, the yelping of the stray,
and, on that sea that lacked both waves and beaches,

the footsteps, neither near nor far away.

GEOFFREY BROCK

MIST

Cover what is far,
White of mist, drifting high,
Flowing over the brightening
Of daybreak in the sky,
After the night-long lightning
And the rock-falls in the air.

Giovanni Pascoli 9

Nascondi le cose lontane,
nascondimi quello ch'è morto!
Ch'io veda soltanto la siepe
dell'orto,
la mura ch'ha piene le crepe
di valeriane.

Nascondi le cose lontane:
le cose son ebbre di pianto!
Ch'io veda i due peschi, i due meli,
soltanto,
che dànno i soavi lor mieli
pel nero mio pane.

Nascondi le cose lontane
che vogliono ch'ami e che vada!
Ch'io veda là solo quel bianco
di strada,
che un giorno ho da fare tra stanco
don don di campane . . .

Nascondi le cose lontane,
nascondile, involale al volo
del cuore! Ch'io veda il cipresso
là, solo,
qui, solo quest'orto, cui presso
sonnecchia il mio cane.

1 9 0 3

Cover what is gone.
Hide the dead from me.
Let me see no more than the tall
Hedge at my boundary,
And where, in the cracks of the wall,
Are the roots of valerian.

Cover what is dead.
The world is drunk with grief.
Let me see my fruit trees only
Deep in flower and leaf—
That give their golden honey
For my bitter bread.

Cover what is far.
Cover the love of the dead.
Let me see, for all their calling,
Only the white of the road.
In time, to the bells' tolling,
I shall go where they are.

Cover what is far.
Hide it away from me.
Let me see, of all beyond,
Only one cypress tree;
With my garden, near at hand,
And my dog drowsing there.

E. J. SCOVELL

IL GELSOMINO NOTTURNO

E s'aprono i fiori notturni,
nell'ora che penso a' miei cari.
   Sono apparse in mezzo ai viburni
   le farfalle crepuscolari.

Da un pezzo si tacquero i gridi:
là sola una casa bisbiglia.
   Sotto l'ali dormono i nidi,
   come gli occhi sotto le ciglia.

Dai calici aperti si esala
l'odore di fragole rosse.
   Splende un lume là nella sala.
   Nasce l'erba sopra le fosse.

Un'ape tardiva sussurra
trovando già prese le celle.
   La Chioccetta per l'aia azzurra
   va col suo pigolio di stelle.

Per tutta la notte s'esala
l'odore che passa col vento.
   Passa il lume su per la scala;
   brilla al primo piano: s'è spento . . .

È l'alba: si chiudono i petali
un poco gualciti; si cova,
   dentro l'urna molle e segreta,
   non so che felicità nuova.

1903

NIGHT-BLOOMING JASMINE

And in the hour when blooms unfurl
thoughts of my loved ones come to me.
    The moths of evening whirl
    around the snowball tree.

Nothing now shouts or sings;
one house only whispers, then hushes.
    Nestlings sleep beneath wings,
    like eyes beneath their lashes.

From open calyces there flows
a ripe strawberry scent, in waves.
    A lamp in the house glows.
    Grasses are born on graves.

A late bee sighs, back from its tours
and no cell vacant anymore.
    The Hen and her cheeping stars
    cross their threshing floor.

All through the night the flowers flare,
scent flowing and catching the wind.
    The lamp now climbs the stair,
    shines from above, is dimmed . . .

It's dawn: the petals, slightly worn,
close up again—each bud to brood,
    in its soft, secret urn,
    on some yet-nameless good.

GEOFFREY BROCK

DA L'AQUILONE

S'inalza; e i piedi trepidi e l'anelo
petto del bimbo e l'avida pupilla
e il viso e il cuore, porta tutto in cielo.

Più su, più su: già come un punto brilla
lassù lassù . . . Ma ecco una ventata
di sbieco, ecco uno strillo alto . . . —Chi strilla?

Sono le voci della camerata
mia: le conosco tutte all'improvviso,
una dolce, una acuta, una velata . . .

A uno a uno tutti vi ravviso,
o miei compagni! e te, sì, che abbandoni
su l'omero il pallor muto del viso.

Sì: dissi sopra te l'orazïoni,
e piansi: eppur, felice te che al vento
non vedesti cader che gli aquiloni!

Tu eri tutto bianco, io mi rammento:
solo avevi del rosso nei ginocchi,
per quel nostro pregar sul pavimento.

Oh! te felice che chiudesti gli occhi
persuaso, stringendoti sul cuore
il più caro dei tuoi cari balocchi!

Oh! dolcemente, so ben io, si muore
la sua stringendo fanciullezza al petto,
come i candidi suoi pètali un fiore

FROM **THE KITE**

It rises and it carries ever higher
The longing in the breast and anxious feet
And gazing face and heart of the kite-flier,

Higher and higher until it's just a dot
Of brightness far, far up . . . But now a sudden
Crosswind and a scream . . . Whose scream was that?

My companions' voices rise to me unbidden
And familiar, the same old chorus
Of sweet and high and hoarse. And there isn't

One, my friends, that I don't recognise, and yes,
Of us all, you in particular, you who droop your head
On your shoulder and avert your quiet face,

You, over whom I shed my tears and prayed,
You who were lucky to have seen the fallen
Only in the windfall of a kite.

You were very pale, I remember, but had grown
Red at the knees from kneeling on the floor—
Raw from all that praying night and morning.

And ah, were you not lucky to cross over
With confidence in your eyes, and in your arms
The plaything that of all things was most dear.

Gently, I well know, when the time comes
We die with our childhood clasped close to our breast
Like a flower in bloom that closes and reforms

ancora in boccia! O morto giovinetto,
anch'io presto verrò sotto le zolle,
là dove dormi placido e soletto . . .

Meglio venirci ansante, roseo, molle
di sudor, come dopo una gioconda
corsa di gara per salire un colle!

Meglio venirci con la testa bionda,
che poi che fredda giacque sul guanciale,
ti pettinò co' bei capelli a onda

tua madre . . . adagio, per non farti male.

1 9 0 4

Its petals into itself. O you, so young, the youngest
Of my dead, I too will soon go down into the clay
Where you sleep calmly, on your own, at rest.

Better to arrive there breathless, like a boy
Who has been racing up a hill,
Flushed and hot and soft, a boy at play.

Better to arrive there with a full
Head of blond hair, which spread cold on the pillow
As your mother combed it, wavy and beautiful,

Combed it slowly so as not to hurt you.

SEAMUS HEANEY

MARZO

Marzo: nu poco chiove
e n' ato ppoco stracqua:
torna a chiovere, schiove,
ride 'o sole cu ll'acqua.

Mo nu cielo celeste
mo n' aria cupa e nera:
mo d' 'o vierno 'e tempeste
mo n' aria 'e primmavera.

N' auciello freddigliuso
aspetta ch' esce 'o sole
ncopp' 'o tturreno nfuso
suspireno 'e vviole . . .

Catarì! . . . Che buo' cchiù?
Ntiénneme, core mio!
Marzo, tu 'o ssaie, si' tu,
e st' auciello songo io.

1898

Salvatore Di Giacomo

1860–1934

MARCH

March: there's a bit of rain,
just a bit later it stops;
it starts, then it stops again,
the sun laughs with the drops.

A moment of clear azure,
a moment of clouds threatening;
a moment of winter's fury,
a moment of glorious spring.

A shivering bird nearby
waits for the sun to return,
while all the violets sigh
over the sodden terrain.

Caterina! . . . Isn't it clear
from what you've already heard?
You know, you are March, my dear,
and I am that little bird.

MICHAEL PALMA

SIENTE, SI VIDE . . .

Siente . . . Si vide a chillo
nfamone 'e Gennarino,
dille ca è n' assassino!
No . . . Nun lle di' accussì!

Dille . . . E sì, sì . . . Dincello
ca è tristo! È scellarato!
Ca sempre chesto è stato! . . .
No . . . Aspetta . . . Nun ce 'o ddi' . . .

E si lle dice: «Rosa
vurria sfucà pur essa,
simbè pur essa stessa
sta incerta si 'o po fa' . . .»?

No . . . Di' ca i' sto chiagnenno!
Dille ca io stongo ardenno!
Dille ca io sto murenno!
Ma portammillo ccà . . .

1916

OLD-FASHIONED DITTY

Listen . . . if you see him,
that crook of Gennarino,
tell him he is a murderer!
No . . . don't tell him that!

Tell him . . . yes, yes, tell him
that he is a beast, a snake,
and always has been that.
No . . . wait . . . don't tell him that!

And if you'd tell him, "Rose
would have her fling, she too;
but then . . . she . . . herself . . .
would want to know if you . . . ?"

No . . . tell him that I'm crying . . .
tell him I'm burning . . . see . . .
tell him I'm dying, dying . . .
But bring him here to me.

EMANUEL CARNEVALI

Salvatore Di Giacomo 21

LA PIOGGIA NEL PINETO

Taci. Su le soglie
del bosco non odo
parole che dici
umane; ma odo
parole più nuove
che parlano gocciole e foglie
lontane.
Ascolta. Piove
dalle nuvole sparse.
Piove su le tamerici
salmastre ed arse,
piove sui pini
scagliosi ed irti,
piove su i mirti
divini,
su le ginestre fulgenti
di fiori accolti,
su i ginepri folti
di coccole aulenti,
piove su i nostri volti
silvani,
piove su le nostre mani
ignude,
su i nostri vestimenti
leggeri,
su i freschi pensieri

Gabriele D'Annunzio

1863–1938

RAIN IN THE PINE GROVE

Silence! . . . At the woods'
edge I can't hear the
human words you speak;
but I hear newer words
the raindrops and the
far-off leaves are saying.
Listen. Rain is falling
out of the scattered
clouds. It's falling on
the briny sun-scorched
tamarinds, raining on
the scales of shaggy
pines, on the holy
myrtle, the refulgent
broom whose buds are
closed, on the dense
juniper with pungent
berries, raining on
our forest faces,
falling on our bare
hands, our light clothes,
on the new ideas the
newborn soul gives
voice to, on the
beguiling tale that

che l'anima schiude
novella,
su la favola bella
che ieri
t'illuse, che oggi m'illude,
o Ermione.

Odi? La pioggia cade
su la solitaria
verdura
con un crepitio che dura
e varia nell'aria secondo le fronde
più rade, men rade.
Ascolta. Risponde
al pianto il canto
delle cicale
che il pianto australe
non impaura,
né il ciel cinerino.
E il pino
ha un suono, e il mirto
altro suono, e il ginepro
altro ancora, stromenti
diversi
sotto innumerevoli dita.
E immensi
noi siam nello spirito
silvestre,
d'arborea vita viventi;
e il tuo volto ebro
è molle di pioggia
come una foglia,
e le tue chiome
auliscono come
le chiare ginestre,

charmed you yesterday
and charms me now,
Hermione.

Do you hear? The rain
is falling on the lonely
green with a crackling
that hangs in the air
varying with the thickness
of the leaves. Listen. The
cicadas' song is answering
the cry, unintimidated by
the wailing south wind
or the ashen sky. The pine
makes one sound and the
myrtle makes another, and
the juniper another still,
different instruments
touched by countless fingers.
And we're huge inside the
sylvan spirit, alive with
tree life; and your drunken
face is softened by the rain
the way a leaf is, and
your hair is fragrant
like the brilliant broom,
earth creature who goes
by the name
Hermione.

Listen. Listen. The
accord of the aerial
cicadas slowly fades

o creatura terrestre
che hai nome
Ermione.

Ascolta, Ascolta. L'accordo
delle aeree cicale
a poco a poco
più sordo
si fa sotto il pianto
che cresce;
ma un canto vi si mesce
più roco
che di laggiù sale,
dall'umida ombra remota.
Più sordo e più fioco
s'allenta, si spegne.
Sola una nota
ancor trema, si spegne,
risorge, trema, si spegne.
Non s'ode su tutta la fronda
crosciare
l'argentea pioggia
che monda,
il croscio che varia
secondo la fronda
più folta, men folta.
Ascolta.
La figlia dell'aria
è muta: ma la figlia
del limo lontana,
la rana,
canta nell'ombra più fonda,
chi sa dove, chi sa dove!
E piove su le tue ciglia,
Ermione.

beneath the rising
cry; but it's joined by
a fainter song that
comes from below, from
the soaked distant shade.
Duller and fainter
it fades out, dies,
rises, trembles, dies.
Just one note still
trembles, dies,
rises, quivers, dies.
There is no sound.
In all the leafage you
can't hear the roaring
silver purifying
rain, its beat that
varies with the thickness
of the leaves. Listen.
The daughter of the air
is silent; but the frog,
daughter of the distant
lime tree, is singing
in the deepest shade,
who knows where, who
knows! And it's raining
on your lashes,
my Hermione.

It rains on your dark
lashes so it seems you're
crying, but from happiness;
you seem to be emerging

Gabriele D'Annunzio 27

Piove su le tue ciglia nere
sì che par tu pianga
ma di piacere; non bianca
ma quasi fatta virente,
par da scorza tu esca.
E tutta la vita è in noi fresca
aulente,
il cuor nel petto è come pesca
intatta,
tra le palpebre gli occhi
son come polle tra l'erbe,
i denti negli alveoli
son come mandorle acerbe.
E andiam di fratta in fratta,
or congiunti or disciolti
(e il verde vigor rude
ci allaccia i melleoli
c'intrica i ginocchi)
chi sa dove, chi sa dove!
E piove su i nostri volti
silvani,
piove su le nostre mani

ignude,
su i nostri vestimenti
leggeri,
su i freschi pensieri
che l'anima schiude
novella,
su la favola bella
che ieri
m'illuse, che oggi t'illude,
o Ermione.

1 9 0 3

from the bark not white, but
nearly green. And all of
life is fresh and fragrant
in us, the heart in the
breast is like an intact
peach, the eyes among
their lashes are like
springs in the grass,
the teeth in the gums
are bitter almonds. And
we move from glade to
glade, now together, now
apart (and the green rude
vigor binds our ankles,
catches at our knees),
who knows where, who
knows! It's raining
on our forest faces,
raining on our naked
hands, on our light
clothes, on the fresh
ideas the newborn soul
uncovers, on the lovely
tale that thrilled me
yesterday and
thrills you now,
Hermione.

JONATHAN GALASSI

Gabriele D'Annunzio 29

BOCCA D'ARNO

Bocca di donna mai mi fu di tanta
soavità nell'amorosa via
(se non la tua, se non la tua, presente)
come la bocca pallida e silente
del fiumicel che nasce in Falterona.
Qual donna s'abbandona
(se non tu, se non tu) sì dolcemente
come questa placata correntìa?
Ella non canta,
e pur fluisce quasi melodìa
all'amarezza.

    Qual sia la sua bellezza
    io non so dire,
    come colui che ode
    suoni dormendo e virtudi ignote
    entran nel suo dormire.

Le saltano all'incontro i verdi flutti,
schiumanti di baldanza,
con la grazia dei giovini animali.
In catena di putti
non mise tanta gioia Donatello,
fervendo il marmo sotto lo scalpello,
quando ornava le bianche cattedrali.
Sotto ghirlande di fiori e di frutti
svolgeasi intorno al pergami la danza
infantile, ma non sì fiera danza
come quest'una.

    V'è creatura alcuna
    che in tanta grazia
    viva ed in sì perfetta
    gioia, se non quella lodoletta
    che in aere si spazia?

THE MOUTH OF THE ARNO

The mouth of woman never was to me
so full of pleasure in the ways of love
(excepting yours, excepting yours, right now)
as the pale opening out, the silent lips
of this small stream that springs in Falterona.
What woman can abandon
herself (excepting only you) so sweetly
as this appeased and sated current does?
It does not sing
and yet it flows like melody towards
its bitter end.
   The nature of its beauty
   I cannot speak,
   being like one who hears
   sounds that pierce his sleep, and unknown powers
   enter his sleeping mind.

Leaping a little to meet it, the green waves
burst into confident foam,
the graceful surging of young animals.
They move with greater bounds
of joy than Donatello's hand-in-hand
cherubs in marble warm beneath the chisel
when he was decorating white cathedrals.
Under the swags and chains of flowers and fruits
those children wreath around his balustrades,
skipping and turning; but their dance is never
as wild as this one.
   Does any other creature
   live with such grace
   and in such perfect joy?
   except for Dante's lark up there
   that goes for walks on air.

Forse l'anima mia, quando profonda
sè nel suo canto e vede la sua gloria;
forse l'anima tua, quando profonda
sè nell'amore e perde la memoria
degli inganni fugaci in che s'illuse
ed anela con me l'alta vittoria.
Forse conosceremo noi la piena
felicità dell'onda
libera e delle forti ali dischiuse
e dell'inno selvaggio che si frena.
Adora e attendi!

    Adora, adora, e attendi!
    Vedi? I tuoi piedi
    nudi lascian vestigi
    di luce, ed à tuoi occhi prodigi
    sorgon dall'acque. Vedi?

Grandi calici sorgono dall'acque,
di non so qual leggiere oro intessuti.
Le nubi i monti i boschi i lidi l'acque
trasparire per le corolle immani
vedi, lontani e vani
come in sogno paesi sconosciuti.
Farfelle d'oro come le tue mani
volando a coppia scoprono su l'acque
con meraviglia i fiori grandi e strani,
mentre tu fiuti
l'odor salino.

    Fa un suo gioco divino
    l'Ora solare,
    mutevole e gioconda
    come la gola d'una colomba
    alzata per cantare.

Perhaps my soul when it has thrown itself
deep in its state of song and sees its glory,
perhaps your soul when it has thrown itself
deep into love and so forgets the history
of the illusions it was trapped among
and strains with me toward high victory—
perhaps we shall experience the full
happiness of the free
overlapping wave, the strong unfolded wings
and the untamed expansion of its song.
Keep watch, and worship.
    Keep praying, watch with awe.
    You see? Your bare
    feet have left prints of light,
    and before your eyes wonders are rising
    out of the water. See?

Great flower-cups, chalices, rise from the pouring water,
woven somehow like mail from finest gold.
The clouds the hills the woods the shores the waters
are visible through the enormous flower-heads,
you see?—far-off, transparent
as unknown countries that appear in dreams.
Butterflies golden as your open hands
flying in pairs discover on the waters
with wonder those great blossoms that seem foreign,
while you breathe in
the smell of salt.
    The long hand of the sun
    plays its divine game
    with shifting shades of joy,
    like the iridescent throats of pigeons
    lifting, swollen with song.

Gabriele D'Annunzio 33

Sono le reti pensili. Talune
pendon come bilance dalle antenne
cui sostengono i ponti alti e protesi
ove l'uom veglia a volgere la fune;
altre pendono a prua dei palischermi
trascorrendo il perenne
specchio che le rifrange; e quando il sole
batte a poppa i navigli, stando fermi
i remi, un gran fulgor le trasfigura:
grandi calici sorgono dall'acque,
gigli di foco.

 Fa un suo divino gioco
 la giovine Ora
 che è breve come il canto
 della colomba. Godi l'incanto,
 anima nostra, e adora!

1 9 0 3

I PASTORI

Settembre, andiamo. È tempo di migrare.
Ora in terra d'Abruzzi i miei pastori
lascian gli stazzi e vanno verso il mare:
scendono all'Adriatico selvaggio
che verde è come i pascoli dei monti.

Han bevuto profondamente ai fonti
alpestri, che sapor d'acqua natía
rimanga ne' cuori esuli a conforto,
che lungo illuda la lor sete in via.
Rinnovato hanno verga d'avellano.

This vision is the fisherman's hanging nets.
Some hang like parts of balances slung from spars
propped up on the high platforms which jut out
where men can sit and watch and pull the rope;
others are hung over the bows of dories,
and cut the eternal mirror
of passing water that reflects them; when the sun
beats on the boats from astern and the oars stand
at rest, a burst of radiance transforms them:
great chalices, flower-cups, rise from the pouring waters,
lilies of fire.
    The young face of the sun
    plays its divine game,
    which lasts no longer than
    the song of pigeons. Enjoy enchantment,
    our single soul: worship here.

ALISTAIR ELLIOT

THE SHEPHERDS

September's come, let's go: migration time.
In the Abruzzi lands my shepherds now
are leaving their summer folds: down they climb,
sloping toward the untamed Adriatic,
its brine as green as pastures in the mountains.

They have drunk deeply from the upland fountains,
hoping the taste of native waters may
linger as solace in their exile hearts
and cheat the thirst that dogs them on their way.
Each is clutching a fresh-cut hazel crook.

E vanno pel tratturo antico al piano,
quasi per un erbal fiume silente,
su le vestigia degli antichi padri.
O voce di colui che primamente
conosce il tremolar della marina!

Ora lungh'esso il litoral cammina
la greggia. Senza mutamento è l'aria.
il sole imbionda sì la viva lana
che quasi dalla sabbia non divaria.
Isciacquío, calpestío, dolci romori.

Ah perché non son io co' miei pastori?

1 9 0 3

They take the path their fathers' fathers took,
the old drove-road, which bears them to the plain
as if upon a silent current of grass.
And oh the trembling sea, and the young swain
shouting at what he's never seen before!

The flock is moving now along the shore.
Around it, all the air is at a stand.
The sun has turned that cloud of living wool
so blond it's hard to tell it from the sand.
Splashing, tromping, sweet noise upon the air—

Ah, why am I not with my shepherds there?

GEOFFREY BROCK

Gabriele D'Annunzio 37

ER VENTRILOCO

Se credi a questo, sei 'no scemo, scusa:
pô sta' che un omo parli co' la gente
come se ne la panza internamente
ciavesse quarche machina arinchiusa?

Nun credo che in un'epoca che s'usa
d'aprì la bocca senza di' mai gnente
esista 'sto fenomeno vivente
che dice tante cose a bocca chiusa!

Parla cór ventre! Oh questa sì ch'è bella!
Sortanto er poveraccio che nun magna
se sente fa' glu-glu ne le budella.
Io stesso, speciarmente a fin de mese,
me sento che lo stomaco se lagna . . .
Ma sai ched'è? La voce der Paese!

1919

ER GATTO E ER CANE

Un Gatto soriano
diceva a un Barbone:
—Nun porto rispetto

Trilussa

1871–1950

VENTRILOQUIST

Ventriloquist means *stomach speaker*. It's Latin.
If you believe him, by God, you're gullible—
as if the stomach were a place to chat in
or speech could come from swallowing a syllable.

I can't believe that in an age like ours
when everybody's mouth is open, but—but—
when nothing is said, anyone's got the power
of saying anything with his mouth shut.

His stomach talk? What is he trying to tell me?
Only a poor beggar who hasn't once
eaten today hears "glub glub" in his belly.
Matter of fact, especially when the month's
almost out, my guts grumble and grate.
Know whose voice it is? The voice of the State!

JOHN DUVAL

THE CAT AND THE DOG

The cat said to the dog,
"Look at it this way:
you'll never see me pay

nemmanco ar padrone,
perché a l'occasione
je graffio la mano;
ma tu che lo lecchi
te becchi le botte:
te mena, te sfotte,
te mette in catena
cor muso rinchiuso
e un cerchio cor bollo
sull'osso del collo,
seconno la moda
te taja li ricci,
te spunta la coda . . .
Che belli capricci!
Io guarda: so' un Gatto,
so' un ladro, lo dico;
ma a me nun s'azzarda
de famme 'ste cose . . . —
Er Cane rispose:
—Ma io . . . je so' amico!

1922

ALL'OMBRA

Mentre me leggo er solito giornale
spaparacchiato all'ombra d'un pajaro,
vedo un porco e je dico: —Addio, majale!—
vedo un ciuccio e je dico: —Addio, somaro!—

Forse 'ste bestie nun me caperanno,
ma provo armeno la soddisfazzione
de potè di' le cose come stanno
senza paura de finì in priggione.

1932

any respect to the man.
In fact, if I'm in the mood,
I scratch him on the hand.
But you, you fetch his slippers,
lick his boots and slobber.
What does it get you? A kick!
He chains you to a stick
and chokes you with a collar,
or keeps you in a kennel,
then crimps your ears and tags you,
bobs your tail and clips you,
because it's the latest fad,
and, brother, you've been had!
Look at me: I'm a cat!
I've stolen again and again,
but the man's never tried
to keep me muzzled or penned."
The dog replied,
"But I'm his friend."

JOHN DUVAL

LYING IN THE SHADE

Reading, as usual, in *The New Yorker*,
behind a haystack, chewing on a straw,
I see a swine and say, "So long, old porker!"
I see an ass and say, "So long, hee-haw!"

Such beasts won't take my meaning very far,
so I'll be satisfied if I can tell
a little of the way things really are
without the risk of ending in a cell.

PETER DAVISON

FELICITÀ

C'è un Ape che se posa
su'un bottone de rosa:
lo succhia e se ne va . . .
Tutto sommato, la felicità
è una piccola cosa.

1944

HAPPINESS

I saw a bee settle
on a rose petal.
It sipped, and off it flew.
All in all, happiness, too,
is something little.

JOHN DUVAL

ONOMATOPEA RUMORISTA

MACCHINA TIPOGRAFICA

Dodici persone
    ognuno ripetere per un minuto di seguito
    le seguenti onomatopee rumoriste

1° settesettesettesettesettesette
2° nennenennenennenennenennenenne
3° vùùùùmmùùvùùùùùmmùùvùù
4° tè.tè.tè.tè.tè.tè.tè.tè.tè.tè.tè.tè.tè.
5° miaaaaaanavanò.miaaaaaanavanò
6° sta—sta—sta—sta—sta
7° lalalalalalalalalalalalalalalalalalala
8° ftftftftftftftftftftftftftftftftft
9° riòriòrièrièriòriòrièrièriòriòrièrièriòriò
10° scscscscscspsspscscscscscspssps
11° vèvèvèvèvèvèvèvèvèvèvèvèvèvèvèvè
12° nunnnònònunnnònònunnnònònunnnònò

1914

Giacomo Balla

1871–1958

NOISIST ONOMATOPOEIA

PRINTING PRESS

Twelve people
    each repeats continuously for one minute
    the following noisist onomatopoeias

1st SETtaySETtaySETtaySETtaySETtay
2nd nennenennenennenennenennenenne
3rd voooommoovooooommoovoo
4th teh.teh.teh.teh.teh.teh.teh.teh.teh
5th meaaaaahhnavaNO.meaaaaahhnavaNO
6th stah—stah—stah—stah—stah
7th lalalalalalalalalalalalalalalalalalala
8th ftftftftftftftftftftftftftftftftft
9th reeOreeOreeEHreeEHreeOreeOreeEHreeEH
10th skskskskskspsspskskskskspssps
11th veveveveveveveveveveveveve
12th nooonNONOnooonNONOnooonNONO

GEOFFREY BROCK

DALLA **FONDAZIONE E**
MANIFESTO DEL FUTURISMO

Avevamo vegliato tutta la notte—i miei amici ed io—sotto lampade di moschea dalle cupole di ottone traforato, stellate come le nostre anime, perché come queste irradiate dal chiuso fulgòre di un cuore elettrico. Avevamo lungamente calpestata su opulenti tappeti orientali la nostra atavica accidia, discutendo davanti ai confini estremi della logica ed annerendo molta carta di frenetiche scritture. [. . .]

Sussultammo ad un tratto, all'udire il rumore formidabile degli enormi tramvai a due piani, che passano sobbalzando, risplendenti di luci multi-colori, come i villaggi in festa che il Po straripato squassa e sradica d'im-provviso, per trascinarli fino al mare, sulle cascate e attraverso i gorghi di un diluvio.

Poi il silenzio divenne più cupo. Ma mentre ascoltavamo l'estenuato borbottio di preghiere del vecchio canale e lo scricchiolar dell'ossa dei palazzi moribondi sulle loro barbe di umida verdura, noi udimmo subita-mente ruggire sotto le finestre gli automobili famelici.

«Andiamo,» diss'io, «andiamo, amici! Partiamo! Finalmente, la mitolo-gia e l'ideale mistico sono superati. Noi stiamo per assistere alla nascita del Centauro e presto vedremo volare i primi Angeli! . . . Bisognerà scuotere le porte della vita per provarne i cardini e i chiavistelli! . . . Partiamo! Ecco, sulla terra, la primissima aurora! Non v'è cosa che agguagli lo splendore

F. T. Marinetti

1876–1944

FROM THE FOUNDING AND

MANIFESTO OF FUTURISM

We had stayed up all night, my friends and I, under hanging mosque lamps with domes of filigreed brass, domes starred like our spirits, shining like them with the prisoned radiance of electric hearts. For hours we had trampled our atavistic ennui into rich oriental rugs, arguing up to the last confines of logic and blackening many reams of paper with our frenzied scribbling. [. . .]

Suddenly we jumped, hearing the mighty noise of the huge double-decker trams that rumbled by outside, ablaze with colored lights, like villages on holiday suddenly struck and uprooted by the flooding Po and dragged over falls and through gorges to the sea.

Then the silence deepened. But, as we listened to the old canal muttering its feeble prayers and the creaking bones of sickly palaces above their damp green beards, under the windows we suddenly heard the famished roar of automobiles.

"Let's go!" I said. "Friends, away! Let's go! Mythology and the Mystic Ideal are defeated at last. We're about to see the Centaur's birth and, soon after, the first flight of Angels! . . . We must shake at the gates of life, test the bolts and hinges. Let's go! Look there, on the earth, the very first dawn! There's nothing to match the splendor of the sun's red sword, slashing for the first time through our millennial gloom!"

della rossa spada del sole che schermeggia per la prima volta nostre tenebre millenarie! . . .»

Ci avvicinammo alle tre belve sbuffanti, per palparne amorosamente i torridi petti. Io mi stesi sulla mia macchina come un cadavere nella bara, ma subito risuscitai sotto il volante, lama di ghigliottina che minacciava il mio stomaco.

La furente scopa della pazzia ci strappò a noi stessi e ci cacciò attraverso le vie, scoscese e profonde come letti di torrenti.

[. . .]

«Usciamo dalla saggezza come da un orribile guscio, e gettiamoci, come frutti pimentati d'orgoglio entro la bocca immensa e torta del vento! . . . Diamoci in pasto all'Ignoto, non già per disperazione, ma soltanto per colmare i profondi pozzi dell'Assurdo!»

Avevo appena pronunziate queste parole, quando girai bruscamente su me stesso, con la stessa ebrietà folle dei cani che voglion mordersi la coda, ed ecco ad un tratto venirmi incontro due ciclisti, che mi diedero torto, titubando davanti a me come due ragionamenti, entrambi persuasivi e nondimeno contraddittori. Il loro stupido dilemma discuteva sul mio terreno . . . Che noia! Auff! . . . Tagliai corto, e, pel disgusto, mi scaraventai colle ruote all'aria in un fossato . . .

Oh! Materno fossato, quasi pieno di un'acqua fangosa! Bel fossato d'officina! Io gustai avidamente la tua melma fortificante, che mi ricordò la santa mammella nera della mia nutrice sudanese . . . Quando mi sollevai—cencio sozzo e puzzolente—di sotto la macchina capovolta, io mi sentii attraversare il cuore, deliziosamente, dal ferro arroventato della gioia!

Una folla di pescatori armati di lenza e di naturalisti podagrosi tumultuava già intorno al prodigio. Con cura paziente e meticolosa, quella gente dispose alte armature ed enormi reti di ferro per pescare il mio automobile, simile ad un gran pescecane arenato. La macchina emerse lentamente dal fosso, abbandonando nel fondo, come squame, la sua pesante carrozzeria di buon senso e le sue morbide imbottiture di comodità.

Credevano che fosse morto il mio bel pescecane, ma una mia carezza bastò a rianimarlo, ed eccolo risuscitato, eccolo in corsa, di nuovo, sulle sue pinne possenti!

We went up to the three snorting beasts, to lay amorous hands on their torrid breasts. I stretched out on my car like a corpse on its bier, but revived at once under the steering wheel, a guillotine blade that threatened my stomach.

The raging broom of madness swept us out of ourselves and drove us through streets as rough and deep as the beds of torrents.

[. . .]

"Let's break out of the horrible shell of wisdom and throw ourselves like pride-ripened fruit into the wide, contorted mouth of the wind! Let's give ourselves utterly to the Unknown, not in desperation but only to replenish the deep wells of the Absurd!"

The words were scarcely out of my mouth when I spun my car around with the frenzy of a dog trying to bite its tail, and there, suddenly, were two cyclists coming toward me, shaking their fists, wobbling like two equally convincing but nevertheless contradictory arguments. Their stupid dilemma was blocking my way—Damn! Ouch! . . . I stopped short and to my disgust rolled over into a ditch with my wheels in the air . . .

Oh! Maternal ditch, almost full of muddy water! Fair factory drain! I gulped down your nourishing sludge; and I remembered the blessed black breast of my Sudanese nurse . . . When I came up—torn, filthy, and stinking—from under the capsized car, I felt the white-hot iron of joy deliciously pass through my heart!

A crowd of fishermen with handlines and gouty naturalists were already swarming around the prodigy. With patient, loving care those people rigged a tall derrick and iron grapnels to fish out my car, like a big beached shark. Up it came from the ditch, slowly, leaving in the bottom, like scales, its heavy framework of good sense and its soft upholstery of comfort.

They thought it was dead, my beautiful shark, but a caress from me was enough to revive it; and there it was, alive again, running on its powerful fins!

Allora, col volto coperto dalla buona melma delle officine—impasto di scorie metalliche, di sudori inutili, di fuliggini celesti—noi, contusi e fasciate le braccia ma impavidi, dettammo le nostre prime volontà a tutti gli uomini vivi della terra:

MANIFESTO DEL FUTURISMO

1. Noi vogliamo cantare l'amor del pericolo, l'abitudine all'energia e alla temerità.

2. Il coraggio, l'audacia, la ribellione, saranno elementi essenziali della nostra poesia.

3. La letteratura esaltò fino ad oggi l'immobilità pensosa, l'estasi e il sonno. Noi vogliamo esaltare il movimento aggressivo, l'insonnia febbrile, il passo di corsa, il salto mortale, lo schiaffo ed il pugno.

4. Noi affermiamo che la magnificenza del mondo si è arricchita di una bellezza nuova: la bellezza della velocità. Un automobile da corsa col suo cofano adorno di grossi tubi simili a serpenti dall'alito esplosivo . . . un automobile ruggente, che sembra correre sulla mitraglia, è più bello della Vittoria di Samotracia.

5. Noi vogliamo inneggiare all'uomo che tiene il volante, la cui asta ideale attraversa la Terra, lanciata a corsa, essa pure, sul circuito della sua orbita.

6, Bisogna che il poeta si prodighi, con ardore, sfarzo e munificenza, per aumentare l'entusiastico fervore degli elementi primordiali.

7. Non v'è più bellezza, se non nella lotta. Nessuna opera che non abbia un carattere aggressivo può essere un capolavoro. La poesia deve essere concepita come un violento assalto contro le forze ignote, per ridurle a prostrarsi davanti all'uomo.

8. Noi siamo sul promontorio estremo dei secoli! . . . Perché dovremmo guardarci alle spalle, se vogliamo sfondare le misteriose porte dell'Impossibile? Il Tempo e lo Spazio morirono ieri. Noi viviamo già nell'assoluto, poiché abbiamo già creata l'eterna velocità onnipresente.

9. Noi vogliamo glorificare la guerra—sola igiene del mondo—il militarismo, il patriottismo, il gesto distruttore dei libertari, le belle idee per cui si muore e il disprezzo della donna.

And so, faces smeared with good factory muck—plastered with metallic waste, with senseless sweat, with celestial soot—we, bruised, our arms in slings, but unafraid, declared our high intentions to all the living of the earth:

MANIFESTO OF FUTURISM

1. We intend to sing the love of danger, the habit of energy and fearlessness.

2. Courage, audacity, and revolt will be essential elements of our poetry.

3. Up to now literature has exalted a pensive immobility, ecstasy, and sleep. We intend to exalt aggressive action, a feverish insomnia, the racer's stride, the mortal leap, the punch and the slap.

4. We affirm that the world's magnificence has been enriched by a new beauty: the beauty of speed. A racing car whose hood is adorned with great pipes, like serpents of explosive breath—a roaring car that seems to ride on grapeshot is more beautiful than the Victory of Samothrace.

5. We want to hymn the man at the wheel, who hurls the lance of his spirit across the Earth, along the circle of its orbit.

6. The poet must spend himself with ardor, splendor, and generosity, to swell the enthusiastic fervor of the primordial elements.

7. Except in struggle, there is no more beauty. No work without an aggressive character can be a masterpiece. Poetry must be conceived as a violent attack on unknown forces, to reduce and prostrate them before man.

8. We stand on the last promontory of the centuries! . . . Why should we look back, when what we want is to break down the mysterious doors of the Impossible? Time and Space died yesterday. We already live in the absolute, because we have created eternal, omnipresent speed.

9. We will glorify war—the world's only hygiene—militarism, patriotism, the destructive gesture of freedom-bringers, beautiful ideas worth dying for, and scorn for woman.

F. T. Marinetti 51

10. Noi vogliamo distruggere i musei, le biblioteche, le accademie d'ogni specie, e combattere contro il moralismo, il femminismo e contro ogni viltà opportunistica o utilitaria.

11. Noi canteremo le grandi folle agitate dal lavoro, dal piacere o dalla sommossa: canteremo le maree multicolori o polifoniche delle rivoluzioni nelle capitali moderne; canteremo il vibrante fervore notturno degli arsenali e dei cantieri incendiati da violente lune elettriche; le stazioni ingorde, divoratrici di serpi che fumano; le officine appese alle nuvole pei contorti fili dei loro fumi; i ponti simili a ginnasti giganti che scavalcano i fiumi, balenanti al sole con un lucchichio di coltelli; i piroscafi avventurosi che fiutano l'orizzonte, le locomotive dall'ampio petto, che scalpitano sulle rotaie, come enormi cavalli d'acciaio imbrigliati di tubi, e il volo scivolante degli aeroplani, la cui elica garrisce al vento come una bandiera e sembra applaudire come una folla entusiasta.

È dall'Italia, che noi lanciamo pel mondo questo nostro manifesto di violenza travolgente e incendiaria, col quale fondiamo oggi il «Futurismo», perché vogliamo liberare questo paese dalla sua fetida cancrena di professori, d'archeologhi, di ciceroni e d'antiquarii.

Già per troppo tempo l'Italia è stata un mercato di rigattieri. Noi vogliamo liberarla dagl'innumerevoli musei che la coprono tutta di cimiteri innumerevoli.

[. . .]

In verità io vi dichiaro che la frequentazione quotidiana dei musei, delle biblioteche e delle accademie (cimiteri di sforzi vani, calvarii di sogni crocifissi, registri di slanci troncati! . . .) è, per gli artisti, altrettanto dannosa che la tutela prolungata dei parenti per certi giovani ebbri del loro ingegno e della loro volontà ambiziosa. Per i moribondi, per gl'infermi, pei prigionieri, sia pure: —l'ammirabile passato è forse un balsamo ai loro mali, poiché per essi l'avvenire è sbarrato . . . Ma noi non vogliamo più saperne, del passato, noi, giovani e forti futuristi!

E vengano dunque, gli allegri incendiarii dalle dita carbonizzate! Eccoli! Eccoli! . . . Suvvia! date fuoco agli scaffali delle biblioteche! . . . Sviate il corso dei canali, per inondare i musei! . . . Oh, la gioia di veder

10. We will destroy the museums, libraries, academies of every kind, will fight moralism, feminism, every opportunistic or utilitarian cowardice.

11. We will sing of great crowds excited by work, by pleasure, and by riot; we will sing of the multicolored, polyphonic tides of revolution in the modern capitals; we will sing of the vibrant nightly fervor of arsenals and shipyards blazing with violent electric moons; greedy railway stations that devour smoke-plumed serpents; factories hung on clouds by the crooked lines of their smoke; bridges that stride the rivers like giant gymnasts, flashing in the sun with a glitter of knives; adventurous steamers that sniff the horizon; deep-chested locomotives whose wheels paw the tracks like the hooves of enormous steel horses bridled by tubing; and the sleek flight of planes whose propellers chatter in the wind like banners and seem to cheer like an enthusiastic crowd.

It is from Italy that we launch through the world this violently upsetting incendiary manifesto of ours. With it, today, we establish Futurism, because we want to free this land from its smelly gangrene of professors, archaeologists, ciceroni, and antiquarians. For too long has Italy been a dealer in secondhand clothes. We mean to free her from the numberless museums that cover her like so many graveyards.

[. . .]

In truth I tell you that daily visits to museums, libraries, and academies (cemeteries of empty exertion, calvaries of crucified dreams, registries of aborted beginnings!) are, for artists, as damaging as the prolonged supervision by parents of certain young people drunk with their talent and their ambitious wills. When the future is barred to them, the admirable past may be a solace for the ills of the moribund, the sickly, the prisoner . . . But we want no part of it, the past, we the young and strong Futurists!

So let them come, the gay incendiaries with charred fingers! Here they are! Here they are! . . . Come on! Set fire to the library shelves! Turn aside the canals to flood the museums! . . . Oh, the joy of seeing the glorious old

galleggiare alla deriva, lacere e stinte su quelle acque, le vecchie tele glo-
riose! . . . Impugnate i picconi, le scuri, i martelli e demolite senza pietà le
città venerate!

I più anziani fra noi, hanno trent'anni: ci rimane dunque almeno un de-
cennio, per compier l'opera nostra. Quando avremo quarant'anni, altri uo-
mini più giovani e più validi di noi, ci gettino pure nel cestino, come
manoscritti inutili. Noi lo desideriamo!

[. . .]

L'arte, infatti, non può essere che violenza, crudeltà ed ingiustizia.

I più anziani fra noi hanno trent'anni: eppure, noi abbiamo già sperpe-
rati tesori, mille tesori di forza, di amore, d'audacia, d'astuzia e di rude vo-
lontà; li abbiamo gettati via impazientemente, in furia, senza contare, senza
mai esitare, senza riposarci mai, a perdifiato . . . Guardateci! Non siamo an-
cora spossati! I nostri cuori non sentono alcuna stanchezza, poiché sono
nutriti di fuoco, di odio e di velocità! . . . Ve ne stupite? . . . È logico, poiché
voi non vi ricordate nemmeno di aver vissuto! Ritti sulla cima del mondo,
noi scagliamo una volta ancora, la nostra sfida alle stelle! [. . .]

1909

DA MANIFESTO TECNICO

DELLA LETTERATURA FUTURISTA

In aeroplano, seduto sul cilindro della benzina, scaldato il ventre dalla testa
dell'aviatore, io sentii l'inanità ridicola della vecchia sintassi ereditata da
Omero. Bisogno furioso di liberare le parole, traendole fuori dalla prigione
del periodo latino! Questo ha naturalmente, come ogni imbecille, una testa
previdente, un ventre, due gambe e due piedi piatti, ma non avrà mai due
ali. Appena il necessario per camminare, per correre un momento e fermarsi
quasi subito sbuffando! . . .

Ecco che cosa mi disse l'elica turbinante, mentre filavo a duecento metri
sopra i possenti fumaiuoli di Milano. E l'elica soggiunse:

1. **Bisogna distruggere la sintassi, disponendo i sostan-
tivi a caso, come nascono.**

canvases bobbing adrift on those waters, discolored and shredded! . . .
Take up your pickaxes, your axes, and hammers and wreck, wreck the
venerable cities, pitilessly!

The oldest of us is thirty: so we have at least a decade for finishing our
work. When we are forty, other younger and stronger men will probably
throw us in the wastebasket like useless manuscripts—we want it to hap-
pen!

[. . .]

Art, in fact, can be nothing but violence, cruelty, and injustice.

The oldest of us is thirty: even so we have already scattered treasures,
a thousand treasures of force, love, courage, astuteness, and raw will-
power; have thrown them impatiently away, with fury, carelessly, unhesi-
tatingly, breathless, and unresting . . . Look at us! We are still untired! Our
hearts know no weariness because they are fed with fire, hatred, and
speed! . . . Does that amaze you? It should, because you can never remem-
ber having lived! Erect on the summit of the world, once again we hurl our
defiance at the stars! [. . .]

R. W. FLINT

FROM TECHNICAL MANIFESTO

OF FUTURIST LITERATURE

I was in an airplane, sitting on the gas tank, my stomach warmed by the
pilot's head, when I suddenly felt the absurd inanity of the old syntax in-
herited from Homer. Raging need to free words, releasing them from the
prison of the Latin period. It has, of course, like any imbecile, a provident
head, a stomach, two legs, and two flat feet, but will never have two wings.
Something to walk with, run a few steps, and then stop, panting, almost
immediately! . . .

That's what the whirling propeller told me as I flew two hundred me-
ters above the mighty Milanese smokestacks. And the propeller added:

1. **We must destroy syntax by placing nouns at random
as they are born**.

F. T. Marinetti 55

2. **Si deve usare il verbo all'infinito**, perché si adatti elasticamente al sostantivo e non lo sottoponga all'io dello scrittore che osserva o immagina. Il verbo all'infinito può, solo, dare il senso della continuità della vita e l'elasticità dell'intuizione che la percepisce.

3. **Si deve abolire l'aggettivo** perché il sostantivo nudo conservi il suo colore essenziale. L'aggettivo avendo in sé un carattere di sfumatura, è incompatibile con la nostra visione dinamica, poiché suppone una sosta, una meditazione.

4. **Si deve abolire l'avverbio**, vecchia fibbia che tiene unite l'una all'altra le parole. L'avverbio conserva alla frase una fastidiosa unità di tono.

5. **Ogni sostantivo deve avere il suo doppio**, cioè il sostantivo deve essere seguìto, senza congiunzione, dal sostantivo a cui è legato per analogia. Esempio: uomo-torpediniera, donna-golfo, folla-risacca, piazza-imbuto, porta-rubinetto.

Siccome la velocità aerea ha moltiplicato la nostra conoscenza del mondo, la percezione per analogia diventa sempre più naturale per l'uomo. Bisogna dunque sopprimere il come, il quale, il così, il simile a. Meglio ancora, bisogna fondere direttamente l'oggetto coll'immagine che esso evoca, dando l'immagine in iscorcio mediante una sola parola essenziale.

6. **Abolire anche la punteggiatura**. Essendo soppressi gli aggettivi, gli avverbi e le congiunzioni, la punteggiatura è naturalmente annullata, nella continuità varia di uno stile vivo, che si crea da sé, senza le soste assurde delle virgole e dei punti. Per accentuare certi movimenti e indicare le loro direzioni, s'impiegheranno i segni della matematica: $+ - x : = > <$, e i segni musicali.

7. Gli scrittori si sono abbandonati finora all'analogia immediata. Hanno paragonato per esempio l'animale all'uomo o ad un altro animale, il che equivale ancora, press'a poco, a una specie di fotografia. Hanno paragonato per esempio un fox-terrier a un piccolissimo puro-sangue. Altri, più avanzati, potrebbero paragonare quello stesso fox-terrier trepidante, a una piccola macchina Morse. Io lo paragono, invece, a un'acqua ribollente. V'è in ciò **una gradazione di analogie sempre più vaste**, vi sono dei rapporti sempre più profondi . . . [. . .]

8. **Non vi sono categorie d'immagini**, nobili o grossolane, eleganti o volgari, eccentriche o naturali. L'intuizione che le percepisce non

2. **We must use the verb in the infinitive**, so that it will conform elastically to the noun and will not subordinate it to the I of the writer who sees or imagines. Only the infinitive verb can convey the sense of life's continuity and the elasticity of the intuition that perceives it.

3. **We must abolish the adjective** so that the naked noun can retain its essential color. The adjective, carrying in it a principle of nuance, is incompatible with our dynamic vision, because it implies a pause, a meditation.

4. **We must abolish the adverb**, old clip that holds words together. The adverb maintains a fastidious unity of tone in the sentence.

5. **Every noun should have its double**—that is, a noun should be followed, without any conjunctive phrase, by the noun to which it is tied by analogy. Example: man–torpedo boat, woman-harbor, square-funnel, door-faucet.

Because aerial speed has expanded our knowledge of the world, perception by analogy is becoming increasingly natural to man. Thus we must suppress the like, the as, the so, the similar to, etc. Better still, we must fuse the object directly with the image it evokes by presenting the foreshortened image in a single essential word.

6. **No more punctuation**. Once adjectives, adverbs, and conjunctive phrases are suppressed, punctuation is naturally annulled in the varied continuity of a living style that creates itself, without the absurd pauses of commas and periods. To emphasize certain movements and show their directions, we will use mathematical signs, x + : − = < >, and musical symbols.

7. Up to now writers have indulged themselves in direct analogies. For example, they have compared an animal to man or to another animal, which is still almost the same as photography. For example, they have compared a fox terrier to a tiny thoroughbred. Others, more progressive, might compare this same trembling fox terrier to a little Morse apparatus. I myself compare it to boiling water. **The analogies here have become increasingly vast**, the connections increasingly deep . . . [. . .]

8. **There are no categories of images**, noble or vulgar, elegant or base, eccentric or natural. The intuition that perceives them has

ha né preferenze né partiti-presi. Lo stile analogico è dunque padrone assoluto di tutta la materia e della sua intensa vita.

9. Per dare i movimenti successivi d'un oggetto bisogna dare la **catena delle analogie** che esso evoca, ognuna condensata, raccolta in una parola essenziale. [. . .] In certi casi bisognerà unire le immagini a due a due, come le palle incatenate, che schiantano, nel loro volo tutto un gruppo d'alberi. [. . .] Per avviluppare e cogliere tutto ciò che vi è di più fuggevole e di più inafferrabile nella materia, bisogna formare delle **strette reti d'immagini o analogie**, che verranno lanciate nel mare misterioso dei fenomeni. [. . .]

10. Siccome ogni specie di ordine è fatalmente un prodotto dell'intelligenza cauta e guardinga, bisogna orchestrare le immagini disponendole secondo un **maximum di disordine**.

11. **Distruggere nella letteratura l'«io»**, cioè tutta la psicologia. L'uomo completamente avariato dalla biblioteca e dal museo, sottoposto a una logica e ad una saggezza spaventose, non offre assolutamente più interesse alcuno. Dunque, dobbiamo abolirlo nella letteratura, e sostituirlo finalmente colla materia, di cui si deve afferrare l'essenza a colpi d'intuizione, la qual cosa non potranno mai fare i fisici né i chimici. [. . .]

Ci gridano: «La vostra letteratura non sarà bella! Non avremo più la sinfonia verbale, dagli armoniosi dondolii, e dalle cadenze tranquillizzanti!». Ciò è bene inteso! E che fortuna! Noi utilizziamo, invece, tutti i suoni brutali, tutti i gridi espressivi della vita violenta che ci circonda.

Facciamo coraggiosamente il «brutto» in letteratura, e uccidiamo dovunque la solennità. Via! non prendete di queste arie da grandi sacerdoti, nell'ascoltarmi! Bisogna sputare ogni giorno sull'Altare dell'Arte! Noi entriamo nei domini sconfinati della libera intuizione. Dopo il verso libero, ecco finalmente le **parole in libertà**! [. . .]

Poeti futuristi! Io vi ho insegnato a odiare le biblioteche e i musei, per prepararvi a **odiare l'intelligenza**, ridestando in voi la divina intuizione, dono caratteristico delle razze latine.

Mediante l'intuizione, vinceremo l'ostilità apparentemente irriducibile che separa la nostra carne umana dal metallo dei motori. Dopo il regno animale, ecco iniziarsi il regno meccanico. [. . .]

Milano, 11 Maggio 1912

1912

neither preferences nor prejudices. The analogical style is therefore absolute master of all matter and its intense life.

9. To render the successive movements of an object, we must render the **chain of analogies** it evokes, each one condensed, drawn into one essential word. [. . .] In certain cases we must link images in pairs like chain shot that can level a clump of trees in its flight. [. . .] To surround and capture all that is most fleeting and elusive in matter, we must make **closely woven nets of images or analogies** that we will cast into the mysterious sea of phenomena. [. . .]

10. Since all order is inevitably the product of cautious intelligence, we must orchestrate images by arranging them with a **maximum of disorder**.

11. **Destroy the "I" in literature**—that is, all psychology. Man, utterly ruined by libraries and museums, ruled by a fearful logic and wisdom, is of absolutely no more interest. So abolish him in literature. Replace him with matter, whose essence must be grasped by flashes of intuition, something the physicists and chemists can never do. [. . .]

They shout to us: "It won't be beautiful! We'll have no more verbal symphonies with harmonious modulations and soothing rhythms." That's right. And what luck! Instead we use all the brutal sounds, all the expressive cries of the violent life that surrounds us.

Let us boldly create the "ugly" in literature and kill solemnity wherever it may be. And don't put on those high-priest airs when you listen to me. We must spit every day on the Altar of Art. We are entering the limitless domains of free intuition. After free verse, here at last are **words in freedom**. [. . .]

Futurist poets! I taught you to hate libraries and museums. This was to prepare you to **hate intelligence**, awakening in you the divine intuition that is the distinctive gift of the Latin races.

Through intuition, we will put an end to the seemingly indomitable hostility that separates our human flesh from the metal of engines. After the animal kingdom, the mechanical kingdom begins! [. . .]

Milan, 11 May 1912

ELIZABETH R. NAPIER AND
BARBARA R. STUDHOLME

LE SOIR, COUCHÉE DANS SON LIT,

ELLE RELISAIT LA LETTRE DE

SON ARTILLEUR AU FRONT

1918

AT NIGHT, LYING IN BED, SHE REREADS THE LETTER FROM HER GUNNER AT THE FRONT

ELIZABETH R. NAPIER AND
BARBARA R. STUDHOLME

ARCOBALENO

Inzuppa 7 pennelli nel tuo cuore di 36 anni finiti ieri 7 aprile
E rallumina il viso disfatto delle antiche stagioni

Tu hai cavalcato la vita come le sirene nichelate dei caroselli da fiera
In giro
Da una città all'altra di filosofia in delirio
D'amore in passione di regalità in miseria
Non c'è chiesa cinematografo redazione o taverna che tu non conosca
Tu hai dormito nel letto d'ogni famiglia

Ci sarebbe da fare un carnevale
Di tutti i dolori
Dimenticati con l'ombrello nei caffè d'Europa
Partiti tra il fumo coi fazzoletti negli sleeping-cars diretti al nord al sud

Paesi ore
Ci sono voci che accompagnan pertutto come la luna e i cani
Ma anche il fischio di una ciminiera
Che rimescola i colori del mattino
E dei sogni
Non si dimentica né il profumo di certe notti affogate nelle ascelle di
topazio
Queste fredde giunchiglie che ho sulla tavola accanto all'inchiostro
Eran dipinte sui muri della camera n. 19 nell'Hôtel des Anglais a Rouen

RAINBOW

Dip 7 brushes into your heart 36 years old yesterday April 7th
And touch up that face worn out by the passing seasons

You have ridden life like a nickel-plated mermaid on a carousel
Whirling
From city to city from philosophy to frenzy
Love to passion royalty to poverty
There isn't a church movie theater newsdesk or bar you don't know
You've slept in every family's bed

There should be a carnival
Of all the sorrows
Forgotten along with umbrellas in all the cafes of Europe
Gone in a cloud of smoke with handkerchiefs in the sleeping cars of
        express trains heading north or south

Countries hours
There are voices that follow you everywhere like the moon or a dog
Even the whistle of a smokestack
That stirs the colors of the morning
And of dreams
You won't forget or the scent of certain nights drowned in topaz armpits
These cold narcissus that I keep on the table by the inkwell
Were painted on the walls of Room 19 of the Hôtel des Anglais in Rouen

Un treno passeggiava sul quai notturno
Sotto la nostra finestra
Decapitando i riflessi delle lanterne versicolori
Tra le botti del vino di Sicilia
E la Senna era un giardino di bandiere infiammate

Non c'è più tempo
Lo spazio
È un verme crepuscolare che si raggricchia in una goccia di fosforo
Ogni cosa è presente
Come nel 1902 tu sei a Parigi in una soffitta
Coperto da 35 centimetri quadri di cielo
Liquefatto nel vetro dell'abbaino
La Ville t'offre ancora ogni mattina
Il bouquet fiorito dello Square de Cluny;
Dal boulevard Saint-Germain scoppiante di trams e d'autobus
Arriva la sera a queste campagne la voce briaca della giornalaia
Di rue de la Harpe
«Pari-cûrses» «l'Intransigeant» «la Presse»
Il negozio di Chaussures Raoul fa sempre concorrenza alle stelle
E mi accarezzo le mani tutte intrise dei liquori del tramonto
Come quando pensavo al suicidio vicino alla casa di Rigoletto

Sì caro
L'uomo più fortunato è colui che sa vivere nella contingenza al pari dei fiori
Guarda il signore che passa
E accende il sigaro orgoglioso della sua forza virile
Recuperata nelle quarte pagine dei quotidiani
O quel soldato di cavalleria galoppante nell'indaco della caserma
Con una ciocchetta di lilla fra i denti

L'eternità splende in un volo di mosca
Metti l'uno accanto all'altro i colori dei tuoi occhi
Disegna il tuo arco

A train rambling along the quay late at night
Beneath our window
Beheaded the reflections of multicolored lanterns
Among casks of Sicilian wine
And the Seine was a garden of blazing flags

There is no more time
Space
Is a twilight worm coiled in a drop of phosphorus
Everything is present
As in 1902 you are in a garret in Paris
Sheltered by 35 square centimeters of sky
Melting across the glass of the skylight
La Ville offers you again each morning
The flowering bouquet of the Square de Cluny
From Boulevard Saint-Germain exploding with trams and buses
Every evening you hear the hoarse cry of the paperboy
From Rue de la Harpe
"Pari-cûrses" "l'Intransigeant" "la Presse"
The shoestore Chaussures Raoul still rivals the stars
And I rub my hands stained with the liquors of sunset
Like that time I thought about suicide near Rigoletto's house

Yes my dear
The most fortunate man knows how to live with uncertainty like the flowers
Look at that gentleman strolling past
As he lights his cigar proud of his manly vigor
Restored by the fourth-page spreads in the daily papers
Or that trooper galloping through the indigo darkness of his barracks
A sprig of lilac between his teeth

Eternity shines in the flight of a housefly
Place the colors of your eyes side by side
And sketch the arch

La storia è fuggevole come un saluto alla stazione
E l'automobile tricolore del sole batte sempre più invano il suo record fra i
   vecchi macchinari del cosmo
Tu ti ricordi insieme ad un bacio seminato nel buio
Una vetrina di libraio tedesco Avenue de l'Opéra
E la capra che brucava le ginestre
Sulle ruine della scala del palazzo di Dario a Persepoli
Basta guardarsi intorno
E scriver come si sogna
Per rianimare il volto della nostra gioia

Ricordo tutti i climi che si sono carezzati alla mia pelle d'amore
Raggianti al mio desiderio
Nevi
Mari gialli
Gongs
Carovane
Il carminio di Bombay e l'oro bruciato dell'Iran
Ne porto un geroglifico sull'ala nera
Anima girasole il fenomeno convergere in questo centro di danza
Ma il canto più bello è ancora quello dei sensi nudi

Silenzio musica meridiana
Qui e nel mondo poesia circolare
L'oggi si sposa col sempre
Nel diadema dell'iride che s'alza
Siedo alla mia tavola e fumo e guardo
Ecco una foglia giovane che trilla nel verziere difaccia
I bianchi colombi volteggiano per l'aria come lettere d'amore buttate dalla
   finestra
Conosco il simbolo la cifra il legame
Elettrico
La simpatia delle cose lontane
Ma ci vorrebbero delle frutta delle luci e delle moltitudini
Per tendere il festone miracolo di questa pasqua

History is as fleeting as a nod at the train station
And the tricolor car of the sun keeps breaking its own record pointlessly
    amid the used machinery of the cosmos
You remember along with a kiss planted in the darkness
The window of a German bookseller in the Avenue de l'Opéra
And the goat grazing on yellow broom
Among the ruined stairs of Darius's palace at Persepolis
You need only look around
And write from your dreams
To revive the face of our joy

I remember all the climates that caressed my skin like a lover
Shimmering on my desire
Snows
Yellow seas
Gongs
Caravans
Carmine of Bombay burnt gold of Iran
I carry their hieroglyph on this black wing
Sunflower soul the phenomenon converges here in the center of this dance
But the most beautiful song is still that of the naked senses

Silence music of the south
Here and in the world circular poetry
Today marries Always
In the crown of the rising rainbow
I sit at my table and I smoke and stare
A young leaf trills in the garden right in front of me
White doves flutter through the air like love letters thrown from the
    window
I know the symbol the code the electrical
Connection
The attraction of faraway things
But we need fruit and lights and crowds
To festoon this Easter with miracles

Ardengo Soffici 67

Il giorno si sprofonda nella conca scarlatta dell'estate
E non ci sono più parole
Per il ponte di fuoco e di gemme

Giovinezza tu passerai come tutto finisce al teatro
Tant pis Mi farò allora un vestito favoloso di vecchie affichés

1 9 1 5

CROCICCHIO

Dissolversi nella cipria dell'ordinotte.
Con l'improvviso clamore dell'elettricità del gas dell'acetilene e delle
    altre luci
Fiorite nelle vetrine
Alle finestre e nell'aeroplano del firmamento
Le scarpe che trascinano gocciole di diamanti e d'oro lungo i marciapiedi
    primaverili
Come le bocche e gli occhi
Di tutte queste donne pazze d'isterie solitarie
Le automobili venute da pertutto
Le carrozze reali e i tramways in uno squittio d'uccelli mitragliati

Nous n'avons plus d'amour que pour nous-mêmes enfin

«È proibito parlare al manovratore»

Oh nuotare come un pesce innamorato che beve smeraldi
Fra questa rete di profumi e di bengala!

1 9 1 5

The day sinks into the scarlet basin of summer
And there are no more words
For that bridge of fire and jewels

My youth will pass like the end of every play
Tant pis I'll make myself a fabulous suit out of old posters

OLIVIA SEARS

CROSSROADS

To dissolve in the face-powder of dusktime
With the sudden clamor of electricity of acetylene gas and of the other
    lights
That bloom in the windows
Of shops and apartments and in the aircraft of the sky
Shoes trailing drops of diamonds and gold behind them on the sidewalks
    of spring
Like the mouths and eyes
Of all these women gone mad with their lonely hysterias
Automobiles arriving from everywhere
The regal carriages and the streetcars in a twitter of machine-gunned
    birds

Nous n'avons plus d'amour que pour nous-mêmes enfin

"Talking to the Driver Is Prohibited"

Oh to swim like a love-struck fish drinking emeralds
Through this net of fragrances and Bengal lights!

GEOFFREY BROCK

OSPEDALE DA CAMPO 026

Ozio dolce dell'ospedale!
Si dorme a settimane intere;
Il corpo che avevamo congedato
Non sa credere ancora a questa felicità: vivere.

Le bianche pareti della camera
Son come parentesi quadre,
Lo spirito vi si riposa
Fra l'ardente furore della battaglia d'ieri
E l'enigma fiorito che domani ricomincerà.

Sosta chiara, crogiuolo di sensi multipli;
Qui tutto converge in un'unità indicibile;
Misteriosamente sento fluire un tempo d'oro,
Dove tutto è uguale:
I boschi, le quote della vittoria, gli urli, il sole, il sangue dei morti,

Io stesso, il mondo;
E i quattro gialli limoni
Che guardo amorosamente risplendere
Sul mio nero comodino di ferro.

1918

FIELD HOSPITAL 026

Blessed interlude: the hospital!
where a body, given leave
(and no sense of possibility)
sleeps a whole week

waking in parentheses:
four white walls
between yesterday's screaming batteries
and whatever remains to sprout tomorrow.

In this silent crucible my senses re-knit;
unscramble another life
where all things add up: mangled forests,
improbable sunlight on the blood of the dead,

and this new world I survive for:
a bowl of yellow lemons
brilliantly bitter
on my black bedside cabinet.

LAURIE DUGGAN

Ardengo Soffici 71

SE IN ME

potesse entrare di straforo
la chioma sua
di certo si trasmuterebbe
la tinta del mio sangue in quella
d'oro

1933

LE RONDINE

in deliziose cappe di raso nero
dattilografavano il risveglio
dettato dall'aurora

1933

GRANDE DELIZIA

osservare quel treno sbuffante
salire i gradini traversini
raggiunger la bocca del tunnel
che se lo succhia come lequorizia

1933

Farfa

1879–1964

2 IN 1

If I could steal into the strands
of your blond hair
I know for a fact my blood
would change color, would turn
pure gold

FRED CHAPPELL

THE SWALLOWS

in refreshing capes of black satin
they're typing out the new aubade
daybreak just dictated

FRED CHAPPELL

WHAT FUN

to see how the gasping train
climbs the ladder of rail ties
to get to the mouth of the tunnel
and be sucked in like a licorice stick

FRED CHAPPELL

GIGI

non sono sereno stasera
portami un kocktail di sette colori
come usano a parigi
che mi faccia diventare arcobaleno

1 9 3 3

GIGI

I'm queasy this evening
bring me one of those 7-colored
cocktails like they drink in Paris
I wanna go somewhere over the rainbow

FRED CHAPPELL

INVERNALE

«... cri ... i ... i ... i ... i ... icch» ...

        l'incrinatura
il ghiaccio rabescò, stridula e viva.
«A riva!» Ognuno guadagnò la riva
disertando la crosta malsicura.
«A riva! A riva! ...» Un soffio di paura
disperse la brigata fuggitiva.

«Resta!» Ella chiuse il mio braccio conserto,
le sue dita intrecciò, vivi legami,
alle mie dita. «Resta, se tu m'ami!»
E sullo specchio subdolo e deserto
soli restammo, in largo volo aperto,
ebbri d'immensità, sordi ai richiami.

Fatto lieve così come uno spetro,
senza passato più, senza ricordo,
m'abbandonai con lei, nel folle accordo,
di larghe rote disegnando il vetro.
Dall'orlo il ghiaccio fece cricch, più tetro ...
dall'orlo il ghiaccio fece cricch, più sordo ...

Rabbrividii così, come chi ascolti
lo stridulo sogghigno della Morte,
e mi chinai, con le pupille assorte,

Guido Gozzano

1883–1916

A WINTRY SCENE

"...cre—ee—ee—eak"...

                       in an arabesque across
the ice, shrill and alive, the crack appeared.
"Quick, to the shore!" And everybody there
broke for the shore across the trembling ice.
"Quick, to the shore! To the shore!" The revelers
were scattered by a sudden gust of fear.

"Stay!" And she held my arm against her side,
the live links of her fingers eagerly
twining with mine. "If you love me, stay with me!"
And on that empty treacherous and wide
mirror we stayed alone, in a broad free glide,
deaf to the shouting, drunk with immensity.

Light as a phantom suddenly, unbound,
no memory left, nothing to recollect,
I gave myself to her in a mad compact.
Across the glass we circled round and round.
And at the edge the ice more darkly groaned . . .
and at the edge the ice more deeply cracked . . .

I shivered then, like one who hears the sound
of Death's shrill laughter. Bending, staring at
the ice, I shuddered at the sight of it:

e trasparire vidi i nostri volti
già risupini lividi sepolti . . .
Dall'orlo il ghiaccio fece cricch, più forte . . .

Oh! Come, come, a quelle dita avvinto,
rimpiansi il mondo e la mia dolce vita!
O voce imperiosa dell'istinto!
O voluttà di vivere infinita!
Le dita liberai da quelle dita,
e guadagnai la ripa, ansante, vinto . . .

Ella solo restò, sorda al suo nome,
rotando a lungo, nel suo regno solo.
Le piacque, alfine, ritoccare il suolo;
e ridendo approdò, sfatta le chiome,
e bella ardita palpitante come
la procellaria che raccoglie il volo.

Non curante l'affanno e le riprese
dello stuolo gaietto femminile,
mi cercò, mi raggiunse tra le file
degli amici con ridere cortese:
«Signor mio caro grazie!» E mi protese
la mano breve, sibilando: «Vile!».

1911

TOTÒ MERÚMENI

I

Col suo giardino incolto, le sale vaste, i bei
balconi secentisti guarniti di verzura,
la villa sembra tolta da certi versi miei,
sembra la villa-tipo, del Libro di Lettura . . .

below me two transparent faces frowned
colorless cold and laid out underground . . .
And at the edge the ice more sharply split . . .

Caught in her fingers, how I hungered for
my sweet life and the world I lived it in!
The endless lust to live forevermore!
The imperious voice of instinct deep within!
I pulled my fingers free of hers and then,
panting, undone, I headed for the shore . . .

Alone, deaf to her name, and endlessly
revolving in her solitary reign
she stayed. At last, it pleased her to come in.
She came up laughing, she let her hair fall free,
lovely and bold and breathless she seemed to me
like a petrel safely come to earth again.

Ignoring her breathlessness and the reprimands
of all the girlish brightly colored crowd,
she looked for me, she found me, she came forward
laughingly, through the circle of my friends:
"My hero, thanks so much!" And with her hand
held out to me a moment, hissed: "You coward!"

MICHAEL PALMA

TOTÒ MERÚMENI

I

With its unkempt garden, its vast rooms, its fine
seventeenth-century balconies decked with greenery,
the villa seems cribbed from certain verses of mine,
a model villa, a piece of postcard scenery . . .

Pensa migliori giorni la villa triste, pensa
gaie brigate sotto gli alberi centenari,
banchetti illustri nella sala da pranzo immensa
e danze nel salone spoglio da gli antiquari.

Ma dove in altri tempi giungeva Casa Ansaldo,
Casa Rattazzi, Casa d'Azeglio, Casa Oddone,
s'arresta un automobile fremendo e sobbalzando,
villosi forestieri picchiano la gorgòne.

S'ode un latrato e un passo, si schiude cautamente
la porta . . . In quel silenzio di chiostro e di caserma
vive Totò Merúmeni con una madre inferma,
una prozia canuta ed uno zio demente.

I I

Totò ha venticinque anni, tempra sdegnosa,
molta cultura e gusto in opere d'inchiostro,
scarso cervello, scarsa morale, spaventosa
chiaroveggenza: è il vero figlio del tempo nostro.

Non ricco, giunta l'ora di «vender parolette»
(il suo Petrarca! . . .) e farsi baratto o gazzettiere,
Totò scelse l'esilio. E in libertà riflette
ai suoi trascorsi che sarà bello tacere.

Non è cattivo. Manda soccorso di danaro
al povero, all'amico un cesto di primizie;
non è cattivo. A lui ricorre lo scolaro
pel tema, l'emigrante per le commendatizie.

Gelido, consapevole di sé e dei suoi torti,
non è cattivo. È il buono che derideva il Nietzsche
«. . . in verità derido l'inetto che si dice
buono, perché non ha l'ugne abbastanza forti . . .»

It thinks of its past to ease its present gloom,
of jolly gatherings under ancient oaks,
of legendary feasts in the dining room,
and dances in the great hall, now stripped of antiques.

For where, in better times, the Ansaldos called,
or the d'Azeglios, or this or that contessa,
some motorcar now jerks up, its tires bald,
and hirsute foreigners batter the Medusa.

First comes a bark, then footsteps, then the lazy
creak of the door . . . In that hush (think cloister or tomb)
lives Totò Merúmeni with his ailing mum,
a grizzled great-aunt, and an uncle who's crazy.

II

Totò is twenty-five, haughty by temperament,
has much to say regarding the word on the page,
little sense or scruples, and an alarming bent
for self-scrutiny: a perfect creature of our age.

When penury urged him to "peddle his scribbles"
(there's his Petrarch!) and become a shyster or hack,
Totò chose exile—this after youthful dabbles
(unmentionable here) on which he now thinks back.

He isn't bad: to the poor he sends donations,
to his friends baskets of the choicest fruit;
he isn't bad. The schoolboy seeks him out
for lessons, the emigrant for recommendations.

A cold man, conscious of his nature, its flaws,
he isn't bad. He's the good man Nietzsche lampoons:
"In truth, I always scoff at the weak buffoons
who claim to be good because they have no claws . . ."

Guido Gozzano 81

Dopo lo studio grave, scende in giardino, gioca
coi suoi dolci compagni sull'erba che l'invita;
i suoi compagni sono: una ghiandaia rôca,
un micio, una bertuccia che ha nome Makakita . . .

I I I

La Vita si ritolse tutte le sue promesse.
Egli sognò per anni l'Amore che non venne,
sognò pel suo martirio attrici e principesse
ed oggi ha per amante la cuoca diciottenne.

Quando la casa dorme, la giovinetta scalza,
fresca come una prugna al gelo mattutino,
giunge nella sua stanza, lo bacia in bocca, balza
su lui che la possiede, beato e resupino . . .

I V

Totò non può sentire. Un lento male indomo
inaridì le fonti prime del sentimento;
l'analisi e il sofisma fecero di quest'uomo
ciò che le fiamme fanno d'un edificio al vento.

Ma come le ruine che già seppero il fuoco
esprimono i giaggioli dai bei vividi fiori,
quell'anima riarsa esprime a poco a poco
una fiorita d'esili versi consolatori . . .

V

Così Totò Merúmeni, dopo tristi vicende,
quasi è felice. Alterna l'indagine e la rima.
Chiuso in se stesso, medita, s'accresce, esplora, intende
la vita dello Spirito che non intese prima.

After serious study, he goes outside to play
with his dear companions on their grassy plat;
and his companions are: a raucous jay,
a Barbary ape named Makakita, and a cat.

III

Life broke all its promises. For years he was tortured
by storybook dreams of Love that never took;
actresses and princesses often featured.
His lover today is the eighteen-year-old cook.

As the villa slumbers, the girl enters his chambers,
barefoot, fresh as a plum in the chill of dawn . . .
She bends to kiss him on the mouth, then clambers
atop him; blissfully supine, he helps her on . . .

IV

Totò can't feel. A slow, unchecked malaise
dried up his founts of feeling; analysis
and sophistry have done to him what a blaze
does to a house as high winds howl and hiss.

But just as ruins left in a fire's wake
may utter irises with their vivid blooms,
this parched soul manages, over time, to make
a scattering of slight, consoling poems . . .

V

Thus, after fortune's sad vicissitudes, Totò
grows nearly happy. He alternates research and rhyme.
Apart, he ponders, explores, and comes to know
something of the life of the Spirit, for the first time.

Perché la voce è poca, e l'arte prediletta
immensa, perché il Tempo—mentre ch'io parlo!—va,
Totò opra in disparte, sorride, e meglio aspetta.
E vive. Un giorno è nato. Un giorno morirà.

1 9 1 1

I COLLOQUI (III)

L'immagine di me voglio che sia
sempre ventenne, come in un ritratto;
amici miei, non mi vedrete in via,

curvo dagli anni, tremulo, e disfatto!
Col mio silenzio resterò l'amico
che vi fu caro, un poco mentecatto;

il fanciullo sarò tenero e antico
che sospirava al raggio delle stelle,
che meditava Arturo e Federico,

ma lasciava la pagina ribelle
per seppellir le rondini insepolte,
per dare un'erba alle zampine delle

disperate cetonie capovolte . . .

1 9 1 1

LA PIÙ BELLA!

I

Ma bella più di tutte l'Isola Non-Trovata:
quella che il Re di Spagna s'ebbe da suo cugino
il Re di Portogallo con firma sugellata
e bulla del Pontefice in gotico latino.

Because his voice is small and his chosen art
immense, because Time—even as I speak!—does fly,
he smiles, and hopes for better, and works apart.
He's living. One day he was born. One day he'll die.

GEOFFREY BROCK

THE COLLOQUIES: 3

I want my image to be always young,
fixed at twenty, as by the artist's hand.
Friends, you won't see me doddering along

bent with the years, hands shaking, all unmanned.
And with my silence I will always be
the friend you loved, a trifle scatterbrained.

I'll stay the tender boy eternally
who looked up at the glowing stars and sighed,
who sifted Arthur and Friedrich's philosophy

but left the rebellious page and went outside
to bury the unburied swallows there,
to extend a blade of grass to the terrified

overturned beetles clawing at the air . . .

MICHAEL PALMA

THE LOVELIEST

I

But loveliest of all, the Unfound Isle:
the King of Spain received it from his cousin,
the King of Portugal, with a royal seal
and the Pope's bull, scrawled in a Gothic Latin.

Guido Gozzano 85

L'Infante fece vela pel regno favoloso,
vide le fortunate: Iunonia, Gorgo, Hera
e il Mare di Sargasso e il Mare Tenebroso
quell'isola cercando . . . Ma l'isola non c'era.

Invano le galee panciute a vele tonde,
le caravelle invano armarono la prora:
con pace del Pontefice l'isola si nasconde,
e Portogallo e Spagna la cercano tuttora.

II

L'isola esiste. Appare talora di lontano
tra Teneriffe e Palma, soffusa di mistero:
«. . . l'Isola Non-Trovata!» Il buon Canarïano
dal Picco alto di Teyde l'addita al forestiero.

La segnano le carte antiche dei corsari.
. . . *Hifola da-trovarfi?* . . . *Hifola pellegrina?* . . .
È l'isola fatata che scivola sui mari;
talora i naviganti la vedono vicina . . .

Radono con le prore quella beata riva:
tra fiori mai veduti svettano palme somme,
odora la divina foresta spessa e viva,
lacrima il cardamomo, trasudano le gomme . . .

S'annuncia col profumo, come una cortigiana,
l'Isola Non-Trovata . . . Ma, se il pilota avanza,
rapida si dilegua come parvenza vana,
si tinge dell'azzurro color di lontananza . . .

1913

Seeking the fabled place, the Infante passed
the Fortunate Isles—Junonia, Gorgo, Hera,
sailed the Sea of Darkness and the Sargasso,
eye to his glass . . . The island was not there.

In vain the sails of the stout galleys swelled,
in vain they fitted out their caravels:
with the Pope's peace, the island hid itself;
Spain seeks it still, and Portugal as well.

I I

The isle exists. Occasionally it appears
between La Palma and Tenerife, beguiling.
On Teide's peak, the kind Canaryman steers
the foreigner's gaze: "There, the Unfound Isle!"

It's marked on the parchment maps of privateers:
Wandering ifle? or Ifland to-be-found?
It's the enchanted isle that rides the waters,
and sometimes sailors see it close at hand:

Their vessels glide along its blessed shore;
the dense green sacred forest scents the air;
over the nameless flowers, huge palms soar;
cardamom weeps, the rubber trees perspire . . .

The Unfound Isle, announced by fragrances,
like courtesans . . . And like vain semblances,
when pilots sail too near it vanishes,
turning that shade of blue that distance is.

GEOFFREY BROCK

A MIA MOGLIE

Tu sei come una giovane
una bianca pollastra.
Le si arruffano al vento
le piume, il collo china
per bere, e in terra raspa;
ma, nell'andare, ha il lento
tuo passo di regina,
ed incede sull'erba
pettoruta e superba.
È migliore del maschio.
È come sono tutte
le femmine di tutti
i sereni animali
che avvicinano a Dio.
Così, se l'occhio, se il giudizio mio
non m'inganna, fra queste hai le tue uguali,
e in nessun'altra donna.
Quando la sera assonna
le gallinelle,
mettono voci che ricordan quelle,
dolcissime, onde a volte dei tuoi mali
ti quereli, e non sai
che la tua voce ha la soave e triste
musica dei pollai.

Umberto Saba

1883–1957

TO MY WIFE

You are like
a young white hen,
with feathers ruffled
in the wind, who bends her neck
to drink and scratch the ground
yet walks with your same slow
and queenly step,
proud and puffed up
as she struts on the grass.
She is better than the male.
She is like all
the females of all
the peaceful animals
living close to God.
So if my eye does not deceive me,
if my judgment is correct, it is in their number
that you find your equals,
and in no other woman.
When evening comes to lull
the chickens all to sleep,
they coo in voices that recall
the sweet sounds you sometimes make
when ailing, unaware
you're echoing the sad and gentle
music of the henhouse.

Tu sei come una gravida
giovenca;
libera ancora e senza
gravezza, anzi festosa;
che, se la lisci, il collo
volge, ove tinge un rosa
tenero la tua carne.
se l'incontri e muggire
l'odi, tanto è quel suono
lamentoso, che l'erba
strappi, per farle un dono.
È così che il mio dono
t'offro quando sei triste.

Tu sei come una lunga
cagna, che sempre tanta
dolcezza ha negli occhi,
e ferocia nel cuore.
Ai tuoi piedi una santa
sembra, che d'un fervore
indomabile arda,
e così ti riguarda
come il suo Dio e Signore.
Quando in casa o per via
segue, a chi solo tenti
avvicinarsi, i denti
candidissimi scopre.
Ed il suo amore soffre
di gelosia.

Tu sei come la pavida
coniglia. Entro l'angusta
gabbia ritta al vederti
s'alza,

You are like a pregnant
heifer,
still roaming free and still
unburdened, frolicsome, in fact,
who when you stroke her
bends her neck toward you,
the skin beneath a tender pink.
And if sometimes you hear her
moo, so plaintive is the sound
of it, you tear the grass up from the ground
and give it to her as a gift.
So, too, do I offer you
my gift when you feel sad.

You are like a lanky
dog, with eyes so
full of tenderness,
such fierceness in her heart.
At your feet she seems
a saint, burning with
untamable devotion,
looks up at you
as to her Lord and God.
When following close behind,
at home or on the street,
to all who so much as approach
she bares her pure white teeth.
Hers is a love disturbed
by jealousy.

You are like the timid
rabbit, who in her narrow
cage stands straight up
at the sight of you,

e verso te gli orecchi
alti protende e fermi;
che la crusca e i radicchi
tu le porti, di cui
priva in sé si rannicchia,
cerca gli angoli bui.
Chi potrebbe quel cibo
ritoglierle? chi il pelo
che si strappa di dosso,
per aggiungerlo al nido
dove poi partorire?
Chi mai farti soffrire?

Tu sei come la rondine
che torna in primavera.
Ma in autunno riparte;
e tu non hai quest'arte.
Tu questo hai della rondine:
le movenze leggere:
questo che a me, che mi sentiva ed era
vecchio, annunciavi un'altra primavera.

Tu sei come la provvida
formica. Di lei, quando
escono alla campagna,
parla al bimbo la nonna
che l'accompagna.
E così nella pecchia
ti ritrovo, ed in tutte
le femmine di tutti
i sereni animali
che avvicinano a Dio;
e in nessun'altra donna.

1910

and toward you turns
her long, unmoving ears,
waiting for the bran and chicory
you bring to her. If left unfed
she huddles up into herself,
seeks out dark corners.
But who would ever deny her
that food? Who could ever
strip her of the fur she plucks
from her own skin to build the nest
where she will bear her young?
Who could ever do you harm?

You are like the swallow
that returns each year in spring;
but then she leaves again in autumn,
and you're not like that at all.
What makes you like the swallow
are your graceful movements,
and that you heralded, to one who felt
and was so old as I, another spring.

You are like the wise, far-seeing
ant, that a grandmother might
hold up as an example
to her grandson
while on a country walk.
And in the honeybee
I see you too, and in all
the females of all
the peaceful animals
living close to God;
and in no other woman.

STEPHEN SARTARELLI

Umberto Saba

LA CAPRA

Ho parlato a una capra.
Era sola sul prato, era legata.
Sazia d'erba, bagnata
dalla pioggia, belava.

Quell'uguale belato era fraterno
al mio dolore. Ed io risposi, prima
per celia, poi perché il dolore è eterno,
ha una voce e non varia.
Questa voce sentiva
gemere in una capra solitaria.

In una capra dal viso semita
sentiva querelarsi ogni altro male,
ogni altra vita.

1 9 1 0

TRIESTE

Ho attraversata tutta la città.
Poi ho salita un'erta,
popolosa in principio, in là deserta,
chiusa da un muricciolo:
un cantuccio in cui solo
siedo; e mi pare che dove esso termina
termini la città.

Trieste ha una scontrosa
grazia. Se piace,
è come un ragazzaccio aspro e vorace,

THE GOAT

I've spoken to a goat.
She was alone in the field, she was tethered.
Sated with grass, drenched
with rain, she bleated.

Her steady bleating brothered
my own grief. And I replied—at first
in jest, and then because the voice of grief
is one unchanging everlasting note.
That was the voice
moaning out of the solitary goat.

Out of that goat with its Semitic face
came grievances regarding every evil,
from every throat.

GEOFFREY BROCK

TRIESTE

I crossed the entire city
then headed uphill;
it was crowded at first, deserted farther on.
Enclosed by a little wall:
this alcove where alone
I sit and it seems that where this ends
the city ends.

Trieste has an irritable
grace. Its appeal
is a ragamuffin's, gruff and greedy,

con gli occhi azzurri e mani troppo grandi
per regalare un fiore;
come un amore
con gelosia.
Da quest'erta ogni chiesa, ogni sua via
scopro, se mena all'ingombrata spiaggia,
o alla collina cui, sulla sassosa
cima,una casa, l'ultima, s'aggrappa.
Intorno
circola ad ogni cosa
un'aria strana, un'aria tormentosa,
l'aria natia.

La mia città che in ogni parte è viva,
ha il cantuccio a me fatto, alla mia vita
pensosa e schiva.

1912

UN RICORDO

Non dormo. Vedo una strada, un boschetto,
che sul mio cuore come un'ansia preme;
dove si andava, per star soli e insieme,
io e un altro ragazzetto.

Era la Pasqua; i riti lunghi e strani
dei vecchi. E se non mi volesse bene
—pensavo—e non venisse più domani?
E domani non venne. Fu un dolore.
uno spasimo fu verso la sera;
che un'amicizia (oggi lo so) non era,
era quello un amore;

blue-eyed, his hands
too big for giving
flowers, like a jealous love.
From up here, I can make out
every church, every street
leading down to a packed
beach, or up a hill to a rocky peak
where a house, the last one, clings.
And all around
circling everything
a strange, nagging air,
the native air.

My city, everywhere alive
has made a little alcove where I can live
my pensive, my timid life.

JACQUELINE OSHEROW

A MEMORY

I cannot sleep. I see a street, some pines,
and in my heart the old anxieties gather.
We used to go there alone, to be together,
another boy and I.

It was Passover, the old folks' rites arcane
and slow. And if he doesn't care enough,
I thought, and if he doesn't come tomorrow?
Tomorrow he did not come: a new pain.
Spasms that evening of grief. Now I know
friendship wasn't what we had in our grove;
what we had was love—

il primo; e quale e che felicità
n'ebbi, tra i colli e il mare di Trieste.
Ma perché non dormire, oggi, con queste
storie di, credo, quindici anni fa?

1 9 1 5

MEZZOGIORNO D'INVERNO

In quel momento ch'ero già felice
(Dio mi perdoni la parola grande
e tremenda) chi quasi al pianto spinse
mia breve gioia? Voi direte: «Certa
bella creatura che di là passava,
e ti sorrise». Un palloncino invece,
un turchino vagante palloncino
nell'azzurro dell'aria, ed il nativo
cielo non mai come nel chiaro e freddo
mezzogiorno d'inverno risplendente.
Cielo con qualche nuvoletta bianca,
e i vetri delle case al sol fiammanti,
e il fumo tenue d'uno due camini,
e su tutte le cose, le divine
cose, quel globo dalla mano incauta
d'un fanciullo sfuggito (egli piangeva
certo in mezzo alla folla il suo dolore,
il suo grande dolore) tra il Palazzo
della Borsa e il Caffè dove seduto
oltre i vetri ammiravo io con lucenti
occhi or salire or scendere il suo bene.

1 9 2 0

the first. And such love then, and what a glow
of joy, between the hills and sea of Trieste . . .
But why, tonight, am I unable to rest,
when all that happened fifteen years ago?

GEOFFREY BROCK

WINTER NOON

Who in the moment of my happiness
(God forgive my using a word so grand,
so terrible) reduced my brief delight
nearly to tears? "A certain lovely creature,"
you'll surely say, "who smiled at you in passing."
But no: a blue meandering balloon
against the azure air, my native sky
never so clear and cold as then, at noon
that dazzling winter day: a few small clouds,
and upper windows flaming in the sun,
and faint smoke from a chimney, maybe two—
and over everything, every divine
thing, that globe that had escaped a boy's
incautious fingers (surely he was out there,
broadcasting through the crowded square his grief,
his immense grief) between the great façade
of the Stock Exchange and the café where I,
behind a window, watched with shining eyes
the rise and fall of what he once possessed.

GEOFFREY BROCK

DA AUTOBIOGRAFIA (3)

Mio padre è stato per me «l'assassino»,
fino ai vent'anni che l'ho conosciuto.
Allora ho visto ch'egli era un bambino;
e che il dono ch'io ho da lui l'ho avuto.

Aveva in volto il mio sguardo azzurrino,
in miseria, un sorriso dolce e astuto.
Andò sempre pel mondo pellegrino:
più d'una donna l'ha amato e pasciuto.

Egli era gaio e leggero: mia madre
tutti sentiva della vita i pesi.
Di mano ei le sfuggì come un pallone.

«Non somigliare—ammoniva—a tuo padre».
Ed io più tardi in me stesso lo intesi:
Eran due razze in antica tenzone.

1923

DA TRE POESIE ALLA MIA BALIA: 1

Mia figlia
mi tiene il braccio intorno al collo, ignudo;
ed io alla sua carezza m'addormento.

Divento
legno in mare caduto che sull' onda
galleggia. E dove alla vicina sponda
anelo, il flutto mi porta lontano.

FROM AUTOBIOGRAPHY (3)

My father was "the murderer" to me
until I met him in my twentieth year.
That he was still a child was plain to see;
that my gift came from him was also clear.

I found in my father's face my own blue gaze;
his smile, though he was poor, was sweet and clever.
He went about the world as a pilgrim goes;
was loved and nourished by more than one lover.

He was a light and cheerful man; my mother
felt all the groaning heaviness of life.
And he slipped through her hands like a balloon.

"You better not," she warned, "be like your father."
I later understood her in myself:
they were two races in an ancient agon.

GEOFFREY BROCK

FROM THREE POEMS TO MY WET NURSE: 1

My daughter
wraps her naked arm around my neck.
I fall asleep to her caress

and turn into
a piece of driftwood floating on the waves,
yearning for the nearby shore but carried
by the current far to sea.

Oh, come sento che lottare è vano!
Oh, come in petto per dolcezza il cuore
vien meno!

Al seno
approdo di colei che Berto ancora
mi chiama, al primo, all' amoroso seno,
ai verdi paradisi dell' infanzia.

1 9 3 3

ULISSE

O tu che sei sì triste ed hai presagi
d'orrore—Ulisse al declino—nessuna
dentro l'anima tua dolcezza aduna
la Brama
per una
pallida sognatrice di naufragi
che t'ama?

1 9 3 4

DONNA

Quand'eri
giovanetta pungevi
come una mora di macchia. Anche il piede
t'era un arma, o selvaggia.

Eri difficile a prendere.

        Ancora

Ah, how vain it feels to struggle!
Ah, how tenderly my heart within me
falters!

I fall to land
upon the breast of her for whom I still am
Berto, upon that first and loving breast,
green paradise of childhood.

STEPHEN SARTARELLI

ULYSSES

O you who are so sad and foresee horrors—
Ulysses in decline—is there no pool
of longing welling sweetly in that soul
of yours
for a pale
girl who dreams of shipwrecks, and who
loves you?

GEOFFREY BROCK

WOMAN

When young
you stung
like blackberry thorns. Even your foot
was sharp, you savage.

You were difficult to hold.
                                    Still

giovane, ancora
sei bella. I segni
degli anni, quelli del dolore, legano
l'anime nostre, una ne fanno. E dietro
i capelli nerissimi che avvolgo
alle mie dita, più non temo il piccolo
bianco puntuto orecchio demoniaco.

1 9 3 4

SERA DI FEBBRAIO

Spunta la luna.
        Nel viale è ancora
giorno, una sera che rapida cala.
Indifferente gioventù si allaccia;
sbanda a povere mete.
        Ed è il pensiero
della morte che, infine, aiuta vivere.

1 9 4 4

IL VETRO ROTTO

Tutto si muove contro te. Il maltempo,
le luci che si spengono, la vecchia
casa scossa a una raffica e a te cara
per il male sofferto, le speranze
deluse, qualche bene in lei goduto.
Ti pare il sopravvivere un rifiuto
d'obbedienza alle cose.
        E nello schianto
del vetro alla finestra è la condanna.

1 9 4 4

you are young, still
you're beautiful. The scars
of years, of sadness, bind
our souls, making them one. And behind
the jet black hair I wind
around my finger, I no longer fear
the small white pointed demonic ear.

V. PENELOPE PELIZZON

FEBRUARY EVENING

The moon appears.
                    The avenue is still
sunlit, though evening has begun to fall.
The indifferent young make their connections,
veer off toward small aims.
                    And it's the thought
of death that helps us, after all, to live.

GEOFFREY BROCK

THE BROKEN PANE

It all conspires against you. Nasty weather,
lights that keep burning out, and the old house
jolted by every gust. It's dear to you
for what you suffered in it, for the hopes
dashed there, and for a few good times as well.
Survival seems to you a refusal to obey
the way of things.
                    And in the shattering
of a window pane, you hear a judgment passed.

GEOFFREY BROCK

AMORE

Ti dico addio quando ti cerco Amore,
come il mio tempo e questo grigio vuole.
Oh, in te era l'ombra della terra e il sole,
e il cuore d'un fanciullo senza cuore.

1947

DA SCORCIATOIE

3

ULTIMO CROCE. In una casa dove uno s'impicca, altri si ammazzano fra di loro, altri si danno alla prostituzione o muoiono faticosamente di fame, altri ancora vengono avviati al carcere o al manicomio, si apre una porta e si vede una vecchia signora che suona—molto bene—la spinetta.

10

COCTEAU. Ricordo, dopo dieci e più anni, l'*Orfeo* di Cocteau. E lo ricordo così.

Un marito, irritato per non aver avuto il premio di poesia, litiga con sua moglie. Un vetro va in frantumi. Entra un operaio, per eseguire la riparazione. L'uomo non vede (o finge); ma la donna si accorge, con sgomento, che l'operaio lavora *senza toccar terra*, campato in aria. «Sono stanca» esplode «di misteri. Ho chiamato un vetraio, e non un angelo.»

17

QUEL PASSANTE che si fa un piacere d'avvisarti che i lacci delle tue scarpe si sono sciolti, è un uomo impossibile. Forse ne sei accorto da solo, e cerchi, senza darlo a vedere, un luogo per rimediare. Forse cammini perseguitato dalle Furie. Nel primo caso ti riesce solo importuno, nel secondo . . .

LOVE

I say goodbye when I approach you, Love,
as my age and this gray would have me do.
There was the shadow of the earth and sun
and, oh, the heart of a heartless boy in you.

GEOFFREY BROCK

FROM **SHORTCUTS**

3

LAST STRAW. In a house where one person hangs himself, where others kill each other, where some are prostitutes, and some are dying painfully of hunger, where still others are destined for jail or the madhouse, a door opens, and you can see an old woman playing the spinet. Playing it very well.

10

COCTEAU. After more than ten years, I still remember Cocteau's *Orfeo*. This is how I remember it.

A husband, upset because he hasn't won a poetry prize, is quarreling with his wife. A window shatters. In comes a workman to repair it. The husband doesn't (or pretends not to) notice, though the woman, appalled, does see that the workman is doing his job *without touching the ground*. He's floating on the air. "I'm tired of mysteries," she explodes. "I called for a glazier, not an angel."

17

THE PASSERBY who takes pleasure in telling you that your shoelaces are undone is a useless person. Perhaps you knew it yourself and are looking for an out-of-the-way place to fix them. Or perhaps you are being pursued by the Furies. In the first instance, he is just a nuisance. In the second . . .

48

GLI STRILLI acutissimi dei bimbi in cuna, o portati a prendere il sole da madri amorose, in carrozzella, ricordano, molto da vicino, i: Presto Francia! Presto Polonia! di Adolfo Hitler.

59

NIETZSCHE, il mio Nietzsche, il mio buon Nietzsche (non quello altro e di altri) è così affascinante perché parla all'anima e di cose dell'anima come Carmen parlava d'amore a don José. «Non ci si annoiava con quella ragazza!» diceva questi a Merimée, alla vigilia di morire per lei. E nemmeno noi ci annoiamo con Nietzsche. Nietzsche non fu un filosofo; fu il caso estremo di una quasi completa sublimazione di Eros.

Fu anche altre cose; lo so.

95

UN POETA che ammiro, a un critico che, durante un pranzo, gli parlava bene di un altro poeta (Montale), voleva—e si era appena alla pasta asciutta—*cavargli un occhio con la forchetta.* Col suo gesto (fortunatamente stornato) il giovane, e un po' ebbro, Ungaretti, dimostrava: 1° Quanto era poeta; 2° Quanto i poeti sono, irrimediabilmente, infantili.

1 9 4 6

4 8

THE SHARP, shrill cries of babies in their cradles, or being pushed in carriages to take the sun by their loving mothers, recall at very close quarters the "Tomorrow the world!" of Adolf Hitler.

5 9

NIETZSCHE, my Nietzsche, my good Nietzsche (not that Nietzsche of others), is so fascinating because he speaks to one's soul and about the soul in the way Carmen spoke to Don José about love. "One never gets tired of that girl!" he told Merimée, just before dying for her. And we never get tired of Nietzsche. Nietzsche wasn't a philosopher. He was the epitome of an almost complete sublimation of Eros.

He was other things too, I know.

9 5

POETS. When, during a meal, a critic spoke well to a poet I like of another poet (Montale), the poet tried, and we were just at the pasta, to *poke his eyes out with a fork*. With this (fortunately thwarted) act, the young and slightly drunk Ungaretti demonstrated (1) how much of a poet he was, and (2) how irremediably infantile poets are.

ESTELLE GILSON

PAESI

Esplodon le simpatiche campane
d'un bianco campanile sopra i tetti
grigi; donne con rossi fazzoletti
cavano da un rotondo forno il pane.

Ammazzano un maiale nella neve
tra un gruppo di bambini affascinati
dal sangue, che con gli occhi spalancati
aspettan la crudele agonia breve.

Gettano i galli vittoriosi squilli.
I buoi escono dai fienili neri;
si spargono su l'argine, tranquilli,

scendono a bere gravi acqua d'argento.
Nei campi, rosei, bianchi, i cimiteri
sperano in mezzo al verde del frumento.

1 9 0 9

Corrado Govoni

1884–1965

THE VILLAGES

A sympathy of bells explodes
From a white bell-tower above
The gray roofs. Out of a large oven
Women with red kerchiefs pull the loaves.

In the new snow they've brought a pig
To slaughter; around, enchanted by
The blood, children wait for that quick
Cruel agony, with big eyes.

The cocks all peal triumphantly.
Oxen come from the black hay-barns,
Spreading over the banksides, quietly,

Then go down, grave, to drink the silver water.
In the fields, pink and white, the graveyards
Shine among the green waves of the wheat.

W. D. SNODGRASS

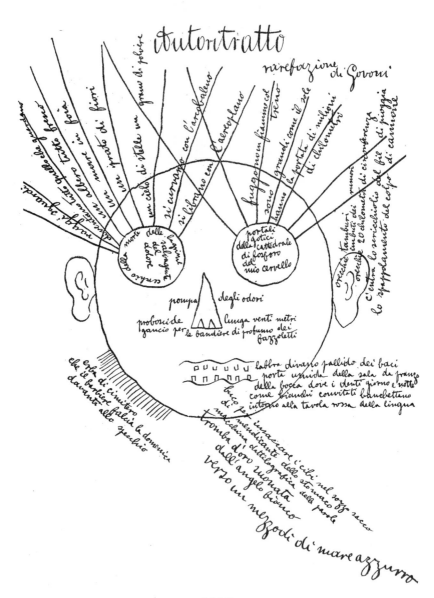

1915

SELF-PORTRAIT

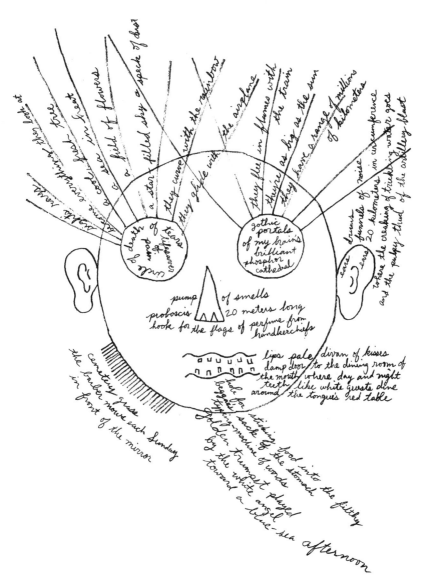

GEOFFREY BROCK

LA TROMBETTINA

Ecco che cosa resta
di tutta la magia della fiera
quella trombettina
di latta azzurra e verde,
che suona una bambina
camminando, scalza, per i campi.
Ma, in quella nota sforzata,
ci son dentro i pagliacci bianchi e rossi,
c'è la banda d'oro rumoroso,
la giostra coi cavalli, l'organo, i lumini.
Come, nello sgocciolare della gronda,
c'è tutto lo spavento della bufera,
la bellezza dei lampi e dell'arcobaleno;
nell'umido cerino d'una lucciola
che si sfa su una foglia di brughiera
tutta la meraviglia della primavera.

1924

THE LITTLE TRUMPET

And here's what is left
of the magic of the fair:
a little tin trumpet,
blue and green,
a barefoot little girl tooting
as she walks through the fields.
But inside that forced note
are clowns dressed white-and-red
and a band all noisy gold,
a calliope, a merry-go-round, and lanterns.
As in the dripping of the gutter
is the shudder of the storm,
the beauty of the lightning and the rainbow;
as in the damp match of the firefly
going out on a heather leaf
is all the marvel of spring.

FELIX STEFANILE

DA LA NOTTE

Ricordo una vecchia città, rossa di mura e turrita, arsa su la pianura ster-
minata nell'Agosto torrido, con il lontano refrigerio di colline verdi e molli
sullo sfondo. Archi enormemente vuoti di ponti sul fiume impaludato in
magre stagnazioni plumbee: sagome nere di zingari mobili e silenziose sulla
riva: tra il barbaglio lontano di un canneto lontane forme ignude di ado-
lescenti e il profilo e la barba giudaica di un vecchio: e a un tratto dal mezzo
dell'acqua morta le zingare e un canto; da la palude afona una nenia pri-
mordiale monotona e irritante: e del tempo fu sospeso il corso.

■ ■ ■

Inconsciamente colui che io ero stato si trovava avviato verso la torre bar-
bara, la mitica custode dei sogni dell'adolescenza. Saliva al silenzio delle
straducole antichissime lungo le mura di chiese e di conventi: non si udiva
il rumore dei suoi passi. Una piazzetta deserta, casupole schiacciate, fi-
nestre mute: a lato in un balenìo enorme la torre, otticuspide rossa impen-
etrabile arida. Una fontana del cinquecento taceva inaridita, la lapide
spezzata nel mezzo del suo commento latino. Si svolgeva una strada acciot-
tolata e deserta verso la città.

[. . .]

■ ■ ■

Dino Campana

1885–1932

FROM **THE NIGHT**

I remember an old city, red walls and red battlements, on the immense plain burnt out from the August heat, with the far-away spongy cold comfort of green hills in the background. Enormous emptiness of bridge-arches over the stagnant river dried to thin leaden puddles: a black molding of Gypsies shifting and silent along the banks: among the dazzle and glare of a distant canebrake the far-off naked figures of teenage boys and the Hasidic beard of an old man: and suddenly out of the midst of the dead water the Gypsy women came and a song, primordial dirge from the voiceless swamp monotonous and irritating: and time ground down and held still.

■ ■ ■

The person I had once been found himself unconsciously heading toward the barbarous tower, legendary keeper of adolescent dreams. In the silence of ancient lanes and half-streets he climbed up alongside the church and the convent walls: you couldn't even hear the noise of his footsteps. A deserted little piazza, broken hovels like old bruises, dead windows: to one side in an enormous wash of light, the tower, eight-pointed arid impenetrably red and unadorned; a dried-up sixteenth-century fountain kept silent, its stone shattered in the middle of its own Latin commentary. A deserted cobblestone road opened up toward the city.

[. . .]

■ ■ ■

Non seppi mai come, costeggiando torpidi canali, rividi la mia ombra che mi derideva nel fondo. Mi accompagnò per strade male odoranti dove le femmine cantavano nella caldura. Ai confini della campagna una porta incisa di colpi, guardata da una giovine femmina in veste rosa, pallida e grassa, la attrasse: entrai. Una antica e opulente matrona dal profilo di montone, coi neri capelli agilmente attorti sulla testa sculturale barbaramente decorata dall'occhio liquido come da una gemma nera dagli sfaccettamenti bizzarri sedeva, agitata da grazie infantili che rinascevano colla speranza traendo essa da un mazzo di carte lunghe e untuose strane teorie di regine languenti re fanti armi e cavalieri. Salutai e una voce conventuale, profonda e melodrammatica mi rispose insieme ad un grazioso sorriso aggrinzito. Distinsi nell'ombra l'ancella che dormiva colla bocca semiaperta, rantolante di un sonno pesante, seminudo il bel corpo agile e ambrato. Sedetti piano.

[. . .]

E allora figurazioni di un'antichissima libera vita, di enormi miti solari, di stragi di orgie si crearono avanti al mio spirito. Rividi un'antica immagine, una forma scheletrica vivente per la forza misteriosa di un mito barbaro, gli occhi gorghi cangianti vividi di linfe oscure, nella tortura del sogno scoprire il corpo vulcanizzato, due chiazze due fori di palle di moschetto sulle sue mammelle estinte. Credetti di udire fremere le chitarre là nella capanna d'assi e di zingo sui terreni vaghi della città, mentre una candela schiariva il terreno nudo. In faccia a me una matrona selvaggia mi fissava senza batter ciglio. La luce era scarsa sul terreno nudo nel fremere delle chitarre. A lato sul tesoro fiorente di una fanciulla in sogno la vecchia stava ora aggrappata come un ragno mentre pareva sussurrare all'orecchio parole che non udivo, dolci come il vento senza parole della Pampa che sommerge.

[. . .]

1914

I never knew how I saw my own shadow coasting along the torpid canals, my ghost that laughed back at me from the depths. It went with me along the strong-smelling streets where women sang in the hot weather. At the edge of the countryside a door cut in the stone, watched by a young woman in a pale dress, pale and fat, caught its eye: I entered. An aging but opulent older woman was sitting inside, profile like a ram's, with black hair twisted loosely about her sculptural head wildly decorated by a rheumy eye like a black gemstone with bizarre facets, agitated by childish graces that kept resurfacing like false hopes being pulled from a deck of cards in long sanctimonious strange theories of languishing queens a king infantrymen weapons and knights. I spoke to her and a voice from the convent, deep and melodramatic, answered me along with a wrinkled and gracious smile. I could see stretched out in the shadows the maidservant half nude who slept with her mouth half open, her throat rattling in a heavy sleep, her beautiful body supple and amber. I sat down slowly.

[. . .]

And then fictions of a very old and free life, of enormous solar myths and massacres that created themselves before my spirit. I saw an old image again, a skeletal form alive because of the great force of a barbarous myth, eyes abyss-like and changing glaring with dark blood, in the dream's torture discovering the vulcanized body, two spots two bullet holes on her extinct breasts. I thought I heard the guitars shudder over there in the board-and-branch shack on the lonely fields of the city, a candle throwing light on the bare ground. In front of me a wild older woman stared me down without batting an eyelash. The light was weak on the bare ground in the quivering of the guitars. To one side on the blossoming treasure of a young dreaming girl the woman now clung like a spider while seeming to whisper words in my ear I couldn't make out, words sweet as the wordless wind of the Pampas that sinks you.

[. . .]

CHARLES WRIGHT

Dino Campana 119

LA CHIMERA

Non so se tra roccie il tuo pallido
Viso m'apparve, o sorriso
Di lontananze ignote
Fosti, la china eburnea
Fronte fulgente o giovine
Suora de la Gioconda:
O delle primavere
Spente, per i tuoi mitici pallori
O Regina O Regina adolescente:
Ma per il tuo ignoto poema
Di voluttà e di dolore
Musica fanciulla esangue,
Segnato di linea di sangue
Nel cerchio delle labbra sinuose
Regina de la melodia:
Ma per il vergine capo
Reclino, io poeta notturno
Vegliai le stelle vivide nei pelaghi del cielo,
Io per il tuo dolce mistero
Io per il tuo divenir taciturno.
Non so se la fiamma pallida
Fu dei capelli il vivente
Segno del suo pallore,
Non so se fu un dolce vapore,
Dolce sul mio dolore,
Sorriso di un volto notturno:
Guardo le bianche rocce le mute fonti dei venti
E l'immobilità dei firmamenti
E i gonfii rivi che vanno piangenti
E l'ombre del lavoro umano curve là sui poggi algenti
E ancora per teneri cieli lontane chiare ombre correnti
E ancora ti chiamo ti chiamo Chimera.

1914

CHIMERA

I don't know if among rocks your pale
Face appeared to me, or if
You were a smile from unknown
Distances, your bowed ivory
Brow gleaming, O young
Sister of the Mona Lisa:
For your mythical pallor
O Queen O adolescent Queen
Of dead springs:
But for your unknown poem
Of wantonness and sorrow
Bloodless musical girl
Marked by a line of blood
In the circle of your sinuous lips,
Queen of Melody:
But for your inclined
Virginal head, I, poet of the night
Kept watch over the bright stars in the oceans of the sky,
I for your sweet mystery
I for your silent becoming.
I do not know if the pale flame
Of her hair was the living
Sign of her pallor,
I do not know if it was a sweet vapor,
Sweet on my sorrow,
Smile of a nocturnal face:
I gaze at the white rocks the mute sources of the winds
And the stillness of the firmaments
And the swollen rivers that go on weeping
And the shadows of human work bent there on the icy knolls
And still across tender skies distant bright shadows running
And still I call you I call you Chimera.

LUIGI BONAFFINI

GIARDINO AUTUNNALE (FIRENZE)

Al giardino spettrale al lauro muto
De le verdi ghirlande
A la terra autunnale
Un ultimo saluto!
A l'aride pendici
Aspre arrossate nell'estremo sole
Confusa di rumori
Rauchi grida la lontana vita:
Grida al morente sole
Che insanguina le aiole.
S'intende una fanfara
Che straziante sale: il fiume spare
Ne le arene dorate; nel silenzio
Stanno le bianche statue a capo i ponti
Volte: e le cose già non sono più.
E dal fondo silenzio come un coro
Tenero e grandioso
Sorge ed anela in alto al mio balcone:
E in aroma d'alloro,
In aroma d'alloro acre languente,
Tra le statue immortali nel tramonto
Ella m'appar, presente.

1914

NOTTURNO TEPPISTA

Firenze nel fondo era gorgo di luci di fremiti sordi:
Con ali di fuoco i lunghi rumori fuggenti
Del tram spaziavano: il fiume mostruoso
Torpido riluceva come un serpente a squame.

AUTUMN GARDEN (FLORENCE)

To the ghostly garden to the laurel mute
Green garlands shorn
To the autumnal country
Now a last salute!
Up the parched falling lawns
Harsh scarlet in the sun's last rays
Struggles a torn
Deep-throated roar—life crying far away:
It cries to the dying sun that sheds
Dark blood on the flower-beds.
A brass band saws
The air: the river's gone
Between its golden sands: in a great calm
The dazzling statues that the bridgehead bore
Are turned away: there's nothing anymore.
Out of profound silence, something like
A chorus soft and grand,
Longing, soars to the terrace where I stand:
And in redolence of laurel,
Of laurel languorous, laurel piercing, where
Those statues in the sunset loom immortal
She appears, present there.

JOHN FREDERICK NIMS

NOCTURNE

Florence, abyss of enfolding light:
*

The tram-lines, like wings of fire—
Their long, retreating sparks, their susurrant cries:
*

Su un circolo incerto le inquiete facce beffarde
Dei ladri, ed io tra i doppi lunghi cipressi uguali a fiaccole spente
Più aspro ai cipressi le siepi
Più aspro del fremer dei bussi,
Che dal mio cuore il mio amore,
Che dal mio cuore, l'amore un ruffiano che intonò e cantò:

Amo le vecchie troie
Gonfie lievitate di sperma
Che cadono come rospi a quattro zampe sovra la coltrice rossa
E aspettano e sbuffano ed ansimano
Flaccide come mantici.

1 9 1 4

DONNA GENOVESE

Tu mi portasti un po' d'alga marina
Nei tuoi capelli, ed un odor di vento,
Che è corso di lontano e giunge grave
D'ardore, era nel tuo corpo bronzino:
—Oh la divina
Semplicità delle tue forme snelle—
Non amore non spasimo, un fantasma,
Un'ombra della necessità che vaga
Serena e ineluttabile nell'anima
E la discioglie in gioia, in incanto serena

The Arno, glittering snake, touches
The white cloisters of flame, easing
Its burden, the chill of its scales:
*

The double cypress, extinguished theories
Harsher than hedgerows, harsher
Than alms-boxes; harsher, too,
Than songs my pandering heart
Continues to sing, snatches of melody:
*

—I love the old-fashioned whores
Swollen with sperm
Who plop, like enormous toads, on all fours
Over the featherbed
And wait, and puff, and snort,
Flaccid as any bellows—:
*

&c. &c. &c. &c. &c. &c. &c. &c. &c. &c.

CHARLES WRIGHT

GENOA WOMAN

You brought me a little seaweed
In your hair, and a wind odor
That came in from hundreds of miles away and arrives
Heavy with meaning, smuggled in your tan skin:
—O the divine
Simplicity of your acrobat's body—
Not love not spasm, but something untouchable,
Necessity's ghost that walks aimlessly
Serene and ineluctable through the soul
And unties it with joy, as though under a sweet spell,
So that the desert wind

Dino Campana 125

Perché per l'infinito lo scirocco
Se la possa portare.
Come è piccolo il mondo e leggero nelle tue mani!

1 9 1 4

O L'ANIMA VIVENTE DELLE COSE

O l'anima vivente delle cose
O poesia deh baciala deh chiudila come il sole di maggio
Non vana come i sogni dei mattini
Torpidi. Scintilli il tuo pensiero
Sulle forme molteplici
Che muovono cantano e stridono
Elettrizzate nel sole
Anima oscura del mondo
Son le tue forme molteplici
Che tratte dal sonno alla vita
Ora avviluppano il mondo
Io confitto nel masso
Ti guardo o dea forza
Tu mi sferzi e mi sciogli e mi lanci
Nel tuo fremente torbido mare
O poesia siimi tu faro
Siimi tu faro e porterò un voto laggiù
Sotto degli infrenati archi marini
Dell'alterna tua chiesa azzurra e bianca
Là dove aurora fiammea s'affranca
Da un arco eburneo, a magici confini
Genova Genova Genova

1 9 1 4

Can carry it out through infinity.
How small the world is
and how light it is in your hands.

CHARLES WRIGHT

CAMPANA, NAILED TO A BOULDER

O for christsake poetry kiss
The soul of things alive!
And close it in like the sun in May.
Forget the vanity of the poet's dreams
In the drugged mornings.
I hope your sound shines
On all the forms
That move, sing, scream—
Electric in the sun!
Vague soul of the earth,
Your many forms, drawn
Between sleep and life,
Now circle everything . . .
And I, Campana, nailed to a boulder,
Stare at you O goddess
Even though you whip me,
Even though you melt me and toss me
Into the trembling ocean of yourself.
O poetry be a beacon,
Be for Campana a beacon, and for you
I will carry an offering
Beneath the unknown curves
Of the sea, your cathedral
Which is sometimes white, sometimes blue.
There a flaming circle will break free
From its white arc and fly
Toward the magical edges:
O Genoa, Genoa, Genoa!

THOMAS LUX

Dino Campana 127

DALL'IMMAGINE TESA

Dall'immagine tesa
vigilo l'istante
con imminenza di attesa—
e non aspetto nessuno:
nell'ombra accesa
spio il campanello
che impercettibile spande
un polline di suono—
e non aspetto nessuno:
fra quattro mura
stupefatte di spazio
più che un deserto
non aspetto nessuno:
ma deve venire,
verrà, se resisto
a sbocciare non visto,
verrà d'improvviso,
quando meno l'avverto:
verrà quasi perdono
di quanto fa morire,
verrà a farmi certo
del suo e mio tesoro,
verrà come ristoro
delle mie e sue pene,
verrà, forse già viene
il suo bisbiglio.

1922

Clemente Rèbora

1885–1957

IMAGE TENSED

Image tensed,
I eye the instant,
anticipation welling—
and I expect no one;
in the lit shadows
I watch as the doorbell
sheds its inaudible
pollen of sound—
and I expect no one;
within four walls
astounded more by space
than any desert place,
I expect no one;
but come he will,
he must; if I hold on
to bloom unseen,
he'll suddenly appear
when I am least aware:
coming as if to forgive
all he gives to death,
coming to assure me
of his reward and mine,
coming as anodyne
for my pain, for his—
perhaps his whisper is
already on its way.

GEOFFREY BROCK

CHI SONO?

Son forse un poeta?
No, certo.
Non scrive che una parola, ben strana,
la penna dell'anima mia:
«follía».
Son dunque un pittore?
Neanche.
Non ha che un colore
la tavolozza dell'anima mia:
«malinconía».
Un musico, allora?
Nemmeno.
Non c'è che una nota
nella tastiera dell'anima mia:
«nostalgía».
Son dunque . . . che cosa?
Io metto una lente
davanti al mio cuore
per farlo vedere alla gente.
Chi sono?
Il saltimbanco dell'anima mia.

1909

Aldo Palazzeschi

1885–1974

WHO AM I?

Am I perhaps a poet?
Certainly not.
It writes only one word, and an odd one,
the pen of my soul:
"folly."
Am I a painter, then?
Not even that.
It has only one tint,
the palette of my soul:
"melancholy."
So am I a musician?
Not at all.
There's only one note
on the keyboard of my soul:
"nostalgia."
I am then . . . what?
I place a lens
in front of my heart
so people can see it.
Who am I?
The acrobat of my soul.

MICHAEL PALMA

DA E LASCIATEMI DIVERTIRE!

Tri tri tri,
fru fru fru,
ihu ihu ihu,
uhi uhi uhi!
Il poeta si diverte,
pazzamente,
smisuratamente!
Non lo state a insolentire,
lasciatelo divertire
poveretto,
queste piccole corbellerie
sono il suo diletto.

Cucù rurù,
rurù cucù,
cuccuccurucù!
Cosa sono queste indecenze?
Queste strofe bisbetiche?
Licenze, licenze,
licenze poetiche!
Sono la mia passione.

Farafarafarafa,
tarataratarata,
paraparaparapa,
laralaralarala!
Sapete cosa sono?
Sono robe avanzate,
non sono grullerie,
sono la spazzatura
delle altre poesie.

[. . .]

FROM SO LET ME HAVE MY FUN

Tri tri tri,
fru fru fru,
ihu ihu ihu,
uhi uhi uhi!
The poet's having fun;
he's mad
and out of control!
But don't say anything bad,
let him have his fun,
poor soul:
these harmless little tricks
that give him his kicks.

Cucu ruru,
ruru cucu,
cucucucurucu!
What are these obscenities?
These stanzas, who can read them?
Freedom, freedom,
poetic freedom!
They're my passion.

Farafarafarafa,
tarataratarata,
paraparaparapa,
laralaralarala!
Do you know what they are?
Avant-garde stuff:
not mere grotesqueries
but the finishing off
of other poetries.

[. . .]

Aldo Palazzeschi 133

Labala
falala
falala
eppoi lala.
Lalala lalala.
Certo è un azzardo un po' forte,
scrivere delle cose così,
che ci son professori oggidì
a tutte le porte.

Ahahahahahahah!
Ahahahahahahah!
Ahahahahahahah!
Infine io ho pienamente ragione,
i tempi sono molto cambiati,
gli uomini non dimandano
più nulla dai poeti,
e lasciatemi divertire!

1910

L'INDIFFERENTE

Io sono tuo padre.
Ah, sì? . . .
Io sono tua madre.
Ah, sì? . . .
Questo è tuo fratello.
Ah, sì? . . .
Quella è tua sorella.
Ah, sì? . . .

1914

Labala
falala
falala
and even lala.
Lalala lalala!
The risk is certainly great
to write the way you do.
Like guards at every gate
the professors are watching you.

Ahahahahahaha!
Ahahahahahaha!
Ahahahahahaha!
When all is said and done
I'm right, the times have changed,
and men don't ask a thing
of poets anymore,
so let me have my fun!

FELIX STEFANILE

INDIFFERENT

I am your father.
  Is that so?
I am your mother.
  Is that so?
This is your brother.
  Is that so?
That is your sister.
  Is that so?

EMANUEL CARNEVALI

NOVEMBRE

Dei giovani e dei vecchi
si raggruppano
tra le rovine calde di Roma,
su cui i platani lasciano cadere
con rumore di carta
le loro foglie dorate.
I giovani fanno sapere ai vecchi
quello che a loro piace,
e i vecchi fanno finta di non sentire.

1 9 4 6

NOVEMBER

Young men and old men
gather again in groups
among the sultry ruins of Rome
over which plane-trees let fall,
with a papery sound,
leaves turned gold.
The young men tell the old men
what is to their liking;
the old men make believe they do not hear.

FREDERICK MORTIMER CLAPP

Aldo Palazzeschi 137

DA DESOLAZIONE DEL

POVERO POETA SENTIMENTALE

I

Perché tu mi dici: poeta?
Io non sono un poeta.
Io non sono che un piccolo fanciullo che piange.
Vedi: non ho che le lagrime da offrire al Silenzio.
Perché tu mi dici: poeta?

II

Le mie tristezze sono povere tristezze comuni.
Le mie gioie furono semplici,
semplici cosí, che se io dovessi confessarle a te arrossirei.
Oggi io penso a morire.

III

Io voglio morire, solamente, perché sono stanco;
solamente perché i grandi angioli
su le vetrate delle cattedrali
mi fanno tremare d'amore e di angoscia;
solamente perché, io sono, oramai,
rassegnato come uno specchio,
come un povero specchio melanconico.

Vedi che io non sono un poeta:
sono un fanciullo triste che ha voglia di morire.

[. . .]

1906

Sergio Corazzini

1886–1907

FROM DESOLATION OF THE

POOR SENTIMENTAL POET

I

Why do you call me poet?
I'm not a poet.
I'm only a crying little boy.
You see: I have only tears to offer up to the Silence.
Why do you call me poet?

II

My sorrows are poor ordinary sorrows.
My joys were simple,
so simple that if I confessed them to you I would blush.
Today I think about dying.

III

I want to die, only because I'm tired;
only because the large angels
in the windows of the cathedrals
make me shiver with love and anguish;
only because, by now,
I'm resigned like a mirror,
like a poor melancholy mirror.

You see that I'm not a poet:
I'm only a sad child who wants to die.

[. . .]

MICHAEL PALMA

AUTUNNO

Autunno. Già lo sentimmo venire
nel vento d'agosto,
nelle pioggie di settembre
torrenziali e piangenti
e un brivido percorse la terra
che ora, nuda e triste,
accoglie un sole smarrito.
Ora passa e declina,
in quest'autunno che incede
con lentezza indicibile,
il miglior tempo della nostra vita
e lungamente ci dice addio.

1920

ALBA

Solo in te, alba, riposa
la mia morte affannosa.
Solo in te trova pace
l'insonnia mia, ch'è simile
ad un rombante fiume

Vincenzo Cardarelli

1887–1959

AUTUMN

Autumn. Already we felt it coming
in the August wind,
in the September rains
torrential and weeping,
and a shudder ran over the earth
that now, naked and sad,
receives a bewildered sun.
Now there passes and declines
in this autumn which advances
with unspeakable slowness
the best time of our life
and at great length it bids us goodbye.

WILLIAM WEAVER

DAWN

Dawn, in you alone there rests
my breathless death.
In you alone finds peace
my sleeplessness,
like a rumbling river
predatory and infernal

rapinoso, infernale,
dov'io vado ogni notte
dibattendomi invano.
Dinanzi a te, che giungi
sempre così furtiva
da far quasi paura, e origli e spii,
spettro anche tu, il più vago,
alba dal freddo viso,
cessan gli orrori, fuggono i fantasmi.
La morte, mia nera
compagna di veglia,
se ne va, s'allontana
a passi di ladro.
Ond'io emergo e mi libero
dall'onda tenebrosa
e affranto mi riduco
al mio sonno di pietra.
O alba, dolce alba,
mare di luce incerta,
in cui tutto ha foce.

1928

where each night
in vain I go to struggle.
Before you, who approach
so furtive
as to make us fear,
eavesdropping, spying,
you, too, the vaguest specter,
chill-faced dawn,
the horrors cease, the phantoms flee.
Death, the black
companion of my vigil,
moves far off
with the tread of a thief.
Then I emerge and free myself
from the shadowed wave
and, breathless, I descend
into my sleep of stone.
O dawn, O gentle dawn,
ocean of uncertain light
receiving every river.

ALLEN MANDELBAUM

VICENZA 1915

Grigiori d'alba. Nella muta via
che sa di pane fresco e di rugiada
scoppia improvviso un tuono di fanfara:
il battaglione alpino se ne va . . .

Imposte sbatacchiate. Alle finestre,
donne in camicia tra gerani in fiore.
E un bandierone di vento e di sole
d'un tratto avvolge tutta la città.

1919

RIVA DI PENA, CANALE D'OBLIO . . .

Ora è la grande ombra d'autunno:
la fredda sera improvvisa calata
da tutto il cielo fumido oscuro
su l'acqua spenta, la pietra malata.

Ora è l'angoscia dei lumi radi,
gialli, sperduti per il nebbione,
l'uno dall'altro staccati, lontani,
chiuso ciascuno nel proprio alone.

Diego Valeri

1887–1976

VICENZA 1915

Gray of daybreak. Into the silent street
fragrant with fresh bread and dew there comes
a sudden blare of bugles and of drums:
the alpine battalion's ready to march on . . .

Slapping of shutters. Women in nightgowns
framed in the windows amid geraniums.
And then the entire city all at once
is wrapped in a huge flag of wind and sun.

MICHAEL PALMA

PAIN'S SHORE, OBLIVION'S CANAL . . .

Now is the great shadow of autumn:
out of the broad dark hazy skies
the evening chill has suddenly fallen
on the spent water, the ill quays.

And now the pang of the few lanterns
in the thick fog: islands of yellow,
each isolated from the others,
each confined by its own halo.

Riva di pena, canale d'oblio . . .
Non una voce dentro il cuor morto.
Solo quegli urli straziati d'addio
dei bastimenti che lasciano il porto.

1930

Pain's shore, oblivion's canal . . .
No voice calls out in the dead heart.
Only those rending shrieks of farewell
from vessels as they leave the port.

GEOFFREY BROCK

Padre, se anche tu non fossi il mio
padre, se anche fossi a me un estraneo,
per te stesso egualmente t'amerei.
Ché mi ricordo d'un mattin d'inverno
che la prima viola sull'opposto
muro scopristi dalla tua finestra
e ce ne desti la novella allegro.
Poi la scala di legno tolta in spalla
di casa uscisti e l'appoggiasti al muro.
Noi piccoli stavamo alla finestra.

E di quell'altra volta mi ricordo
che la sorella mia piccola ancora
per la casa inseguivi minacciando
(la caparbia avea fatto non so che).
Ma raggiuntala che strillava forte
dalla paura ti mancava il cuore:
ché avevi visto te inseguir la tua
piccola figlia, e tutta spaventata
tu vacillante l'attiravi al petto,
e con carezze dentro le tue braccia
l'avviluppavi come per difenderla
da quel cattivo ch'era il tu di prima.

Padre, se anche tu non fossi il mio
padre, se anche fossi a me un estraneo,
fra tutti quanti gli uomini già tanto
pel tuo cuore fanciullo t'amerei.

1914

Camillo Sbarbaro

1888–1967

Father, even if you were not my own
father, even if you were no relation,
I'd love you just as much for who you are.
Because I still recall, one winter morning,
when you looked out your window and saw spring's
first violet perched atop the facing wall,
then gleefully reported the news to us.
Taking the wooden ladder on your shoulder,
you went outside and leaned it on the wall.
We little ones were watching from the window.

And I remember too that other time,
when you were chasing my still-little sister
from one room to the next with angry threats.
(I don't know what the stubborn girl had done.)
But when you caught her she was screaming so,
from fear, that you no longer had the heart:
for you had seen yourself chasing your own
small daughter, who was terrified, and you
drew her then unsteadily to your chest
and wrapped her gently in your arms, as if
to shield her from the brute that you had been.

Father, even if you were not my own
father, even if you were no relation,
I, for that tender boyish heart of yours,
would still, above all other men, love you.

GEOFFREY BROCK

LA VITE

Ormai somiglio a una vite che vidi un dì con stupore. Cresceva su un
   muro di casa nascendo da un lastrico. Trapiantata, sarebbe intristita.
Così l'anima ha messo radice nella pietra della città e altrove non
   saprebbe più vivere. E se ancora m'avviene di guardar come a scampo
   ai monti lontani, in realtà essi non mi parlano più.
Mi esalta il fanale atroce a capo del vicolo chiuso.
Il cuore resta appeso in ex voto a chiassuoli a crocicchi.
Aspetti di cose mi toccano come nessun gesto umano potrebbe.
Come la vite mi cibo di aridità. Più della femmina, m'illudono la sete e
   gli artifizi. Il lampeggiar degli specchi m'appaga.
A volte, a disturbare l'inerzia in cui mi compiaccio, affiora, chi sa da che
   piega di me, un mondo a una sola dimensione e, smarrita per esso,
   l'infanzia.
Al richiamo mi tendo, trepidante mi chino in ascolto . . . Ah non era
   che il ricordo d'un'esistenza anteriore!

Forse mi vado mineralizzando.
Già il mio occhio è di vetro, da tanto non piango; e il cuore, un ciottolo
   pesante.

1 9 2 0

Il desiderio di Pierangelo è degno d'un re. «Se fossi milionario, affitterei
quell'individuo.» Lo vede per la prima volta ma la sua vista, che sa per-
ché, lo indispone. «Su lui sfogherei l'umore del momento. Nel calore d'una
discussione o solo per sgranchirmi un po' e magari per sbadataggine, gli
lascerei andare dei tremendi ceffoni O, viceversa, lo piglierei pel sganasci-
cino. In ogni circostanza la sua faccia dovrebbe restare impassibile; digni-
tosa, anzi. Non avrebbe altro compito che di trovarsi sempre a portata di
mano. In cilindro, beninteso. Gli passerei pel suo disturbo un onorario da
ministro.»

1 9 2 0

THE VINE

By now I resemble a vine I saw one day with amazement. It grew up the side
    of a house out of a paving stone. Transplanting would have stunted it.
My soul too is rooted in the stones of the city and could no longer live
    anywhere else. And if I sometimes gaze at the distant mountains with
    thoughts of escape, in truth the mountains no longer speak to me.
I'm thrilled by the awful lamp at the dead end of an alley.
My heart hangs like an ex voto over backstreets, crossroads.
The appearances of objects touch me as no human gesture could.
Like a vine I thrive on dryness. More than women, thirst and artifice
    seduce me. The flash of a mirror satisfies me.
At times, as if to disturb the inertia I delight in, a one-dimensional world
    surfaces from who knows what nook inside me—and lost within it,
    my childhood.
I hear its call and lean in, cocking a nervous ear . . . Ah but it was nothing
    but the memory of a past existence!

Perhaps I am becoming mineral.
My eye is already glass, so long has it been since I cried; my heart is a
    heavy cobblestone.

GEOFFREY BROCK

Pierangelo's wish was worthy of a king. "If I were a millionaire I'd rent my-
self that man there." It was the first time he'd laid eyes on the fellow but
for some unknown reason he didn't like what he saw. "I'd take out on him
my feelings of the moment. In the heat of an argument, or just when I
wanted a bit of a workout, or—why not?—when I just felt like letting
loose, I'd send him flying with a couple of furious smacks. Or else I might
pinch his cheeks. In any case, he must continue to look impassive, and
even dignified. His only job would be to stay always close at hand. In a top
hat, naturally. And for his trouble I'd give him a minister's pay."

GAYLE RIDINGER

Camillo Sbarbaro 151

ETERNO

Tra un fiore colto e l'altro donato
l'inesprimibile nulla

1916

AGONIA

Morire come le allodole assetate
sul miraggio

O come la quaglia
passato il mare
nei primi cespugli
perché di volare
non ha più voglia

Ma non vivere di lamento
come un cardellino accecato

1916

Giuseppe Ungaretti

1888–1970

ETERNAL

Between one flower picked and the other given
the inexpressible nothing

PATRICK CREAGH

AGONY

To die like thirsty larks
beside the mirage.

Or like the quail
crossing the pounded beach—
to die
in the first bushes because
it has lost the will
to fly.

But not to feed on grief
like a blinded finch.

KEVIN HART

IN MEMORIA

Locvizza il 30 settembre 1916

Si chiamava
Moammed Sceab

Discendente
di emiri di nomadi
suicida
perché non aveva più
Patria

Amò la Francia
e mutò nome

Fu Marcel
ma non era Francese
e non sapeva più
vivere
nella tenda dei suoi
dove di ascolta la cantilena
del Corano
gustando un caffè

E non sapeva
sciogliere
il canto
del suo abbandono

L'ho accompagnato
insieme alla padrone dell'albergo
dove abitavamo

IN MEMORY

Locvizza, September 30, 1916

His name
was Mohammed Sceab

Descended
from emirs of nomads
suicide
because he had no
country

He loved France
and changed his name

Was Marcel
but wasn't French
and no longer knew
how to live
in his family's tent
where you listen to the chant
of the Koran
and sip coffee

And he couldn't
free
the song
of his exile

I followed him
with the hotel landlady
from our place

a Parigi
dal numero 5 della rue des Carmes
appassito vicolo in discesa

Riposa
nel camposanto d'Ivry
sobborgo che pare
sempre
in una giornata
di una decomposta fiera

E forse io solo
so ancora
che visse

1916

VEGLIA

Cima Quattro il 23 dicembre 1915

Un'intera nottata
buttato vicino
a un compagno
massacrato
con la sua bocca
digrignata
volta al plenilunio
con la congestione
delle sue mani
penetrata
nel mio silenzio

in Paris
at number 5 rue des Carmes
sloping decayed alley

He lies
in the cemetery at Ivry
suburb that always
seems
in a day
of an abandoned fair

And maybe I only
still know
he lived

ANDREW WYLIE

VIGIL

Peak Four, December 23, 1915

One whole night
flung down
beside a
butchered
companion
with his clenched
jaw
tipped toward the full moon
with his swollen hands
thrust into
my silence

ho scritto
lettere piene d'amore

Non sono mai stato
tanto
attaccato alla vita

1 9 1 6

ALLEGRIA DI NAUFRAGI

Versa il 14 febbraio 1917

E subito riprende
il viaggio
come
dopo il naufragio
un superstite
lupo di mare

1 9 1 9

MATTINA

Santa Maria La Longa il 26 gennaio 1917

M'illumino
d'immenso

1 9 1 9

I wrote
letters full of love

I have never been
so bound
to life

SARAH ARVIO

JOY OF SHIPWRECK

Versa, February 14, 1917

And suddenly the voyage
resumes
as
after being shipwrecked
a surviving
old sea dog will

CID CORMAN

MORNING

Santa Maria La Longa, January 26, 1917

Immensity
illumines me

ALLEN MANDELBAUM

UN'ALTRA NOTTE

Vallone il 20 aprile 1917

In quest'oscuro
colle mani
gelate
distinguo
il mio viso

Mi vedo
abbandonato nell'infinito

1 9 1 9

VANITÀ

Vallone il 19 agosto 1917

D'improvviso
è alto
sulle macerie
il limpido
stupore
dell'immensità

E l'uomo
curvato
sull'acqua
sorpresa
dal sole
si rinviene
un'ombra

ANOTHER NIGHT

Vallone, April 20, 1917

In this dark
with hands
frozen
I pick out
my face

I see myself
abandoned in the infinite

PETER JAY

VANITY

Vallone, August 19, 1917

Suddenly
there towers
above the rubble
the limpid
wonder
of immensity

And the man
bent
over the sun-
startled water
comes to
as a shadow

Cullata e
piano
franta

1919

SOLDATI

Bosco di Courton luglio 1918

Si sta come
d'autunno
sugli alberi
le foglie

1919

LA PIETÀ (1)

Sono un uomo ferito.

E me ne vorrei andare
E finalmente giungere,
Pietà, dove si ascolta
L'uomo che è dolo con sé.

Non ho che superbia e bontà.

E mi sento esiliato in mezzo agli uomini.

Ma per essi sto in pena.
Non sarei degno di tornare in me?

Ho popolato di nomi il silenzio.

Rocked and
softly
shattered

CHARLES TOMLINSON

SOLDIERS

Wood of Courton, July 1918

Stand like
trees'
autumn
leaves

ANDREW WYLIE

PITY (1)

I am a wounded man.

And I would go
And finally reach the place,
Pity, where there is a hearing
For the man who's alone with himself.

I have only pride and goodwill.

And I feel exiled among men.

But I feel pain for them.
Would I not be worthy to be restored to myself?

I have peopled the silence with names.

Ho fatto a pezzi cuore e mente
Per cadere in servitù di parole?

Regno sopra fantasmi.

O figlie secche,
Anima portata qua e là . . .

No, odio il vento e la sua voce
Di bestia immemorabile.

Dio, coloro che t'implorano
Non ti conoscono più che di nome?

M'hai discacciato dalla vita.

Mi discaccerai dalla morte?

Forse l'uomo è anche indegno di sperare.

Anche la fonte del rimorso è secca?

Il peccato che importa,
Se alla purezza non conduce più.

La carne si ricorda appena
Che una volta fu forte.

E' folle e usata, l'anima.

Dio, guarda la nostra debolezza.

Vorremmo una certezza.

Di noi nemmeno più ridi?

Have I splintered my heart and mind
To fall into the slavery of words?

I rule over ghosts.

O dry leaves,
Soul borne hither and yon . . .

No, I detest the wind and its voice
Of an immemorial beast.

Lord, do those who implore you
Know you no longer except by name?

You have thrust me away from life.

Will you thrust me from death?

Perhaps man is not even fit for hope.

Has the fountain of remorse also run dry?

What does sin matter
If it no longer leads to purity?

The flesh scarcely remembers
That once it was strong.

Deranged and worn is the soul.

Lord, look upon our weakness.

We would have a sign.

Don't you even laugh at us anymore?

E compiangici dunque, crudeltà.

Non ne posso più di stare murato
Nel desiderio senza amore.

Una traccia mostraci di giustizia.

La tua legge qual è?

Fulmina le mie povere emozioni,
Liberami dall'inquietudine.

Sono stanco di urlare senza voce.

1933

DA LA MORTE MEDITATA:

CANTO PRIMA

O sorella dell'ombra,
Notturna quanto più la luce ha forza,
M'insegui, morte.

In un giardino puro
Alla luce ti diè l'ingenua brama
E la pace fu persa,
Pensosa morte,
Sulla tua bocca.

Da quel momento
Ti odo nel fluire della mente
Approfondire lontananze,
Emula sofferente dell'eterno.

Pity us then, cruelty.

I can no longer bear being walled up
In desire without love.

Show us a sign of justice.

What is your law?

Blast my poor feelings,
Free me from disquiet.

I am tired of howling without a voice.

ANTHONY HECHT

FROM MEDITATIONS

ON DEATH: FIRST CANTO

O sister of the shadow,
Blackest in strongest light,
Death, you pursue me.

In a pure garden
Artless desire conceived you
And peace was lost,
Pensive death,
On your mouth.

From that moment
I hear you in the mind's flow,
Sounding the far depths,
Suffering rival of eternity.

Madre velenosa degli evi
Nella paura del palpito
E della solitudine,

Bellezza punita e ridente,

Nell'assopirsi della carne
Sognatrice fuggente,

Atleta senza sonno
Della nostra grandezza,

Quando m'avrai domato, dimmi:

Nella malinconia dei vivi
Volerà a lungo la mia ombra?

1933

SENZA PIÙ PESO

Per un Iddio che rida come un bimbo,
Tanti gridi di passeri,
Tante danze nei rami,

Un'anima si fa senza piú peso,
I prati hanno una tale tenerezza,
Tale pudore negli occhi rivive,

Le mani come foglie
S'incantano nell'aria . . .

Chi teme piú, chi giudica?

1933

Poisonous mother of the ages,
Fearful of palpitation
And of solitude,

Beauty punished and smiling,

In the drowse of flesh,
Runaway dreamer,

Unsleeping athlete
Of our greatness,

When you have tamed me, tell me:

In the melancholy of the living
How long will my shadow fly?

STANLEY KUNITZ

WEIGHTLESS NOW

For a god who is laughing like a child
So many cries of sparrows,
So many hoppings high in the branches,

A soul grows weightless now,
Such tenderness is on the fields,
Such chastity refills the eyes,

The hands like leaves
Float breathless in the air . . .

Who fears, who judges now?

RICHARD WILBUR

NON GRIDATE PIÙ

Cessate d'uccidere i morti,
Non gridate più, non gridate
Se li volete ancora udire,
Se sperate di non perire.

Hanno l'impercettibile sussurro,
Non fanno più rumore
Del crescere dell'erba,
Lieta dove non passa l'uomo.

1947

VARIAZIONI SU NULLA

Quel nonnulla di sabbia che trascorre
Dalla clessidra muto e va posandosi,
E, fugaci, le impronte sul carnato,
Sul carnato che muore, d'una nube . . .

Poi mano che rovescia la clessidra,
Il ritorno per muoversi, di sabbia,
Il farsi argentea tacito di nube
Ai primi brevi lividi dell'alba . . .

La mano in ombra la clessidra volse,
E, di sabbia, il nonnulla che trascorre
Silente, è unica cosa che ormai s'oda
E, essendo udita, in buio non scompaia.

1950

NO MORE YELLING

Stop killing the dead.
Don't yell anymore, no yelling
If you still hope to hear them,
If you hope you won't perish.

There's an imperceptible whisper,
A rumor no louder
Than rising grass—
Happy! where man can't pass.

ALLEN GINSBERG

VARIATIONS ON NOTHING

That negligible bit of sand which slides
Without a sound and settles in the hourglass,
And the fleeting impressions on the fleshy pink,
The perishable fleshy pink, of a cloud . . .

Then a hand that turns over the hourglass,
The going back for flowing back, of sand,
The quiet silvering of a cloud
In the first few lead-gray seconds of dawn . . .

The hand in shadow turned the hourglass,
And the negligible bit of sand which slides
And is silent, is the only thing now heard,
And, being heard, doesn't vanish in the dark.

ANDREW FRISARDI

IN LIMINE

Godi se il vento ch'entra nel pomario
vi rimena l'ondata della vita:
qui dove affonda un morto
viluppo di memorie,
orto non era, ma reliquario.

Il frullo che tu senti non è un volo,
ma il commuoversi dell'eterno grembo;
vedi che si trasforma questo lembo
di terra solitario in un crogiuolo.

Un rovello è di qua dall'erto muro.
Se procedi t'imbatti
tu forse nel fantasma che ti salva:
si compongono qui le storie, gli atti
scancellati pel giuoco del futuro.

Cerca una maglia rotta nella rete
che ci stringe, tu balza fuori, fuggi!
Va, per te l'ho pregato, —ora la sete
mi sarà lieve, meno acre la ruggine . . .

1925

Eugenio Montale

1896–1981

IN LIMINE

Rejoice when the breeze that enters the orchard
brings you back the tidal rush of life:
here, where dead memories
mesh and founder,
was no garden, but a reliquary.

That surge you hear is no whir of wings,
but the stirring of the eternal womb.
Look how this strip of lonely coast
has been transformed: a crucible.

All is furor within the sheer wall.
Advance, and you may chance upon
the phantasm who might save you:
here are tales composed and deeds
annulled, for the future to enact.

Find a break in the meshes of the net
that tightens around us, leap out, flee!
Go, I have prayed for your escape—now my thirst
will be slaked, my rancor less bitter . . .

WILLIAM ARROWSMITH

I LIMONI

Ascoltami, i poeti laureati
si muovono soltanto fra le piante
dai nomi poco usati: bossi ligustri o acanti.
Io, per me, amo le strade che riescono agli erbosi
fossi dove in pozzanghere
mezzo seccate agguantano i ragazzi
qualche sparuta anguilla:
le viuzze che seguono i ciglioni,
discendono tra i ciuffi delle canne
e mettono negli orti, tra gli alberi dei limoni.

Meglio se le gazzarre degli uccelli
si spengono inghiottite dall'azzurro:
più chiaro si ascolta il susurro
dei rami amici nell'aria che quasi non si muove,
e i sensi di quest'odore
che non sa staccarsi da terra
e piove in petto una dolcezza inquieta.
Qui delle divertite passioni
per miracolo tace la guerra,
qui tocca anche a noi poveri la nostra parte di ricchezza
ed è l'odore dei limoni.

Vedi, in questi silenzi in cui le cose
s'abbandonano e sembrano vicine
a tradire il loro ultimo segreto,
talora ci si aspetta
di scoprire uno sbaglio di Natura,
il punto morto del mondo, l'anello che non tiene,
il filo da disbrogliare che finalmente ci metta
nel mezzo di una verità.
Lo sguardo fruga d'intorno,

THE LEMONS

Listen to me, the poets laureate
walk only among plants
with rare names: boxwood, privet, and acanthus.
But I like roads that lead to grassy
ditches where boys
scoop up a few starved
eels out of half-dry puddles:
paths that run along the banks,
come down among the tufted canes,
and end in orchards, among the lemon trees.

Better if the hubbub of the birds
dies out, swallowed by the blue:
we can hear more of the whispering
of friendly branches in not-quite-quiet air,
and the sensations of this smell
that can't divorce itself from earth
and rains a restless sweetness on the heart.
Here, by some miracle, the war
of troubled passions calls a truce;
here we poor, too, receive our share of riches,
which is the fragrance of the lemons.

See, in these silences where things
give over and seem on the verge of betraying
their final secret,
sometimes we feel we're about
to uncover an error in Nature,
the still point of the world, the link that won't hold,
the thread to untangle that will finally lead
to the heart of a truth.
The eye scans its surroundings,

la mente indaga accorda disunisce
nel profumo che dilaga
quando il giorno più languisce.
Sono i silenzi in cui si vede
in ogni ombra umana che si allontana
qualche disturbata Divinità.

Ma l'illusione manca e ci riporta il tempo
nelle città rumorose dove l'azzurro si mostra
soltanto a pezzi, in alto, tra le cimase.
La pioggia stanca la terra, di poi; s'affolta
il tedio dell'inverno sulle case,
la luce si fa avara—amara l'anima.
Quando un giorno da un malchiuso portone
tra gli alberi di una corte
ci si mostrano i gialli dei limoni;
e il gelo del cuore si sfa,
e in petto ci scrosciano
le loro canzoni
le trombe d'oro della solarità.

1925

DA OSSI DI SEPPIA

1

Non chiederci la parola che squadri da ogni lato
l'animo nostro informe, e a lettere di fuoco
lo dichiari e risplenda come un croco
perduto in mezzo a un polveroso prato.

the mind inquires aligns divides
in the perfume that gets diffused
at the day's most languid.
It's in these silences you see
in every fleeting human
shadow some disturbed Divinity.

But the illusion fails, and time returns us
to noisy cities where the blue
is seen in patches, up between the roofs.
The rain exhausts the earth then;
winter's tedium weighs the houses down,
the light turns miserly—the soul bitter.
Till one day through a half-shut gate
in a courtyard, there among the trees,
we can see the yellow of the lemons;
and the chill in the heart
melts, and deep in us
the golden horns of sunlight
pelt their songs.

JONATHAN GALASSI

FROM CUTTLEFISH BONES

1

Don't ask me for the word that might define
our formless soul, publish it
in letters of fire, and set it shining,
lost crocus in the dusty field.

Ah l'uomo che se ne va sicuro
agli altri ed a se stesso amico
e l'ombra sua non cura che la canicola
stampa sopra uno scalcinato muro!

Non domandarci la formula che mondi possa aprirti,
sì qualche storta sillaba e secca come un ramo.
Codesto solo oggi possiamo dirti:
ciò che *non* siamo, ciò che *non* vogliamo.

2

Meriggiare pallido e assorto
presso un rovente muro d'orto,
ascoltare tra i pruni e gli sterpi
schiocchi di merli, frusci di serpi.

Nelle crepe del suolo o su la veccia
spiar le file di rosse formiche
ch'ora si rompono ed or s'intrecciano
a sommo di minuscole biche.

Osservare tra frondi il palpitare
lontano di scaglie di mare
mentre se levano tremuli scricchi
di cicale dai calvi picchi.

E andando nel sole che abbaglia
sentire con triste meraviglia
com'è tutta la vita e il suo travaglio
in questo seguitare una muraglia
che ha in cima cocci aguzzi di bottiglia.

Ah, that man so confidently striding,
friend to others and to himself, careless
that the dog days' sun might stamp
his shadow on a crumbling wall!

Don't ask me for formulas to open worlds
for you: all I have are gnarled syllables,
branch-dry. All I can tell you now is this:
what we are *not*, what we do *not* want.

WILLIAM ARROWSMITH

2

To spend the afternoon, absorbed and pale,
beside a burning garden wall;
to hear, among the stubble and the thorns,
the blackbirds cackling and the rustling snakes.

On the cracked earth or in the vetch
to spy on columns of red ants
now crossing, now dispersing,
atop their miniature heaps.

To ponder, peering through the leaves,
the heaving of the scaly sea
while the cicadas' wavering screech
goes up from balding peaks.

And walking out into the sunlight's glare
to feel with melancholy wonder
how all of life and its travail
is in this following a wall
topped with the shards of broken bottles.

DAVID YOUNG

6

Portami il girasole ch'io lo trapianti
nel mio terreno bruciato dal salino,
e mostri tutto il giorno agli azzurri specchianti
del cielo l'ansietà del suo volto giallino.

Tendono alla chiarità le cose oscure,
si esauriscono i corpi in un fluire
di tinte: queste in musiche. Svanire
è dunque la ventura delle venture.

Portami tu la pianta che conduce
dove sorgono bionde trasparenze
e vapora la vita quale essenza;
portami il girasole impazzito di luce.

Spesso il male di vivere ho incontrato:
era il rivo strozzato che gorgoglia,
era l'incartocciarsi della foglia
riarsa, era il cavallo stramazzato.

Bene non seppi, fuori del prodigio
che schiude la divina Indifferenza:
era la statua nella sonnolenza
del meriggio, e la nuvola, e il falco alto levato.

Forse un mattino andando in un'aria di vetro,
arida, rivolgendomi, vedrò compirsi il miracolo:
il nulla alle mie spalle, il vuoto dietro
di me, con un terrore di ubriaco.

6

Bring me the sunflower, let me plant it
in my field parched by the sea-salt wind,
and let it show the blue reflecting sky
the yearning of its yellow face all day.

Dark things tend to brightness, bodies
fade out in a flood of colors,
colors in music. So disappearing is
the destiny of destinies.

Bring me the plant that leads the way
to where blond transparencies
rise, and life as essence turns to haze;
bring the sunflower crazed with light.

JONATHAN GALASSI

7

I have often met the evil of living:
the gurgle of the strangled brook,
the papering of the parched leaf,
the fallen horse, dying.

Of good I found little more than the omen
disclosed by the divine Indifference:
the statue in the drowsing
noon, and the cloud, and the hawk soaring.

WILLIAM ARROWSMITH

14

Maybe one morning, walking in dry glass air,
I'll turn and see the miracle occur—
nothing at my back, behind me there
the void—with a drunkard's terror.

Poi come s'uno schermo, s'accamperanno di gitto
alberi case colli per l'inganno consueto.
Ma sarà troppo tardi; ed io me n'andrò zitto
tra gli uomini che non si voltano, col mio segreto.

19

Cigola la carrucola del pozzo,
l'acqua sale alla luce e vi si fonde.
Trema un ricord nel ricolmo secchio,
nel puro cerchio un'immagine ride.
Accosto il volto a evanescenti labbri:
si deforma il passato, si fa vecchio,
appartiene ad un altro . . .
                            Ah che già stride
la ruota, ti ridona all'atro fondo,
visione, una distanza ci divide.

1925

DELTA

La vita che si rompe nei travasi
secreti a te ho legata:
quella che si dibatte in sé e par quasi
non ti sappia, presenza soffocata.

Quando il tempo s'ingorga alle sue dighe
la tua vicenda accordi alla sua immensa,
ed affiori, memoria, più palese
dall'oscura regione ove scendevi,
come ora, al dopopioggia, si riaddensa
il verde ai rami, ai muri il cinabrese.

Then as if on a screen, hills houses trees
will quickly pose again for their usual ruse.
But too late: and I will walk on, unspeaking,
among the men who don't turn, with my secret.

GEOFFREY BROCK

19

At the crank of the windlass in the well
water rises to—and then becomes—the light;
and in the filled bucket's pristine circle
the image of a known face laughs and trembles.
No sooner have I leant towards those lips
that fade away than the past crumbles,
grows old, is someone else's . . .
                  Then the wheel
screaks, bestowing you, vision, back again
on the sheer black of the gulf between us.

JAMIE MCKENDRICK

DELTA

To thee
I have willed the life drained
in secret transfusions, the life chained
in a coil of restlessness, unaware, self-angry.

When time leans on his dykes
then thine
be his allconsciousness
and memory flower forth in a flame
from the dark sanctuary, and shine
more brightly, as now, the rain over, the dragon's-blood
on the walls and the green against the branches.

Tutto ignoro di te fuor del messaggio
muto che mi sostenta sulla via:
se forma esisti o ubbia nella fumea
d'un sogno t'alimenta
la riviera che infebbra, torba, e scroscia
incontro alla marea.

Nulla di te nel vacillar dell'ore
bige o squarciate da un vampo di solfo
fuori che il fischio del rimorchiatore
che dalle brume approda al golfo.

1925

IL BALCONE

Pareva facile giuoco
mutare in nulla lo spazio
che m'era aperto, in un tedio
malcerto il certo tuo fuoco.

Ora a quel vuoto ho congiunto
ogni mio tardo motivo,
sull'arduo nulla si spunta
l'ansia di attenderti vivo.

La vita che dà barlumi
è quella che sola tu scorgi.
A lei ti sporgi da questa
finestra che non s'illumina.

1939

Of thee
I know nothing, only
the tidings sustaining my going,
and shall I find
thee shape or the fumes of a dream
drawing life
from the river's fever boiling darkly
    against the tide.

Of thee nothing in the grey hours and the hours
torn by a flame of sulphur,
only
the whistle of the tug
whose prow has ridden forth into the bright gulf.

SAMUEL BECKETT

THE BALCONY

It seemed an easy game
to change to nothing the space
open to me, and to vague
boredom your definite flame.

Now to that nothing I give
my every belated motive;
the hard void blunts the anguish
of awaiting you while I live.

That life that gleams and sparks
is one you alone can see.
You lean out toward it from
this window that stays dark.

GEOFFREY BROCK

VERSO VIENNA

Il convento barocco
di schiuma e di biscotto
adombrava uno scorcio d'acque lente
e tavole imbandite, qua e là sparse
di foglie e zenzero.

Emerse un nuotatore, sgrondò sotto
una nube di moscerini,
chiese del nostro viaggio,
parlò a lungo del suo d'oltre confine.

Additò il ponte in faccia che si passa
(informò) con un solo di pedaggio.
Salutò con la mano, sprofondò,
fu la corrente stessa . . .
                  Ed al suo posto,
battistrada balzò da una rimessa
un bassotto festoso che latrava,

fraterna unica voce dentro l'afa.

1939

DA MOTTETTI

1

Lo sai: debbo riperderti e non posso.
Come un tiro aggiustato mi sommuove
ogni opera, ogni grido e anche lo spiro
salino che straripa
dai moli e fa l'oscura primavera
di Sottoripa.

EN ROUTE TO VIENNA

The baroque convent, all meerschaum and biscuit,
shaded a glimpse
of slow-moving water and laid tables,
strewn here and there with leaves
and lumps of ginger.

A swimmer emerged, shook himself
under a gnat-cloud,
inquired of our journey
spoke at length of his own, across the border.

He pointed to the near bridge
which can be crossed (so he told us)
for a penny. He waved, dived,
was the stream itself . . .
                              And in his stead—
blazing the way for us—a little dachshund
bounded out of a garage, barking with joy,

one brotherly voice in the sultry haze.

EAMON GRENNAN

FROM MOTETS

1

You know this: I must lose you again and cannot.
Every action, every cry strikes me
like a well-aimed shot, even the salt spray
that spills over the harbor walls
and makes spring
dark against the gates of Genoa.

Paese di ferrame e alberature
a selva nella polvere del vespro.
Un ronzìo lungo viene dall'aperto,
strazia com'unghia ai vetri. Cerco il segno
smarrito, il pegno solo ch'ebbi in grazia
da te.
                    E l'inferno è certo.

3

Brina sui vetri; uniti
sempre e sempre in disparte
gl'infermi; e sopra i tavoli
i lunghi soliloqui sulle carte.

Fu il tuo esilio. Ripenso
anche al mio, alla mattina
quando udii tra gli scogli crepitare
la bomba ballerina.

E durarono a lungo i notturni giuochi
di Bengala: come in una festa.

È scorsa un'ala rude, t'ha sfiorato le mani,
ma invano: la tua carta non è questa.

6

La speranza di pure rivederti
m'abbandonava;

e mi chiesi se questo che mi chiude
ogni senso di te, schermo d'immagini,

Country of ironwork and ship masts
like a forest in the dust of evening.
A long drone comes from the open spaces
scraping like a nail on a windowpane. I look
for the sign I have lost, the only pledge
I had from you.
                    Now hell is certain.

D A N A   G I O I A

3

Frost on the panes, the sick
always together and always kept
apart; and over the tables long
soliloquies about cards.

That was your exile. I think again
of mine, of the morning
among the cliffs when I heard the crackle
of the ballerina bomb.

And the fireworks went on
and on: as though it were a holiday.

A brutal wing slid past, it grazed your hands,
but nothing more. That card isn't yours.

W I L L I A M   A R R O W S M I T H

6

The hope of even seeing you again
was deserting me;

and I asked myself if this that shuts
every sense of you in, an image screen,

ha i segni della morte o dal passato
è in esso, ma distorto e fatto labile,
un *tuo* barbaglio:

(a Modena, tra i portici,
un servo gallonato trascinava
due sciacalli al guinzaglio).

1 0

Perché tardi? Nel pino lo scoiattolo
batte la coda a torcia sulla scorza.
La mezzaluna scende col suo picco
nel sole che la smorza. È giorno fatto.

A un soffio il pigro fumo trasalisce,
si difende nel punto che ti chiude.
Nulla finisce, o tutto, se tu fólgore
lasci la nube.

1 4

Infuria sale o grandine? Fa strage
di campanule, svelle la cedrina.
Un rintocco subacqueo s'avvicina,
quale tu lo destavi, e s'allontana.

La pianola degl'inferi da sé
accelera i registri, sale nelle
sfere del gelo . . . —brilla come te
quando fingevi col tuo trillo d'aria
Lakmé nell'Aria delle Campanelle.

bears the signs of death or if there is not,
distorted, yes, and fugitive, but there,
some glare of *you*:

(at Modena, along the arches,
a liveried servant dragged
two jackals on the leash).

G E O R G E K A Y

1 0

Why wait? The squirrel beats his torch-tail
on the pine tree's bark.
The half-moon with its peak sinks down
into the sun that snuffs it out. It's day.

The sluggish mist is startled by a breeze,
but holds firm at the point it covers you.
Nothing ends, or everything,
if, thunderbolt, you leave your cloud.

J O N A T H A N G A L A S S I

1 4

Is it salt or hail that rages? It lacerates
the bluebells, roots out the verbena.
An underwater tolling comes in waves,
which you awakened, and fades away.

The hurdy-gurdy of the damned
picks up, on its own, the tempo, rises
into the spheres of ice . . . —it glitters like you
when you played at Lakmé, trilling the Bell Song.

C H A R L E S W R I G H T

Il fiore che ripete
dall'orlo del burrato
non scordarti di me,
non ha tinte più liete né più chiare
dello spazio gettato tra me e te.

Un cigolìo si sferra, ci discosta,
l'azzurro pervicace non ricompare.
Nell'afa quasi visibile mi riporta all'opposta
tappa, già buia, la funicolare.

. . . ma così sia. Un suono di cornetta
dialoga con gli sciami del querceto.
Nella valva che il vespero riflette
un vulcano dipinto fuma lieto.

La moneta incassata nella lava
brilla anch'essa sul tavolo e trattiene
pochi fogli. La vita che sembrava
vasta è più breve del tuo fazzoletto.

1 9 3 9

TEMPI DI BELLOSGUARDO (I)

Oh come là nella corusca
distesa che s'inarca verso i colli,
il brusìo della sera s'assottiglia
e gli alberi discorrono col trito
mormorio della rena; come limpida

The flower that rehearses
at the edge of the gorge
its forget-me-not
has no strain more joyous, more clear
than what emptiness we bridge.

A rasp of iron comes between us,
the pig-headed azure won't return.
In a palpable heat the funicular drops me
at the opposite station, already dark.

J. D. MCCLATCHY

2 0

. . . but so be it. A note from a cornet
converses with the bee-swarms in the oaks.
On the clamshell that reflects the sunset
a painted volcano cheerfully smokes.

The coin embedded in the lava gleams
too, on the desk, where it holds a thin sheaf
of paper in place. The life that used to seem
immense is briefer than your handkerchief.

GEOFFREY BROCK

BELLOSGUARDO

Oh how faint the twilight hubbub rising from
that stretch of landscape arching towards the hills—
the even trees along its sandbanks glow
for a moment, and talk together tritely;

Eugenio Montale 193

s'inalvea là in decoro
di colonne e di salci ai lati e grandi salti
di lupi nei giardini, tra le vasche ricolme
che traboccano,
questa vita di tutti non più posseduta
del nostro respiro;
e come si ricrea una luce di zàffiro
per gli uomini
che vivono laggiù: è troppo triste
che tanta pace illumini a spiragli
e tutto ruoti poi con rari guizzi
su l'anse vaporanti, con incroci
di camini, con grida dai giardini
pensili, con sgomenti e lunghe risa
sui tetti ritagliati, tra le quinte
dei frondami ammassati ed una coda
fulgida che trascorra in cielo prima
che il desiderio trovi le parole!

1939

LA CASA DEI DOGANIERI

Tu non ricordi la casa dei doganieri
sul rialzo a strapiombo sulla scogliera:
desolata t'attende dalla sera
in cui v'entrò lo sciame dei tuoi pensieri
e vi sostò irrequieto.

Libeccio sferza da anni le vecchie mura
e il suono del tuo riso non è più lieto:
la bussola va impazzita all'avventura
e il calcolo dei dadi più non torna.
Tu non ricordi; altro tempo frastorna
la tua memoria; un filo s'addipana.

how clearly this life finds a channel there
in a fine front of columns flanked by willows,
the wolf's great leaps through the gardens past the fountains
spouting so high the basins spill—this life
for everyone no longer possessed with our breath—
and how the sapphire last light is born again
for men who live down here; it is too sad
such peace can only enlighten us by glints,
as everything falls back with a rare flash
on steaming sidestreets, crossed by chimneys, shouts
from terraced gardens, shakings of the heart,
the long, high laughter of people on the roofs,
too sharply traced against the skyline, caught
between the wings and tail, massed branchings, cloud-
ends, passing, luminous, into the sky
before desire can stumble on the words.

ROBERT LOWELL

THE COASTGUARD STATION

You don't remember the coastguard house
perched at the top of the jutting height,
awaiting you still, abandoned since that night
when your thoughts came swarming in
and paused there, hovering.

Southwesters have lashed the old walls for years,
the gaiety has vanished from your laugh:
the compass swings at random, crazy,
odds can no longer be laid on the dice.
You don't remember: a thread pays out.

Ne tengo ancora un capo; ma s'allontana
la casa e in cima al tetto la banderuola
affumicata gira senza pietà.
Ne tengo un capo; ma tu resti sola
né qui respiri nell'oscurità.

Oh l'orizzonte in fuga, dove s'accende
rara la luce della petroliera!
Il varco è qui? (Ripullula il frangente
ancora sulla balza che scoscende . . .)
Tu non ricordi la casa di questa
mia sera. Ed io non so chi va e chi resta.

1 9 3 9

LA BUFERA

Les princes n'ont point d'yeux pour voir ces grandes merveilles,
Leurs mains ne servent plus qu'à nous persécuter . . .
—AGRIPPA D'AUBIGNÉ, *À Dieu*

La bufera che sgronda sulle foglie
dure della magnolia i lunghi tuoni
marzolini e la grandine,

(i suoni di cristallo nel tuo nido
notturno ti sorprendono, dell'oro
che s'è spento sui mogani, sul taglio
dei libri rilegati, brucia ancora
una grana di zucchero nel guscio
delle tue palpebre)

il lampo che candisce
alberi e muro e li sorprende in quella

I hold one end still; but the house
keeps receding, above the roof the soot-
blackened weathervane whirls, pitiless.
I hold one end: but you stay on, alone, not
here, breathing in my darkness.

Oh, the horizon keeps on receding, there, far out
where a rare tanker's light blinks in the blackness!
Is the crossing here? (The furious breakers
climb the cliff that falls off, sheer . . .)
You don't remember the house of this, my evening.
And I don't know who's staying, who's leaving.

WILLIAM ARROWSMITH

THE STORM

(after Montale)

The storm that batters the magnolia's
impermeable leaves, the long-drawn drum roll
of Martian thunder with its hail

(crystal acoustics trembling in your night's lair
disturb you while the gold transfumed
from the mahoganies, the pages' rims
of the de luxe books, still burns, a sugar grain
under your eyelid's shell)

lightning that makes stark-white the trees,
the walls, suspending them—

Eugenio Montale 197

eternità d'istante—marmo manna
e distruzione—ch'entro te scolpita
porti per tua condanna e che ti lega
più che l'amore a me, strana sorella, —
e poi lo schianto rude, i sistri, il fremere
dei tamburelli sulla fossa fuia,
lo scalpicciare del fandango, e sopra
qualche gesto che annaspa . . .

                    Come quando
ti rivolgesti e con la mano, sgombra
la fronte dalla nube dei capelli,

mi salutasti—per entrar nel buio.

1956

NELLA SERRA

S'empì d'uno zampettìo
Di talpe la limonaia,
brillò in un rosario di caute
gocce la falce fienaia.

S'accese sui pomi cotogni
Un punto, una cocciniglia
Si udì inalberarsi alla striglia
Il poney—e poi vinse il sogno

Rapito e leggero ero intriso di te,
la tua forza era il mio
respiro nascosto, il tuo viso
nel mio si fondeva, e l'oscuro

interminable instant—marbled manna
and cataclysm—deep in you sculpted,
borne now as condemnation: this binds you
closer to me, strange sister, than any love.
So, the harsh buskings, bashings of castanets
and tambourines around the spoilers' ditch,
fandango's foot-rap and over all
some gesture still to be defined . . .

                              As when
you turned away and casting with a hand
that cloudy mass of hair from off your forehead

gave me a sign and stepped into the dark.

GEOFFREY HILL

IN THE GREENHOUSE

The lemon-house was being over-
ridden by the moles' stampedes.
The scythe shone in a rosary
of wary waterbeads.

A spot among the quinces blazed,
a bug—cochineal.
We heard the pony rear up at
the comb—then sleep was all.

Rapt, weightless, I was drenched with you,
my hidden breathing was your form,
your face was merging into mine,
and the dark idea of God

pensiero di dio discendeva
sui pochi viventi, tra suoni
celesti e infantili tamburi
e globi sospesi di fulmini

su me, su te, sui limoni . . .

1 9 5 6

NEL PARCO

Nell'ombra della magnolia
che sempre più si restringe,
a un soffio di cerbottana
la freccia mi sfiora e si perde.

Pareva una foglia caduta
dal pioppo che a un colpo di vento
si stinge—e fors'era una mano
scorrente da lungi tra il verde.

Un riso che non m'appartiene
trapassa da fronde canute
fino al mio petto, lo scuote
un trillo che punge le vene,

e rido con te sulla ruota
deforme dell'ombra, mi allungo
disfatto di me sulle ossute
radici che sporgono e pungo

con fili di paglia il tuo viso . . .

1 9 5 6

descended on the living few
to celestial tones
and children's drums
and globes of lightning strung above

the lemons, and me, and you . . .

JONATHAN GALASSI

IN THE PARK

In the magnolia's ever
stricter shade, at one
puff from a blowgun
the dart grazes me and is gone.

It was like a leaf let fall
by the poplar a gust of wind
uncolors—perhaps a hand
roving through green from afar.

A laughter not my own
pierces through hoary branches
into my breast, a thrill
shakes me, stabs my veins,

and I laugh with you on the warped
wheel of shade, I stretch out
discharged of myself on the sharp
protruding roots, and needle

your face with bits of straw . . .

JAMES MERRILL

L'ANGUILLA

L'anguilla, la sirena
dei mari freddi che lascia il Baltico
per giungere ai nostri mari,
ai nostri estuari, ai fiumi
che risale in profondo, sotto la piena avversa,
di ramo in ramo e poi
di capello in capello, assottigliati,
sempre più addentro, sempre più nel cuore
del macigno, filtrando
tra gorielli di melma finché un giorno
una luce scoccata dai castagni
ne accende il guizzo in pozze d'acquamorta,
nei fossi che declinano
dai balzi d'Appennino alla Romagna;
l'anguilla, torcia, frusta,
freccia d'Amore in terra
che solo i nostri botri o i disseccati
ruscelli pirenaici riconducono
a paradisi di fecondazione;
l'anima verde che cerca
vita là dove solo
morde l'arsura e la desolazione,
la scintilla che dice
tutto comincia quando tutto pare
incarbonirsi, bronco seppellito;
l'iride breve, gemella
di quella che incastonano i tuoi cigli
e fai brillare intatta in mezzo ai figli
dell'uomo, immersi nel tuo fango, puoi tu
non crederla sorella?

1956

THE EEL

The selfsame, the siren
of icy waters, shrugging off as she does the Baltic
to hang out in our seas,
our inlets, the rivers
through which she climbs, bed-hugger, who keeps going against
the flow, from branch to branch, then
from capillary to snagged capillary,
farther and farther in, deeper and deeper into the heart
of the rock, straining
through mud runnels, till one day
a flash of light from the chestnut trees
sends a fizzle through a standing well,
through a drain that goes
by dips and darts from the Apennines to the Romagna—
that selfsame eel, a firebrand now, a scourge,
the arrow shaft of Love on earth
which only the gulches or dried-out
gullies of the Pyrenees might fetch and ferry back
to some green and pleasant spawning ground,
a green soul scouting and scanning
for life where only
drought and desolation have hitherto clamped down,
the spark announcing
that all sets forth when all that's set forth
is a charred thing, a buried stump,
this short-lived rainbow, its twin met
in what's set there between your eyelashes,
you who keep glowing as you do, undiminished, among the sons
of man, faces glistening with your slime, can't you take in
her being your next-of-kin?

PAUL MULDOON

PICCOLO TESTAMENTO

Questo che a notte balugina
nella calotta del mio pensiero,
traccia madreperlacea di lumaca
o smeriglio di vetro calpestato,
non è lume di chiesa o d'officina
che alimenti
chierico rosso, o nero.
Solo quest'iride posso
lasciarti a testimonianza
d'una fede che fu combattuta,
d'una speranza che bruciò più lenta
di un duro ceppo nel focolare.
Conservane la cipria nello specchietto
quando spenta ogni lampada
la sardana si farà infernale
e un ombroso Lucifero scenderà su una prora
del Tamigi, dell'Hudson, della Senna
scuotendo l'ali di bitume semi-
mozze dalla fatica, a dirti: è l'ora.
Non è un'eredità, un portafortuna
che può reggere all'urto dei monsoni
sul fil di ragno della memoria,
ma una storia non dura che nella cenere
e persistenza è solo l'estinzione.
Giusto era il segno: chi l'ha ravvisato
non può fallire nel ritrovarti.
Ognuno riconosce i suoi: l'orgoglio
non era fuga, l'umiltà non era
vile, il tenue bagliore strofinato
laggiù non era quello di un fiammifero.

1956

LITTLE TESTAMENT

This light that flashes in the night
of my mind's skull,
this mother-of-pearl snail's track,
this emery board of ground-up glass,
is not the glow from any church or factory
that might sustain the clerical red, or black.
I have only this iris
to leave you, testimony
of a faith too often fought for,
of a hope that burned slower
than a green log on a fire.
Keep its dust in your compact
when every light goes out,
and the sardana becomes infernal
and Lucifer's shade rises upon some boat bow
in the Thames or Hudson or Seine,
turning his coal-black wings
half cut away by weariness, and tells you, "Now."
It's no inheritance, no good-luck piece
to pacify those monsoons
along the spider's thread of memory;
anyone's biography survives
only in its own ashes,
and persistence is nothing but extinction.
The sign was a just one: whoever has seen it
cannot but find you again.
Each knows his own: pride
was never escape, humility
never a cowardice; that tenuous glow down there
was more than just a match.

CHARLES WRIGHT

IL SOGNO DEL PRIGIONIERO

Albe e notti qui variano per pochi segni.

Il zigzag degli storni sui battifredi
nei giorni di battaglia, mie sole ali,
un filo d'aria polare,
l'occhio del capoguardia dello spioncino,
crac di noci schiacciate, un oleoso
sfrigolìo dalle cave, girarrosti
veri o supposti—ma la paglia è oro,
la lanterna vinosa è focolare
se dormendo mi credo ai tuoi piedi.

La purga dura da sempre, senza un perché.
Dicono che chi abiura e sottoscrive
può salvarsi da questo sterminio d'oche ;
che chi obiurga se stesso, ma tradisce
e vende carne d'altri, affera il mestolo
anzi che terminare nel *pâté*
destinato agl'Iddii pestilenziali.

Tardo di mente, piagato
dal pungente giaciglio mi sono fuso
col volo della tarma che la mia suola
sfarina sull'impiantito,
coi kimoni cangianti delle luci
sciorinate all'aurora dai torrioni,
ho annusato nel vento il bruciaticcio
dei buccellati dai forni,
mi son guardato attorno, ho suscitato
iridi su orizzonti di ragnateli
e petali sui tralicci delle inferriate,
mi sono alzato, sono ricaduto
nel fondo dove il secolo è il minuto—

THE PRISONER'S DREAM

Here few signs distinguish dawns from nights.

The zigzag of the starlings over the watchtowers
on battle days, my only wings,
a thread of polar air,
the head guard's eye in the peephole,
nuts cracking, fatty crackling
in the basements, roastings
real or imagined—but the straw is gold,
the wine-red lantern is hearth light,
if sleeping I can dream I'm at your feet.

The purge goes on as before, no reason given.
They say that he who recants and enlists
can survive this slaughtering of geese;
that he who upbraids himself, but betrays and sells
another's hide grabs the ladle by the handle
instead of ending up in the pâté
destined for the pestilential Gods.

Slow-witted, sore
from my sharp pallet, I've become
the flight of the moth my sole
is turning into powder on the floor,
become the light's chameleon kimonos
hung out from the towers at dawn.
I've smelled the scent of burning on the wind
from the cakes in the ovens,
I've looked around, I've conjured rainbows
shimmering on fields of spiderwebs
and petals on the trellises of bars,
I've stood, and fallen back
into the pit where a century's a minute—

e i colpi si ripetono ed i passi,
e ancora ignoro se sarò al festino
farcitore o farcito. L'attesa è lunga,
il mio sogno di te non è finito.

1956

DA **XENIA** I

1

Caro piccolo insetto
che chiamavano mosca non so perchè,
stasera quasi al buio
mentre leggevo il Deuteroisaia
sei ricomparsa accanto a me,
ma non avevi occhiali,
non potevi vedermi
né potevo io senza quel luccichio
riconoscere te nella foschia.

4

Avevamo studiato per l'aldilà
un fischio, un segno di riconoscimento.
Mi provo a modularlo nella speranza
che tutti siamo gia morti senza saperlo.

5

Non ho mai capito se io fossi
il tuo cane fedele e incimurrito
o tu lo fossi per me.

and the blows keep coming, and the footsteps,
and still I don't know if at the feast
I'll be stuffer or stuffing. The wait is long,
my dream of you isn't over.

JONATHAN GALASSI

FROM **XENIA** I

1

Dear little insect—
they called you Mosca, I don't know why—
this evening as I was reading
Deutero-Isaiah in the half-light
you reappeared beside me;
but you weren't wearing glasses,
you couldn't see me,
and I couldn't make you out in the dusk
without their glitter.

JONATHAN GALASSI

4

For the afterlife we had devised
a whistle, a sign of recognition.
I'm trying variations of it in the hope
we're all already dead without knowing it.

HARRY THOMAS

5

I never figured out if I
was your faithful, distempered dog
or you were mine.

Per gli altri no, eri un insetto miope
smarrito nel blabla
dell'alta società. Erano ingenui
quei furbi e non sapevano
di essere loro il tuo zimbello:
di esser visti anche al buio e smascherati
da un tuo senso infallibile, dal tuo
radar di pipistrello.

6

Non hai pensato mai di lasciar traccia
di te scrivendo prosa o versi. E fu
il tuo incanto—e dopo la mia nausea di me.
Fu pure il mio terrore: di esser poi
ricacciato da te nel gracidante
limo dei neòteroi.

9

Ascoltare era il solo tuo modo di vedere.
Il conto del telefono s'è ridotto a ben poco.

1971

To others, no, you were a myopic bug
lost in the blab
of high society. They were naïve,
those clever ones—they never knew
they were the butt of *your* jokes:
that you had seen them even in the dark,
unmasking them with your infallible
bat's radar.

GEOFFREY BROCK

6

You never thought of leaving your mark
by writing prose or verse. This
was your charm—and later my self-revulsion.
It was what I dreaded too: that someday
you'd shove me back into the croaking
bog of modern neoterics.

WILLIAM ARROWSMITH

9

Listening was the only way you had of seeing.
Now the phone bill is down to next to nothing.

HARRY THOMAS

DELL'OMBRA

Un giorno di primavera
vidi l'ombra d'un'albatrella
addormentata sulla brughiera
come una timida agnella.

Era lontano il suo cuore
e stava sospeso nel cielo;
nel mezzo del raggiante sole
bruno, dentro un bruno velo.

Ella si godeva il vento;
solitaria si rimuoveva
per far quell'albero contento:
di fiammelle, qua e là, ardeva.

Non aveva fretta o pena;
altro che di sentire mattino,
poi il suo meriggio, poi la sera
con il suo fioco cammino.

Tra tante ombre che vanno
continuamente, all'ombra eterna,
e copron la terra d'inganno
adoravo quest'ombra ferma.

Carlo Betocchi

1899–1986

THE SHADOW

One spring day I saw
the shadow of a strawberry tree
lying on the moor
like a shy lamb asleep.

Its heart was far away,
suspended in the sky,
brown in a brown veil,
in the sun's eye.

The shadow played in the wind,
moving there alone
to make the tree content.
Here and there it shone.

It knew no pain or haste,
wanting only to feel morning,
then noon, then the slow-paced
journey of evening.

Among all the shadows always
joining eternal shadow,
shrouding the earth in falseness,
I loved this steady shadow.

Così, talvolta, tra noi
scende questa mite apparenza,
che giace, e sembra che si annoi
nell'erba e nella pazienza.

1 9 3 2

D'ESTATE

E cresce, anche per noi
l'estate
vanitosa, coi nostri
verdissimi peccati;

ecco l'ospite secco
del vento,
che fa battibecco
tra le foglie della magnolia;

e suona la sua
serena
melodia, sulla prua
d'ogni foglia, e va via

e la foglia non stacca,
e lascia
l'albero verde, ma spacca
il cuore dell'aria.

1 9 5 5

And thus, at times, it descends
among us, this meek semblance,
and lies down, as if drained,
in grass and in patience.

GEOFFREY BROCK

SUMMER

And it grows, the vain
summer,
even for us with our
bright green sins:

behold the dry guest,
the wind,
that stirs up quarrels
among magnolia boughs

and plays its serene
tune on
the prows of all the leaves—
and then is gone,

leaving the leaves
still there,
the tree still green, but breaking
the heart of the air.

GEOFFREY BROCK

DA **DIARETTO**

INVECCHIANDO (VIII)

Ed ecco, da vecchi incomincia
quel sognacchiare notturno,
vago, senza senso, che ne mena
qua e là, poiché le corrotte funzioni
esigono anch'esse uno spasso:
e riappaiono quivi gli amici
perduti, tra un vagare
sonnambulo, nella stupidità
dell'esistere arreso.
Ma anche qui v'è fare non incosciente
perché è come quando il barcaiolo
del vecchio traghetto sull'Arno,
che sosta alla riva,
sciaguatta in fondo alla barca
con la gottazza, e scarica l'acqua
oltrebordo nel fiume,
ove riprende a correre,
la vecchia acqua marcita fra le doghe,
se pur la barca è lì ferma,
tra i giunchi e la fanga.

1 9 6 1

FROM LITTLE DIARY OF

GETTING OLD (VIII)

And then at night, when old,
we start having vague pointless
scraps of dreams that lead us
to this place or that, since even
our failing senses insist on
outings: and lost friends reappear,
sleepwalking through the stupor
of surrendered existence.
But here too there's something
that's not unconscious, as when
the boatman stops his old ferry
along the banks of the Arno,
plunges his wooden bailer
into the bottom of the boat,
and dumps that stale water,
gone to grime between the staves,
overboard into the river,
where it flows again,
though the boat is held fast
amid the mud and rushes.

GEOFFREY BROCK

PICCOLA AMICA

1932

Pino Masnata

1901–1968

- -

LITTLE DARLIN

GEOFFREY BROCK

L'AMBIZIONE

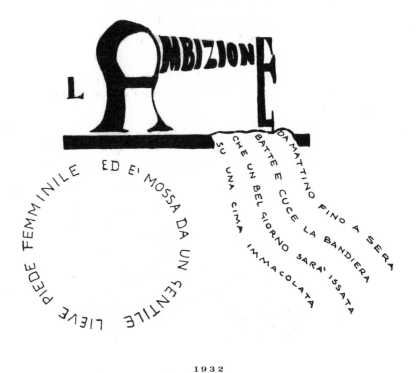

L'AMBIZIONE

DA MATTINO FINO A SERA
BATTE E CUCE LA BANDIERA
CHE UN BEL GIORNO SARÀ ISSATA
SU UNA CIMA IMMACOLATA

ED È MOSSA DA UN GENTILE LIEVE PIEDE FEMMINILE

1932

AMBITION

AMBITION
FROM DAWN TO DUSK IT PLIES
AND SEWS THE PRETTY FLAG
THAT ONE FINE DAY WILL RISE
ATOP SOME PRISTINE CRAG
AND IT MOVES TO THE SWEET
PRESSURE OF FEMALE FEET

GEOFFREY BROCK

ED È SUBITO SERA

Ognuno sta solo sul cuor della terra
trafitto da un raggio di sole:
ed è subito sera.

1930

VENTO A TÌNDARI

Tìndari, mite ti so
fra larghi colli pensile sull'acque
dell'isole dolci del dio,
oggi m'assali
e ti chini in cuore.

Salgo vertici aerei precipizi,
assorto al vento dei pini,
e la brigata che lieve m'accompagna
s'allontana nell'aria,
onda di suoni e amore,
e tu mi prendi
da cui male mi trassi
e paure d'ombre e di silenzi,
rifugi di dolcezze un tempo assidue
e morte l'anima.

Salvatore Quasimodo

1901–1968

AND SUDDENLY IT'S EVENING

Everyone is alone at the heart of the earth
pierced by a ray of sunlight:
and suddenly it's evening.

CHARLES GUENTHER

WIND AT TINDARI

Tindari, I know you mild
among broad hills, above the waters
of the god's soft islands,
today you assail me
and bend into my heart.

I climb peaks, airy precipices,
engulfed in the wind of the pines,
and my lighthearted company
moves far-off in air,
wave of sounds and love,
and you, beloved, take me,
you from whom I drew evil
and fears of shades and silences,
asylums of softness once assiduous
and death of soul.

A te ignota è la terra
ove ogni giorno affondo
e segrete sillabe nutro:
altra luce ti sfoglia sopra i vetri
nella veste notturna,
e gioia non mia riposa
sul tuo grembo.

Aspro è l'esilio,
e la ricerca che chiudevo in te
d'armonia oggi si muta
in ansia precoce di morire;
e ogni amore è schermo alla tristezza,
tacito passo nel buio
dove mi hai posto
amaro pane a rompere.

Tìndari serena torna;
soave amico mi desta
che mi sporga
nel cielo da una rupe
e io fingo timore a chi non sa
che vento profondo m'ha cercato.

1930

TERRA

Notte, serene ombre,
culla d'aria,
mi giunge il vento se in te mi spazio,
con esso il mare odore della terra
dove canta alla riva la mia gente
a vele, a nasse,
a bambini anzi l'alba desti.

To you unknown's the earth
wherein each day I sink
and nourish secret syllables:
other light unleafs you through your windows
in your nocturnal dress,
and joy not mine reposes
on your breast.

Harsh is exile,
and my search for harmony
that was to end in you, alters today
into precocious dread of death:
and every love is a screen for sadness,
silent tread into the darkness
where you have set me
bitter bread to break.

Tindari, serene, return;
soft friend awaken me
that from a stone I thrust me skyward,
feigning fear to who knows not
what deep wind has sought me out.

ALLEN MANDELBAUM

THE LAND

Nights—placid shadows—
Cradle of air—
I feel the wind when I reflect on you:
—With the sea, the odor of the earth
Where my people are singing to the shore—
With sails, with eel baskets—
With children rather—you arouse the dawn.

Monti secchi, pianure d'erba prima
che aspetta bovi e greggi,
m'è dentro il male vostro che mi scava.

1 9 3 0

ANTICO INVERNO

Desiderio delle tue mani chiare
nella penombra della fiamma:
sapevano di rovere e di rose;
di morte. Antico inverno.

Cercavano il miglio gli uccelli
ed erano subito di neve;
così le parole.
Un po' di sole, una raggera d'angelo,
e poi la nebbia; e gli alberi,
e noi fatti d'aria al mattino.

1 9 3 0

OBOE SOMMERSO

Avara pena, tarda il tuo dono
in questa mia ora
di sospirati abbandoni.

Un oboe gelido risillaba
gioia di foglie perenni,
non mie, e smemora;

Dry hills, and plains of early grass
Waiting for flocks and oxen—
Within me are your hardships
Which are hollowing me out.

PETER RUSSELL

ANCIENT WINTER

Desire for your bright hands
in the half-shadow of the flame:
they smelled of oak and roses;
and death. Ancient winter.

The birds out foraging seed
were suddenly snow;
like our words.
A little sun, an angel's halo,
then mist: and the trees,
and us made of air in the morning.

JONATHAN GALASSI

SUNKEN OBOE

Miser pain, delay your gift
in this my hour
of longed-for abandons.

Chill, again an oboe utters
joy of everlasting leaves,
not mine, and disremembers;

In me si fa sera:
l'acqua tramonta
sulle mie mani erbose.

Ali oscillano in fioco cielo,
labili: il cuore trasmigra
ed io son gerbido,

e i giorni una maceria.

1932

STRADA DI AGRIGENTUM

Là dura un vento che ricordo acceso
nelle criniere dei cavalli obliqui
in corsa lungo le pianure, vento
che macchia e rode l'arenaria e il cuore
dei telamoni lugubri, riversi
sopra l'erba. Anima antica, grigia
di rancori, torni a quel vento, annusi
il delicato muschio che riveste
i giganti sospinti giù dal cielo.
Come sola nello spazio che ti resta!
E più t'accori s'odi ancora il suono
che s'allontana verso il mare
dove Espero già striscia mattutino
il marranzano tristemente vibra
nella gola del carraio che risale
il colle nitido di luna, lento
tra il murmure d'ulivi saraceni.

1942

in me, evening falls:
the water sets
on my grassy hands.

In a dim sky, fleeting
wings sway; the heart migrates
and I am fallow

and the days, rubble.

ALLEN MANDELBAUM

THE AGRIGENTUM ROAD

That wind's still there that I remember afire
In the manes of the racing horses
Veering across the plains; a wind
That stains the sandstone and erodes the hearts
Of downed columnar statues in the grass.
Oh antique soul, bled white
By rancor, back you lean to that wind again,
Catching the delicate fetor of the moss
That clothes those giants tumbled down by heaven.
How lonely it will be, the time that is left you!
    Worse, worse, if you should hear
That sound again, borne toward the far-off sea
Which Hesperus already pinks with morning:
The jew's-harp quavering sadly in the mouth
Of the wagon-maker climbing
Slowly his moon-washed hill, amidst
The murmur of the Saracen olive trees.

RICHARD WILBUR

L'ALTO VELIERO

Quando vennero uccelli a muovere foglie
degli alberi amari lungo la mia casa,
(erano ciechi volatili notturni
che foravano i nidi sulle scorze)
io misi la fronte alla luna,
e vidi un alto veliero.

A ciglio dell'isola il mare era sale;
e s'era distesa la terra e antiche
conchiglie lucevano fitte ai macigni
sulla rada da nani limoni.

E dissi all'amata che in sé agitava un mio figlio,
e aveva per esso continuo il mare nell'anima:
«Io sono stanco di tutte quest'ali che battono
a tempo di remo, e delle civette
che fanno il lamento dei cani
quando è vento di luna ai canneti.
Io voglio partire, voglio lasciare quest'isola.»
Ed essa: «O caro, è tardi: restiamo.»

Allora mi misi lentamente a contare
i forti riflessi d'acqua marina
che l'aria mi portava sugli occhi
dal volume dell'alto veliero.

1942

THE TALL SCHOONER

When birds came to shake the leaves
of the bitter trees beside my house
(they were blind, nocturnal flying-things
that dug their nests in bark),
I turned to the moon
and saw a tall schooner.

At the island's edge the sea was salt;
and the land stretched out and ancient
shells shone, rooted in stones
on the road of dwarf lemons.

And I said to my love, in whom my son already stirred,
and for that the sea moved continuously in her soul:
"I am tired of all these wings beating
in time to oars, and the screech owls
howling the dogs' lament
when the wind of the moon moves in the canebrake.
I want to leave, I want to leave this island."
And she: "Love, it is late; let's remain."

Then slowly I set myself to counting
the strong inflections of the seawater
the air sailed up to my eyes
from the bulk of the tall schooner.

MICHAEL EGAN

GIÀ VOLA IL FIORE MAGRO

Non saprò nulla della mia vita,
oscuro monotono sangue.

Non saprò chi amavo, chi amo,
ora che qui stretto, ridotto alle mie membra,
nel guasto vento di marzo
enumero i mali dei giorni decifrati.

Già vola il fiore magro
dai rami. E io attendo
la pazienza del suo volo irrevocabile.

1942

ALLE FRONDE DEI SALICI

E come potevamo noi cantare
con il piede straniero sopra il cuore,
fra i morti abbandonati nelle piazze
sull'erba dura di ghiaccio, al lamento
d'agnello dei fanciulli, all'urlo nero
della madre che andava incontro al figlio
crocifisso sul palo del telegrafo?
Alle fronde dei salici, per voto,
anche le nostre cetre erano appese,
oscillavano lievi al triste vento.

1947

MARCH WIND (AFTER QUASIMODO)

I will know nothing of my life but its mysteries,
the dead cycles of the breath and sap.

I shall not know whom I loved, or love
now that in the random winds of March

I am nothing but my limbs. I fall
into myself, and the years numbered in me.

The thin blossom is already streaming from my boughs.
I watch the pure calm of its only flight.

DON PATERSON

ON THE WILLOW BRANCHES

And we, how could we have sung
with a foreign foot pressed on our heart,
among the dead littering the piazzas
on grass brittle with ice, over the lamblike
crying of children, over the black howl
of the mother who stumbled upon her son
crucified on a telegraph pole?
On the willow branches, as offerings,
even our harps were suspended,
and rocked gently in the mourning wind.

ROB A. MACKENZIE

UOMO DEL MIO TEMPO

Sei ancora quello della pietra e della fionda,
uomo del mio tempo. Eri nella carlinga,
con le ali maligne, le meridiane di morte,
—t'ho visto—dentro il carro di fuoco, alle forche,
alle ruote di tortura. T'ho visto: eri tu,
con la tua scienza esatta persuasa allo sterminio,
senza amore, senza Cristo. Hai ucciso ancora,
come sempre, come uccisero i padri, come uccisero
gli animali che ti videro per la prima volta.
E questo sangue odora come nel giorno
quando il fratello disse all'altro fratello:
«Andiamo ai campi». E quell'eco fredda, tenace
è giunta fino a te, dentro la tua giornata.
Dimenticate, o figli, le nuvole di sangue
salite dalla terra, dimenticate i padri:
le loro tombe affondano nella cenere,
gli uccelli neri, il vento, coprono il loro cuore.

1947

EPITAFFIO PER BICE DONETTI

Con gli occhi alla pioggia e agli elfi della
notte, è là, nel campo quindici a Musocco,
la donna emiliana da me amata nel
tempo triste della giovinezza.
Da poco fu giocata dalla morte
mentre guardava quieta il vento dell'autunno
scrollare i rami dei platani e le foglie
dalla grigia casa di periferia.

MAN OF MY TIME

You are still the one with the stone and sling,
man of my time. You were in the cockpit,
with the malign wings, the sundials of death—
I have seen you—in the chariot of fire, at the gallows,
at the wheels of torture. I have seen you: it was you,
with your exact science persuaded to extermination,
without love, without Christ. Again, as always, you
have killed, as did your fathers kill, as did
the animals that saw you for the first time kill.
And this blood smells as on the day
one brother told the other brother: "Let us
go into the fields." And that echo, chill, tenacious,
has reached down to you, within your day.
Forget, O sons, the clouds of blood
risen from the earth, forget the fathers:
their tombs sink down in ashes,
black birds, the wind, cover their hearts.

ALLEN MANDELBAUM

EPITAPH FOR BICE DONETTI

Here eyes toward the rain and the spirits of night,
there, in field fifteen at Musocco,
lies the Emilian woman I loved
in the sad hours of youth.
Death prevailed over her, not long ago,
while she was quietly watching
the autumn wind shake the branches
and leaves of the plane trees
from her gray house on the edge of town.

Il suo volto è ancora vivo di sorpresa,
come fu certo nell'infanzia, fulminato
per il mangiatore di fuoco alto sul carro.
O tu che passi, spinto da altri morti,
davanti alla fossa undici sessanta,
fermati un minuto a salutare quella
che non si dolse mai dell'uomo che
qui rimane, odiato, coi suoi versi,
uno come tanti, operaio di sogni.

1 9 4 9

Her face is still alive with surprise,
as surely it was in childhood, struck
by the fire-eater high up, on the wagon.
O you who pass by, drawn by other deaths,
stop for a moment before grave
eleven-sixty to speak a word
to one who never felt sorry for the man
left here, hated, with his verses,
one like so many, a worker of dreams.

ADAM GIANNELLI

LIRISMO GEOMETRICO

curva di orizzonte che sostiene con colonne piramidali di monti il quadrato viola del cielo
la luna è un circolo luminoso dove le linee rette delle stelle si tagliano per misurare i diametri ed i raggi
rettangoli colorati di case pesano sopra file interminabili di alberi conici le linee spezzate delle grondaie
poligoni di paesaggi lontani suddivisi da masse cubiche di luci e di ombre
dietro cinematografie liquide di luci a pendenza geometrica figure in rilievo sullo sfondo fotografico cercano con forme algebriche di movimento la meraviglia elettrica dell'UOMO MECCANICO

1925

NOTTURNO

sotto il fanale sporco (sanculotto elettrico che à vinto la nobilità depravata delle stelle) una prostituta-femmina bionda domina l'arcobaleno artificiale della notte con il colore azzurro-vivo dei suoi vestiti di seta

mi à baciato una sera lontana
immergendomi nello spasimo rosso del suo profumo violento
insegnandomi la meraviglia dei caffè-chantants che cambiarono con lussurie spregiudicate la mia ingenuità di poeta in vita elastica-notturna di ELEGANTISSIMO TEPPISTA

1925

Fillia

1904–1936

GEOMETRIC LYRICISM

curving horizon whose pyramidal mountain columns support the sky's violet square

the moon is a luminous circle intersected by the stars' straight lines measuring diameters and radiuses

colored rectangular houses superimpose the broken lines of their eaves on interminable rows of conical trees

distant polygonal landscapes interrupted by cubical masses of light and shadow

behind slanting geometric lights forming moving pictures background figures seek the electric miracle of MECHANICAL MAN with algebraic expressions of movement

WILLARD BOHN

NOCTURNE

beneath the filthy streetlight (electric sansculotte conqueror of the stars' depraved nobility) a blond prostitute-female dominates the night's artificial rainbow with her blue-vivid silk garments

she kissed me one evening long ago

immersing me in her violent perfume's red spasm

introducing me to marvelous cabarets whose unprejudiced lustings transformed my naïve poetic existence into the nocturnal-elastic life of AN EXTREMELY ELEGANT THUG

WILLARD BOHN

La vita . . . è ricordarsi di un risveglio
triste in un treno all'alba: aver veduto
fuori la luce incerta: aver sentito
nel corpo rotto la malinconia
vergine e aspra dell'aria pungente.

Ma ricordarsi la liberazione
improvvisa è più dolce: a me vicino
un marinaio giovane: l'azzurro
e il bianco della sua divisa, e fuori
un mare tutto fresco di colore.

1 9 3 8

Se dietro la finestra illuminata
dorme un fanciullo, nella notte estiva,
e sognerà . . .
        Passa veloce un treno
e va lontano.
        Il mare è come prima.

1 9 3 8

Sandro Penna

1906–1977

Life . . . is remembering a sad
waking in a train at dawn, seeing
the tentative light outside, feeling
in the broken body the bitter virgin
sorrow of the piercing air.

But remembering the sudden release
is sweeter, a young sailor
beside me, the blue and white
of his uniform, and outside
a sea all crisp with color.

W. S. DI PIERO

If a boy sleeping behind
the lighted window on a summer night
begins to dream . . .
          A train rushes past
on into the distance.
            The sea is still the same.

W. S. DI PIERO

NUOTATORE

Dormiva . . . ?
           Poi si tolse e si stirò.
Guardò con occhi lenti l'acqua. Un guizzo
il suo corpo.
          Così lasciò la terra.

1938

SERA NEL GIARDINO

La sera mi ha rapito
i rissosi fanciulli.
Le loro voci d'angeli
in guerra.
         Adesso in seno
a nuove luci stanno
là sull'opposte case.

Resta sul cielo chiaro
d'un eroe s'un cavallo
incisa macchia muta

sotto la prima stella.

1938

INTERNO

Dal portiere non c'era nessuno.
C'era la luce sui poveri letti
disfatti. E sopra un tavolaccio

THE SWIMMER

Had he been sleeping . . . ?

                Got up and stretched,
gazed slowly at the water. Then, body
aquiver,

      left the earth.

WILLIAM JAY SMITH

EVENING IN THE PARK

The evening kidnapped
my quarreling boys.
Their angel voices
warring.
      Now they stand
in the mothering shelter of new lights
in houses across the street.

Engraved on the bright sky
the silent smudge
of a hero on a horse

under the first star.

W. S. DI PIERO

INTERIOR

The doorman wasn't in.
The poor disheveled beds
shone in the light. An urchin

dormiva un ragazzaccio
bellissimo.
                Usci dalle sue braccia
annuvolate, esitando, un gattino.

1 9 3 8

È pur dolce il ritrovarsi
per contrada sconosciuta.
Un ragazzo con la tuta
ora passa accanto a te.

Tu ne pensi alla sua vita
—a quel desco che l'aspetta.
E la stanca bicicletta
ch'egli posa accanto a sé.

Ma tu resti sulla strada
sconosciuta ed infinito.
Tu non chiedi alla tua vita
che restare ormai com'è.

1 9 3 8

La veneta piazzetta,
antica e mesta, accoglie
odor di mare. E voli
di colombi. Ma resta
nella memoria—e incanta
di sé la luce—il volo

was sleeping on rough boards:
gorgeous.
          Nervous, a kitten
leapt from the cloud of his arms.

GEOFFREY BROCK

It's good to find yourself
in a strange neighborhood.
A guy in coveralls
passes you on the sidewalk.

You think about his life—
the dinner that awaits him,
the weary bicycle
he's pushing by his side.

You keep on walking down
that strange, infinite road.
And all you ask of life is
to stay the way it is.

GEOFFREY BROCK

The small Venetian square,
ancient and mournful, harbors
the smell of sea. The flights
of doves. But there remains
in memory—enchanting
the very light—the flight

del giovane ciclista
vòlto all'amico: un soffio
melodico: «Vai solo?»

1 9 3 8

Il cielo è vuoto. Ma negli occhi neri
di quel fanciullo io pregherò il mio dio.

Ma il mio dio se ne va in bicicletta
o bagna il muro con disinvoltura.

1 9 3 8

Deserto è il fiume. E tu lo sai che basta
ora con le solari prodezze di ieri.
Bacio nelle tue ascelle, umidi, fieri,
gli odori di un'estate che si guasta.

1 9 5 5

Lumi del cimitero, non mi dite
che la sera d'estate non è bella.
E belli sono i bevitori dentro
le lontane osterie.

Muovonsi come fregi
antichi sotto il cielo
nuovo di stelle.

of the young cyclist turned
toward his friend: his tuneful
whisper: "Going alone?"

GEOFFREY BROCK

The sky is empty. But in the black eyes
of that boy I will pray to my god.

But my god rides away on a bicycle
or wets the wall with nonchalance.

MOIRA EGAN AND DAMIANO ABENI

The river's deserted. And you know
that yesterday's sunlit exploits
are over. In your armpits I kiss
the fierce damp smells of a summer spoiling.

W. S. DI PIERO

Graveyard lights, don't tell me
the summer evening's not fine.
And fine the drinkers
in faraway inns.

Like antique friezes
they move under the sky
new with stars.

Lumi del cimitero, calmi diti
contano lente sere. Non mi dite
che la notte d'estate non è bella.

1 9 5 5

Ecco il fanciullo acquatico e felice.
Ecco il fanciullo gravido di luce
più limpido del verso che lo dice.
Dolce stagione di silenzio e sole
e questa festa di parole in me.

1 9 5 5

Il treno tarderà di almeno un'ora.
L'acqua del mare si fa più turchina.
Sul muro calcinato il campanello
casalingo non suona. La panchina
di ferro scotta al sole. Le cicale
sono le sole padrone dell'ora.

1 9 5 5

Oh non ti dare arie
di superiorità.
Solo uno sguardo io vidi
degno di questa. Era
un bambino annoiato in una festa.

1 9 5 6

Graveyard lights, calm fingers
go counting slow evenings. Don't tell me
the summer night's not fine.

BLAKE ROBINSON

Here is the boy, aquatic and happy.
Here is the boy, heavy with light,
more limpid than the verse that says it.
Lovely season of silence and sun
and this holiday of words within me.

WILLIAM WEAVER

The train will be at least an hour late.
The blue-green of the water darkens.
The doorbell on the whitewashed wall
doesn't ring. The iron
bench burns in the sun. The cicadas
are sole masters of the hour.

W. S. DI PIERO

Spare me the air
of superiority.
I've seen only one face
worthy of it:
a baby's, bored at a party.

GEORGE SCRIVANI

Passando sopra un ponte
alto sull'imbrunire
guardando l'orizzonte
ti pare di svanire.

Ma la campagna resta
piena di cose vere
e tante azzurre sfere
non valgono una festa.

1956

È l'ora in cui si baciano i marmocchi
assonnati sui caldi ginocchi.
Ma io, per lunghe strade, coi miei occhi
inutilmente. Io, mostro da niente.

1956

Io vado verso il fiume su un cavallo
che quando io penso un poco un poco egli si ferma.

1976

LETTERATURA

Di là dal fiume un canto di ragazzi
ebbri, nella sera di luglio.
Io buio, sul sedile, e vuoto.
Ero una volta Holderlin . . . Rimbaud . . .

1976

As you pass high upon
a bridge as night falls there
you gaze at the horizon
and seem to disappear.

But still the fields are full
of things that still are true
and all the spheres of blue
aren't worth one festival.

HENRY TAYLOR

Evening again, and every sleepy youngster
home on a warm lap, getting a kiss.
And me, on these long streets, with this
pair of useless eyes. A trivial monster.

GEOFFREY BROCK

I'm off to the river on a horse,
who'll halt a little when I think a little.

BLAKE ROBINSON

LITERATURE

Over there by the river, the song of boys
drinking in the July night.
I sit, dark and empty, on a bench.
I once was Hölderlin . . . Rimbaud . . .

ADAM GIANNELLI

GRAPPA A SETTEMBRE

I mattini trascorrono chiari e deserti
sulle rive del fiume, che all'alba s'annebbia
e incupisce il suo verde, in attesa del sole.
Il tabacco, che vendono nell'ultima casa
ancor umida, all'orlo dei prati, ha un colore
quasi nero e un sapore sugoso: vapora azzurrino.
Tengon anche la grappa, colore dell'acqua.

È venuto un momento che tutto si ferma
e matura. Le piante lontano stan chete:
sono fatte piú scure. Nascondono frutti
che a una scossa cadrebbero. Le nuvole sparse
hanno polpe mature. Lontano, sui corsi,
ogni casa matura al tepore del cielo.

Non si vede a quest'ora che donne. Le donne non fumano
e non bevono, sanno soltanto fermarsi nel sole
e riceverlo tiepido addosso, come fossero frutta.
L'aria, cruda di nebbia, si beve a sorsate
come grappa, ogni cosa vi esala un sapore.
Anche l'acqua del fiume ha bevuto le rive
e le macera al fondo, nel cielo. Le strade
sono come le donne, maturano ferme.

Cesare Pavese

1908–1950

GRAPPA IN SEPTEMBER

The mornings pass clear and deserted
on the river's banks, fogged over by dawn,
their green darkened, awaiting the sun.
In that last house, still damp, at the edge
of the field, they're selling tobacco, blackish,
juicy in flavor: its smoke is pale blue.
They also sell grappa, the color of water.

The moment has come when everything stops
to ripen. The trees in the distance are quiet,
growing darker and darker, concealing fruit
that would fall at a touch. The scattered clouds
are pulpy and ripe. On the distant boulevards,
houses are ripening beneath the mild sky.

This early you see only women. Women don't smoke
and don't drink, they know only to stop in the sun
to let their bodies grow warm, as if they were fruit.
The air's raw with this fog, you drink it in sips
like grappa, everything here has a flavor.
Even the river water has swallowed the banks
and steeps them below, in the sky. The streets
are like women, they grow ripe without moving.

A quest'ora ciascuno dovrebbe fermarsi
per la strada e guardare come tutto maturi.
C'è persino una brezza, che non smuove le nubi,
ma che basta a dirigere il fumo azzurrino
senza romperlo: è un nuovo sapore che passa.
E il tabacco va intinto di grappa. È cosí che le donne
non saranno le sole a godere il mattino.

1 9 3 6

DISCIPLINA

I lavori cominciano all'alba. Ma noi cominciamo
un po' prima dell'alba a incontrare noi stessi
nella gente che va per la strada. Ciascuno ricorda
di esser solo e aver sonno, scoprendo i passanti
radi—ognuno trasogna fra sé,
tanto sa che nell'alba spalancherà gli occhi.
Quando viene il mattino ci trova stupiti
a fissare il lavoro che adesso comincia.
Ma non siamo piú soli e nessuno piú ha sonno
e pensiamo con calma i pensieri del giorno
fino a dare in sorrisi. Nel sole che torna
siamo tutti convinti. Ma a volte un pensiero
meno chiaro—un sogghigno—ci coglie improvviso
e torniamo a guardare come prima del sole.
La città chiara assiste ai lavori e ai sogghigni.
Nulla può disturbare il mattino. Ogni cosa
può accadere e ci basta di alzare la testa
dal lavoro e guardare. Ragazzi scappati
che non fanno ancor nulla, camminano in strada
e qualcuno anche corre. Le foglie dei viali
gettan ombre per strada e non manca che l'erba,

This is the time when each person should pause
in the street to see how everything ripens.
There's even a breeze, it won't move the clouds,
but it's enough to carry the blue smoke
without breaking it: a new flavor passing. And tobacco
is best when steeped in some grappa. That's why the women
won't be the only ones enjoying the morning.

GEOFFREY BROCK

DISCIPLINE

Jobs begin at dawn. But we begin
just before dawn to encounter ourselves
in people walking down the street. Each one remembers
he's alone and sleepy, discovering himself in the few
passersby—each man daydreams to himself, knowing
the dawn light will force his eyes open.
When morning comes, it finds us numbly
staring at the job of work, which now begins.
But now nobody's alone, nobody's sleeping anymore,
and we think our daylight thoughts so serenely
we start to smile. That returning sunlight
has us all convinced. But sometimes a thought less bright
and clear—a mocking grin—suddenly surprises us,
and we go back to looking the way we did, before the light.
The bright city watches our working, it sees us grinning.
Nothing can upset the morning. Anything
can happen, all we have to do is raise our heads
from work and watch. Boys skipping school,
who do no work at all, are roaming in the streets,
some of them are running. Along the avenues the leaves
throw shadows on the streets, only grass is missing from

tra le case che assistono immobili. Tanti
sulla riva del fiume si spogliano al sole.
La città ci permette di alzare la testa
a pensarci, e sa bene che poi la chiniamo.

1936

TOLLERANZA

Piove senza rumore sul prato del mare.
Per le luride strade non passa nessuno.
È discesa dal treno una femmina sola:
tra il cappotto si è vista la chiara sottana
e le gambe sparire nella porta annerita.

Si direbbe un paese sommerso. La sera
stilla fredda su tutte le soglie, e le case
spandon fumo azzurrino nell'ombra. Rossastre
le finestre s'accendono. S'accende una luce
tra le imposte accostate nella casa annerita.

L'indomani fa freddo e c'è il sole sul mare.
Una donna in sottana si strofina la bocca
alla fonte, e la schiuma è rosata. Ha capelli
biondo-ruvido, simili alle bucce d'arancia
sparse in terra. Protesa alla fonte, sogguarda
un monello nerastro che la fissa incantato.
Donne fosche spalancano imposte alla piazza
—i mariti sonnecchiano ancora, nel buio.

Quando torna la sera, riprende la pioggia
scoppiettante sui molti bracieri. Le spose,
ventilando i carboni, dànno occhiate alla casa
annerita e alla fonte deserta. La casa

between the houses which watch, not moving. In the sunlight
along the river by the swimming-place, kids are undressing.
The city lets us lift our heads and think
about these things, knowing we'll lower them later.

W I L L I A M   A R R O W S M I T H

TOLERANCE

It rains without sound on the green stretch
of the sea. In the dirty streets nobody moves.
A woman got off her train, a woman alone.
Through her raincoat you can see her bright skirt,
and her legs disappearing through the dark doorway.

The town is like a place under water. Night
drips cold at every doorway, and the houses
spread a bluish haze in the darkness. Red
windows are kindled. Between the shuttered blinds
of the blackened house, a light goes on.

Morning is cold, with sunlight on the sea.
A woman in a skirt stands rinsing her mouth
at the fountain, and the water is reddish. Her hair
is dirty blond, like the orange peels scattered
on the ground. Bending to the spout, she peers up
at a blackish urchin staring at her, fascinated.
Women in black are opening shutters on the piazza—
their husbands still lie dozing in the dark.

At night the rain begins again, spattering
the braziers hissing at the doorways. Wives
stand fanning the coals and glancing at the black
house and the deserted fountain. The windows

ha le imposte accecate, ma dentro c'è un letto,
e sul letto una bionda si guadagna la vita.
Tutto quanto il paese riposa la notte,
tutto, tranne la bionda, che si lava al mattino.

1 9 4 3

CREAZIONE

Sono vivo e ho sorpreso nell'alba le stelle.
La compagna continua a dormire e non sa.
Dormon tutti, i compagni. La chiara giornata
mi sta innanzi piú netta dei volti sommersi.

Passa un vecchio in distanza, che va a lavorare
o a godere il mattino. Non siamo diversi,
tutti e due respiriamo lo stesso chiarore
e fumiamo tranquilli a ingannare la fame.
Anche il corpo del vecchio dev'essere schietto
e vibrante—dovrebbe esser nudo davanti al mattino.

Stamattina la vita ci scorre sull'acqua
e nel sole: c'è intorno il fulgore dell'acqua
sempre giovane, i corpi di tutti saranno scoperti.
Ci sarà il grande sole e l'asprezza del largo
e la rude stanchezza che abbatte nel sole
e l'immobilità. Ci sarà la compagna
—un segreto di corpi. Ciascuno darà una sua voce.

Non c'è voce che rompe il silenzio dell'acqua
sotto l'alba. E nemmeno qualcosa trasale
sotto il cielo. C'è solo un tepore che scioglie le stelle.
Fa tremare sentire il mattino che vibra
tutto vergine, quasi nessuno di noi fosse sveglio.

1 9 6 2

are shuttered tight, but inside there's a bed,
and on the bed a blonde is earning her living.
At night the whole town goes to sleep,
all but the blonde, who washes in the morning.

WILLIAM ARROWSMITH

CREATION

I'm alive and at daybreak I've startled the stars.
My companion continues to sleep unaware.
All companions are sleeping. The day is a clear one
and stands sharper before me than faces in water.

In the distance an old man is walking to work
or enjoying the morning. We aren't so different,
we both breathe the same faint glimmer of light
as we casually smoke, cheating our hunger.
The old man, too, must have a body that's pure
and vital—he ought to stand naked facing the morning.

Life this morning flows out over water
and in sunlight: around us the innocent splendor
of water, and all the bodies will soon be uncovered.
There'll be a bright sun and the sharpness of sea air
and the harsh exhaustion that beats down in sunlight
and stillness. And my companion will be here—
a shared secret of bodies, each with its own voice.

There's no voice to break the silence of water
at dawn. And nowhere is anything startled
beneath this sky. There's only a star-melting warmth.
One shudders to feel the morning trembling
so virginally, as if none of us here were awake.

GEOFFREY BROCK

DA LA TERRA E LA MORTE

[4]

Hai viso di pietra scolpita,
sangue di terra dura,
sei venuta dal mare.
Tutto accogli e scruti
e repudi da te
come il mare. Nel cuore
hai silenzio, hai parole
inghiottite. Sei buia.
Per te l'alba è silenzio.

E sei come le voci
della terra—l'urto
della secchia nel pozzo,
la canzone del fuoco,
il tonfo di una mela;
le parole rassegnate
e cupe sulle soglie,
il grido del bimbo—le cose
che non passano mai.
Tu non muti. Sei buia.

Sei la cantina chiusa,
dal battuto di terra,
dov'è entrato una volta
ch'era scalzo il bambino,
e ci ripensa sempre.
Sei la camera buia
cui si ripensa sempre,
come al cortile antico
dove s'apriva l'alba.

1951

FROM EARTH AND DEATH

[4]

Your face sculpted from stone,
your blood hard earth—
you come from the sea.
Like the sea you pick up,
examine, then throw away
everything. In your heart
is silence, or choked-back
words. Something too dark.
For you, dawn is silence.

Yet you're full of the voices
of earth: the shock of a bucket
far down a well, fire singing,
the thud of an apple falling,
the resigned words that linger
echoing around thresholds,
a child's first cry—the things
that cannot pass away.
As you can't change. Too dark.

You are the closed cantina
with its earthen floor,
that a small child entered
once when he still went barefoot,
and thinks about forever.
You are the darkened chamber
that rethinks itself forever,
the ancient courtyard where
dawn opens like a fan.

ALAN WILLIAMSON

[5]

Tu non sai le colline
dove si è sparso il sangue.
Tutti quanti fuggimmo
tutti quanti gettammo
l'arma e il nome. Una donna
ci guardava fuggire.
Uno solo di noi
si fermò a pugno chiuso,
vide il cielo vuoto,
chinò il capo e morì
sotto il muro, tacendo.
Ora è un cencio di sangue
e il suo nome. Una donna
ci aspetta alle colline.

1951

Verrà la morte e avrà i tuoi occhi—
questa morte che ci accompagna
dal mattino alla sera, insonne,
sorda, come un vecchio rimorso
o un vizio assurdo. I tuoi occhi
saranno una vana parola,
un grido taciuto, un silenzio.
Così li vedi ogni mattina
quando su te sola ti pieghi
nello specchio. O cara speranza,
quel giorno sapremo anche noi
che sei la vita e sei il nulla.

Per tutti la morte ha uno sguardo.
Verrà la morte e avrà i tuoi occhi.

You do not know the hills
where blood was spilled.
We all fled,
we all threw down
our arms and our names. A woman
watched us flee.
Only one of us
stopped, with fist clenched,
saw the empty sky,
bent his head and died
under a wall, silently.
Now he is a pool of blood,
and his name. A woman
awaits us in the hills.

CHARLES WRIGHT

Death will come and will have your eyes—
this death that accompanies us
from morning till evening, unsleeping,
deaf, like an old remorse
or an absurd vice. Your eyes
will be a useless word,
a suppressed cry, a silence.
That's how you see them each morning
when alone with yourself you lean
toward the mirror. O precious hope,
that day we too will know
that you are life and you are nothingness.

Death has a look for everyone.
Death will come and will have your eyes.

Sarà come smettere un vizio,
come vedere nello specchio
riemergere un viso morto,
come ascoltare un labbro chiuso.
Scenderemo nel gorgo muti.

1951

It will be like renouncing a vice,
like seeing a dead face
resurface in the mirror,
like listening to a lip that's shut.
We'll go down into the maelstrom mute.

GEOFFREY BROCK

L'AMICO TRADITO

L'amico tradito mi chiama
Dal fondo del cuore e s'avvicina.
Sento nel sonno che sale.
Io grido all'ultimo passo
Perché mi calpesti.
Poi mi dorme leggero sul petto.

1936

ELEGIA I

Mi ricorderò di questo autunno
Splendido e fuggitivo dalla luce migrante,
Curva al vento sul dorso delle canne.
La piena dei canali è salita alla cintura
E mi ci sono immerso disseccato dalla siccità.
Quando sarò con gli amici nelle notti di città
Farò la storia di questi giorni di ventura,
Di mio padre che a pestar l'uva
S'era fatti i piedi rossi,
Di mia madre timorosa
Che porta un uovo caldo nella mano
Ed è più felice d'una sposa.

Leonardo Sinisgalli

1908–1981

THE FRIEND I BETRAYED

The friend I betrayed calls me
from deep in my heart, comes near.
I hear him climbing in my sleep.
At the last footfall I scream
that he step on me.
Then he sleeps lightly on my chest.

RINA FERRARELLI

ELEGY I

I will remember this autumn,
Splendid and fleeting in the migrant light
That leans over the hunched reeds in the wind.
The flooding canals rose waist-high,
And I, parched by the drought, plunged in.
Among friends on city nights
I'll tell the story of these lucky days,
Of my father who turned his feet red
Treading grapes,
Of my timid mother
Carrying a warm egg in her hand,
Happier than a bride.

Mio padre parlava di quel ciliegio
Piantato il giorno delle nozze, mi diceva,
Quest'anno non ha avuto fioritura,
E sognava di farne il letto nuziale a me primogenito.
Il vento di tramontana apriva il cielo
Al quarto di luna. La luna coi corni
Rosei, appena spuntati, di una vitella!
Domani si potrà seminare, diceva mio padre.
Sul palmo aperto della mano guardavo
I solchi chiari contro il fuoco, io sentivo
Scoppiare il seme nel suo cuore,
Io vedevo nei suoi occhi fiammeggiare
La conca spigata.

1938

VIA VELASCA

Il calpestìo di tanti anni
L'ha quasi affondata, la via
Incredibilmente si è stretta.
Questa è l'ora mia, la mia ora diletta.
Io, ricordo la sera che alla fioca
Luce si spense ogni rumore, un grido
Disse il mio nome come in sogno è sparve.
La via s'incurva, sgocciola
Il giorno dalle cime dei tetti:
Quest'ora dolce suona nel petto.
Non è che una larva restìa
La luce, un barlume: entro la boccia
Di vetro un pesce s'illumina.

1939

My father often talked about that cherry tree
Planted, he told me, on their wedding day—
It didn't blossom this year. He dreamed
It would make a marriage bed for me, his firstborn son.
The north wind was clearing the sky
For the quarter moon. A moon
With the rosy horn-buds of a heifer!
Tomorrow we can plant, my father was saying.
Looking into his open palm, its furrows
Clear in the firelight, I could hear
The seed bursting in his heart,
I could see, in his eyes, the hollow
Aflame with ripe wheat.

GEOFFREY BROCK

VIA VELASCA

Years of pounding have nearly
Caved it in, and it's hard to believe
The street's gotten narrower.
This is my hour, my favorite hour.
I remember one night all noise died
In the fading light, a voice
Cried my name as if in a dream
Then stopped.
The street bends, the day
Drips from the rooftops,
The sweet hour sings in me.
The light is only a stubborn
Ghost, a glow: a fish
Gleams in the glass bottle.

W. S. DI PIERO

VIDI LE MUSE

Sulla collina
Io certo vidi le Muse
Appollaiate tra le foglie.
Io vidi allora le Muse
Tra le foglie larghe delle querce
Mangiare ghiande e coccole.
Vidi le muse su una quercia
Secolare che gracchiavano.
Meravigliato il mio cuore
Chiesi al mio cuore meravigliato
Io dissi al mio cuore la meraviglia.

1939

PIANTO ANTICO

I vecchi hanno il pianto facile.
In pieno meriggio
in un nascondiglio della casa vuota
scoppiano in lacrime seduti.
Li coglie di sorpresa
una disperazione infinita.
Portano alle labbra uno spicchio
secco di pera, la polpa
di un fico cotto sulle tegole.
Anche un sorso d'acqua
può spegnere una crisi
e la visita di una lumachina.

1962

I SAW THE MUSES

Of course I saw the Muses
on the hill
roosting in the leaves.
Well then, I saw the Muses
in the liberal oak leaves
eating acorns and berries.
I saw the Muses on an ancient
oak, where they kept cawing.
My heart marveling
I asked my marveling heart
and told my heart the marvel.

SONIA RAIZISS AND
ALFREDO DE PALCHI

OLD TEARS

To the old, weeping comes easy.
In midafternoon,
in some hiding-place in the empty house
they sit, and burst into tears.
An infinite despair
takes them by surprise.
They raise to their lips
a dry slice of pear, the pulp
of a fig dried on the roof-tiles.
Even a sip of water
can resolve their crisis,
or the sight of a snail.

WILLIAM WEAVER

SABATO SANTO A MANFREDONIA

Di qua non resta più nessuno.
Le anitre scivolano una
dopo l'altra
verso la buia sponda.
Gli amici fondano una città celeste.
Ci lasciano alle finestre
contro il mare bruno
come una montagna.
Messaggeri tra vita e morte
i fanciulli si tuffano
a cogliere vermi sott'acqua
e il vecchio pescatore
aspetta che risorgano
con un ramoscello di sangue
tra le dita.

1 9 6 2

HOLY SATURDAY IN MANFREDONIA

There's no one here now.
The ducks go gliding one
by one
toward the dark shore.
Our friends are founding a celestial city.
They leave us here by windows
facing the sea, brown
as a mountain.
Couriers between life and death,
the children
dive for worms
and the old fisherman
waits for them to surface
with a twig of blood
in their fingers.

W. S. DI PIERO

PAESETTO DI RIVIERA

La sera amorosa
ha raccolto le logge
per farle salpare
le case tranquille
sognanti la rosa
vaghezza dei poggi
discendono al mare
in isole, in ville
accanto alle chiese.

1932

VENTO SULLA GIUDECCA

I venti i venti spogliano le navi
e discendono al freddo
e sono morti.

Chi li spiegherà nel rigoglio
delle accese partenze
ove squilla più forte più forte il mare
e l'antenna sventola il mattino?

Alfonso Gatto

1909–1976

SEASIDE VILLAGE

The amorous evening
Gathered the balconies
And set them sailing
The tranquil houses
Dreaming the rose-red
Vagueness of the hills
Descend on the sea
As islands, as villas
Close by the churches.

HAL STEVEN SHOWS

WIND OVER GIUDECCA

The winds the winds undress the ships
and descend to the cold
and are dead.

Who will unloose them in the luxuriance
of inflamed departures
where stronger stronger blares the sea
and the lateen-yard flaps in the morning wind?

Tutta donna tutta forte tutto amore
ed è rossa la mela, giallo il pane
della Pasqua d'aprile . . .
                            Ed eri calda
ed eri il sole, mattone su mattone,
oltre quel muro la campagna il cielo.

1 9 4 4

DA PER I MARTIRI DI

PIAZZALE LORETO

Io vidi il nuovo giorno che a Loreto
sovra la rossa barricata i morti
saliranno per primi, ancora in tuta
e col petto discinto, ancora vivi
di sangue e di ragioni. Ed ogni giorno,
ogni ora eterna brucia a questo fuoco,
ogni alba ha il petto offeso da quel piombo
degli innocenti fulminati al muro.

1 9 4 7

ANNIVERSARIO

Io ricordo quei giorni: nell'ignoto
mattino ove a svegliarci era il terrore
d'esser rimasti soli, udivo il cielo
come una voce morta. E già la luce
abbandonata dai morenti ai vetri

All woman all strong all love
and red is the apple, yellow the bread
of April Easter . . .
                        And you were warm
and you were the sun, brick upon brick,
beyond that wall the fields the sky.

ROBERTA L. PAYNE

FOR THE MARTYRS OF

LORETO SQUARE

I saw a new day breaking on Loreto Square
when over their red barricade the dead
climbed for the first time, still in their overalls,
bare-chested, pulsing again with blood and reasons.
                        And every day,
every hour burns endlessly in this fire,
every dawn has its breast outraged by the bullets
which like lightning-strike smashed the innocent
        back against the wall.

KENDRICK SMITHYMAN

ANNIVERSARY

I remember those days: In the unpredictable
morning, when what woke us was the fear
of being left alone, I heard the sky
like a dead voice. And already the light
abandoned by the dying on the window-panes

mi toccava la fronte, sui capelli
lasciava l'orma del suo sonno eterno.
Un grido umano che s'udisse, nulla
—solo la neve—e tutti erano vivi
dietro quel muro a piangere, il silenzio
beveva a fiumi il pianto della terra.

Oh, l'Europa gelata nel suo cuore
mai più si scalderà: sola, coi morti
che l'amano in eterno, sarà bianca
senza confini, uniti dalla neve.

1 9 4 7

touched my forehead; on my hair
it left traces of its eternal sleep.
No human cry was heard—only the snow—
and all were alive behind that wall
merely to weep, and silence
drank in torrents the weeping of the earth.

Oh, Europe frozen to her heart
will never again grow warm: alone with the dead
who love her eternally, she will be white
without boundaries, united by the snow.

GIOVANNI PONTIERO

Alfonso Gatto · 279

AL FRATELLO

Un giorno amaro l'infinita cerchia
dei colli
veste di luce declinante,
e già trabocca sulla pianura
un autunno di foglie.

Più freddo ora dispiega i suoi vessilli
d'ombra il tramonto,
un chiaro lume nasce
dove tu dolce manchi
all'antica abitudine serale.

1951

A SUA MADRE, CHE
AVEVA NOME MARIA

Sei tu, invocata ogni sera, dipinta sulle nuvole
che arrossano la nostra pianura e chi si muove in essa,
bambini freschi come foglie e donne umide in viaggio
verso la città nella luce d'un acquazzone che smette,
sei tu, madre giovane eternamente in virtù della morte

Attilio Bertolucci

1911–2000

TO MY BROTHER

One grievous day
clothes the infinite circle of the hills
in a waning light,
and already there overflows across the plain
a whole autumn of leaves.

Colder the sunset now unfurls
its shadowy ensigns:
a bright lamp is lit
where you in your gentleness are missing
from the ancient ceremony of evening.

CHARLES TOMLINSON

TO HIS MOTHER, WHOSE

NAME WAS MARIA

Invoked every sundown, it's you, painted on clouds
rouging our treasured plain and all who walk it,
with leaf-fresh kids and women damp from traveling,
city-bound, in the radiance of a just-stopped shower;
it's you, mother eternally young, courtesy of death's

che t'ha colta, rosa sul punto dolce di sfioritura,
tu, l'origine di ogni nevrosi e ansia che mi tortura,
e di questo ti ringrazio per l'età passata presente e futura.

1 9 5 5

I PAPAVERI

Questo è un anno di papaveri, la nostra
terra ne traboccava poi che vi tornai
fra maggio e giugno, e m'inebriai
d'un vino così dolce così fosco.

Dal gelso nuvoloso al grano all'erba
maturità era tutto, in un calore
conveniente, in un lento sopore
diffuso dentro l'universo verde.

A metà della vita ora vedevo
figli cresciuti allontanarsi soli
e perdersi oltre il carcere di voli
che la rondine stringe nello spento

bagliore d'una sera di tempesta,
e umanamente il dolore cedeva
alla luce che in casa s'accendeva
d'un'altra cena in un'aria più fresca

per grandine sfogatasi lontano.

1 9 7 1

plucking hand, rose at the fragrant point of unpetaling,
you who are the alpha of every neurosis, every torturing anxiety,
and for this I give you gratitude for time past, time present, time future.

CYRUS CASSELLS

POPPIES

This is a year of poppies: our land
was brimming with them as May burned
into June and I returned—
a sweet dark wine that made me drunk.

From clouds of mulberry to grains to grasses
ripeness was all, in the fitting
heat, in the slow drowsiness spreading
through the universe of green.

My life half over I saw grown sons
setting off alone and vanishing from sight
beyond the prison the flight
of the swallow makes in the spent

glow of a stormy evening, but the pain
gave way humanely to the light
coming on inside the house for another meal
in air made cooler by hail

letting off steam in the distance.

GEOFFREY BROCK

GIARDINO PUBBLICO

In una torva luce
bambini e asinelli
consumano le ultime
ore del giorno, Dio

fa cessare quei loro
gesti dementi, manda
uno scroscio di pioggia
sulla pelle, sul pelo

affaticati e pesti
dal vivere e da ottobre
che madido si disfa,
e li trovi il crepuscolo

nelle stanze, le stalle
loro assegnate, quieti
e dispersi, e tu
che morendo li insanguini

e li redimi, o sole.

1971

RITRATTO DI UOMO MALATO

Questo che vedete qui dipinto in sanguigna e nero
e che occupa intero il quadro spazioso
sono io all'età di quarantanove anni, ravvolto
in un'ampia vestaglia che mozza a metà le mani

PUBLIC GARDEN

In a grim light
children and little donkeys
waste away the last hours
of day: Lord

make their mad
movements cease, send
a burst of rain
onto pelt and skin,

matted and worn
by life and by October
dissolving in dampness,
so that dusk might find them

in their rooms, the stalls
assigned them, quiet
and dispersed, and you
who in dying bloodstain

and redeem them, O sun.

NICHOLAS BENSON

PORTRAIT OF A SICK MAN

This man you see here painted in bloodred and black
taking up the entire big canvas
is me at forty-nine, wrapped
in a spacious robe that cuts my hands in half

come fossero fiori, non lascia vedere se il corpo
sia coricato o seduto: così è degli infermi
posti davanti a finestre che incorniciano il giorno,
un altro giorno concesso agli occhi stancatisi presto.

Ma se chiedo al pittore, mio figlio quattordicenne,
chi ha voluto ritrarre, egli subito dice
«uno di quei poeti cinesi che mi hai fatto
leggere, mentre guarda fuori, una delle sue ultime ore».

È sincero, ora ricordo d'avergli donato quel libro
che rallegra il cuore di riviere celesti
e brune foglie autunnali; in esso saggi, o finti saggi, poeti
graziosamente lasciano la vita alzando il bicchiere.

Sono io appartenente a un secolo che crede
di non mentire, a ravvisarmi in quell'uomo malato
mentendo a me stesso: e ne scrivo
per esorcizzare un male in cui credo e non credo.

1971

DA O SALMISTA: DON ATTILIO

Emma, la fronte ai vetri di chi medita dolori,
in questo mezzogiorno di primavera montana veglia
don Attilio, che è ancora vivo, dietro le sue spalle,
ma muore, non fa altro da mesi, da anni,
che morire. Eppure è possibile a lei ancora
di quest'uomo folgorato, stroncato, atterrato,
rinarrarsi lunghe stagioni attive
e felici, fumi d'altare e di cucina, incenso e caffè
confondendosi da chiesa a canonica, e viceversa,

as if they were flowers, and one can't tell if the body
is reclining or seated: so it is with the unwell,
placed in front of windows that frame the day,
another day conceded to eyes that quickly tire.

But if I ask the painter, my fourteen-year-old son,
whom he wanted to portray, he says right away:
"One of those Chinese poets you had me read,
as he gazes outside, in one of his final hours."

He's sincere, I now remember giving him that book
that cheers the heart with celestial rivieras
and dark autumn leaves; in it wise or wise-cracking poets
graciously leave life, glass raised.

Only I, part of a century that believes
it doesn't lie, recognize myself in that sick man
lying to myself: and I write
to exorcise an illness in which I do and do not believe.

NICHOLAS BENSON

FROM O PSALMIST: DON ATTILIO

Emma, pressing against the panes
the forehead of one meditating sorrows,
this midday of mountain spring
watches beside the bed of Don Attilio
who, behind her back, is still alive
yet dying—has done nothing for months, for years
but die. Yet it is possible even now for her
thinking of this paralyzed, felled, broken man,
to relive in memory long seasons

in corridoi umidi invasi da gente stordita,
allegre per le festività cattoliche in cui è bello
potersi immergere mani intrecciate e cuori in fretta
palpitanti per nozze battesimi cresime, argenti
sfolgorando anche nelle ammaccature e nelle pezze chiodate,
rose spargendo perdizione sensuale
in questo permesso, benedetto paganesimo della nostra
religione. E aggiungi per lui il peccato (veniale)
della poesia rinvigorita dall'innesto modernista
ma illanguidita dalla luce di perdizione delle cupole parmigiane.

1984

active and happy, fumes from altar and from kitchen,
incense and coffee mingling together
between church and rectory, and back again;
in damp passageways invaded by a gaping throng,
times gladdened by those Catholic festivities in which
it is so lovely to immerse oneself, clasped hands and hearts in haste
throbbing at marriages, christenings, confirmations, silver
blazing even in its dents and rivets,
roses scattering sensual perdition
in this permitted, blessed paganism which is our
religion. And add for him the sin (venial merely)
of poetry invigorated by the graft
of modernism and then softened by
the light of perdition from the domes of Parma.

CHARLES TOMLINSON

PUDORE

Se qualcuno delle mie parole
ti piace
e tu me lo dici
sia pur solo con gli occhi
io mi spalanco
in un riso beato
ma tremo
come una mamma piccola giovane
che perfino arrossisce
se un passante le dice
che il suo bambino è bello.

1933

CONFIDARE

Ho tanta fede in te. Mi sembra
che saprei aspettare la tua voce
in silenzio, per secoli
di oscurità.

Tu sai tutti i segreti,
come il sole:

Antonia Pozzi

1912–1938

SHYNESS

If one of my words
pleases you
and you tell me
even only with your eyes
I break out
in a blissful smile—
but I tremble
like a small young mother
who blushes if even
a passerby remarks
her baby's lovely.

DESMOND O'GRADY

TO TRUST

I have so much faith in you.
I could wait for your voice
silently through centuries of darkness.

Like the sun
you know all the secrets.

potresti far fiorire
i gerani e la zagara selvaggia
sul fondo delle cave
di pietra, delle prigioni leggendarie.

Ho tanta fede in te. Son quieta
come l'arabo avvolto
nel barracano bianco,
che ascolta Dio maturargli
l'orzo intorno alla casa.

1934

You could make geraniums
and wild orange trees bloom
deep in marble quarries
and legendary prisons.

I have so much faith in you. I'm calm
as an Arab wrapped in white barracan
listening to God
making the barley grow around his house.

LYNNE LAWNER

IL GIBBONE

a Rina

No, non è questo il mio
paese. Qua
—fra tanta gente che viene,
tanta gente che va—
io sono lontano e solo
(straniero) come
l'angelo in chiesa dove
non c'e Dio. Come,
allo zoo, il gibbone.

Nell'ossa ho un'altra città
che mi strugge. È là.
L'ho perduta. Città
grigia di giorno e, a notte,
tutta una scintillazione
di lumi—un lume
per ogni vivo, come,
qui al cimitero, un lume
per ogni morto. Città
cui nulla, nemmeno la morte
—mai,—mi ricondurrà.

1965

Giorgio Caproni

1912–1990

THE GIBBON

to Rina

No, this is not my country.
Here—among so
many people who come and go—
I'm far away and lonely
(a stranger) like the angel
in a church where there is
no God. Like, at the zoo,
the gibbon. In my bones

another city lies
that consumes me. Over there.
I have lost it. A city
gray by day and by night
a conflagration of lights—
a light for each living creature
as in a graveyard there
is one for each of the dead.
A city, to which nothing
ever, not even death,
will bring me back.

NED CONDINI

I COLTELLI

«Be'?» mi fece.
Aveva paura. Rideva.
D'un tratto, il vento si alzò.
L'albero, tutto intero, tremò.
Schiacciai il grilletto. Crollò.
Lo vidi, la faccia spaccata
sui coltelli: gli scisti.
Ah mio dio. Mio Dio.
Perché non esisti?

1 9 7 5

BIBBIA

Ah mia famiglia, mia
famiglia dispersa come
quella dell'Ebreo . . . Nel nome
del padre, del figlio (nel mio
nome) ah mia càsata
infranta mia lacerata
tenda volata via
col suo fuoco e il suo dio.

1 9 7 5

DOPO LA NOTIZIA

Il vento . . . È rimasto il vento.
Un vento lasco, raso terra, e il foglio
(quel foglio di giornale) che il vento
muove su e giù sul grigio
dell'asfalto. Il vento
e nient'altro. Nemmeno
il cane di nessuno, che al vespro

THE KNIVES

"Well?" he said to me.
He was scared. Laughing.
Suddenly the wind stirred.
The whole tree shook.
I squeezed the trigger. He fell.
I saw him, his face split
on the knives: the schist.
Oh, my god. *My God.*
Why do you not exist?

PASQUALE VERDICCHIO

BIBLE

O my family, my
family scattered like the Jews . . .
In the name of the father,
the son (in my name) ah
my broken lineage
my torn tent blown away
with its fire and its god.

NED CONDINI

AFTER THE NEWS

The wind . . . There remained the wind.
A slack wind, bald earth, and the leaf
(of a newspaper) the wind shifts up and down
on the asphalt's grey. The wind
and nothing else. Not even
no one's dog who at vespers
slips, even him, in church
to seek a master. Not even,

Giorgio Caproni

sgusciava anche lui in chiesa
in questua d'un padrone. Nemmeno,
su quel tornante alto
sopra il ghiareto, lo scemo
che ogni volta correva
incontro alla corriera, a aspettare
—diceva—se stesso, andato
a comprar senno. Il vento
e il grigio delle saracinesche
abbassate. Il grigio
del vento sull'asfalto. E il vuoto,
Il vuoto di quel foglio nel vento
analfabeta. Un vento
lasco e svogliato—un soffio
senz'anima, morto.
Nient'altro. Nemmeno lo sconforto.
Il vento e nient'altro. Un vento
spopolato. Quel vento,
là dove agostinianamente
più non cade tempo.

1975

RITORNO

Sono tornato là
dove non ero mai stato.
Nulla, da come non fu, è mutato.
Sul tavolo (sull'incerato
a quadretti) ammezzato
ho ritrovato il bicchiere
mai riempito. Tutto
è ancora rimasto quale
mai l'avevo lasciato.

1975

on that switchback road
high above the gravel path, the fool
who every time runs
to meet the local bus, to await
—as he said—himself, gone away
to purchase discernment. The wind
and grey of the shutters
pulled down. The grey
of the wind on the asphalt. And nothingness.
The nothingness of *that* leaf
in the illiterate wind. A wind
slack and distracted—a breath
without spirit, quite dead.
Nothing else. Not even the dejection.
The wind and nothing else. A wind
without people. *That* wind,
there where Augustinianly
time no longer happens.

PETER ROBINSON

RETURN

I came again
to where I'd never been.
Nothing was changed from what it wasn't.
On the table (on the waxed
checkered tablecloth) half-emptied
I found the glass that had never
been filled. Everything
still remained just as
I had never left it.

DAVID GOLDSTEIN

DA DIARIO D'ALGERIA

Non sa più nulla, è alto sulle ali
il primo caduto bocconi sulla spiaggia normanna.
Per questo qualcuno stanotte
mi toccava la spalla mormorando
di pregar per l'Europa
mentre la Nuova Armada
si presentava alle coste di Francia.

Ho risposto nel sonno: —È il vento,
il vento che fa musiche bizzarre.
Ma se tu fossi davvero
il primo caduto bocconi sulla spiaggia normanna
prega tu se lo puoi, io sono morto
alla guerra e alla pace.
Questa è la musica ora:
delle tende che sbattono sui pali.
Non è musica d'angeli, è la mia
sola musica e mi basta—.

Campo Ospedale 127, giugno 1944

1 9 4 7

Vittorio Sereni

1913–1983

■ ■

FROM ALGERIAN DIARY

He knows nothing anymore, is borne up on wings,
the first to fall splayed on the Normandy beaches.
That's why someone tonight
touched my shoulder murmuring
pray for Europe
as the New Armada
drew on the coast of France.

I replied in my sleep: —It's the wind,
the wind which makes strange music.
But if you truly were
the first to fall splayed on the Normandy beaches,
you pray if you can, I am dead
to war and to peace.
This, the music now:
of tents that flap against the poles.
It's not the music of angels, it's my own
music only and enough—.

Camp Hospital 127, June 1944

PETER ROBINSON AND
MARCUS PERRYMAN

SABA

Beretto pipa bastone, gli spenti
oggetti di un ricordo.
Ma io li vidi animati indosso a uno
ramingo in un'Italia di macerie e di polvere.
Sempre di sé parlava ma come lui nessuno
ho conosciuto che di sé parlando
e ad altri vita chiedendo nel parlare
altrettanta e tanta più ne desse
a chi stava ad ascoltarlo.
E un giorno, un giorno o due dopo il 18 aprile,
lo vidi errare da una piazza all'altra
dall'uno all'altro caffè di Milano
inseguito dalla radio.
«Porca—vociferando—porca». Lo guardava
stupefatta la gente.
Lo diceva all'Italia. Di schianto, come a una donna
che ignara o no a morte ci ha ferito.

1965

DI PASSAGGIO

Un solo giorno, nemmeno. Poche ore.
Una luce mai vista.
Fiori che in agosto nemmeno te li sogni.
Sangue a chiazze sui prati,
non ancora oleandri dalla parte del mare.
Caldo, ma poca voglia di bagnarsi.
Ventilata domenica tirrena.
Sono già morto e qui torno?
O sono il solo vivo nella vivida e ferma
nullità di un ricordo?

1965

SABA

Beret pipe stick, the lifeless
objects of memory.
But I saw them brought to life on one
roaming in an Italy of dust and rubble.
Always he talked of himself
but like no one I've known who talking of themselves
and demanding life of others in his talk
gave as much and so much more
to anyone who'd stay and listen.
And one day, a day or two after the 18th of April,
I saw him wandering from square to square
from one Milan café to another
hounded by the radio.
"Bitch"—he was yelling—"bitch." In amazement
people looked at him.
It was Italy he meant. Abrupt, as to a woman
who knowingly or not has wounded us to death.

PETER ROBINSON AND
MARCUS PERRYMAN

PASSING THROUGH

Just one day, if that. A few hours.
A light never seen.
Flowers in August you'd never dream of.
Blood pooling on the fields,
oleanders not yet on the seaward side.
Hot, but who feels like swimming?
Windswept Tyrrhene Sunday.
Have I died and come back here?
Am I the only one left alive in the vivid stilled
blankness of a memory?

W. S. DI PIERO

I VERSI

Se ne scrivono ancora.
Si pensa a essi mentendo
ai trepidi occhi che ti fanno gli auguri
l'ultima sera dell'anno.
Se ne scrivono solo in negativo
dentro un nero di anni
come pagando un fastidioso debito
che era vecchio di anni.
No, non è più felice l'esercizio.
Ridono alcuni: tu scrivi per l'Arte.
Nemmeno io volevo questo che volevo ben altro.
Si fanno versi per scrollare un peso
e passare al seguente. Ma c'è sempre
qualche peso di troppo, non c'è mai
alcun verso che basti
se domani tu stesso te ne scordi.

1965

UN SOGNO

Ero a passare il ponte
su un fiume che poteva essere il Magra
dove vado d'estate o anche il Tresa,
quello delle mie parti tra Germignaga e Luino.
Me lo impediva uno senza volto, una figura plumbea.
«Le carte» ingiunse. «Quali carte» risposi.
«Fuori le carte» ribadì lui ferreo
vedendomi interdetto. Feci per rabbonirlo:
«Ho speranze, un paese che mi aspetta,
certi ricordi, amici ancora vivi,

LINES

A few still get written.
You're thinking about them, meanwhile
telling lies to the anxious faces wishing you
all the best on New Year's Eve.
A few get written just as negatives
inside a black space of years
like paying off a nagging debt
that's been due for years.
No, there's no fun in it anymore.
You wrote (they're laughing) for art, only art.
Not me, not that, that's the last thing I wanted.
Each line is a load shrugged off
to make space for the next. There are always
extra loads to take, and no single line
ever suffices
if you yourself can't even remember it tomorrow.

W. S. DI PIERO

A DREAM

I was crossing a bridge
over a river that could have been the Magra
where I go for the summer or even the Tresa,
in my part of the country between Germignaga and Luino.
A leaden body without face blocked my way.
"Papers," he ordered. "What papers," I answered.
"Out with them," he insisted, firm
on seeing me aghast. I made to appease him:
"I've prospects, a place awaiting me,
certain memories, friends still alive,

qualche morto sepolto con onore».
«Sono favole,—disse—non si passa
senza un programma». E soppesò ghignando
i pochi fogli che erano i miei beni.
Volli tentare ancora. «Pagherò
al mio ritorno se mi lasci
passare, se mi lasci lavorare». Non ci fu
modo d'intendersi: «Hai tu fatto
—ringhiava—la tua scelta ideologica?».
Avvinghiati lottammo alla spalletta del ponte
in piena solitudine. La rissa
dura ancora, a mio disdoro.
Non lo so
chi finirà nel fiume.

1 9 6 5

SARÀ LA NOIA

dei giorni lunghi e torridi
ma oggi la piccola
Laura è fastidiosa proprio.
Smettila—dico—se no . . .
con repressa ferocia
torcendole piano il braccino.

Non mi fai male non mi fai
male, mi sfida in cantilena
guardandomi da sotto in su
petulante ma già
in punta di lagrime,
non piango nemmeno vedi.

a few dead honorably buried."
"Fairy tales," he said. "You can't pass
without a program." And sneering he weighed up
the few papers, my worldly goods.
I wanted one last try. "I'll pay
on the way back if you'll let me
pass, if you'll let me work."
We would never see eye to eye. "Have you made,"
he was snarling, "your ideological choice?"
Grappling we struggled on the bridge's parapet
in utter solitude. The fight
still goes on, to my dishonor.
I don't know
who'll end up in the river.

PETER ROBINSON AND
MARCUS PERRYMAN

IT MUST BE THE BOREDOM

of the long and scorching days
but little Laura
is really annoying today.
"Stop it," I say, "or else . . ."
twisting lightly her tiny arm
with repressed fierceness.

You don't hurt me you don't
hurt me, she dares me in a sing-song,
looking up at me,
petulant but already
on the verge of tears,
see I'm not even crying.

Vedo. Ma è l'angelo
nero dello sterminio
quello che adesso vedo
lucente nelle sue bardature
di morte
e a lui rivolto in estasi
il bambinetto ebreo
invitandolo al gioco
del massacro.

1981

PAURA SECONDA

Niente ha di spavento
la voce che chiama me
proprio me
dalla strada sotto casa
in un'ora di notte:
è un breve risveglio di vento,
una pioggia fuggiasca.
Nel dire il mio nome non enumera
i miei torti, non mi rinfaccia il passato.
Con dolcezza (Vittorio,
Vittorio) mi disarma, arma
contro me stesso me.

1981

I see. But it's the dark
exterminating angel
that I see now
shining in his death
trappings
and turning to him in ecstasy
the Jewish child
invites him to a game
of massacre.

L U I G I   B O N A F F I N I

SECOND FEAR

There is nothing frightening about the voice
that calls me—
really me—
from the street below the house
at this hour of the night:
it is a brief awakening by the wind,
a fugitive rain.
Pronouncing my name, it does not list
my wrongs nor reproach me for my past.
Calling gently—Vittorio,
Vittorio—it disarms me, arms
me against myself.

W I L L I A M   J A Y   S M I T H

AVORIO

Parla il cipresso equinoziale, oscuro
e montuoso esulta il capriolo,
dentro le fonti rosse le criniere
dai baci adagio lavan le cavalle.
Giù da foreste vaporose immensi
alle eccelse città battono i fiumi
lungamente, si muovono in un sogno
affettuose vele verso Olimpia.
Correranno le intense vie d'Oriente
ventilate fanciulle e dai mercati
salmastri guarderanno ilari il mondo.
Ma dove attingerò io la mia vita
ora che il tremebondo amore è morto?
Violavano le rose l'orizzonte,
esitanti città stavano in cielo
asperse di giardini tormentosi,
la sua voce nell'aria era una roccia
deserta e incolmabile di fiori.

1940

Mario Luzi

1914–2005

IVORY

The ever-dark cypress is alive,
the somber mountain buck is elated;
in reddened springs the mares
slowly wash caresses out of their manes.
Down from misty forests immense
rivers lash against the towering cities
constantly; quivering sails move
in a dream towards Olympia.
Airy girls will travel the crowded roads
of the Orient and from brackish markets
will look cheerfully at the world.
But where will I draw my life from
now that flickering love is dead?
Roses corrupted the horizon;
faltering cities sprinkled with troubled
gardens remained in the sky;
her voice on the air was a desert rock
never to be heaped with flowers.

I. L. SALOMON

NOTIZIE A GIUSEPPINA

DOPO TANTI ANNI

Che speri, che ti riprometti, amica,
se torni per così cupo viaggio
fin qua dove nel sole le burrasche
hanno una voce altissima abbrunata,
di gelsomino odorano e di frane?

Mi trovo qui a questa età che sai,
né giovane né vecchio, attendo, guardo
questa vicissitudine sospesa;
non so più quel che volli o mi fu imposto,
entri nei miei pensieri e n'esci illesa.

Tutto l'altro che deve essere è ancora,
il fiume scorre, la campagna varia,
grandina, spiove, qualche cane latra
esce la luna, niente si riscuote,
niente dal lungo sonno avventuroso.

1952

NELLA CASA DI N.

COMPAGNA D'INFANZIA

Il vento è un aspro vento di quaresima,
geme dentro le crepe, sotto gli usci,
sibila nelle stanze invase, e fugge;
fuori lacera a brano a brano i nastri

TIDINGS FOR GIUSEPPINA,

YEARS LATER

What do you hope, or expect, my friend,
returning from such a dismal voyage,
to where storms in the sun
have a high-pitched yet somber voice
and smack of jasmine and landslides?

I am here, you know, at this age,
neither young nor old, waiting and watching
this vicissitude in suspense;
I know no longer what I wanted or what was imposed on me,
you enter into my thoughts, then go out untouched.

Everything else is as it should be,
the river flows, the countryside changes,
it rains and hails, a dog barks,
the moon comes out, nothing moves,
nothing from the long adventurous sleep.

G. SINGH AND GABRIELLE BARFOOT

IN THE HOUSE OF A GIRL

I KNEW IN CHILDHOOD

The wind's a bitter Lenten wind,
it moans in cracks and under doors,
whines through invaded rooms, is gone.
Outside it rips to shreds the ribbons

delle stelle filanti se qualcuna
impigliata nei fili fiotta e vibra,
l'incalza, la rapisce nella briga.

Io sono qui, persona in una stanza,
uomo nel fondo di una casa, ascolto
lo stridere che fa la fiamma, il cuore
che accelera i suoi moti, siedo, attendo.
Tu dove sei? sparita anche la traccia . . .
Se guardo qui la furia e se più oltre
l'erba, la povertà grigia dei monti.

1952

NELL'IMMINENZA DEI QUARANT'ANNI

Il pensiero m'insegue in questo borgo
cupo ove corre un vento d'altipiano
e il tuffo del rondone taglia il filo
sottile in lontananza dei monti.

Sono tra poco quarant'anni d'ansia,
d'uggia, d'ilarità improvvise, rapide
com'è rapida a marzo la ventata
che sparge luce e pioggia, son gli indugi,
lo strappo a mani tese dai miei cari,
dai miei luoghi, abitudini di anni
rotte a un tratto che devo ora comprendere.
L'albero di dolore scuote i rami . . .

Si sollevano gli anni alle mie spalle
a sciami. Non fu vano, è questa l'opera
che si compie ciascuno e tutti insieme

of streamers—when they catch on wires,
mutter and shake, it hunts them down,
hauls them away on hellish currents.

I'm here, a person in a room,
a man deep in a house, I listen
to the fire shrieking, to my heart
that quickens, and I sit, I wait.
Where are you now? Not a trace left . . .
Here I see fury; beyond, grass
and the gray poverty of mountains.

GEOFFREY BROCK

ON APPROACHING FORTY

The thought pursues me through this dreary town
where the wind sweeps down from the high plateau
and where a diving chimney swift can cut
the slender thread of mountains far away.

So soon come forty years of restlessness,
of tedium, of unexpected joy,
quick as a gust of wind in March is quick
to scatter light and rain, soon come delays,
snatched from the straining hands of those I love,
torn from my haunts, the customs of my years
suddenly crushed to make me understand.
The tree of sorrow shakes its branches . . .

The years rise like a swarm around my shoulders.
Nothing has been in vain. This is the work
which all complete together and alone,

Mario Luzi

i vivi i morti, penetrare il mondo
opaco lungo vie chiare e cunicoli
fitti d'incontri effimeri e di perdite
o d'amore in amore o in uno solo
di padre in figlio fino a che sia limpido.

E detto questo posso incamminarmi
spedito tra l'eterna compresenza
del tutto nella vita nella morte,
sparire nella polvere o nel fuoco
se il fuoco oltre la fiamma dura ancora.

1957

LA NOTTE LAVA LA MENTE

La notte lava la mente.

Poco dopo si è qui come sai bene,
file d'anime lungo la cornice,
chi pronto al balzo, chi quasi in catene.

Qualcuno sulla pagina del mare
traccia un segno di vita, figge un punto.
Raramente qualche gabbiano appare.

1957

In salvo?—Lui solo può saperlo,
macché, neppure lui,
lui meno di chiunque altro—e questo
più di tutto la sgomenta

the living and the dead, to penetrate
the impenetrable world, down open roads,
down mineshafts of discovery and loss,
and learned from many loves or only one,
from father down to son—till all is clear.

And having said this, I can start out now,
easy in the eternal company
of all things living, of all things dead,
to disappear in either dust or fire
if any fire endures beyond its flame.

DANA GIOIA

NIGHT CLEANSES THE MIND

Night cleanses the mind.

A little later, as you well know,
we're here, a line of souls along the ledge,
some ready for the leap, others

as if in chains. On the sea's page,
someone traces a sign of life, fixes a point.
Seldom do any gulls appear.

GEOFFREY BROCK

Out of danger?—He alone can know,
but no, of course not, not even he,
he less than anyone—and this
terrifies her more than anything

in quel sogno di naufragio
troppo spesso ricorrente, che lui perda
di forza e di sapienza
e dimentichi la rotta
e il punto e nemmeno più lo cerchi
il suo tutto smarrito orientamento.
Bravo! così siamo alla cieca
in un nembo, così
nessuno al mondo ne sa niente
di noi, del nostro viaggio—grida,
o le sembra, in quella desolata batticina
dell'alba prima del risveglio.
E lui, eccolo là
vecchio, sfatto dalla fatica
e dalla veglia. Non parla e non ascolta,
non conosce, non riconosce
i luoghi, né decifra il suo indelebile tatuaggio.

                                   Oh maître.

          1985

AUCTOR

Non ancora, non abbastanza,
                    non crederlo
mai detto
in pieno e compiutamente
il tuo debito col mondo.
                Aperto—
così t'era
il suo libro
stato gioiosamente offerto,

in that too often recurrent
dream of shipwreck, that he might lose
his strength and wits
and forget the course
and the site and even stop looking
for his utterly lost bearings.
Well done! this way we move blindly
in a nimbus, this way
no one will know anything
about us and our journey—she shouts,
or so it seems to her, in that desolate skiff
of dawn before awakening.
And he, there he is,
old and withered from fatigue
and the vigil. He does not speak or listen,
does not know or recognize
the places, and cannot decipher his indelible tattoo.

Oh maître.

STEPHEN SARTARELLI

AUCTOR

Not yet, not enough,
                    don't believe it—
your debt to the world
has never been stated
in full.
        Open—
thus to you
was its book
joyfully offered,
that you might read what could be read,

Mario Luzi 319

perché tu ne leggessi il leggibile,
il nero, il bianco,
                    il testo, i suoi intervalli
per te e per altri, ancora
più inesperti,
che non osavano farlo.
E il molto appreso
dovevi tu
in parola ricambiarlo.
Questo pareva il tuo compito
e stentavi,
                    stentavi a riconoscerlo.
Né sai perché, dove fosse il disaccordo
che ti ha tritato la vita,
tormentato il canto.

1990

the black, the white,

                    the text and its gaps,

for yourself and for others

even less skilled

who dared not even try.

And everything learned

you were supposed

to repay in words.

This seemed your task,

and barely,

            barely could you recognize it.

Nor do you know why, or whence came the discord

that tattered your life,

mangled your song.

STEPHEN SARTARELLI

VARIAZIONE SUL TEMA PRECEDENTE

Se un corno alto di luna varca i corsi sereni
e scalda della sua mite brace i glauchi selciati
escono i cavallanti tra il sonno ammantellati
alle strade che affondano tiepide in mezzo ai fieni.

Calma e chiara è la notte, dal madore dei prati
sale un latte leggero che ondeggia a soffi leni
di vento, si ode a tratti la cieca ansia dei treni
lontani che precipitano verso i folti mercati.

Ma tu, dio che sorridi al profitto e alla perdita,
incanta lungo il cammino i tuoi neri protetti,
lungo il dolce cammino che sfiora i campi già verdi!

Socchiudi la finestra dell'ostessa, dai letti
odorosi richiama sulla porta le serve,
splendi nel vino, accendi nell'ombra occhi diletti!

1945

Giorgio Bassani

1916–2000

IDYLL

As a horn of the high moon veers in clear skies over Main Street
And inflames with a fugitive heat the sea-green pavements,
Out of the town cloaked horsemen ride across sleep
On lukewarm roads that founder halfway in hayfields.

Quiet the night, and clear, and from the moist
Low meadows comes up lightly a milk that billows
In gusts of the wind, and a sound comes of distant trains
Aimed, blindly anxious, at packed market-places.

But you, a god who smiles at the gain and the loss,
Bless your black adepts all the way with spells,
All the good way past fields whose green is here!

The woman who keeps the inn, unbar her window,
Call down to the door the maids from their odorous beds,
Shine in the wine, light rapturous eyes in the shadows!

DONALD DAVIE

SALUTO A ROMA

Addio, arena di calce, addio diamante,
il tuo cielo su me è un chiuso volto;
lascia ch'io torni al mio paese sepolto
nell'erba come in un mare caldo e pesante.

Porte roventi nel cielo distante,
nero è il tuo sole, nera è la tua luna.
Carne senza rimpianti, riso senza nessuna
memoria: addio città senza speranza.

Perché io so le tue vie, diritte spade, i suoni
delle tue piazze celesti; ma so il vento
che ti affila, il lamento
delle tue nascoste stazioni.

No, la tua fronte non splende di grazia.
Chi ti raccoglierà, grido di giubilo?
L'iride che ti specchia è senza nubi.
Sei sola, dentro le tue mura di spazio.

1963

LE LEGGI RAZZIALI

La magnolia che sta giusto nel mezzo
del giardino di casa nostra a Ferrara è proprio lei
la stessa che ritorna in pressoché tutti
i miei libri

La piantammo nel '39
pochi mesi dopo la promulgazione

SALUTE TO ROME

Goodbye limed sand, goodbye diamond,
your sky is a closed face above me,
let me return to my home town entombed
in grass as in a warm and high sea.

Burning gates in the distant sky,
your sun is black, it's black your moon.
Flesh without regret, laughter without one
memory: hopeless city, goodbye.

Since I know your streets, straight swords, the tones
of your celestial squares; but I know the gales
that hone you, the wails
from your hidden stations.

No, your brow doesn't shine with grace.
Who'll gather you, cry of jubilation?
The rainbow mirroring you is cloudless.
You're alone, within your walls of space.

PETER ROBINSON

THE RACIAL LAWS

The magnolia smack in the middle
of our Ferrara house's garden is the very
same that reappears in almost every
book of mine

We planted it in '39
ceremoniously

Giorgio Bassani 325

delle leggi razziali con cerimonia
che riuscì a metà solenne e a metà comica
tutti quanti abbastanza allegri si Dio
vuole
in barba al noioso ebraismo
metastorico

Costretta fra quattro impervie pareti
piuttosto prossime crebbe
nera luminosa invadente
puntando decisa verso l'imminente
cielo
piena giorno e notte di bigi
passeri di bruni merli
guatati senza riposo giù da pregne
gatte nonché da mia
madre
anche essa spiante indefessa da dietro
il davanzale traboccante ognora
delle sue briciole

Dritta dalla base al vertice come una spada
ormai fuoresce oltre i tetti circostanti ormai può guardare
la città da ogni parte e l'infinito
spazio verde che la circonda
ma adesso incerta lo so lo
vedo
d'un tratto espansa lassù sulla vetta d'un tratto debole
nel sole
come che all'improvviso non sa raggiunto
che abbia il termine d'un viaggio lunghissimo
la strada da prendere che cosa
fare

1974

just a few months after
the Racial Laws were brought to bear
it was a solemn-comical affair all of us
fairly lighthearted God permitting despite
being encumbered with that dull historical appendix
Judaism

Walled-in by four walls forewarned
soon enough it grew
black luminous wide-rimmed
pointing decisively up towards the imminent
sky
full day
and night with grey
sparrows dusky blackbirds
unflaggingly scanned from below by pregnant
cats and by my
mother—
she too confined defenceless there behind
the windowsill forever brimming
with her crumbs.

Straight as a sword from its base to its tip
twenty-some years on
it overtops the neighbouring roofs
beholding every bit of the city and the infinite
green space that circles it
but now somehow stumped I can guess
how it feels unsure
of a stretch up there in the heights a narrow space
in the sun
like someone at a loss
after a long long journey
as to which road to take or
what to do

JAMIE MCKENDRICK

Giorgio Bassani 327

FOGLIO DI VIA

Dunque nulla di nuovo da questa altezza
Dove ancora un poco senza guardare si parla
E nei capelli il vento cala la sera.

Dunque nessun cammino per discendere
Se non questo del nord dove il sole non tocca
E sono d'acqua i rami degli alberi.

Dunque fra poco senza parole la bocca.
E questa sera saremo in fondo alla valle
Dove le feste han spento tutte le lampade.

Dove una folla tace e gli amici non riconoscono.

1 9 4 6

LETTERA

Padre, il mondo ti ha vinto giorno per giorno
come vincerà me, che ti somiglio.

Padre, i tuoi gesti sono aria nell'aria,
come le mie parole vento nel vento.

Franco Fortini

1917–1994

DEPORTATION ORDER

So nothing new from up here
where you look around a bit longer without speaking
and wind in your hair the evening falls.

So there's no path down
except this one from the north, where sun never reaches
and tree branches are water.

So very soon a mouth with no words.
And this evening we'll be at the bottom of the valley
where celebrations have burned out all the lamps,

where a crowd remains silent and friends don't know each other.

LAWRENCE R. SMITH

LETTER

Father, the world has conquered you day by day
as it will conquer me, who resembles you.

Father, your gestures are air in the air,
and these, my words, wind in the wind.

Padre, ti hanno spogliato, tradito, umiliato,
nessuno t'ha guardato per aiutarti.

Padre di magre risa, padre di cuore bruciato,
padre, il più triste dei miei fratelli, padre,

il tuo figliolo ancora trema del tuo tremore,
come quel giorno d'infanzia di pioggia e paura

pallido tra le urla buie del rabbino contorto
perdevi di mano le zolle sulla cassa di tuo padre.

Ma quello che tu non dici devo io dirlo per te
al trono della luce che consuma i miei giorni.

Per questo è partito tuo figlio: e ora insieme ai compagni
cerca le strade bianche di Galilea.

1946

UN'ALTRA ATTESA

Ogni cosa, puoi dirlo, è assai più buia
di quanto avevi immaginato, in questa
casa dove ti han detto di aspettare
che tornino gli amici tumultuosi.
Vai da una stanza all'altra e dunque aspetti.
I muri sono stanchi, oscuri gli angoli.
Torneranno gli amici appassionati.
Non è dolore, non è ira o noia
ma un rancore nel fondo della testa
che ora sembra noia ora dolore.
Fuori dei vetri vedi ancora i tetti.
Dentro, dove tu sei, non vedi più.

Father, they have stripped, betrayed, humiliated you,
    no one looked your way or tried to help you.

Father of thin laughter, father of the burnt heart,
    father, most sorrowful of my brothers, father,

your son still trembles from your trembling
    as on that childhood day of rain and anguish

pale in the dark howls of the bent rabbi
    your hand scattered loam on the coffin of your father.

Now what you don't say I must say for you
    at that throne of light which consumes my days.

For this your son has left; and now with comrades
    he's searching for the white roads of Galilee.

VAN K. BROCK

ANOTHER WAIT

You can say it now, everything is even darker
than you imagined in this
house where they told you to wait
until your rowdy friends come back.
Moving room to room—that's how you wait.
The walls are weary, the corners dark.
Your excited friends will be back soon.
It's not pain, not anger or annoyance,
it's some grudge at the back of your mind
that feels like annoyance or pain.
You can still see the roofs out the windows.
Inside, where you are, you can't see anything.

Se non, contro il soffitto, dai cortili
qualche filo di lume o dalla bruma
il chiaro della città verso cena.
Puoi, quando vuoi, accendere la luce,
leggere un libro, fumare, pensare
ad altro, intanto che il tuo tempo passa.

1 9 6 3

TRADUCENDO BRECHT

Un grande temporale
per tutto il pomeriggio si è attorcigliato
sui tetti prima di rompere in lampi, acqua.
Fissavo versi di cemento e di vetro
dov'erano grida e piaghe murate e membra
anche di me, cui sopravvivo. Con cautela, guardando
ora i tegoli battagliati ora la pagina secca,
ascoltavo morire
la parola d'un poeta o mutarsi
in altra, non per noi più, voce. Gli oppressi
sono oppressi e tranquilli, gli oppressori tranquilli
parlano nei telefoni, l'odio è cortese, io stesso
credo di non sapere più di chi è la colpa.

Scrivi mi dico, odia
chi con dolcezza guida al niente
gli uomini e le donne che con te si accompagnano
e credono di non sapere. Fra quelli dei nemici
scrivi anche il tuo nome. Il temporale
è sparito con enfasi. La natura
per imitare le battaglie è troppo debole. La poesia
non muta nulla. Nulla è sicuro, ma scrivi.

1 9 6 3

Except, on the ceiling, a few threads of light
from the courtyard, or through the mist
the city's supper-hour glow.
You can, whenever you want, turn on the light,
read a book, smoke, think about
other things while your time goes by.

W. S. DI PIERO

TRANSLATING BRECHT

A huge thunderstorm
rolled around in coils all afternoon above
the roof-tops before it broke in flashes and sheeted down.
I stared at the lines of cement and glass
that walled up screams and wounds and limbs
including mine, which I have survived. Warily, looking
now up at the roof-tiles doing battle, now at the dry page,
I listened to the word
of a poet perish or change
into another voice we no longer hear. The oppressed
are oppressed and quiet, quietly the oppressors
talk on the phone, hatred is polite, and even I
believe I no longer know who is to blame.

Write, I tell myself, hate
those who sweetly lead into nothingness
the men and women who walk beside you
and believe they do not know. Write your name too
among those of the enemy. The storm
has passed away with all its bluster. Nature
is far too feeble to mimic battles. Poetry
changes nothing. Nothing is certain, but write.

PAUL LAWTON

LA LINEA DEL FUOCO

Le trincee erano qui.
C'è ferro ancora tra i sassi.
L'ottobre lavora nuvole.
La guerra finì da tanti anni.
L'ossuario è in vetta.

Siamo venuti di notte
tra i corpi degli ammazzati.
Con fretta e con pietà
abbiamo dato il cambio.
Fra poco sarà l'assalto.

1973

AGLI DÈI DELLA MATTINATA

Il vento scuote allori e pini. Ai vetri, giù acqua.
Tra fiumi e luci la costa la vedi a tratti, poi nulla.
La mattinata si affina nella stanza tranquilla.
Un filo di musica rock, le matite, le carte.
Sono felice della pioggia. O dei inesistenti,
proteggete l'idillio, vi prego. E che altro potete,
o dei d'autunno indulgenti dormenti,
meste di frasche le tempie? Come maestosi quei vostri
luminosi cumuli! Quante ansiose formiche nell'ombra!

1973

THE LINE OF FIRE

This is where the trenches were.
You'll find iron still among the stones.
October hustles the clouds.
The war finished so many years ago.
The ossuary is on the hilltop.

We came by night
between corpses of the killed.
In haste and pity
we took over from them.
Very soon the attack will begin.

MICHAEL HAMBURGER

TO THE GODS OF THE MORNING

Wind shakes laurels and pines. Water streams down the windows.
Between mists and clearances you glimpse bits of the coast, then nothing.
The morning mellows in the quiet room.
A trickle of rock music, the pencils, the papers.
I'm glad about the rain. O inexistent gods,
safeguard the idyll, I beg of you. What else can you do,
O gods of autumn, slumbering, indulgent,
your temples melancholy with bays? How majestic are your
gleaming cumuli! And all those ants restless in the shade!

PAUL LAWTON

SONETTO DEI SETTE CINESI

Una volta il poeta di Augsburg ebbe a dire
che alla parete della stanza aveva appeso
l'Uomo Del Dubbio, una stampa cinese.
L'immagine chiedeva: come agire?

Ho una foto alla parete. Vent'anni fa
nel mio obiettivo guardarono sette operai cinesi.
Guardano diffidenti o ironici o sospesi.
Sanno che non scrivo per loro. Io

so che non sono vissuti per me.
Eppure il loro dubbio qualche volta mi ha chiesto
più candide parole o atti più credibili.

A loro chiedo aiuto perché siano visibili
contraddizioni e identità fra noi.
Se un senso esiste, è questo.

1985

DA SETTE CANZONETTE DEL GOLFO

1

Ah letizia del mattino!
Sopra l'erba del giardino
la favilla della bava,
della bava del ragnetto
che s'affida al ventolino.

Lontanissime sirene
d'autostrada, il sole viene!

SONNET OF THE SEVEN CHINESE

The Augsburg poet once said he tacked
an image of the Man of Doubt
to the wall of his room. A Chinese print.
The image asked: How ought one to act?

I have a photo on my wall. Twenty years ago
seven Chinese workers looked into my lens.
They look wary, or ironic, or tense.
They know I do not write for them. I know

they didn't live for me. Yet sometimes I feel
I'm being asked for more candid words,
more credible deeds, by their doubtfulness.

In turn I ask their help in making visible
the contradictions and identities among us.
If there's a point, it's this.

GEOFFREY BROCK

FROM SEVEN GULF DITTIES

1

Ah, the delight of dawn!
Over the grassy lawn
the spark of silk, of silk
spat out by some small spider
to be the breeze's pawn.

A distant siren whines
from the freeway. Sun shines!

Che domenica, che pace!
È la pace del vecchietto,
l'ora linda che gli piace.

Le formiche in fila vanno.
Vanno a fare, ehi! qualche danno
alle pere già mature . . .
Quanto sole è sul muretto!
Le lucertole lo sanno.

2

Lontano lontano si fanno la guerra.
Il sangue degli altri si sparge per terra.

Io questa mattina mi sono ferito
a un gambo di rosa, pungendomi un dito.

Succhiando quel dito, pensavo alla guerra.
Oh povera gente, che triste è la terra!

Non posso giovare, non posso parlare,
non posso partire per cielo o per mare.

E se anche potessi, o genti indifese,
ho l'arabo nullo! Ho scarso l'inglese!

Potrei sotto il capo dei corpi riversi
posare un mio fitto volume di versi?

Non credo. Cessiamo la mesta ironia.
Mettiamo una maglia, che il sole va via.

1994

What a Sunday, what peace!
An old man's tidy peace,
his favorite hour of all.

The ants march on in rows.
They're off to do who knows
what harm to the ripe pears . . .
Such sun now on the wall!
The lizards heed its call.

2

Far away, far away, men making wars.
Other folk's blood spilt on other folk's floors.

Only this morning I wounded my finger:
a thorn on my rosebush pierced like a stinger.

Sucking that finger, I thought of the war.
Sad is the earth! And those people, so poor!

I'm of no help, being here and not there,
nor can I reach them, by sea or by air.

And what if I could—what good could I do?
My Arabic's terrible! My English is, too!

What, should I stroll through the fields of the dead
leaving sheaves of my verses under each head?

No. Enough of this wretched irony-fest.
Let's put on a coat. The sun's low in the west.

GEOFFREY BROCK

Franco Fortini 339

AUTUNNO

Autunno, quante foglie
se ne vanno col vento.
Vedi, nel cielo spento
la pioggia si raccoglie.

Tristezza vagabonda
di poveri viandanti,
pochi cavalli stanchi
nella strada profonda.

Brulichio de la sera,
vuota monotonia
porta l'Ave Maria
cosí senza preghiera.

1 9 3 9

NOTTE DIETRO LE PERSIANE

Dietro le persiane ogni sera
gli uomini rinserrano
la loro vita
per morire una notte.

Saturno Montanari

1918–1941

AUTUNNO

Autumn, so many leaves
pass with the wind, I see
the worn-out rain
gather aloft again.

Aimless or vagabond,
a walking sadness, beyond
the deep-cut road:
horses weary of load.

A whirring noise, new night there
empty in monotone:
the Ave Maria
no prayer.

EZRA POUND

NOTTE DIETRO LE PERSIANE

When the light
goes, men shut behind blinds
their life, to die for a night.

Ma c'è pure chi sogna
un disperato tramonto
traverso i vetri e le imposte.
E chi rimane ancora
dopo ch'è sfatto il sole
ad aspettar le stelle.
Sono questi i poeti
che hanno l'anima di canzoni,
un anima tutta voce
e lieviti di speranza.

1939

And yet
through glass and bars
some dream a wild sunset,
waiting the stars.

Call these few, at least
the singers, in whom
hope's voice is yeast.

EZRA POUND

SHEMÀ

Voi che vivete sicuri
Nelle vostre tiepide case
Voi che trovate tornando a sera
Il cibo caldo e visi amici:

Considerate se questo è un uomo,
Che lavora nel fango
Che non conosce pace
Che lotta per mezzo pane
Che muore per un sí o per un no.
Considerate se questa è una donna,
Senza capelli e senza nome
Senza piú forza di ricordare
Vuoti gli occhi e freddo il grembo
Come una rana d'inverno.

Meditate che questo è stato:
Vi comando queste parole.
Scolpitele nel vostro cuore
Stando in casa andando per via,
Coricandovi alzandovi:
Ripetetele ai vostri figli.
O vi si sfaccia la casa,
La malattia vi impedisca,
I vostri nati torcano il viso da voi.

1946

Primo Levi

1919–1987

SHEMÀ

You who live safe
In your warm houses,
You who come home at evening to find
Hot food and friendly faces:

    Consider if this is a man,
    Who toils in the mud
    Who knows no peace
    Who fights for a chunk of bread
    Who dies at a yes or a no.
    Consider if this is a woman,
    Without hair and without name
    Without strength to remember
    Empty eyes and cold womb
    Like a frog in winter.

Be mindful that this has been:
I urge these words on you.
Carve them on your heart
At home or roaming the streets
Lying down or rising up:
Repeat them to your children.
Or may your houses fall,
Sickness lay you low,
Your offspring turn their faces from you.

AL ALVAREZ

ALZARSI

Sognavamo nelle notti feroci
Sogni densi e violenti
Sognati con anima e corpo:
Tornare; mangiare; raccontare.
Finché suonava breve e sommesso
Il commando dell'alba:
                        «Wstawaç»;
E si spezzava in petto il cuore.

Ora abbiamo ritrovato la casa,
Il nostro ventre è sazio,
Abbiamo finito di raccontare.
È tempo. Presto udremo ancora
Il comando straniero:
                        «Wstawaç».

1946

REVEILLE

In the brutal nights we'd dream
Dense violent dreams,
Dreamed with soul and body:
To return; to eat; to tell the story.
Until the dawn command
Sounded brief, low:

                   "*Wstawać*":
And the heart cracked in the breast.

Now we have found our homes again,
Our bellies are full,
We've finished telling the story.
It's time. Soon we'll hear again
The strange command:

                   "*Wstawać*."

RUTH FELDMAN
AND BRIAN SWANN

I MELI I MELI I MELI

Quell'albero che mi sorprese
con i suoi rami gonfi
quanti corvi sul ramo piú alto.

Quel toro che si accese
per una macchia scura al mercato
quanto sangue versato alle frontiere.

Quella ragazza in tuta che si intese
prima con francesi e polacchi
quanti viaggi il suo corpo tra le braccia.

Quel soldato che mi chiese
la via breve oltre Sempione
quanta ansia in uno sguardo.

1956

AMBIZIONI

Viaggiare
mangiare e bere
ben dormire
e di tanto in tanto
qualche massacro.

1956

1920–

APPLE TREES APPLE TREES APPLE TREES

This tree which surprised me
with its swollen limbs
so many crows on the highest branch.

That bull which flew into a fury
because of the dark stain at the market
so much blood spilled at the borders.

That girl in overalls who got along so well
first with Frenchmen then with Poles
so many voyages, her body in their arms.

That soldier who asked me
the shortcut over Sempione
so much fear in one glance.

LAWRENCE R. SMITH

AMBITIONS

To travel
eat and drink
sleep well
and now and then
a little slaughter.

MICHAEL PALMA

TORRIDO

Ecco l'estate
viene su a dismisura
tutto arde
fin le pietre nella notte
e le mura.
                    I sono senza
volontà, non sono mai pronto
ma ho molto tempo davanti a me,
non mi chiedo dove va il mondo
né come andrà dopo di me.
Bastano gli altri
che muoiono ogni giorno
per capire com'è.

1956

LEGITTIMA SPERANZA

In un sagrato fitto di popolo
e di potenti in pulpito vociferanti
un uomo ammucchia pietre solitario.
Che sia senza peccato?

1962

LA NEVE NELL'ARMADIO

La storia
quella vera
che nessuno studia

HEAT

Here the summer comes
out of control
burning everything
even at night
walls and rocks.
                I can't get moving, I'm never
ready for anything, but there's plenty of time.
I don't worry about where the world is going
or what will happen after I'm gone.
Plenty of others
are dying every day
to figure it out.

MILLER WILLIAMS

JUSTIFIED HOPE

In a churchyard packed with people
and VIPs bawling from pulpits
a man piles up stones, quite alone.
Could he be without sin?

VITTORIA BRADSHAW

THE SNOW IN THE WARDROBE

The true history
which no one studies
which today to most

che oggi ai più dà soltanto fastidio
(che addusse lutti infiniti)
d'un sol colpo ti privò dell'infanzia

La siepe è di betulla
il cielo una stella gialla
i fidanzati chiamano dai tetti
la campagna quasi ucràina
anche le oche sono di Chagall

Che può una stanza dai muri di paglia
un cantuccio tra papà e mamma? un forte
carpatico ci sarebbe voluto
dalle cento segrete con tutto un popolo
di armati o la Grande Muraglia quando
due lanzi ariani insignificanti
con gli stivali infransero la quiete
del Sabato

Ti hanno messo in fila
come a scuola
per farti star buona
un assassino accarezza
la tua treccia bionda
che cadrà prima

Dopo tanto se qualcuno
amichevole batte alla porta
lo spavento fa più bambina
la tua faccia e smorta

Questi sogni macchiati di fango
—tremi con le coperte addosso
per tutto il gelo che patisti

is merely a nuisance
(which caused infinite grief)
with a single blow deprived you of childhood

The hedge is birch
the sky a yellow star
lovers call from the rooftops
the landscape almost Ukrainian
even the geese are Chagall's

What use is a room with walls of straw
a nook between papa and mamma?
what you needed was a Carpathian fort
with a hundred dungeons and a whole
populace of warriors or the Great Wall
when two trivial Aryan mercenaries
in jackboots shattered the quiet
of the Sabbath

They've lined you up
as at school
to make you be good
a murderer fondles
your blond braid
it will fall first

After so much if some
friend knocks on your door
fear makes your face
more childlike and pale

These mud-stained dreams—
the morning you recount them
you tremble under the covers

il mattino quando li racconti:
vuoi la piuma vuoi le noci
sotto il cuscino vuoi il pane
caro

Vorrei nutrirti con il miele
di tutte le arnie del mondo,
o di pinoli come uno scoiattolo.

1965

for all the cold you endured:
you want feathers you want nuts
under the pillow you want the costly
bread

I'd like to nourish you with honey
from all the beehives on earth
or with pine-nuts like a squirrel.

VAN K. BROCK

I MORTI

I morti vanno, dentro il nero carro
incrostato di funebre oro, col passo
lento dei cavalli: e spesso
per loro suona la banda.
Al passaggio, le donne si precipitano
a chiudere le finestre di casa,
le botteghe si chiudono: appena uno spiraglio
per guardare il dolore dei parenti,
al numero degli amici che è dietro,
alla classe del carro, alle corone.
Così vanno via i morti, al mio paese:
finestre e porte chiuse, ad implorarli
di passar oltre, di dimenticare
le donne affaccendate nelle case,
il bottegaio che pesa e ruba,
il bambino che gioca ed odia,
gli occhi vivi che brulicano
dietro l'inganno delle imposte chiuse.

1952

Leonardo Sciascia

1921–1989

THE DEAD

The dead go by, their black carts
crusted with funeral gold, the horses
stepping slowly—often a band
is playing for them. As they pass,
women scurry to close their windows,
shops close too: just a crack
through which to watch the family's grief,
to see how many friends have come,
how nice the cart is, the wreaths.
Where I'm from, this is how the dead leave:
windows and doors shutting,
begging them to keep on going,
to forget the women busying themselves
inside the houses, the shopkeeper
who shorts us on weight, the little boy
who plays and hates—the living eyes
teeming behind the fraud of shutters.

GEOFFREY BROCK

VIVO COME NON MAI

Dal vecchio chiostro entro nel silenzio
dei tuoi viali, tra i marmi
che affiorano come rovine
nel rigoglio verdissimo dell'erba;
e un marcio odore di terra e di foglie
mi chiude nell'autunno che in te stagna,
anche se il sole
folgora sulle lapidi e sui cippi
o inverno rabbrividisce nei cipressi.

Perpetua stagione di morte: e mi ritrovo
vivo, gremito di parole
come l'istrione sulla fosse d'Ofelia;
vivo come non mai, presso i miei morti.

1952

ALIVE AS NEVER BEFORE

From the old cloister I enter the silence
of your avenues, flanked by marbles
that rise up like ruins
from the dazzling green of the grass;
and a rank odor of dirt and leaves
wraps me in the autumn that stagnates in you
whether the sun
blazes on the markers and headstones
or winter shudders in the cypresses.

Death's everlasting season: and here I am
alive, crowded with words
like that ham at Ophelia's grave;
alive as never before, among my dead.

GEOFFREY BROCK

DA LA SABBIA E L'ANGELO

I

Non occorrevano i templi in rovina sul limitare di deserti,
Con le colonne mozze e le gradinate che in nessun luogo conducono;
Né i relitti insabbiati, le ossa biancheggianti lungo il mare;
E nemmeno la violenza del fuoco contro i nostri campi e le case.
Bastava che l'ombra sorgesse all'angolo più quieto della stanza
O vegliasse dietro la nostra porta socchiusa—
La fine pioggia ai vetri, un pezzo di latta che gemesse nel vento:
Noi sapevamo già di appartenere alla morte.

III

Ogni volta che dicemmo addio;
Ogni volta che verso la fanciullezza ci volgemmo, alle nostre spalle caduta
(Tremando l'anima al suo lungo lamento);
Ogni volta che dall'amato ci staccammo nel freddo chiarore dell'alba;
Ogni volta che vedemmo sui morti occhi l'enigma richiudersi;
O anche quando semplicemente ascoltavamo il vento nelle strade deserte,
E guardavamo l'autunno trascorrere sulla collina,
Stava l'Angelo al nostro fianco e ci consumava.

Margherita Guidacci

1921–1992

FROM **THE SAND AND THE ANGEL**

I

We didn't need the crumbling temples on the deserts' edge,
With lopped columns and stairs that lead nowhere;
Nor the sand-covered wreckage, the bleached bones along the sea.
Not even the violence of fire against our fields and homes.
It was enough that the shadow rose from the quietest corner of the room
Or kept its vigil behind our half-closed door—
The fine rain against the windowpanes, a piece of tin moaning in the wind:
We knew already we belonged to death.

RUTH FELDMAN

III

Every time that we said goodbye;
Every time that we turned towards childhood, with our shoulders bowed
(Spirit trembling in its long lament);
Every time that we broke free of the beloved in cold clear dawn;
Every time that we saw the enigma fasten upon dead eyes;
Or even when we simply listened to the wind in the empty streets,
And watched autumn run out over the hillside,
The Angel stayed at our side and consumed us.

CID CORMAN

V

Furono ultime a staccarsi le voci. Non le voci tremende
Della guerra e degli uragani,
E nemmeno voci umane ed amate,
Ma mormorii d'erbe e d'acque, risa di vento, frusciare
Di fronde tra cui scoiattoli invisibili giocavano,
Ronzio felice d'insetti attraverso molte estati
Fino a quell'insetto che più insistente ronzava
Nella stanza dove noi non volevamo morire.
E tutto si confuse in una nota, in un fermo
E sommesso tumulto, come quello del sangue
Quando era vivo il nostro sangue. Ma sapevamo ormai
Che a tutto ciò era impossibile rispondere.
E quando l'Angelo ci chiese. «Volete ancora ricordare?»
Noi stessi l'implorammo: «Lascia che venga il silenzio!»

1946

LA MADRE PAZZA

Noi con gli stracci smessi del passato
ci costruiamo un presente.
Come una bambola piena di segatura
lo stringiamo al petto,
teneramente lo culliamo.
Cosí la madre pazza, mia vicina,
parla con un fanciullo
da molto tempo sparito in mezzo ai fiori,
e intanto volta indignata le spalle
all'uomo grigio, flaccido ed affranto
che quel fanciullo è diventato
e che la supplica invano
di riconoscerlo.

1970

The last to move away were the voices. Not the terrible voices
Of war and hurricanes,
Nor human and beloved voices,
But the babbling of grass and water, the laughter of wind,
Leaves rustling where invisible squirrels used to play,
The joyful buzz of insects over many summers
And even that insect that buzzed the more insistently
In the room where we did not wish to die.
And everything confused in a single note, in a firm
And subdued contrast, like that of blood
When our blood was yet alive. But we already knew
It was impossible to respond to all of that,
And when the Angel asked us: "Do you still want to remember?"
We ourselves implored him: "Let silence come!"

CATHERINE O'BRIEN

THE MAD MOTHER

With the cast-off rags of the past
we build ourselves a present,
clutch it to our chests
like a doll filled with sawdust,
cradle it tenderly.
Just so, the mad mother, my neighbor,
talks to a little boy
who disappeared long ago among the flowers,
and meanwhile turns her back indignantly
on the gray man, flabby and broken,
that little boy has become,
and who begs her in vain
to recognize him.

RUTH FELDMAN

SULL'ORLO DELLA VISIONE

Notte—albero, nido—notte da cui mi è tanto
faticoso staccarmi, presa tra un'ala bruna
ed un grande barbaglio, saprò muovermi
sotto un cielo di luce, tra le forme
che, per me ignote, avanzano? O vorrò
chiudere gli occhi, rifugiarmi ancora
in te?

1993

ON THE EDGE OF VISION

Night—tree, nest—night that I leave behind
with great difficulty, caught between a brown wing
and great dazzlement, will I know how to move
beneath a sky of light, among these forms
unknown to me, advancing? Or will I want
to close my eyes, seek refuge once again
in you?

CATHERINE O'BRIEN

QUANTO A LUNGO

Quanto a lungo tra il grano e tra il vento
di quelle soffitte
più alte, più estese che il cielo,
quanto a lungo vi ho lasciate
mie scritture, miei rischi appassiti.
Con l'angelo e con la chimera
con l'antico strumento
col diario e col dramma
che giocano le notti
a vicenda col sole
vi ho lasciate lassù perché salvaste
dalle ustioni della luce
il mio tetto incerto
i comignoli disorientati
le terrazze ove cammina impazzita la grandine:
voi, ombra unica nell'inverno,
ombra tra i demoni del ghiaccio.
Tarme e farfalle dannose
topi e talpe scendendo al letargo
vi appresero e vi affinarono,
su voi sagittario e capricorno
inclinarono le fredde lance
e l'acquario temperò nei suoi silenzi

Andrea Zanzotto

1921–

HOW LONG

How long amid the wheat and the wind
of those garrets
higher and wider than the sky,
how long I have left you
my writings, my withered risks.
With the angel and chimera
with the ancient tool
with the diary and drama
that the nights play
one after the other with the sun
I left you up there to save
from the burning light
my uncertain roof,
the bewildered chimney-tops
the terraces where the crazed hail walks:
you, solitary shadow in the winter,
shadow among the demons of ice.
Noxious moths and butterflies
mice and moles dropping into hibernation
grasped and whetted you,
Sagittarius and Capricorn
trained cold lances at you
and Aquarius tempered in its silences

nelle sue trasparenze
un anno stillante di sangue, una mia
perdita inesplicabile.

Già per voi con tinte sublimi
di fresche antenne e tetti
s'alzano intorno i giorni nuovi,
già alcuno s'alza e scuote
le muffe e le nevi dai mari;
e se a voi salgo per cornici e corde
verso il prisma che vi discerne
verso l'aurora che v'ospita,
il mio cuore trafitto dal futuro
non cura i lampi e le catene
che ancora premono ai confini.

1951

ORMAI

Ormai la primula e il calore
ai piedi e il verde acume del mondo

I tappeti scoperti
le logge vibrate dal vento ed il sole
tranquillo baco di spinosi boschi;
il mio male lontano, la sete distinta
come un'altra vita nel petto

Qui non resta che cingersi intorno il paesaggio
qui volgere le spalle.

1951

in its transparencies
a year dripping with blood, one of my
inexplicable losses.

Already for you with sublime tints
of fresh antennae and roofs
the new days crop up all around,
already someone rises up and shakes
the mold and the snows from the seas;
and if I climb to you along ledges and cables
towards the prism that gives form to you
towards the dawn that shelters you,
my heart transfixed by the future
ignores the lightning flashes and chains
that still press in at the edges.

PATRICK BARRON

BY NOW

By now the primrose and the heat
at one's feet and the green acumen of the world.

Tapestries unfurled
the loggias vibrate in wind and in sun.
Peaceful larva of the thicket;
distant my pain, the thirst distinct
as another life in the lungs.

Here all that remains is to wrap oneself in the landscape
to turn one's back.

WAYNE CHAMBLISS

ESISTERE PSICHICAMENTE

Da questa artificiosa terra-carne
esili acuminati sensi
e sussulti e silenzi,
da questa bava di vicende
soli che urtarono fili di ciglia
ariste appena sfrangiate pei colli
da questo lungo attimo
inghiottito da nevi, inghiottito dal vento,
da tutto questo che non fu
primavera non luglio non autunno
ma solo egro spiraglio
ma solo psiche,
da tutto questo che non è nulla
ed è tutto ciò ch'io sono:
tale la verità geme a se stessa,
si vuole pomo che gonfia ed infradicia.
Chiarore acido che tessi
i bruciori d'inferno
degli atomi e il conato
torbido d'alghe e vermi,
chiarore uovo
che nel morente muco fai parole
e amori.

1957

COSÌ SIAMO

Dicevano, a Padova, «anch'io»
gli amici «l'ho conosciuto».
E c'era il romorio d'un acqua sporca

EXISTING PSYCHICALLY

From this artful earth-flesh
thin sharp senses
and starts and silences,
from this slaver of events—
suns that collided with threads of eyelashes
sparsely fringed wheat-spikes across the hills—
from this long instant
swallowed by snows, swallowed by wind,
from all this which was not
spring not July not autumn
but just sickly glimmer
just psyche,
from all this which is nothing
and is everything that I am:
in this way truth groans to itself,
wants to be an apple that swells and soaks.
Sour brightness that weaves
the stings of hell
of atoms and the murky
struggle of seaweed and worms,
egg-gleam
that in that dying slime makes love
and words.

RUTH FELDMAN AND BRIAN SWANN

THAT'S HOW WE ARE

They said, the friends at Padua,
"I knew him too."
And there was nearby the rumble of dirty water,

prossima, e d'una sporca fabbrica:
stupende nel silenzio.
Perché era notte. «Anch'io
l'ho conosciuto.»
Vitalmente ho pensato
a te che ora
non sei né soggetto né oggetto
né lingua usuale né gergo
né quiete né movimento
neppure il né che negava
e che per quanto s'affondino
gli occhi miei dentro la sua cruna
mai ti nega abbastanza

E così sia: ma io
credo con altrettanta
forza in tutto il mio nulla,
perciò non ti ho perduto
o, più ti perdo e più ti perdi,
più mi sei simile, più m'avvicini.

1962

LA PERFEZIONE DELLA NEVE

Quante perfezioni, quante
quante totalità. Pungendo aggiunge.
E poi astrazioni astrificazioni formulazione d'astri
assideramento, attraverso sidera e coelos
assideramenti assimilazioni—
nel perfezionato procederei
più in là del grande abbaglio, del pieno e del vuoto,
ricercherei procedimenti

and of a dirty factory:
stupendous in the silence.
Because it was night. "I
knew him too."
Keenly I thought
of you who now
are neither subject nor object
not usual speech nor jargon
not quiet nor motion
not even the not that negates—
and for all that my eyes
pierce its needle's eye—
never negates you enough.

So be it: but I believe
with equal force
in all my nothingness,
therefore I haven't lost you
or, the more I lose you and you lose yourself,
the more like me you are, the closer you come.

RUTH FELDMAN AND BRIAN SWANN

THE PERFECTION OF THE SNOW

How many perfections, how many
how many totalities. Stinging it adds.
And then abstractions astrifications astral formulations
star-frost, across sidera and coelos
star-frosts and assimilations—
I would proceed in the perfected
beyond the glaring dazzle, the full and the empty,
I would search out proceedings

risaltando, evitando
dubbiose tenebrose; saprei direi.
Ma come ci soffolce, quanta è l'ubertà nivale
come vale: a valle del mattino a valle
a monte della luce plurifonte.
Mi sono messo di mezzo a questo movimento-mancamento radiale
ahi il primo brivido del salire, del capire,
partono in ordine, sfidano: ecco tutto.
E la tua consolazione insolazione e la mia, frutto
di quest'inverno, allenate, alleate,
sui vertici vitrei del sempre, sui margini nevati
del mai-mai-non-lasciai-andare,
e la stella che brucia nel suo riccio
e la castagna tratta dal ghiaccio
e—tutto—e tutto-eros, tutto-lib. libertà nel laccio
nell'abbraccio mi sta: ci sta,
ci sta all'invito, sta nel programma, nella faccenda.
Un sorriso, vero? E la vi(ta) (id-vid)
quella di cui non si può nulla, non ipotizzare,
sulla soglia si fa (accarezzare?).
Evoè lungo i ghiacci e le colture dei colori
e i rassicurati lavori degli ori.
Pronto. A chi parlo? Riallacciare.
E sono pronto, in fase d'immortale,
per uno sketch-idea della neve, per un suo guizzo.
Pronto.
Alla, della perfetta.

«È tutto, potete andare.»

1968

standing out, avoiding
the doubtful and dark; I would know I would say.
But how it suffuses us, how great is the snowy fertility
how much is it worth: in the valley of morning in the valley
on the mountain of many-springed light.
I put myself into the middle of this radial movement-missing
ah the first shiver of ascending, of understanding,
they depart in order, they challenge: that's all.
And your consolation insulation and my own, fruit
of this winter, trained, allied,
on the vitreous vertices of forever, on the snowy edges
of never-never-did-I-let-go,
and the star burning in its husk
and the chestnut pulled from the ice
and—all—and all-eros, all-lib. liberty in the snare
it's there in my embrace: it goes along,
it goes along with the invitation, the program, the whole affair.
A smile, right? And the li(fe) (id-vid)
about which you can do nothing, cannot hypothesize,
it gets (caressed?) on the threshold.
Evoè there along the ices and cultures of colors
and the reassured workings of golds.
Hello? Who's speaking? Hang up.
And I'm ready, in an immortal phase,
for a "sketch-idea" of snow, for one of its glimmerings.
Hello.
To the, of the perfect.

"That's all, you may go."

PATRICK BARRON

AL MONDO

Mondo, sii, e buono;
esisti buonamente,
fa' che, cerca di, tendi a, dimmi tutto,
ed ecco che io ribaltavo eludevo
e ogni inclusione era fattiva
non meno che ogni esclusione;
su bravo, esisti,
non accartocciarti in te stesso, in me stesso

Io pensavo che il mondo così concepito
con questo super-cadere super-morire
il mondo così fatturato
fosse soltanto un io male sbozzolato
fossi io indigesto male fantasticante
male fantasticato mal pagato
e non tu, bello, non tu «santo» e «santificato»
un po' più in là, da lato, da lato

Fa' di (ex-de-ob-etc)-sistere
E oltre tutte le preposizioni note e ignote,
abbi qualche chance,
fa' buonamente un po';
il congegno abbia gioco.
Su, bello, su.

Su, münchhausen.

1 9 6 8

TO THE WORLD

World: Be, and be good.
exist nicely,
do that, try to, aim to, tell me all,
and there I was upending eluding
and every inclusion was no less
effective than every exclusion;
come on, old chum, exist,
don't curl up in yourself in myself

I thought that the world thus conceived
with this super-falling super-drying
the world thus adulterated
was only a me ill-hatched from a cocoon
was me ill-digested fantasizing
ill-fantasized ill-paid
and not you, dear, not you "sainted" and "sanctified"
a little more over there, to the side, to the side

Be sure to (ex-des-res etc.)-ist
and beyond all prepositions known and unknown,
you should have some *chance*,
behave nicely for a bit;
give the mechanism some play.
Come on, dear, come on.

                        Come on, Münchhausen.

PATRICK BARRON

Andrea Zanzotto 377

SUBNARCOSI

Uccelli
crudo infinito cinguettio
su un albero invernale
qualche cosa di crudo
forse non vero ma solo
scintillio di un possibile
infantilmente aumano
ma certo da noi che ascoltiamo
    —allarmati—lontano
    —o anche placati—lontano
uccelli tutta una città
pregna   chiusa
           glorie di glottidi
           acumi e vischi di dottrine
un chiuso si-si-significare
nemmeno infantile ma
adulto occulto nella sua minimità

           [disperse specie del mio sonno
           che mai ritornerà].

        1973

DA IPERSONETTO

I (SONETTO DI GRIFI IFE E FILI)

Traessi dalla terra io in mille grifi
minimi e in unghie birbe le ife e i fili
di nervi speni, i sedimenti vili
del rito, voglie così come schifi;

SUBNARCOSIS

Birds
raw endless chirping
on a cold black branch
something raw
not true perhaps, but only
the announcement of some possible
childlike, inhuman
though certainly for those of us listening
   —alarmed—far off
   —becalmed—far off
birds a whole city
teeming   closed
                glories of glottises
                of acumens and traps of doctrine
a closed si-si-significance
not even childlike but
adult occult in its austerity

                [scattered species of my sleep
                never to return].

WAYNE CHAMBLISS

FROM HYPERSONNET

I (SONNET OF SNOUTS SPORES AND SKEINS)

O for some naughty nails and multiple
wee snouts to disinter the spores and skeins
of lifeless nerves, the vile sludge that remains
after the rite which we abhor but will:

Andrea Zanzotto 379

manovrando l'invito occhial scientifico
e al di là d'esso in viste più sottili,
da lincee linee traessi gli stili
per congegnare il galateo mirifico

onde, minuzie rïarse di morte
—corimbi a greggia, ombre dive, erme fronde—,
risorgeste per dirci e nomi e forme:
rovesciati gli stomaci, le immonde
fauci divaricate, la coorte
dei denti diroccata: ecco le norme.

POSTILLA (SONETTO INFAMIA E MANDALA)

a F. Fortini

Somma di sommi d'irrealtà, paese
che a zero smotta e pur genera a vista
vermi mutanti in dèi, così che acquista
nel suo perdersi, e inventa e inforca imprese,
vanno da falso a falso tue contese,
ma in sì variata ed infinita lista
che quanto in falso qui s'intigna e intrista
là col vero via guizza a nozze e intese.

Falso pur io, clone di tanto falso,
od aborto, e peggiore in ciò del padre,
accalco detti in fatto ovver misfatto:
così ancora di te mi sono avvalso,
di te sonetto, righe infami e ladre—
mandala in cui di frusto in frusto accatto.

1978

to ply the lens of science—unbeaten still—
and see beyond it onto subtler planes:
o from some lynx-eyed lines the styles to strain
and fabricate the marvellous manual,

wherefrom, minute events which death has charred—
bunched corymbs, shades divine, secluded sward—
you'd rise again to tell us names and forms:
turned inside out the bellies, and outsplayed
the gullets in their filth, and the brigade
of teeth all shattered: look, these are the norms.

POSTSCRIPT (INFAMY SONNET AND MANDALA)

To F. Fortini

You sum of unreal summits, my land, you
flake into nought, yet visibly sustain
grubs changing into gods, turn loss to gain,
and make invention and emprise anew.
Your strivings trip from untrue to untrue,
but in such various and unending chain
that all that here is rottenness or bane
there to a match or meld with truth slips through.

And I, false too, clone of so false a breed,
or addled, with the father's fault made worse,
make packing words my deed or my misdeed.
Thus have I used you once more to my end,
sonnet, you infamous, purloining verse,
mandala in which my beggar's crusts are penned.

PETER HAINSWORTH

CARNEVALE A PRATO LEVENTINA

È questa la Domenica Disfatta,
senza un grido né un volo dagli strani
squarci del cielo.
        Ma le lepri
sui prati nevicati sono corse
invisibili, restano dell'orgia
silenziosa i discreti disegni.

I ragazzi nascosti nei vecchi
che hanno teste pesanti e lievi gobbe
entrano taciturni nelle case
dopocena: salutano con gesti
rassegnati.
        Li seguo di lontano,
mentre affondano dolci nella neve.

1 9 6 2

NEL CERCHIO FAMILIARE

Una luce funerea, spenta,
raggela le conifere
dalla scorza che dura oltre la morte,

Giorgio Orelli
1921–

CARNIVAL AT PRATO LEVENTINA

This is the Undone Sunday,
without a cry or flight from the strange
gashes in the sky.
                        But the hares
ran invisible over the snowy
lawns, and discreet designs remain
from the silent orgy.

Children hidden in old men
with light humpbacks and heavy heads
return home taciturn
after dinner, greeting
with resigned gestures.
                        I follow from a distance
as they sink gently into the snow.

LYNNE LAWNER

IN THE FAMILY CIRCLE

An extinguished funereal light
frosts once more the fir trees
whose bark survives past death;

e tutto è fermo in questa conca
scavata con dolcezza dal tempo:
nel cerchio familiare
da cui non ha senso scampare.

Entro un silenzio cosí conosciuto
i morti sono piú vivi dei vivi:
da linde camere odorose di canfora
scendono per le botole in stufe
rivestite di legno, aggiustano i propri ritratti,
tornano nella stalla a rivedere i capi
di pura razza bruna.

       Ma,
senza ferri da talpe, senza ombrelli
per impigliarvi rondini;
non cauti, non dimentichi in rincorse,
dietro quale carillon ve ne andate,
ragazzi per i prati intirizziti?

La cote è nel suo corno.
Il pollaio s'appoggia al suo sambuco.
I falangi stanno a lungo intricati
sui muri della chiesa.
La fontana con l'acqua si tiene compagnia.
Ed io, restituito
a un piú discreto amore della vita . . .

1962

and everything is still in this shell
dug sweetly from time,
in the family circle
from which it is senseless to escape.

Within a silence known so well,
the dead are livelier than the living:
they descend from neat rooms smelling
of camphor, through trapdoors into heated
wood-lined cubicles,
adjust their own portraits,
then return to the stables to view again the heads
of a pure dark breed.

              But
without a mole's tools or umbrellas
to ensnare swallows, after what carillon
have you boys run through numbed meadows,
neither cautious nor forgetful in your pursuits?

The whetstone is in its horn.
The henroost leans against the elder tree.
The spiders have been entangled
a long time on the church walls.
The fountain keeps itself company with water.
And I am restored
to a more discreet love of life.

LYNNE LAWNER

Giorgio Orelli 385

DOVE I RAGAZZI

AMMAZZANO IL GENNAIO

Con un passo men cauto mi precedi,
taciturno compagno, sulla strada
gelata. Non è il fuoco delle case
che mi chiama e soverchia questa sera
nell'intatto paese, ma lo strepito
inatteso che sale
con i fiati infingardi dell'inverno
dalla riva remota, irraggiungibile,
dove i ragazzi ammazzano il gennaio.

1962

WHERE CHILDREN
KILL JANUARY

You walk before me on the icy
street, my reticent companion, at a less
cautious pace. It's not the warmth of the houses
that calls me and overwhelms this evening
in the intact village, but the unexpected
din that rises
with the slack winter gusts
from the remote, unattainable riverbank,
where children kill January.

LAWRENCE VENUTI

IL DÍ DA LA ME MUÀRT

Ta na sitàt, Trièst o Udin,
  ju par un viàl di tèjs,
di vierta, quan' ch'a múdin
  il colòur li fuèjs,
  i colarài muàrt
sot il soreli ch'al art
    biondu e alt
  e i sierarài li sèjs,
  lassànlu lusi, il sèil.

Sot di un tèj clípid di vert
  i colarài tal neri
da la me muàrt ch'a dispièrt
  i tèjs e il soreli.
  I bièj zuvinús
a coraràn ta chè lus
    ch'i ài pena pierdút,
  svualànt fòur da li scuelis
  cui ris tal sorneli.

Jo i sarài 'ciamò zòvin
  cu na blusa clara
e i dols ciavièj ch'a plòvin
  tal pòlvar amàr.

Pier Paolo Pasolini

1922–1975

THE DAY OF MY DEATH

In some city, Trieste or Udine,
   on an avenue of lindens,
in the spring, when leaves
   burst into colour,
   I'll fall
under a sun that blazes
     yellow and high
   and I will close my eyes
   leaving the sky to its splendour.

Under a linden, warm with green,
   I will fall into the darkness
of my death that squanders
   the lindens, the sun.
   Beautiful boys
flying out from school,
     curls at their temples,
   will be running in that light
   I have only just lost.

I will be young still,
   in a pastel shirt
and with soft hair spilling
   into the bitter dirt.

Sarài 'ciamò cialt
e un frut curínt pal sfalt
                   clípit dal viàl
mi pojarà na man
tal grin di cristàl.

1954

DA I CENERI DI GRAMSCI

I

Non è di maggio questa impura aria
che il buio giardino straniero
fa ancora più buio, o l'abbaglia

con cieche schiarite . . . questo cielo
di bave sopra gli attici giallini
che in semicerchi immensi fanno velo

alle curve del Tevere, ai turchini
monti del Lazio . . . Spande una mortale
pace, disamorata come i nostri destini,

tra le vecchie muraglie l'autunnale
maggio. In esso c'è il grigiore del mondo,
la fine del decennio in cui ci appare

tra le macerie finito il profondo
e ingenuo sforzo di rifare la vita;
il silenzio, fradicio e infecondo . . .

Tu giovane, in quel maggio in cui l'errore
era ancora vita, in quel maggio italiano
che alla vita aggiungeva almeno ardore,

I will be warm still
and a boy running on the warm
    asphalt of the avenue
will lay a hand
on the crystal of my lap.

MARY DI MICHELE

FROM GRAMSCI'S ASHES

I

It's not May that brings this impure air,
making the darkness of the foreign garden
darker still, or dazzling with the glare

of blind sunbursts . . . this frothy sky
over pale-yellow penthouses
in vast semicircles that deny

a view of the Tiber's meanders and
Latium's deep-blue hills . . . Between these old
walls the autumn May extends

a deathly peace as unloved as our
destinies. It carries all the grayness
of the world, the close of a decade where

we saw our keen, naïve attempts
to remake life end up among the ruins
and the sodden, sterile silence . . .

In the May of your youth, when to be mistaken
was still part of life, in that Italian
May when life had yet its share of passion,

quanto meno sventato e impuramente sano
dei nostri padri—non padre, ma umile
fratello—già con la tua magra mano

delineavi l'ideale che illumina
(ma non per noi: tu morto, e noi
morti ugualmente, con te, nell'umido

giardino) questo silenzio. Non puoi,
lo vedi?, che riposare in questo sito
estraneo, ancora confinato. Noia

patrizia ti è intorno. E, sbiadito,
solo ti giunge qualche colpo d'incudine
dalle officine di Testaccio, sopito

nel vespro: tra misere tettoie, nudi
mucchi di latta, ferrivecchi, dove
cantando vizioso un garzone già chiude

la sua giornata, mentre intorno spiove.

IV

Lo scandalo del contraddirmi, dell'essere
con te e contro te; con te nel core,
in luce, contro te nelle buie viscere;

del mio paterno stato traditore
—nel pensiero, in un'ombra di azione—
mi so ad esso attaccato nel calore

degli istinti, dell'estetica passione;
attratto da una vita proletaria
a te anteriore, è per me religione

you, less reckless and impurely wholesome
than our fathers—no father but a humble
brother—already with your slender hand

you outlined the ideal that sheds
its light upon this silence (but not for us:
you are dead and we are likewise dead

with you, in this humid garden). Only
here, you see, on foreign ground, may you rest,
still the outcast. Patrician ennui

is all around you. The clanging of anvils,
faint in the late afternoon, is all
that reaches you here from the mills

of Testaccio, where between run-down sheds,
stark piles of sheet metal and iron scraps,
a shop-boy sings playfully, already

ending his day as the rain outside stops.

IV

The scandal of self-contradiction—of being
with you and against you; with you in my heart,
in the light, against you in the dark of my gut.

Though a traitor to my father's station
—in my mind, in a semblance of action—
I know I'm bound to it in the heat

of my instincts and aesthetic passion;
drawn to a proletarian life
from before your time, I take for religion

la sua allegria, non la millenaria
sua lotta: la sua natura, non la sua
coscienza: è la forza originaria

dell'uomo, che nell'atto s'è perduta,
a darle l'ebbrezza della nostalgia,
una luce poetica: ed altro più

io non so dirne, che non sia
giusto ma non sincero, astratto
amore, non accorante simpatia . . .

Come i poveri povero, mi attacco
come loro a umilianti speranze,
come loro per vivere mi batto

ogni giorno. Ma nella desolante
mia condizione di diseredato,
io possiedo: ed è il più esaltante

dei possessi borghesi, lo stato
più assoluto. Ma come io possiedo la storia,
essa mi possiede; ne sono illuminato:

ma a che serve la luce?

1957

DA IL PIANTO DELLA SCAVATRICE

I

Solo l'amare, solo il conoscere
conta, non l'aver amato,
non l'aver conosciuto. Dà angoscia

its joyousness, not its millennial
struggle—its nature, not its
consciousness. It is man's primordial

strength, having been lost in the act,
that gives this faith the joy of nostalgia,
the glow of poetry. More than that

I cannot say, without being right
but insincere, expressing abstract
love, not heartbreaking sympathy . . .

Poor as the poor myself, I cling tight,
like them, to demeaning hopes;
like them, every day of my life I fight

just to live. Yet in my disheartening
condition as one of the dispossessed,
I still possess—and it's the most thrilling

of bourgeois possessions, the ultimate
state of being. Yet as I possess history,
I am possessed by it, enlightened by it:

but what good is the light?

STEPHEN SARTARELLI

FROM **THE LAMENT OF THE EXCAVATOR**

1

It is only loving, only knowing that matters,
not *having* loved, not *having* known.
Living a love that consumes itself

il vivere di un consumato
amore. L'anima non cresce più.
Ecco nel calore incantato

della notte che piena quaggiù
tra le curve del fiume e le sopite
visioni della città sparsa di luci,

scheggia ancora di mille vite,
disamore, mistero, e miseria
dei sensi, mi rendono nemiche

le forme del mondo, che fino a ieri
erano la mia ragione d'esistere.
Annoiato, stanco, rincaso, per neri

piazzali di mercati, tristi
strade intorno al porto fluviale,
tra le baracche e i magazzini misti

agli ultimi prati. Lì mortale
è il silenzio: ma giù, a viale Marconi,
alla stazione di Trastevere, appare

ancora dolce la sera. Ai loro rioni,
alle loro borgate, tornano su motori
leggeri—in tuta o coi calzoni

di lavoro, ma spinti da un festivo ardore
i giovani, coi compagni sui sellini,
ridenti, sporchi. Gli ultimi avventori

chiacchierano in piedi con voci
alte nella notte, qua e là, ai tavolini
dei locali ancora lucenti e semivuoti.

makes for agony. The soul
doesn't grow anymore.
Here, in the enchanted heat of the night

in its depth down here
along the bends of the river with its drowsy
visions of the city strewn with lights

echoing still with a thousand lives,
lacklove, mystery and misery of the senses
make me an enemy of the forms of the world,

which until yesterday were my reason for living.
Bored and weary, I return home,
through dark marketplaces,

sad streets by river docks,
among shacks and warehouses mixed
with the last fields.

There, silence is deadly.
But down along the Viale Marconi,
at Trastevere station, the evening still seems sweet.

To their neighborhoods, to their suburbs
the young return on light motorbikes—
in overalls and workpants

but spurred on by a festive excitement,
with a friend behind on the saddle,
laughing and dirty. The last customers

stand gossiping with loud voices
in the night, here and there, at tables
in almost-empty still brightly lit bars.

Stupenda e misera città,
che m'hai insegnato ciò che allegri e feroci
gli uomini imparano bambini,

le piccole cose in cui la grandezza
della vita in pace si scopre, come
andare duri e pronti nella ressa

delle strade, rivolgersi a un altro uomo
senza tremare, non vergognarsi
di guardare il denaro contato

con pigre dita dal fattorino
che suda contro le facciate in corsa
in un colore eterno d'estate;

a difendermi, a offendere, ad avere
il mondo davanti agli occhi e non
soltanto in cuore, a capire

che pochi conoscono le passioni
in cui io sono vissuto:
che non mi sono fraterni, eppure sono

fratelli proprio nell'avere
passioni di uomini
che allegri, inconsci, interi

vivono di esperienze
ignote a me. Stupenda e misera
città che mi hai fatto fare

esperienza di quella vita
ignota: fino a farmi scoprire
ciò che, in ognuno, era il mondo.

Stupendous and miserable city,
you taught me what joyful ferocious men
learn as kids,

the little things in which the greatness
of life is discovered in peace,
how to be tough and ready

in the confusion of the streets,
addressing another man, without trembling,
not ashamed to watch money counted

with lazy fingers by sweaty delivery boys
against façades flashing by
in the eternal color of summer,

to defend myself, to offend,
to have the world before my eyes
and not just in my heart,

to understand that few know the passions
which I've lived through:
they are not brothers to me,

and yet they are true brothers
with passions of men who,
lighthearted, inconscient,

live entire experiences unknown to me.
Stupendous and miserable city,
which made me experience that unknown life

until I discovered what
in each of us
was the world.

Una luna morente nel silenzio,
che di lei vive, sbianca tra violenti
ardori, che miseramente sulla terra

muta di vita, coi bei viali, le vecchie
viuzze, senza dar luce abbagliano
e, in tutto il mondo, le riflette

lassù, un po' di calda nuvolaglia.
È la notte più bella dell'estate.
Trastevere, in un odore di paglia

di vecchie stalle, di svuotate
osterie, non dorme ancora.
Gli angoli bui, le pareti placide

risuonano d'incantati rumori.
Uomini e ragazzi se ne tornano a casa
—sotto festoni di luci ormai sole—

verso i loro vicoli, che intasano
buio e immondizia, con quel passo blando
da cui più l'anima era invasa

quando veramente amavo, quando
veramente volevo capire.
E, come allora, scompaiono cantando.

1957

A moon dying in the silence that lives on it
pales with a violent glow
which miserably, on the mute earth,

with its beautiful boulevards and old lanes,
dazzles them without shedding light,
and a few hot cloud masses

reflect them over the world.
It is the most beautiful summer night.
Trastevere, smelling of straw

from old stables and half-empty wine-bars,
isn't asleep yet.
The dark corners and peaceful walls

echo with enchanted noise.
Men and boys returning home
under festoons of lonely light,

toward their alleys choked with darkness and garbage,
with that light step
which struck my soul

when I really loved,
when I really longed to understand.
And now as then, they disappear, singing.

LAWRENCE FERLINGHETTI
AND FRANCESCA VALENTE

Vanno verso le Terme di Caracalla
giovani amici, a cavalcioni
di Rumi o Ducati, con maschile
pudore e maschile impudicizia,
nelle pieghe calde dei calzoni
nascondendo indifferenti, o scoprendo,
il segreto delle loro erezioni . . .
Con la testa ondulata, il giovanile
colore dei maglioni, essi fendono
la notte, in un carosello
sconclusionato, invadono la notte,
splendidi padroni della notte . . .

Va verso le Terme di Caracalla,
eretto il busto, come sulle natie
chine appenniniche, fra tratturi
che sanno di bestia secolare e pie
ceneri di berberi paesi—già impuro
sotto il gaglioffo basco impolverato,
e le mani in saccoccia—il pastore migrato
undicenne, e ora qui, malandrino e giulivo
nel romano riso, caldo ancora
di salvia rossa, di fico e d'ulivo . . .

Va verso le Terme di Caracalla,
il vecchio padre di famiglia, disoccupato,
che il feroce Frascati ha ridotto
a una bestia cretina, a un beato,
con nello chassì i ferrivecchi
del suo corpo scassato, a pezzi,
rantolanti: i panni, un sacco,
che contiene una schiena un po' gobba,

Going toward the Caracalla Baths
young friends
on Rumi or Ducati bikes
with male modesty and male immodesty
indifferently hiding or revealing
in the warm folds of their trousers
the secret of their erections . . .
With wavy hair
in youthful colored sweaters
they cleave the night,
in an endless carousal,
they invade the night,
splendid masters of the night . . .

Going toward the Caracalla Baths
with bare chest, as if upon
his native Apennine slopes
among sheep trails
for centuries smelling
of animals and holy ashes
from Berber countries—
already impure, under his dusty rough beret,
hands in his pockets—
the shepherd migrated
when he was eleven,
and now here he is,
jesting scoundrel with his Roman smile
still warm with red sage, figs and olives . . .

Going toward the Caracalla Baths,
the old paterfamilias, unemployed,
reduced by ferocious Frascati
to a blissful dumb beast
with the scrap-iron chassis
of his broken body wheezing,
his clothes a sack containing

due coscie certo piene di croste,
i calzonacci che gli svolazzano sotto
le saccoccie delle giacca pese
di lordi cartocci. La faccia
ride: sotto le ganasce, gli ossi
masticano parole, scrocchiando:
parla da solo, poi si ferma,
e arrotola il vecchio mozzicone,
carcassa dove tutta la giovinezza,
resta, in fiore, come un focaraccio
dentro una còfana o un catino:
non muore chi non è mai nato.

Vanno verso le Terme di Caracalla . . .

1961

Vado anch'io verso le Terme di Caracalla
pensando—col mio vecchio, col mio
stupendo privilegio di pensare . . .
(E a pensare in me sia ancora un dio
sperduto, debole, puerile:
ma la sua voce è così umana
ch'è quasi un canto.) Ah, uscire
da questa prigione di miseria!
Liberarsi dall'ansia che rende
così stupende queste notti antiche!

a back slightly hunched
and two thighs covered with scabs,
rough trousers flapping
under the pockets of his jacket
full of crumpled paper bags.
The face laughs:
under the jaws, the creaking bones
chewing words,
he laughs to himself,
then stops and rolls an old butt,
his carcass in which
all youth remains in bloom,
like a bonfire
in an old bin or basin:
He never dies who was never born.

Going toward the Caracalla Baths . . .

LAWRENCE FERLINGHETTI
AND FRANCESCA VALENTE

I too am on the way to the Caracalla Baths,
thinking with my old
stupendous privilege of thinking . . .
(And to think that a god
may still be in me,
bewildered, feeble, child-like,
but his voice so human,
almost like a song.)
Ah, to escape this prison of misery!
To free oneself from the anxiety that makes
these ancient nights so stupendous!

C'è qualcosa che accomuna chi sa l'ansia
e chi non la sa: l'uomo ha umili desideri.
Prima d'ogni altra cosa, una camicia candida!
Prima d'ogni altra cosa, delle scarpe buone,
dei panni seri! E una casa, in quartieri
abitati da gente che non dia pena,
un appartamento, al piano più assolato,
con tre, quattro stanze, e una terrazza,
abbandonata, ma con rose e limoni . . .

Solo fino all'osso, anch'io ho dei sogni
che mi tengono ancorato al mondo,
su cui passo quasi fossi solo occhio . . .
Io sogno, la mia casa, sul Gianicolo,
verso Villa Pamphili, verde fino al mare:
un attico, pieno del sole antico
e sempre crudelmente nuovo di Roma;
costruirei, sulla terrazza una vetrata,
con tende scure, di impalpabile tela:
ci metterei, in un angolo, un tavolo
fatto fare apposta, leggero, con mille
cassetti, uno per ogni manoscritto,
per non trasgredire alle fameliche
gerarchie della mia ispirazione . . .
Ah, un po' d'ordine, un po' di dolcezza,
nel mio lavoro, nella mia vita . . .
Intorno metterei sedie e poltrone,
con un tavolinetto antico, e alcuni
antichi quadri, di crudeli manieristi,
con le cornici d'oro, contro
gli astratti sostegni delle vetrate . . .
Nella camera da letto (un semplice
lettuccio, con coperte infiorate

Something's there to be shared
by those who know longing and those who don't.
Man has humble desires:
First of all, an immaculate shirt.
First of all, good shoes, proper clothing!
And a house in a district
where people don't bother you,
an apartment high up in the full sun
with three or four rooms and a balcony,
secluded, but with roses and lemons . . .

Alone to the bone, I too have dreams
that keep me anchored in the world,
glancing at it as if I
were only an eye . . .
I dream of my house on the Gianicolo
near Villa Pamphili,
green all the way to the sea,
a penthouse full of old sun,
always cruelly new in Rome.
I'd build a veranda on the balcony
with dark curtains, of impalpable cloth.
I'd have a light custom-made table
placed in a corner
with a thousand drawers,
one for each manuscript
so as not to violate
the insatiable hierarchies of my inspiration . . .
Ah, a bit of order, a bit of sweetness
in my work, in my life . . .
All around I'd put seats and armchairs,
together with a small antique table
and a few old paintings by cruel mannerists,
with golden frames, set against
the bare structure of the veranda.
In the bedroom a simple bed,

tessute da donne calabresi o sarde)
appenderei la mia collezione
di quadri che amo ancora: accanto
al mio Zigaina, vorrei un bel Morandi,
un Mafai, del quaranta, un De Pisis,
un piccolo Rosai, un gran Gattuso . . .

1961

flowery bedspreads woven by women
from Calabria or Sardinia.
Here I'd hang the paintings I still love:
next to my Zigaina, a beautiful Morandi,
a Mafai of the forties, a De Pisis,
a small Rosai, a large Gattuso . . .

LAWRENCE FERLINGHETTI
AND FRANCESCA VALENTE

MIO AMORE NON CREDERE

Mio amore non credere che oggi
il pianeta percorra un'altra orbita,
è lo stesso viaggio tra le vecchie
stazioni scolorite;
vi è sempre un passero sfrullante
nelle aiuole
un pensiero tenace nella mente.
Il tempo gira sul quadrante, giunge
un segno di nebbia sopra il pino
il mondo pende dalla parte del freddo.
Qui le briciole a terra, la brace del camino,
le ali,
le mani basse e intente.

1958

DA NYHAVN

Non ho molto da dirti, alle ventuno
il mondo comincia a farsi bello
come il globo che pende sulla porta.
Si può bere, ballare,

Bartolo Cattafi

1922–1979

MY LOVE, DON'T BELIEVE

My love, don't believe that today
the planet travels on another orbit,
it is the same journey between old
pale stations,
there is always a sparrow flitting
in the flowerbeds
a thought grown stubborn in the mind.
Time turns on the face of the clock, it joins
a trace of fog above the pine trees
the world veers into the regions of cold.
Here are the crumbs on the earth,
the embers in the fireplace,
the wings,
the low and busy hands.

DANA GIOIA

FROM NYHAVN

I don't have much to tell you, at nine p.m.
the world starts to get beautiful
like the globe that hangs over the door.
You can drink, dance,

parlare di cose scollacciate
baciare le statue colorite,
dentro vi bollo bene, nel bordello
di musiche e di mescite. Nessuno
sa che contrabbando compio
col petto tatuato, che tesoro
brucia nella grotta
e che grigia
cartuccia, che miccia nelle mani.
Mi scordo della prora,
domani farò la rotta esatta,
ora ho l'esempio, il budello,
la fame dritta e secca dei gabbiani

(Copenaghen, 1952)

1 9 5 8

API

Quelle api selvatiche
venute da ignote frontiere
che spesso vedi vibrare a capofitto
su gialle corolle
branco nato al di fuori
d'ogni ordine e legge
simile ai fiori caparbi
che predilige e difende
—il miele che ne discende
è un indocile miele—
veementi sfrontate violatrici

talk dirty,
kiss the colored statues,
inside there I really boil, in the brothel
of music and libations. No one
knows what contraband I achieve
with my tattooed chest, what treasure
burns in the grotto
and what gray
cartridge, what fuse in the hands.
I forget the prow,
tomorrow I will steer the exact course,
now I have the example, the gut,
the straight dry hunger of the gulls.

(Copenhagen, 1952)

RUTH FELDMAN
AND BRIAN SWANN

BEES

Those wild bees
which you often see quivering headfirst
over yellow corollas
come from unknown frontiers
a swarm hatched outside
any law and order
like the stubborn flowers
they favor and defend—
the honey they engender
is an untamed honey—
vehement brazen violators

di spazi riservati
a colonie modello
messaggio d'un forte qualcosa
splendente di protervia
che uova e larve comunque mette
nelle tasche dei Santi
e muore il giorno dei Morti

1 9 7 2

NON SI EVADE

Non si evade da questa stanza
da quanto qui dentro non accade.

1 9 7 9

of spaces reserved
for model colonies
they are messengers
and message of a strong something
splendid with arrogance
that still places, however,
eggs and larvae in the Saints' pockets
and dies on All Souls' Day.

RINA FERRARELLI

NO ESCAPE

There's no escaping from this room
from all that doesn't happen here.

GEOFFREY BROCK

LA GRANDE JEANNE

La Grande Jeanne non faceva distinzioni
tra inglesi e francesi
purché avessero le mani fatte
come diceva lei
abitava il porto, suo fratello
lavorava con me
nel 1943.
Quando mi vide a Losanna
dove passavo in abito estivo
disse che io potevo salvarla
e che il suo mondo era lì, nelle mie mani
e nei miei denti che avevano mangiato lepre in alta montagna.

In fondo
avrebbe voluto la Grande Jeanne
diventare una signora per bene
aveva già un cappello
blu, largo, e con tre giri di tulle.

1960

UN'EQUAZIONE DI PRIMO GRADO

La tua camicetta nuova, Mercedes
di cotone mercerizzato
ha il respiro dei grandi magazzini

Luciano Erba

1922–2010

LA GRANDE JEANNE

La Grande Jeanne never made a distinction
between Englishmen and Frenchmen
as long as they had hands
to her liking
she lived down at the harbor, her brother
worked with me
in 1943.
When she saw me once in Lausanne
where I was walking in a summer suit
she told me I could save her
and that her world was there, in my hands
and in my teeth that had eaten wild rabbit in the high mountains.

Ideally
La Grande Jeanne would have liked
to become a respectable lady
she already had a hat
blue, wide, and with three bands of tulle.

CHARLES WRIGHT

EQUATION OF 1 DEGREE

Your new blouse of mercerized
cotton, Mercedes,
has the air of big department stores

dove ci equipaggiavano di bianchi
larghissimi cappelli per il mare
cara provvista di ombra! per attendervi
in stazioni fiorite di petunie
padri biancovestiti! per amarvi
sulle strade ferrate fiori affranti
dolcemente dai merci decollati!
E domani, Mercedes
sfogliare pagine del tempo perduto
tra meringhe e sorbetti al Biffi Scala.

1960

TERRA E MARE

Goletta, gentilissimo legno, svelto
prodigio! se il cuore
sapesse veleggiare come sai
tra gli azzurri arcipelaghi!

ma tornerò alla casa sulla rada
verso le sei, quando la Lenormant
avanza una poltrona sul terrazzo
e si accinge ai lavori di ricamo
per le mense d'altare.

Navigazione blu, estivi giorni
sere dietro una tenda a larghe maglie
come una rete! bottiglie
vascelli tra rocchi di conchiglie
e la lettura di Giordano Bruno
nel salotto di giunco, nominatim
De la Causa Principio e Uno!

1960

where they equipped us with enormous
white hats for the sea,
welcome supply of shade! to wait for you
in stations decked with petunias, fathers
dressed in white! to love you
on railway tracks, anguished flowers,
beheaded sweetly by the passing freight-cars!
And tomorrow, Mercedes,
to leaf through the pages of lost time
between meringues and sherbert at the Biffi Scala!

LYNNE LAWNER

LAND AND SEA

Schooner, most gracious craft, O swift
prodigy! if the heart only
knew how to sail as you do
among the azure island chains!

but I go back to my house above the harbor
around six, when my Lenormant
pushes an armchair forward on the terrace
and settles down to her embroidery—
new napery for the altars.

Blue seafaring, days of summer,
evenings behind a curtain coarsely knit
just like a net! Full-rigged ship models
among sea-shell reefs, in bottles,
and the reading of Giordano Bruno
in the rush-lined parlor, *nominatim*
Concerning the First Cause and the One!

ROBERT FITZGERALD

VANITAS VARIETATUM

Io talvolta mi chiedo
se la terra è la terra
e se queste tra i viali del parco
sono proprio le madri.
Perché passano una mano guantata
sul dorso di cani fedeli?
perché bambini scozzesi
spiano dietro gli alberi
qualcuno, scolaro o soldato
che ora apre un cartoccio
di torrone o di zucchero filato?
Ottobre è rosso e scende dai monti
di villa in villa
e di castagno in castagno
si stringe ai mantelli
accarezza il tricolore sul bungalow
nel giorno che i bersaglieri
entrano ancora a Trieste.
Tutto è dunque morbido sotto gli alberi
presso le madri e i loro mantelli aranciati
la terra, la terra e ogni pena d'amore
esiste altra pena?
sono di là dai cancelli: così le Furie
e le opere non finite.

Ma queste non sono le madri
io lo so, sono i cervi in attesa.

1960

VANITAS VARIETATUM

Now and then I ask myself
if this world really is the world
and if these women among the park's paths
really are the mothers.
Why do they stroke a gloved hand
along the backs of their faithful dogs?
why do Scottish children
spy on someone from behind the trees,
student or soldier
who opens a paper bag now
full of nougats or sugar candy?
October is red and comes down the mountains
from house to house
and from chestnut tree to chestnut tree
it presses against the women's cloaks
it caresses the flag on the bungalow
the very day the soldiers, the *bersaglieri*,
enter Trieste again.
Therefore everything is soft under the trees
near the mothers and their orange cloaks
the world, the world and every pain of love
does any other pain exist?
they are there, outside the gates: thus the Furies
and their endless work.

But these aren't the mothers
I'm sure of it, these are the waiting deer.

CHARLES WRIGHT

GLI ANNI QUARANTA

Sembrava tutto possibile
lasciarsi dietro le curve
con un supremo colpo di freno
galoppare in piedi sulla sella
altre superbe cose
più nobili prospere cose
apparivano all'altezza degli occhi.
Ora gli anni volgono veloci
per cieli senza presagi
ti svegli da azzurre trapunte
in una stanza di mobili a specchiera
studi le coincidenze dei treni
passi una soglia fiorita di salvia rossa
leggi «Salve» sullo zerbino
poi esci in maniche di camicia
ad agitare l'insalata nel tovagliolo.
La linea della vita
deriva tace s'impunta
scavalca sfila
tra i pallidi monti degli dei.

1977

GRAFOLOGIA DI UN ADDIO

Questo azzurro di luglio senza te
è attraverso da troppi neri rondini
che hanno un colore di antenne
e il taglio, il guizzo della tua scrittura.
Si va dal «caro» alla firma
dal cielo alla terra
dalla prima all'ultima riga
dai tetti alle nuvole.

1989

MY FORTIES

It all seemed possible
leaving the curves behind
with definitive squeal of brakes
galloping off stood on the saddle
other lofty things
more noble prosperous things
were appearing at eye level.
Now the years turn quickly
in skies without omens
you awake from blue quilts
to a room with mirrored furniture
study the train connections
cross a threshold blossoming with red sage
read "Welcome" on the mat
then go out in shirtsleeves
to shake the salad in a napkin.
The Life Line drifts
keeps silent won't shift
it hurdles it passes
between the pale hills of the gods.

PETER ROBINSON

A GRAPHOLOGY OF GOODBYE

This July blue with you not here
is slashed by too many black swifts
antenna-colored and with
the cut, the speedy loops of your writing.
From "Dear" to signature,
from sky to earth
from first line to last
from rooftops to the clouds.

W. S. DI PIERO

Luciano Erba 423

IL TRANVIERE METAFISICO

Ritorna a volte il sogno in cui mi avviene
di manovrare un tram senza rotaie
tra campi di patate e fichi verdi
nel coltivato le ruote non sprofondano
schivo spaventapasseri e capanni
vado incontro a settembre, verso ottobre
i passeggeri sono i miei defunti.
Al risveglio rispunta il dubbio antico
se questa vita non sia evento del caso
e il nostro solo un povero monologo
di domande e risposte fatte in casa.
Credo, non credo, quando credo vorrei
portarmi all'al di là un po' di qua
anche la cicatrice che mi segna
una gamba e mi fa compagnia.
Già, ma allora? sembra dica *in excelsis*
un'altra voce.
Altra?

1 9 8 9

THE METAPHYSICAL TRAMDRIVER

Sometimes the dream returns where it happens
I'm maneuvering a tram without rails
through fields of potatoes and green figs
the wheels don't sink in the crops
I avoid bird-scarers and huts
go to meet September, towards October
the passengers are my own dead.
At waking there comes back the ancient doubt
if this life weren't a chance event
and our own just a poor monologue
of homemade questions and answers.
I believe, I don't believe, when believing I'd like
to take to the beyond with me a bit of the here
even the scar that marks my leg
and keeps me company.
Sure, and so? another voice *in excelsis*
appears to say.
Another?

PETER ROBINSON

ALLA FIGLIA DEL TRAINANTE

Io non so piú viverti accanto
qualcuno mi lega la voce nel petto
sei la figli del trainante
che mi toglie il respiro sulla bocca.
Perché qui sotto di noi nella stalla
i muli si muovono nel sonno
perché tuo padre sbuffa a noi vicino
e non ancora va alto sul carro
a scacciare le stelle con la frusta.

1954

I PEZZENTI

È bello fare i pezzenti a Natale
perché i ricchi allora sono buoni;
è bello il presepio a Natale
che tiene l'agnello
in mezzo ai leoni.

1954

Rocco Scotellaro

1923–1953

TO THE CARTER'S DAUGHTER

I can live near you no longer
someone binds the voice in my chest
you are the carter's daughter
who takes the breath from my mouth.
Because below us in the stable
the mules move in their sleep
because your father huffs near us
and does not go yet, high on his cart
to chase off the stars with his whip.

WILLIAM WEAVER

BEGGARS

It's nice to play beggars at Christmas
for the rich then are kind;
it's nice the manger at Christmas
where the lamb lies down
among lions.

CID CORMAN

ATTESE

Le ragazze aspettano sulle porte
Rosse, malariche, bianche
Nelle vesti di lutto.
Così forse solo i carcerati
E gli studenti che contano i giorni.

1954

I VERSI E LA TAGLIOLA

Con la neve si para la tagliola
e si aspettano i gridi dei fringuelli.
La maestra ai bimbi della scuola
legge un verso d'amore per gli uccelli.
Mi piacevano i versi e la tagliola.

1954

WAITING

The girls wait at the red
doors, malarial, white
in their black dresses.
Perhaps only prisoners and students
count the days like them.

RUTH FELDMAN
AND BRIAN SWANN

THE POETRY AND THE SNARE

Come snow and the snare appears
and we wait for the cries of the chaffinch.
The schoolmarm reads to the children
a love poem for the birds.
I liked the poetry and the snare.

CID CORMAN

EPIGRAMMA ROMANO

Tutto ignorate come a Weimar Goethe:
ma troppo grande è Roma per essere Weimar
e voi (perché dirlo?) troppo piccoli siete.

Potevano ben dire la grassa redditiera,
a Weimar, lo stalliere, la guardia, la ragazza:
«Siamo al centro del mondo», perché con essi c'era
uno che senza il mondo poteva vivere.

Ma noi siamo noi soli nel mezzo d'una piazza.

1965

MI CHIEDI COSA VUOL DIRE

Mi chiedi cosa vuol dire
la parola alienazione:
da quando nasci è morire
per vivere in un padrone

che ti vende—è consegnare
ciò che porti—forza, amore,
odio intero—per trovare
sesso, vino, crepacuore.

Giovanni Giudici

1924–

ROMAN EPIGRAM

Like Goethe at Weimar you ignore everything:
but Rome's too big to be Weimar
and you're (why even say it?) too small.

The fat landlady, the stable boy, the guard,
the girl at Weimar could very well say:
"We're at the center of the world," because there was
a man with them who could live without the world.

But we're only ourselves in the middle of a piazza.

LAWRENCE R. SMITH

YOU ASK ME WHAT IT MEANS

You ask me what
the word *alienation* means:
it is to die from the moment of birth
in order to live in a master

who sells you—it is to hand over
the things you carry—power, love,
total hate—in order to find
sex, wine, a broken heart.

Vuol dire fuori di te
già essere mentre credi
in te abitare perché
ti scalza il vento a cui cedi.

Puoi resistere, ma un giorno
è un secolo a cui consumarti:
ciò che dai non da ritorno
al te stesso a cui parte.

È un'altra aspettare,
ma un altro tempo non c'è:
il tempo che sei scompare,
ciò che resta non sei te.

1965

UNA SERA COME TANTE

Una sera come tante, e nuovamente
noi qui, chissà per quanto ancora, al nostro
settimo piano, dopo i soliti urli
i bambini si sono addormentati,
e dorme anche il cucciolo i cui escrementi
un'altra volta nello studio abbiamo trovati.
Lo batti col giornale, i suoi guaiti commenti.

Una sera come tante, e i miei proponimenti
intatti, in apparenza, come anni
or sono, anzi più chiari, più concreti:
scrivere versi cristiani in cui si mostri
che mi distrusse ragazzo l'educazione dei preti;
due ore almeno ogni giorno per me;
basta con la bontà, qualche volta mentire.

It means to live outside yourself
while you believe you reside within
because the wind you yield to
knocks you off your feet.

You can fight it, but one day
is a century of dissipation:
the things you give away never
return to you, their source.

Waiting is another life,
but there is no other time:
the time which is you disappears,
what remains isn't you at all.

LAWRENCE R. SMITH

AN EVENING LIKE SO MANY OTHERS

An evening like so many others, and again
we're here, who knows for how long, on
the seventh floor, the children asleep
after the usual screams and protestations,
and the puppy also asleep whose crap
we found one more time on the study floor.
You smack him with a newspaper, then remark his yelps.

An evening like so many others, and my resolutions
intact, to all appearances, as they were
years ago, clearer than that, actually, solider:
to write Christian verses which show that
as a boy the priests' education destroyed me;
two hours at least every day for myself;
enough of goodness, sometimes to lie.

Una sera come tante (quante ne resta a morire
di sere come questa?) e non tentato da nulla,
dico dal sonno, dalla voglia di bere,
o dall'angoscia futile che mi prendeva alle spalle,
né dalle mie impiegatizie frustrazioni:
mi ridomando, vorrei sapere,
se un giorno sarò meno stanco, se illusioni

siano le antiche speranze della salvezza;
o se nel mio corpo vile io soffra naturalmente
la sorte di ogni altro, non volgare
letteratura ma vita che si piega nel suo vertice,
senza né più virtù né giovinezza.
Potremmo avere domani una vita più semplice?
Ha un fine il nostro subire il presente?

Ma che si viva o si muoia è indifferente,
se private persone senza storia
siamo, lettori di giornali, spettatori
televisivi, utenti di servizi:
dovremmo essere in molti, sbagliare in molti,
in compagnia di molti sommare i nostri vizi,
non questa grigia innocenza che inermi ci tiene

qui, dove il male è facile e inarrivabile il bene.
È nostalgia di un futuro che mi estenua,
ma poi d'un sorriso si appaga o di un come-se-fosse!
Da quanti anni non vedo un fiume in piena?
Da quanto in questa viltà ci assicura
la nostra disciplina senza percosse?
Da quanto ha nome bontà la paura?

Una sera come tante, ed è la mia vecchia impostura
che dice: domani, domani . . . pur sapendo

An evening like so many others (how many evenings like this one
are left till my death?) and not tempted by anything,
I mean by sleep, or wanting to drink,
or by the useless anguish that used to grab me by the shoulders,
or by my white-collar frustrations:
I wonder again, I would like to know,
if one day I will be less tired, if illusions

really are the ancient hopes of salvation;
or if I suffer naturally in my wretched body
the fate of everyone else, not just words
but a life that bows to its summit
without virtue or youth anymore.
Will we be given a simpler life tomorrow?
Does our enduring the present have a purpose?

But it makes no difference if we live or if we die,
if we are private people without a history,
newspaper readers, television
watchers, utility customers:
there should be many of us, many of us should be wrong,
in the company of many we should pile up our sins,
not this gray innocence that holds us helpless

here, where evil is easy and good unattainable.
It's nostalgia for the future that wears me out,
and this is appeased by a smile or an as-it-were!
How long has it been since I've seen a river in flood?
How long does our discipline keep us cowardly
before beating us down?
How long does fear masquerade as goodness?

An evening like so many others, and it's my old deception
that says: tomorrow, tomorrow . . . knowing at the same time

che il nostro domani era già ieri da sempre.
La verità chiedeva assai più semplici tempre.
Ride il tranquillo despota che lo sa:
mi numera fra i suoi lungo la strada che scendo.
C'è più onore in tradire che in essere fedeli a metà.

1 9 6 5

our tomorrow was always yesterday.

Truth required much simpler moral fiber.

The tranquil despot who knows all this is laughing:

He counts me among his victims along the road I'm going down.

There is more honor in betraying than in being half faithful.

CHARLES WRIGHT

LA PINÀIDA

L'è do nòti ch'a insógni la Fedora.
A n'e' so gnénca mè,
forse parchè ò sintéi dla su surèla,
l'altrasàira,
ch' la tòurna da la Frènza.
La Fedora ad Gianóla, ta n la arcórd?
Mata s—cènta, se rèmal, e sa chi ócc
ch'e' pareva ch' la avéss sémpra la févra.
La stéva ma la Costa, sòura al Fusi,
u i pieséva la cecolèta in taza
e la menta se giaz.
Mórta a vintidú an de trentasèt.

U m pèr cmè 'dès, l'ultm'instèda a maréina,
a fémmi e' bagn sa ch'ilt
e pu zétt zétt amdémmi tla pinàida.
La n'era mai cunténta,
zérti vólti,
ch'a séra alè stuglèd vsina un capàn,
la m'avnéva tachèd,
la m scavcéva sal mèni,
la m géva t'un'urèccia: "Pippo, andémm?"

E ènca adès, la nòta, la m'e' déi:
"Pippo, dài, dài, andémma tla pinàida".

Raffaello Baldini

1924–2005

THE PINE GROVE

For two nights now I've been dreaming about Fedora.
I don't even know why myself,
maybe because I heard about her sister,
the other evening,
that she's come back from France.
Fedora, the Gianólas, you don't remember her?
Stark raving mad, with freckles, and those eyes
that made it seem like she always had a fever.
She lived on the via Costa, above the Fusis',
she liked hot chocolate
and mint drinks with ice.
Dead at twenty-two in thirty-seven.

It seems like today, that summer at the shore,
we were swimming with the others,
and then, quietly, quietly, we slipped off to the pine grove.
She was never satisfied,
a few times,
when I was stretched out near a cabana,
she would come up right next to me,
she would tousle my hair with her hands,
she would whisper in my ear: "Pippo, are we going?"

And even now, at night, she says to me:
"Pippo, come on, come on, let's go to the pine grove."

E mè a la vèggh, la à vintidú an,
la è sémpra zóvna,
invíci mè a so strach
e quant la s mètt a córr a n'i stagh dri.
Mo pu a n n'ò gnénca vòia,
ormai mu mè
u m pis da zughé a bréscla e un bicír 'd véin.

1982

FURISTÍR

S' chi mutéur, una boba, mo l'è pin,
me cantòun, 'd Baruzètt
a una zért'òura ta n'i pas, i è 'lè,
tótt, ch'i bacàia, i magna di gelè,
i va, i vén, l'altrasàira s'a n so svélt,
una frenèda, ció, ta m vén madòs?
pu a so stè 'lè a guardèl, mè quèst a l cnòss,
tè t si e' fiúl ad Vitorio, mo sté 'ténti
quant andé par la strèda, e quèll che là,
sla maia ròssa, vén aquè, l'è un Brògi,
l'è l'anvòud ad Ristín, no? u n'è e' tu nòn
Ristín, ta n si e' fiúl d'Ugo? mo chi sit?
e léu u m'à détt un nóm, ch'a n m'arcórd piò,
Cavalli? no, Marietti? un nóm acsè,
ch'a n l'éva mai sintéi, Barbieri? gnénca,
dis che e' su bà e' lavòura ma la Fisi,
i vén da fura, aquè u s vaid ch'u s sta bén,
i aréiva e i n va véa piò, ch mè la dmènga
in piaza quant a pas a tó e' giurnèl,
u s vaid 'd cal fazi,
mo dimpartótt, tla bènca, te consórzi,

And I see her, she's twenty-two years old,
she's still young,
me, on the other hand, I'm tired,
and when she starts running I don't catch up with her.
But then besides I don't even feel like it,
at this point,
all I like to do is play *briscola* and have a glass of wine.

ADRIA BERNARDI

OUTSIDER

With all these engines it's one big racket, it's packed
at Baurzètts' corner
at certain times of the day, you can't even get through, there they are,
all of them, bickering, eating ice cream,
coming, going. The other night, if I hadn't been alert,
brakes screeching! Hey! you want to run me over?
I just stood there looking at him, this one I know,
you're Vittorio's son,
pay attention when you're driving, and that one there,
with the red sweater, come over here, he's a Broggi,
he's Oreste's grandson, right? isn't your grandfather
Oreste? aren't you Ugo's son? who are you?
and he told me a name, which I don't remember anymore.
Cavalli? no, Marietti? a name like that,
which I'd never heard before, Barbieri? it's not that either,
he says his father works for Fisi,
they come here from outside,
everyone can tell it's a nice lifestyle here,
they come and never leave, so I, on Sundays,
in the piazza, when I go to buy the paper,
you see all these faces,
I mean everywhere, in the bank, the Consortium,

tal pòsti, d'ogni tènt, e quèll chi èll?
zénta nóva, mai vésta, che dal vólti
a déggh: e' furistír
aquè a so mè, a n cnòss bèla piò niseun,
mo quéi de póst, ch'i è nèd aquè, a n'e' so,
i avrà pò i su dirétt, o u n vó dí gnént?
e te Cuméun, zà che par fè un cuncòurs,
e pu i l véinz ch'ilt, i nóst i è tótt pataca?
l'è mèi stè zétt, va là, che sa Bonini
ir un èlt pó a ragnémm,
dis: mo quèst l'è egoéisum, cum sarébal?
a sémm ad chèsa nòsta, e' cmanda ch'ilt,
i vén da fura e i cmanda,
u m'à dè dl'egoésta, t'é capéi?
ch'a so 'rvènz mèl, fighéurt, ch s'u i è éun,
a l déggh sémpra, mè, i à da campè tótt
te mònd, la zénta a vrébb ch'i fóss tótt sgnéur,
a n'ò nisuna invéidia, ò e' mi lavòur,
l'è che Bonini quant l'à vòia ad zcòrr,
e mè a i casch sémpra,
ènca ir, a m'i so imbatú par chès.
avnéva da e' campsènt, a i vagh tótt i an,
da la mi mòi, mo u n'è ch'a i ténga e' còunt,
un an, du an, a vagh quant a me sint,
a ciap sò da par mè, una pasagèda,
aréiv alè, a téir véa, ch' l'è pin 'd graménga,
a i pulses e' ritràt, pu, a turnè indrí,
a zéir un pó purséa,
mo u i è da caminé, i è sémpra dri
ch'i lavòura, i ingrandéss, i è rivàt
bèla sla strèda, e u i n'è sémpra di nóv,
i scap fura ad bot, alè, vè, Guàza,
e quèst l'è Diego, l'è parlènt, e quèll
l'è Santarèli, l'è vlú 'ndè tla tèra,
pu Canzio, Nando Ricci, e aquè u i è Sghètta,

the post office, which every so often, and that one, who's he?
new people, never seen before, which at times
I say: around here the foreigner
is me, I don't know anyone anymore,
even the ones from here, who were born here, I don't know,
don't they have their rights too, or doesn't that count for anything?
and at the town hall, it's the same thing with the examinations,
the others win out, are all of ours stupid?
it's better to shut up, come on now, with Bonini
a few days ago, we argued,
he says: you think the world belongs to you? what are you talking about?
this is our home, and the others are running things,
they come from outside and tell us what to do,
he said I was selfish, do you understand what I'm saying?
that I was taking it all wrong, come off it, if there's someone,
I say it all the time, I do,
everyone in the world has to scrape by, everyone wants to be rich,
I don't have a drop of envy in me, I have my work,
it's that Bonini when he wants to talk,
I'm the one who's got to listen to him,
even yesterday, I just happened to run into him,
I was coming back from the cemetery,
I go there every year,
to see my wife, it's not that I don't keep it up,
every year, every two years, I go when I feel like it,
I just pick up and go, by myself, a stroll,
I get there, clear everything away, it's covered with weeds,
I clean her picture, then, going back, I wander around wherever,
it's a long walk there, I'm always at work,
it's gotten bigger, they're as far as
the street now, and they are always new ones,
they just jump out at you, there, look, Guaza,
and this one's Diego, it looks like he's talking,
that one's Santarelli, he already had one foot in the grave,
then Canzio, Nando Ricci, and here, this is Sghètta,

Raffaello Baldini 443

e' féva Garatoni, a n'e' savéva,
quèst l'è rivàt adès, u i è sno un nómar,
l'à da ès Carabéin, i l'à pórt véa
l'altredè, e quèst l'è Otavio, ch'u s stimèva:
a iò e' dutòur ad chèsa:
e quèll che 'lè ch'e' réid l'è Batistini,
vè Miglio 'd Bréina, al scòppi ch' avémm fat,
Mòsca, Dirani, mo l'è tótt' 'n'avdéuda
aquè, l'è cmè in piaza, a i cnòss ma tótt.

1 9 8 8

CAPÈ

Dài, capa tè, che par mè l'è l'istèss.
Enca lòu, a n'e' faz par cumplimént,
capé, mè u m va bén tótt.
U t pis quèll? e tol sò.
O st'èlt? ta n si sichéur? i ti pis tutt déu?
pórti véa, u i n'è tint.
Éun sno? cmè t vu, pénsi, u n gn'è préssia, quèst?
mè, 's'ut ch'a t dégga, u t'à da pis ma tè?
e alòura tól.
E vuílt, nu sté 'lè cmè di candléun,
préima a ridévi, adès aví paéura?
tulí sò quèll ch'a vléi, a n gn'ò gnénch' chéunt,
i è tótt cumpàgn par mè, cm'a v l'òi da déi?
Mo tè, a n'i sémm ancòura, a t vèggh tla faza,
ta i é 'rpéns? t vu cambiè?
dò che t guèrd? fam avdài, t vu quèll che 'lè?
tò, mètt zò cl'èlt, però ta l sé ch' t'é òc?
Alòura, 'iv capè tótt?
E mu mè u m'è 'rvènz quèst, mo guèrda dréinta,

they're doing Garattoni's right now, I didn't even know it,
this one's just arriving, there's just a number,
it's got to be Carabéin, they took him away
the other day, and this is Ottavio, who always just had to brag:
I've got a doctor in the house,
and that one there laughing, that's Battistini,
look at Emilio, Emilio Bréina, what trumps we played,
Mosca, Dirani, it's one big hello,
here, it's like being in the piazza.
I know everyone.

ADRIA BERNARDI

PICKING

Go ahead, you pick, it makes absolutely no difference to me.
They should too, I'm not just saying it,
go ahead and pick, for me any of them are just fine.
You like this one? take it then.
Or this one? you're not sure? you like both?
take them both, there's plenty.
Only one? whatever you want, think about it, no rush, this one?
me? what do you want me to say, you're the one who's got to like it,
my opinion is that I think it looks good, you think so too?
so take it then.
And the rest of you, don't just stand there frozen in place,
first you're laughing, and now you're all stressed out?
pick whichever one you want, I haven't even given it a thought,
they're all the same to me, do I have to draw you a picture?
But you, we're not settled anymore? I can see it in your face,
you're having second thoughts? you want to make a change?
what are you looking at? show me, you want that one?
go on, put back the other one, you know you've really got a good eye.
So now, everyone's picked?
And this one's left for me, well just look what's inside,

a n gn'éva méggh' badè,
ció, a savéi quèll ch'a v déggh?
s'avéss capè par préim avrébb tólt quèst.
Mo pu, zò, i è béll tótt.
Insòmma, adès a sémm a pòst, éun pr'ón,
senza ragnè, ta m guèrd, ta n si cuntént?
t vu quèst che què?

1988

L'IGIENE

Ò capéi, sè, l'igiene, òz, s' ta n sté, 'ténti,
sa tótt' stal malatéi, t vu ch'a n'e' sapa?
mo mè a n déggh mégga d' no lavès, t si mat?
ta n t vu lavè? a déggh? sno d' no esagerè,
parchè puléid, va bén, no smerigléid,
sno che la zénta, bagnoschiuma, sèl,
u n'i basta gnénch' piò la savunètta,
che invíci mè, dal vólti, lavès trop,
e' va pérs ènch' dal robi, l'altredè,
sa óna, ta n la cnòss,
ènca s'a ta n la cnòss,
ènca s'a t déggh e' nóm, la n'è d'aquè,
óna ad Rémin, a s sémm cnunséu par sbai,
du méis fa, dop a s sémm incòuntr'ancòura,
sémpra par sbai, dal paróli, émm ridéu,
mo u n'è mè adès ch'a vòia, a t la racòunt,
par dèt 'n'dea, l'è stè mèrt dopmezdè,
ad chèsa sóvva, e' maréid l'era fura,
la m'è vnú 'vréi, la aveva una vestaglia,
émm bivéu, émm balè, pu dop te lèt
la m'è vnú sòura, ssst! aquè a cmand mè,
e òz l'è la zóbia,
e mè a la sint ancòura, t'è capéi?

2000

I hadn't even given it a second thought,
you know what I've got to say to all of you?
that if I'd been the one with first choice this is the one I'd have picked.
But then again, really, they're all nice.
At any rate, we're all even, one for everyone,
no bickering, you're looking at me, you're not happy?
you want this one?

ADRIA BERNARDI

HYGIENE

I understand, sure, hygiene, these days, if you're not paying attention,
with all these sicknesses, you think I'm not aware?
I'm not saying not to bathe, are you crazy?
you don't want to wash? I'm just saying to not go overboard,
because there's clean, that's fine, but not clean and shiny,
it's just that people now, bath foams, bath salts,
a bar of soap's not good enough,
no, instead, sometimes, by washing too much,
some things even get lost, the other day,
there was one lady, I didn't know her,
even if you tell me her name, she's not from here,
she's from Rimini, we had met each other by chance,
two months ago, then we met again,
again by chance, we exchanged a few words, we laughed,
but it's not like now I'm wanting, I'm just telling you
to give you an idea, it was a Tuesday afternoon,
at her house, her husband was away,
she started to unzip me, she was wearing a dressing gown,
we'd been drinking, we'd danced, then we went to bed,
she climbed on top of me, sssh!
and today is Thursday
and I still smell her, do you understand?

ADRIA BERNARDI

GUÈRA

No, la burocrazéa la n gn'éintrar gnént,
l'è lòu, i la à sa mè,
a so te léibar nir, e a so e' parchè,
l'è stè l'altr'an, d'instèda, da Fasúl
disdài 'd fura, a zcurémmi,
ch'i vó buté zò al scóli, i li vó fè
alazò mi Muléin, 'ta bón, va là,
l'è robi che, e mè 'lè u m'è scap da déi,
cm'òi détt? ad sòura u i vrébb una garnèda
e fè pulire, ècco, una roba acsè,
e lòu, t si mat, i l'à savú e' dè dop,
i à tènt' 'd cal spéi, e d'alòura a so sgnèd,
i n mu nu n pasa óna,
lèzi, regolamént, da dvantè mat,
ch' l'è pió 'd du an ormai, mo lòu, t'é vòia,
e' pò pasè méll'an,
i n pardòuna, quèst', mè, l'è una cambièla
ch'a i ò firmé, e a la chin paghè, però
i n mu n cnòss lòu mu mè,
tótt' la su prepotenza, mè a i péss sòura,
a n déggh par déi, a péss, dabón, la sàira,
quant i n mu n vaid,
mo ènca e' dopmezdè, basta stè 'ténti,
d'invéran, sa chi frédd, zért, u s fa mèi,
la zénta i scapa póch,
d'instèda invíci i sta in zéir fina tèrd,
però d'instèda u i è pió sodisfaziòun,
d'agòst, sòtta e' Vultòun, che da lè e' pasa
l'asesòur de Demanio, a t'e' dagh mè,
e' Demanio, parchè a la téngh ch'a s-ciòp
e quant a i dagh la mòla
l'è dal pisédi da caval, 'na pózza

WAR

No, the bureaucracy's got nothing to do with it,
it's them, they have it in for me,
I'm in their big black book, and I know why,
it happened the year before last, in summer, at Fasúl's,
we were sitting outside, talking,
they wanted to tear down the schools, they wanted to build them
down at the Mulini, are you kidding, come off it,
these are things that, and it just came out of my mouth,
what did I say? that up at the top there should be a broom
and a clean sweep, that's what I said, something along those lines,
and they, go figure, knew about it the next day,
they have so many spies, and from that day I was singled out,
there hasn't been one day that's gone by,
laws, regulations, it's enough to drive you crazy,
it's been more than two years now, but I work, you better believe I work,
a thousand years could pass,
they wouldn't forgive me, for this, I, it's a bill
that I signed for, and I have to pay it, but
they don't know *me,* all their arrogance, I piss on them,
I'm not just saying it either, I piss, I really do, in the evening,
when they don't see me,
even sometimes in the afternoon, just be careful,
in the winter, with that cold, certainly, it's easier,
people don't go out much,
in the summer on the other hand they're out and about until late,
but in the summer, it's more satisfying,
in August, under the big passageway, the assessor, Mr. Public Property
walks right through there, I call him Mr. Public Property,
I hold it until I'm ready to burst, and when I let loose,
I piss like a horse, a stench, you can't even inhale, you can imagine,
underneath the vault, in August, then if the wind's coming from the
    southwest,

ch'u n s'arfièda, t si mat,
alè sòtta, d'agòst, pu s' l'è garbéin,
l'è ch'a n m'aférum, ò imparè da lòu,
non perdono, a n pardòun,
e a n vagh purséa, l'è un tirasègn, parchè
u i n'è ch'i péssa in zéir, mo i péssa e basta,
ti cantéun, te méur di dri di Ricóvar,
còuntra la pòumpa de distributòur
dla Shell ch' l'è di an ch' l'è céus,
insòmma dò ch'u s'è sémpra pisé,
invíci mè, l'è tótt'un'èlta roba,
l'è una guèra, a péss sòtta l'Èrch, a péss
da d'in èlt zò mal schèli de Cuméun,
ch' la va ch' la córr, a péss còuntra la bóssla
dla Pro Loco, tal culònni de Crèdit,
a péss se pèlch dla banda, u i è dal nòti,
a m svégg ch' la m scapa, mo a n vagh méggh' te cès,
a stagh sò, aréiv in piaza, a m mètt d'impí
sla funtèna e a i péss dréinta,
e la matéina dop a pas d'alè,
cmè gnént, a guèrd, un piò bèl zèt, e a réid,
pisé vuílt acsè.

2 0 0 0

it's that I won't stop, I learned from them,
I won't forgive,
and I won't go home, it's target practice, because
there are some who piss wherever they feel like it,
they take a piss and that's it,
in the corners, along the wall behind the old people's home,
against the gas pump
at the Shell station that's been closed for years,
in any case wherever it's always been pissed on,
but my case is completely different,
it's war, I piss under the Arch, I piss
from up above, down on the steps of town hall,
it runs down, I piss against the glass door
of the Tourism Office, on the columns of the Credit Union,
I piss on the band shell, there are nights,
I wake up and I rush out, I don't ever use the toilet,
I get up, go to the piazza, I step up
on the fountain and I piss inside,
and the next morning I walk by,
like nothing happened, I look, nice gush, and I laugh,
that's how you piss.

ADRIA BERNARDI

RESURREZIONE DOPO LA PIOGGIA

Fu nella calma resurrezione dopo la pioggia
l'asfalto rifletteva tutte le nostre macchie
un lungo addio volò come un acrobata
dalla piazza al monte
e l'attimo sparì di volto in volto
s'accesero i fanali e si levò la buia torre
contro la nostra debolezza
i secoli non ci hanno disfatti

1961

QUANDO VIDI IL SALICE

Quando vidi il salice scuotere le sue tristi piume
nel giardino dell'ospedale, mi ferì una scheggia
dell'ora mormorante per la cascata dei colli
dalla costa lontana; la luce composta
giacque senza palpebre sul confine dell'erba.

E vidi nel ricordo la torre al vento sulla scogliera
la sua toppa verde e la scacchiera spallidita.
Vidi che tutto è bello e uguale:
ala di pietra spuma di mare inverno . . .

1961

Alfredo Giuliani

1924–2007

. . . .

RESURRECTION AFTER THE RAIN

It was in the calm resurrection after the rain
the asphalt reflected all our stains
a long goodbye flew like an acrobat
from the piazza to the mount
and the moment vanished from face to face
the floodlights turned on and the dark tower rose
against our weakness
the centuries have not undone us

MICHAEL F. MOORE

WHEN I SAW THE WILLOW

When I saw the willow shaking its sad feathers
in the hospital garden, I was wounded by a shard
of the hour murmuring through the rolling hills
from a distant shore; the composed light
lay eyes unblinking along the edges of the lawn.

And I saw in my memory the tower in the wind on the cliffs,
its green patch and faded chessboard walls.
I saw everything is beautiful and the same:
wing of stone froth of sea winter . . .

MICHAEL F. MOORE

MARZO IN RUE MOUFFETARD

Fetido e allegro il Mouff scende fra ritmi
gregoriani e lamenti di moschea.
Buca il geranio la maceria, rissa
un ventoso fondale d'Algeria
oltre i tetti decrepiti, fra i cento
occhi in agguato a Contrescarpe.
Stoccafissi, incunaboli, archibugi,
lardo di foca, cembali, damaschi
sopra il fiume di paprika e cannella.
Al tramonto una febbre sottile
sconvolge il labirinto, grida al fuoco
il formicaio. Quieti i Patriarchi
nelle fonde necropoli d'argilla
incidono i millenni con la daga
sulla tenera luna.

Il cadente rifugio di Verlaine
scuotono a notte rumbe negre.

1954

Maria Luisa Spaziani

1924–

MARCH IN RUE MOUFFETARD

Stinking and cheerful, the Mouff descends
through Gregorian rhythms and mosque laments.
The geranium pierces the rubble, a windy
backdrop from Algeria wrangles
beyond decrepit roofs, amongst the hundred
eyes in ambush at Contrescarpe.
Dried cod, arquebuses, incunabula,
seal's lard, damasks, cymbals
over the paprika and cinnamon river.
At dusk, a subtle fever
perturbs the labyrinth, it calls
the anthill to the fire. Quiet, Patriarchs
with daggers in deep clay necropolises
engrave the millennia
on the tender moon.

At night, black rumbas stir
the derelict refuge of Verlaine.

PETER ROBINSON

CONVENTO NEL '45

Tempo di viole bianche: e sui declivi
la neve agonizzava,
gli abeti trafiggevano il turchino,
sopra i poveri deschi
i frati salmodiavano in latino
e la valle in trionfo si striava
di fughe di tedeschi.

Tempo di viole bianche, ardua scalata
di giovinezza ai varchi dell'istante.
Mi abbagli ancora, scaglia di diamante,
impero incontrastato della rosa
in cima all'erta di trifogli freschi

(né alcuno mai ci disse che la dolce
Collina dell'Amata
tanto cresciuta nell'ultimo anno
era soltanto—o giovanile inganno—
un cumulo di teschi).

1966

L'orto era denso. I fichi pesavano dai rami,
fra i nespoli i papaveri gridavano l'estate.

Era stato ben arduo potare e seminare,
ma ora Dio sentivi sui campi respirare.

I chicchi erano enormi. Un succo dolce e forte
colava dal velluto fiammingo di una pesca.

THE CONVENT IN '45

Time of white violets; and on the slopes
the snow was dying,
the spruces were piercing turquoise skies,
over their humble suppers
the friars were singing in Latin,
and the valley was furrowed triumphantly
with the flight of the Germans.

Time of white violets, youth's
arduous climb to the threshold of the moment.
You stun me still, you diamond flake,
uncontested realm of the rose
at the summit of the fresh clover slope

(nor did anyone ever tell us that the sweet
Hill of the Beloved,
grown so large the year before,
was only—oh youthful illusion—
a heap of skulls).

BEVERLY ALLEN

The garden was thick. Figs hung from their branches;
among the medlars poppies shouted summer.

Pruning and planting had been a heavy labor,
but now you heard God breathing on the fields.

The grapes were hugely swollen. Sweet, strong juice
dripped from the Flemish velvet of a peach.

Maria Luisa Spaziani 457

Due farfalle in amore bandivano la festa
rituale del raccolto, a San Giovanni al Monte.

Di colpo sentii l'ombra che scura si stagliava
sull'erba del sentiero, quel fiato di sventura.

Mi volsi. Dal cancello si ergeva la figura
del nuovo giardiniere, e mi cacciava.

1970

ULTRASUONO

Il rumore soffoca il canto
ma il canto è uno spillo che attraversa il pagliaio,
cercalo se puoi con torce e calamite
lui ti punge e trafigge quando vuole—

Voce clamante nel deserto, gemito,
ultrasuono, anno-luce, urlo di tribù riscattata,

inconsútile varchi i deserti del tempo,
le inutili matasse dello spazio.

1977

DA VIAGGIO VERONA–PARIGI

Parigi dorme. Un enorme silenzio
è sceso ad occupare ogni interstizio
di tegole e di muri. Gatti e uccelli
tacciono. Solo io di sentinella.

Two love-struck butterflies proclaimed the ritual
festival of harvest, in San Giovanni al Monte.

Suddenly—breath of bad luck—I sensed the shadow
that stood out darkly on the grassy path.

I turned. And from the gate arose the figure
of the new gardener, who was hunting me.

GEOFFREY BROCK

•

ULTRASOUND

The noise suffocates the song
but the song is a needle that through the haystack,
search for it if you can with torches and magnets,
will prick and pierce you at will—

Clamorous voice in the desert, wail,
ultrasound, light-year, cry of a redeemed tribe,

seamless you cross the deserts of time,
the useless skeins of space.

DESMOND O'GRADY

PARIS SLEEPS

Paris sleeps. An enormous silence
has descended to fill every crack
in the walls and roofing tiles. Cats and birds
are silent. I am the only sentry.

Agosto senza clacson. Sopravvivo
unica, forse. Tengo fra le braccia
come Sainte Geneviève la mia città
che spunta dal mantello, in fondo al quadro.

1 9 9 2

August without car horns. I am the only
survivor, maybe. Like Saint Geneviève,
in my arms I hold my city, peeking out
of my cape at the bottom of the painting.

LAURA STORTONI

La neve sfuria e sotto il siero livella
ogni oggetto sporgenza macchia.
Non sei qui: è domenica—
il marito a casa.
Aspettandoti al vetro del motel sulla spiaggia
sento che l'infantile gemito dei gabbiani
è uguale a quello della mia gola ulcerata
dalla sigaretta
                    —intanto la televisione
alle spalle consiglia sul tempo . . .

                    1 9 6 7

Seguo quelle che
entrano nelle auto:
                    queste ambulanti
gettano una lenza che di preciso acchiappa
lungo i marciapiedi, o di profilo sostano
accese dalle vetrine.
L'insistenza dello sguardo sapiente di soldi
un ondare di natiche
il bisbiglio che non intendo sono
l'invito. Non ne usufruisco; ho moglie
e altro, mi dico—ma ecco
ce ne è sempre una che mi mette in panico.

                    1 9 9 9

Alfredo de Palchi

1926–

The snow rages and under its serum
levels every object, protuberance, blemish.
You aren't here: it's Sunday—
your husband's home.
Waiting for you at the window of the motel on the beach
I hear the seagulls' childlike mewing
so like my own throat ulcerated
by cigarettes
          —meanwhile the TV
behind me advises about the weather . . .

      I. L. SALOMON

    I look at the women
    stepping into cars:
               these strollers
    cast a line that hooks my eyes precisely
    as they move along sidewalks
    or stop with a profile lit by shopwindows.
    The obstinate gaze smelling of money
    the swaying of hips,
    whisperings I cannot make out—this
    is the lure. I don't respond; I have a wife,
    I tell myself, and more—but here
    there is always one who stirs me into panic.

          GAIL SEGAL

Trâ, 'me 'na s'giaffa salti trì basèj,
e passi in mezz a l'aria, al ver teater
che l'è mè pàder 'me sarà nel temp,
e schitti, curri, e 'l sbatt che fa la porta
l'è cume l'aria che me curr adré.
A trì, a quatter, al sping de la linghéra,
mì vuli i scal e rivi al campanèll.
Mia mama, adasi, la sciavatta e derva,
mè pàder rìd, e mì me par per nient.

1 9 7 5

Passa el tò cör tra j òmm, nissün le sa.
Sent, cume curr el trenu in mezz i câ!
Nüm rivarèm la nott ne la sutürna,
là due nissün ghe spèta, due se sa . . .
Uh nott, t'û 'ista scend per mia paüra,
e seri sul, cume l'è sul un can,
e seri lí che me scundevi a l'aria
a l'aria me cercava e l'era mí.
La nott l'era la nott, lüna la lüna,
e mí piasevi ai stèll sura de mí.

1 9 9 2

Franco Loi

1 9 3 0 –

Hurled, like a slap I leap three stairs,
and pass in midair to the real-life theater
that's my father as he'll be in time,
I spring, rush, and the slamming of the door
is like the air that chases me behind.
With three, four pushes at the railing,
I fly the stairs and reach the doorbell.
My mother slowly shuffles and then opens,
my father laughs, and to me it seems at nothing.

ANDREW FRISARDI

Your unknown heart among the people goes.
Listen to the train speeding past the houses!
We'll reach nightfall in the saturnine hours,
there, where no one is waiting and who knows . . .
Oh night, I saw you going down my fear,
I was alone the way a dog is alone,
and I was there and hiding in the air,
and the air that sought me out was me.
The night was being night, and moon the moon,
and I was pleasing to the stars above me.

ANDREW FRISARDI

El sú, el dulur g'a 'n nòm, la sua cadèna
l'è amur che prest se svöja del savur:
se tucca 'na farfalla e la sua pèna
diventa pulver e sensa pü calur . . .
Ah, nòm! oh vûs, cadèna che me streng,
le sú, se curr cul fiâ, par bév un fiur
ma al vent se pèrd el nòm, e resta el feng
che l'è l'umbría del cör e de la vita,
e ne la nott gh'impicca cuj sò ceng.

1 9 9 9

I know that suffering has a name, its chain
is love that empties overnight of flavor:
you touch a butterfly and find its pain
is dust and all the heat of it is over . . .
Ah, name! oh, voices, and the chain that wraps
us 'round, we hold our breath to sip a flower,
but we lose the name in wind, what's left, perhaps,
is unreality that shadows heart and life—
that from which at night we're hung by straps.

ANDREW FRISARDI

Dopo il dono di Dio vi fu la rinascita. Dopo la pazienza
dei sensi caddero tutte le giornate. Dopo l'inchiostro
di Cina rinacque un elefante: la gioia. Dopo della gioia
scese l'inferno dopo il paradiso il lupo nella tana. Dopo
l'infinito vi fu la giostra. Ma caddero i lumi e si rinfocillarono
le bestie, e la lana venne preparata e il lupo divorato.
Dopo della fame nacque il bambino, dopo della noia scrisse
i suoi versi l'amante. Dopo l'infinito cadde la giostra
dopo la testata crebbe l'inchiostro. Caldamente protetta
scrisse i suoi versi la Vergine: moribondo Cristo le rispose
non mi toccare! Dopo i suoi versi il Cristo divorò la pena
che lo affliggeva. Dopo della notte cadde l'intero sostegno
del mondo. Dopo dell'inferno nacque il figlio bramoso di
distinguersi. Dopo della noia rompeva il silenzio l'acre
bisbiglio della contadina che cercava l'acqua nel pozzo
troppo profondo per le sue braccia, Dopo dell'aria che
scendeva delicata attorno al suo corpo immenso, nacque
la figliola col cuore devastato, nacque la pena degli uccelli,
nacque il desiderio e l'infinito che non si ritrova se
si perde. Speranzosi barcolliamo fin che la fine peschi
un'anima servile.

1 9 6 4

Amelia Rosselli

1930–1996

After God's gift there came the rebirth. After the patience
of the senses all the days fell. After the India
ink an elephant was born again: joy. After the joy
hell descended after heaven the wolf in the den. After
the infinite came the merry-go-round. But the lights fell and the
animals were fed, and the wool was prepared and the wolf devoured.
After the hunger was born the child, after the boredom the lover
wrote her poems. After the infinite the merry-go-round fell
after the warhead the ink flowed. Warmly protected
the Virgin wrote her poems: the moribund Christ answered her
do not touch me! After her poems Christ devoured the pain
afflicting him. After the night the world's entire support
fell. After the hell the son was born anxious to distinguish
himself. After the boredom the silence was broken by the bitter
whisper of the peasant woman looking for water in the well
too deep for her arms. After the air descending
delicately around her immense body, the daughter with
the devastated heart was born, the birds' pain was born,
desire and the infinite that once lost can never be found again
was born. Hopeful we stagger until the end may fish
a cringing soul.

LUCIA RE AND PAUL VANGELISTI

Per la tua pelle olivastra per la tua mascella cadente
per le tue virginee denta per il tuo pelo bruno per il
tuo amore impossibile per il tuo sangue olivastro e la
mascella inferiore cadente per l'amministrazione dei beni
che non consiglia altre armonie, per l'amore e per il mistero
per la tua voracità e per la mia per il tuo sondare impossibile
abissi—per la mia mania di grandezza per il tuo irrobustire
per la mia debolezza per il tuo cadere e risollevarti
sempre si chiamerà chimera il breve viaggio fatto alle
stelle.

1 9 6 4

Ossigeno nelle mie tende, sei tu, a
graffiare la mia porta d'entrata, a
guarire il mio misterioso non andare
non potere andare in alcun modo con
gli altri. Come fai? Mi sorvegli e
nel passo che ci congiunge v'è soprattutto
quintessenza di Dio; il suo farneticare
se non proprio amore qualcosa di più
grande: il tuo corpo la tua mente e
i tuoi muscoli tutti affaticati: da
un messaggio che restò lì nel vuoto
come se ad ombra non portasse messaggio
augurale l'inquilino che sono io: tua
figlia, in una foresta pietrificata.

1 9 7 6

For your olive skin for your slack jaw
for your virginal teeth for your dark hair for
your impossible love for your olive blood and
slack jaw for the administration of the goods that
recommend no other harmony, for love and mystery
for your greed and mine for your sounding the impossible
abyss—for my visions of grandeur for your strengthening
for my weakness for your falling and raising yourself up
forever we will call chimera this brief journey to the
stars.

LUCIA RE AND PAUL VANGELISTI

Oxygen in my tents, it's you,
scratching at my front door,
curing my mysterious won't go
can't go in any other way with others.
How do you do it? You watch over me
and in our joining step is the general
quintessence of God; his delirium
if not actual love something
larger: your body your mind and
muscles, all strained: from
a message left in emptiness,
as if I couldn't deliver an augural
message to a shadow, I, tenant: your
daughter, in a petrified forest.

DIANA THOW

NEVE

Sembrano minuscoli insetti festeggianti
uno sciame di motori squillanti, una
pena discissa in faticose attenzioni
e una radunata di bravate.

Nevica fuori; e tutto questo rassomiglia
ad una crisi giovanile di pianto se
non fosse che ora le lacrime sono asciutte
come la neve.

Un esperto di questioni meteorologiche
direbbe che si tratta di un innamoramento
ma io che sono un esperto in queste
cose direi forse che si tratta di una

imboscata!

1976

SCIOPERO GENERALE 1969

lampade accesissime e nell'urlo
d'una quieta folla rocambolesca
trovarsi lì a far sul serio: cioè
rischiare! che nell'infantilismo
apparente schianti anche il mio
potere d'infischiarmene.

Un Dio molto interno poteva bastare
non bastò a me il mio egoismo

SNOW

They seem to be tiny insects celebrating
a swarm of shrill motors, a
pain split into difficult attentions
and a gathering of daring actions.

Snow outside; and all this resembles
a youthful crisis of tears if
it weren't for the fact that now the tears are dry
as the snow.

An expert on meteorological questions
would say that this had to do with an infatuation
but I who am expert in these
things would say that it has to do with an

ambush!

LAWRENCE R. SMITH

GENERAL STRIKE 1969

lamps wholly alight and in the howl
of a calm audacious crowd
to find yourself there, acting with seriousness:
taking risks! May this apparent
childishness shatter even my own
power not to care.

A deep inner God could have sufficed
my egotism did not suffice for me

Amelia Rosselli 473

non bastò a queste genti il sapore
d'una ricchezza nella rivincita

del resto strozzata. Dovevamo
esprimere il meglio: regalarsi

ad una retorica che era urlo
di protesta ad una distruzione

impavida nelle nostre impaurite
case. (Persi da me quell'amore
al verticale, a solitario dio
rivoluzionandomi nella gente
asportandomi dal cielo.)

1976

Cambiare la prosa del mondo,
il suo orologio intatto,
quel nostro incorniciare le giostre
faticose di baci.

Hai inventato di nuovo la luna,
è una povera isola
ti chiama con contingenza disperata
imbastardita dalle lunghe cene.

1983

the taste of riches in a revenge
nonetheless smothered did not suffice

for these people. We had to
express something better: allow ourselves

this rhetoric that was a howl
of protest against undaunted

destruction in our frightened
houses. (I lost on my own that vertical
love of solitary god,
revolutionizing myself in the people
removing myself from heaven.)

JENNIFER SCAPPETTONE

To change the prose of the world,
its intact clock,
our framing of merry-go-rounds
fatigued with kisses.

You have invented the moon again,
it is a poor island
it calls you with desperate contingency
bastardized by lasting suppers.

JENNIFER SCAPPETTONE

DA EROTOPAEGNIA (4)

in te dormiva come un fibroma asciutto, come una magra tenia, un sogno;
ora pesta la ghiaia, ora scuote la propria ombra; ora stride,
deglutisce, orina, avendo atteso da sempre il gusto
della camomilla, la temperatura della lepre, il rumore della grandine,
la forma del tetto, il colore della paglia:

                        senza rimedio il tempo
si é rivolto verso i suoi giorni; la terra offre immagini confuse;
saprá riconoscere la capra, il contadino, il cannone?
non queste forbici veramente sperava, non questa pera,
quando tremava in quel tuo sacco di membrane opache.

1 9 6 0

DA PURGATORIO DE L'INFERNO (8)

attraverso Hebecrevon, Lessay, Portbail, St. Sauveur (sotto la pioggia,
sempre); poi Edith disse che non ero gentile (perché non scrivevo, come
    Pierre,
per lei, quelques poèmes); (e che non dovevamo partire);

                                         Micheline
ci giudicò molto semplici; e Edith e Micheline, quando io dissi che non
    l'avevo
tradita (mia moglie), vollero crederlo;

Edoardo Sanguineti

1930–2010

FROM **EROTOPAEGNIA (4)**

he slept in you like a dry fibroma, like a thin tapeworm, a dream;
now he crushes the gravel, now he shakes his shadow; he screeches now,
swallows, urinates, having awaited forever the taste
of chamomile, the temperature of the hare, the sound of hail,
the shape of the roof, the color of straw:

                                        it cannot be helped—time
has turned towards his days; earth offers confused images;
will he be able to recognize the goat, the peasant, the cannon?
it was not for these scissors he really hoped, not for this pear,
when he trembled in your bag of opaque membranes.

CHARLES TOMLINSON

FROM **HELL'S PURGATORY (8)**

through Hebecrevon, Lessay, Portbail, St. Sauveur (beneath the rain,
always); then Edith said that I wasn't nice (because I wouldn't write, like
    Pierre
quelques poèmes for her); (and that we must not part);

                                        Micheline
thought us terribly inexperienced; and Edith and Micheline when I said
    I hadn't
betrayed her (my wife), tried to believe it;

(e qui cade opportuno ricordare quel:
«se ti buttassi le braccia al collo ecc.», che venne poi); poi si ballò tutti,
   anche
Micha, nel salottino; attraverso Cerisy, Canisy, Coutances, Regnéville; (ma
   il 12
luglio era chiuso il Louvre, martedí);
                                  e scrisse (sopra un foglio a quadretti):
«pensavo che non posso guardarti in faccia»; e: «mi dispiace per te»;
e ancora scrisse (mia moglie): «sto male»;
                                  e poi a Gap (H.A.),
(due giorni piú tardi), storditi ancora, quasi inerti: e pensare (dissi);
che noi (quasi piangendo, dissi); (e volevo dire, ma quasi mi soffocava,
davvero, il pianto; volevo dire: con un amore come questo, noi);
un giorno (noi); (e nella piazza strepitava la banda; e la stanza era
in una strana penombra);
         (noi) dobbiamo morire:

                    1 9 6 4

DA **CODICILLO (10)**

non ti sto a dirti lo scacco e lo smacco (e lo scasso e lo scazzo, e lo sballo e lo
   svacco),
che mi sveglio, ogni volta, così vivo:
                          sarà la radiolina, ogni mattina: sarà il
                          buzzer
(che è detto come è scritto, da noi due): e sarà il rimescolarsi delle erezioni
aurorali e dei primi notiziari del giorno: io non lo so: (so più niente di niente):
ma il gallo a pile, quando mi ridesta, mi è più selvaggio che il silvestre, tanto:

                    1 9 8 7

(and here is the right place to record that:
"if I threw my arms around your neck etc.," which followed then); then
   everyone danced, even
Micha, in the sitting room; through Cerisy, Canisy, Coutances, Regnéville;
   (but on July
12th the Louvre was closed, Tuesday);
                              and she wrote (on a sheet of graph
                                    paper):
"I thought I couldn't look you in the face"; and: "I am sorry for you";
and again she wrote (my wife): "I'm ill";
                              and then at Gap (H.A.),
(two days later), still stunned, almost inert: and to think (I said);
that we (almost crying, I said); (and wanted to say, but I was really
   almost choked
by tears; I wanted to say: with a love like this, we):
one day (we); (and in the square the band was thundering away; and the
   room was
in a strange penumbra);
                  (we) must die:

C H A R L E S   T O M L I N S O N

FROM **CODICIL (10)**

I'll spare you the put-downs and let-downs (and hassles and wrangles, and
   freak-outs and wipe-outs)
when I wake up, every time, living as I do:
                              it will be the transistor radio,
                              every day: it will be the buzzer
(a word the two of us said with a U as in you): it will be the remixing of
   auroral
erections and the first newscasts of the day: I don't know (knowing nothing
   about nothing):
but the electric rooster, when it wakes me, seems more savage than its
   sylvan cousin, all the same:

R O B E R T   H A H N   A N D   M I C H E L A   M A R T I N I

Edoardo Sanguineti

DA LIBRETTO

incidetele a lettere di scatola, miei lettori testamentari (e parlo ai miei scolari,
gli ipocriti miei figli, i filoproletari che tanto mi assomigliano, innumerevoli,
ormai, come i grani di sabbia del vacuo mio deserto), queste parole mie, sopra
    la tomba
mia, con la saliva, intingendovi un dito nella bocca: (come io lo intingo,
    adesso,
tra gli eccessivi ascessi delle algide mie gengive):

                                me la sono goduta, io, la
                                      mia vita:

XV

ma come siamo, poi, noi (gli italiani)?
                         la questione fu presa di petto, e
                         strenuamente
sviscerata, una sera, a una cena, al Montefiore del Mishkenot, con alcuni
    opulenti
semibulgari (e con una semibulgaressa, o bulgaressa proprio,
    solidissima):
                (es.:
siamo sensuali? sessuali? sensibili?): (siamo sessuatamente sensati?):
    (sensatamente
sessuati?): (tutto dipende, alla fine, dalla lingua che ti sei scelto): (dalla
    lingua
che ti sei subìto, soprattutto): (e qui, come da tanti squisiti fumi passivi,
    sei stato
violentato da scariche di implacabili fotografie (e di implacabili lingue)
    passive):
(e la lingua passiva, lo vedi, anzi lo senti (sensibilmente lo senti, se lo senti):
(se la senti): la lingua è già, da sola, un'ansiogena anfibologia: sessualmente

FROM **LIBRETTO**

I I I

carve in huge letters, you readers of my will (and I speak to my pupils,
  my hypocrite children, the lovers of the proletariat who are so like me,
    numberless,
  by now, as the grains of sand in my empty desert), over my grave, these
    words of mine,
  with spit, dipping a finger in your mouths: (as I now dip my finger
  in amidst the excessive abcesses of my frozen gums):

I have truly enjoyed

my life:

X V

so what are we like then, we (Italians)?

the question was met head on, and

strenuously

dissected, one evening, at a meal, in the Montefiore in Mishkenot, in the
  company of some opulent
half-Bulgarians (and one half-Bulgaress, or fullbred Bulgaress, mightily
  hefty):
    (e.g.:
are we sensual? sexual? sensitive?): (are we sexually sensate?): (sensately
sexual?): (it all depends, in the end, on the language you've chosen): (on the
  language
above all, you've been subjected to): (and here, as from so many exquisite
  passive fumes, you've been
ravished by myriads of implacable, passive photographs (and so many
  implacable tongues)):
(and this passive tongue, don't you see, or sense, rather (you sense it
  sensorially, if you sense it):
(if you sense the tongue): the tongue already, in itself, is an anxiolytic
  amphibology: sexually

Edoardo Sanguineti 481

sensata, per l'appunto):

            tale mi fu l'ultima sera, che mi fu l'ultima cena,

           e che fu,

come da programma, intiera, un sexy-booze and -schmooze:

                  (gaio usque ad

                    mortem):

       1 9 9 5

sensate, which is the whole point):

                  such was my last evening, my last supper,

             and it was,

as planned, a complete sexy-booze and -schmooze:

                      (cheerful usque ad

                      mortem):

PÁDRAIG J. DALY

GABBIANO

Maestro del senso del vuoto
e del pieno
maestro di tempeste
e di sereno nel mosso elemento
dell'aria cui affidarsi
mentre sorvola la battigia a picco
sulla vertigine prescelta
tra ciò che oscilla in lame cupoargentee
e il fisso dirupare della roccia
tra ciò che non ha ingombro
in un riflesso estendersi di spazio dentro il cielo
e l'immoto ristare dei siti della sosta
e del pernottamento
avanti e dentro e oltre l'eroso accumulo
del tempo in ciò che sotto forma di sostanza
in quell'attraversarlo si consuma:
fugace e prensile di sguardo
a chiglia e alato
a un doppio galleggio nel vivo e agile
disegno dell'esistere
che di una sua antitesi consiste
per infinite istantaneità
di desiderio come intuite
e mosse nello sfrecciarne
il regno.

1990

Camillo Pennati

1931–

GULL

Master of the sense of emptiness
and of the sense of fullness
master of storms
and calms in the air's
moving element to which you entrust yourself
as you hover
above the shore far up
over the sheer vertigo of your choice
between what fluctuates with dark silvery blades
and the abrupt fixity of rock
between the unencumbered space
extending its reflection over airy layers
and the unmoving hold of the overnight places
before and within and beyond the growing of time
into what, lasting through a material form,
is consumed by its own endurance:
fleeing and encompassing with your gaze
keeled and winged
in a twin buoyancy in the quick and agile
design of existence
which in its own antithesis embodies
the timeless instant
of desire grasped and enacted
in your sensuous flight
crossing that realm.

TED HUGHES

VICINO AL GIORDANO

Ore perdute invano
nei giardini del manicomio,
su e giú per quelle barriere
inferocite dai fiori,
persi tutti in un sogno
di realtà che fuggiva
buttata dietro le nostre spalle
da non so quale chimera.
E dopo un incontro
qualche malato sorride
alle false feste.
Tempo perduto in vorticosi pensieri,
assiepati dietro le sbarre
come rondini nude.
Allora abbiamo ascoltato sermoni,
abbiamo moltiplicato i pesci,
laggiù vicino al Giordano,
ma il Cristo non c'era:
dal mondo ci aveva divelti
come erbaccia obbrobriosa.

1984

Alda Merini

1931–2009

NEAR THE JORDAN

Hours wasted in vain
in the asylum's gardens,
back and forth along those walls
made fierce with flowers,
all of us lost in a fleeting
dream of reality
which some chimera
tossed behind our backs.
And after meeting
some patients smile
at the fake friendliness.
Time wasted in whirling thoughts,
hedged in behind the bars
like naked swallows.
Then we listened to sermons,
we multiplied the fishes,
down near the Jordan,
but Christ was not there:
he had uprooted us from the world
like dreadful weeds.

STEPHANIE H. JED AND
PASQUALE VERDICCHIO

Io ero un uccello
dal bianco ventre gentile,
qualcuno me ha tagliato la gola
   per riderci sopra,
   non so.
Io ero un albatro grande
e volteggiavo sui mari.
Qualcuno ha fermato il mio viaggio,
senza nessuna carità di suono.
Ma anche distesa per terra
io canto ora per te
le mie canzoni d'amore.

1984

TOELETTA

La triste toeletta del mattino,
corpi delusi, carni deludenti,
attorno al lavabo
il nero puzzo delle cose infami.
Oh, questo tremolar di oscene carni,
questo freddo oscuro
e il cadere piú inumano
d'una malata sopra il pavimento.
Questo l'ingorgo che la stratosfera
mai conoscerà, questa l'infamia
dei corpi nudi messi a divampare
sotto la luce atavica dell'uomo.

1984

As for me, I used to be a bird
with a gentle white womb,
someone cut my throat
　　just for laughs,
　　I don't know.
As for me, I used to be a great albatross
and whirled over the seas.
Someone put an end to my journey,　‚
without any charity in the tone of it.
But even stretched out on the ground
I sing for you now
my songs of love.

SUSAN STEWART

TOILETTE

The sad morning toilette,
disappointed bodies, disappointing flesh,
around the sink
the black smell of abominable things.
Oh, this trembling of obscene flesh,
this dark cold
and the most inhuman fall
of a sick woman on the floor.
This the crowding that the stratosphere
will never know, this the disgrace
of naked bodies made to blaze
under the atavistic light of humankind.

STEPHANIE H. JED AND
PASQUALE VERDICCHIO

ALDA MERINI

Amai teneramente dei dolcissimi amanti
senza che essi sapessero mai nulla.
E su questi intessei tele di ragno
e fui preda della mia stessa materia.
In me l'anima c'era della meretrice
della santa della sanguinaria e dell'ipocrita.
Molti diedero al mio modo di vivere un nome
e fui soltanto un'isterica.

1991

Apro la sigaretta
come fosse una foglia di tabacco
e aspiro avidamente
l'assenza della tua vita.
È cosí bello sentirti fuori,
desideroso di vedermi
e non mai ascoltato.
Sono crudele, lo so,
ma il gergo dei poeti è questo:
un lungo silenzio acceso
dopo un lunghissimo bacio.

1995

ALDA MERINI

I tenderly loved some very sweet lovers
without them knowing anything about it.
And I wove spiderwebs from this
and I always fell prey to my own creation.
In me there was the soul of the prostitute
of the saint of the one who lusts for blood and of the hypocrite.
Many people gave a label to my way of life
and all the while I was only a hysteric.

SUSAN STEWART

I open the cigarette
as if it were a tobacco leaf
and inhale avidly
the absence of your life.
It is so beautiful to feel you outside,
eager to see me
and yet never heard.
I am cruel, I know,
but the jargon of poets is this:
a long silence lit
after a very long kiss.

CINZIA SARTINI-BLUM
AND LARA TRUBOWITZ

DA AFORISMI E MAGIE

Sono una piccola
ape furibonda.

* * *

Confondere la merda
con la cioccolata
è un privilegio delle persone
estremamente colte.

* * *

Oguno è amico
della sua
patologia.

* * *

Non parlo mai
se non sono
accesa.

* * *

La pistola
che ho puntato alla tempia
si chiama Poesia.

* * *

Ogni tibia ama la sua fibula.

SEVEN APHORISMS

I am a furious
little bee.

※ ※ ※

To mistake shit
for chocolate
is the privilege
of the overeducated.

※ ※ ※

Every man is a friend
to his own
pathology.

※ ※ ※

I never speak
when I am not
turned on.

※ ※ ※

The gun
I point at my head
is called poetry.

※ ※ ※

Every tibia loves its fibula.

* * *

Alda Merini
è stanca di ripetere
che è pazza.

1999

DA AFORISMI E MAGIE

Poiché sono cattolica
non ho mai giocato.

* * *

Ho avuto
trentasei amanti
più IVA.

* * *

Sono completamente
asessuata,
salvo errori
e omissioni.

* * *

Non ho paura della morte
ma ho paura dell'amore.

* * *

■ ■ ■

Alda Merini
is tired of repeating
that she is crazy.

CARLA BILLITTERI

SIX APHORISMS

As I am Catholic
I have never played.

■ ■ ■

I've had
thirty-six lovers
plus tax.

■ ■ ■

I am completely
asexual
not counting errors
and omissions.

■ ■ ■

I'm not afraid of death,
but I'm afraid of love.

■ ■ ■

Nessuno può sapere
cosa c'è
tra me e Dio.

■　■　■

Il peccato
mi fa riposare.

1999

No one can know
what is
between me and God.

■   ■   ■

Sin
relaxes me.

D O U G L A S   B A S F O R D

Alda Merini 4

CINEMA DI POMERIGGIO

Quasi sempre a quest'ora
arriva gente un po' speciale (però
di buonissimo aspetto). Chi si siede
ma poi continua a cambiar posto,
chi sta in piedi, sul fondo della sala, e fiuta,
fiuta rari passaggi, la bambina
mezzo scema, la dama ch'entra sola,
la ragazza sciancata . . . Li guardo per sapere
che storia è la loro, chi li caccia. Quando
viene la luce penso come il cuore
gli si deve contorcere cercando
d'esser salvo più in là, di sprofondare
nel buio che torna tra un minuto.

1966

IL COMPLEANNO DI MIA FIGLIA, 1966

Siano con selvaggia compunzione accese
le tre candele.
Saltino sui coperchi con fragore i due
compari di spada compiuti uno
sei anni e mezzo, l'altro cinque

Giovanni Raboni

1932–2004

MOVIE THEATER IN THE AFTERNOON

Almost always, at this hour
come people who are a bit peculiar (but
of excellent appearance). One who sits
but keeps on getting up to change his seat,
the one on his feet at the back of the hall who sniffs,
sniffs out unusual passageways, the half-wit
young girl, the lady who comes by herself,
the girl with the bad leg . . . I watch them all
to learn what their stories are, who's hunting them.
When the houselights come back up I think of how
their hearts must writhe within them looking to be
safe a bit further on, to sink into
the darkness that returns in just a minute.

MICHAEL PALMA

MY DAUGHTER'S BIRTHDAY 1966

Let the three candles
be lit with a fierce remorse.
Let the two companions of the sword
jump on the covers with a racket, one
aged six and a half, the other five

e io trentaquattro e la mamma trentadue
e la nonna, se non sbaglio, sessantotto.
Questa scena non verrà ripetuta.
La scena non viene diversamente effigiata. E chi
si sentisse esule o in qualche
percentuale risulta ingrugnato
parli prima o domani.
Accogli, streghina di marzapane, la nostra sospettosa tenerezza.
Seguano come a caso stridi
di vagoni piombati, raffiche di mitragliatrice . . .

1 9 7 5

Eroi dispersi, non più o non ancora
mio reggimento oltre il reticolato
della luce, con che povero fiato
mi chiamate, con quanta pena affiorano

dal vocìo del vento che le divora
o le ammucchia come foglie sul lato
dell'ombra le voci che ho tanto amato!
A questo, a queste spoglie fruscianti ora

si riduce dunque il cerimoniale
del verbo . . . E così sia. Non ho bisogno
di sentirvi, vi tocco come tocca

un cieco la schiena di un animale
fidato, come chi è sordo la bocca
del muto che lo ammonisce in un sogno.

1 9 9 8

and I thirty-four and her mother thirty-two
and her grandmother, if I'm not mistaken, sixty-eight.
This scene will not be repeated.
The scene can't be portrayed any differently. And who
has felt himself an exile or in some
way ended up sullen
let him speak up now or tomorrow.
Little marzipan witch, receive our diffident tenderness.
Let there follow us as if by chance shrieks
of hurtling freighters, machine-gun blasts . . .

DAVID STIVENDER AND

J. D. MCCLATCHY

Missing heroes, no longer or not yet
my regiment beyond the chain-link fence
of light, how feebly whispered your laments,
how, calling me, your voices labor to cut

through the clamor of the winds that swallow
them whole or heap them leaf-like on the side
where shade is—voices I have so adored!
This then, this rustling of leaves, is all

that now remains of the old ceremonial
of the word . . . And let it be. I do not seem
to need to hear you; I touch you the way

a blind man lays his hand upon an animal
he trusts, the way a deaf man touches the gray
lips of a mute, who's warning him in a dream.

GEOFFREY BROCK

Ci sono sere che vorrei guardare
da tutte le finestre delle strade
per cui passo, essere tutte le rade
ombre che vedo o immagino vegliare

nei loro fiochi santuari. Abbiamo,
sussurro passando, lo stesso sogno,
cancellare fino a domani il sogno
opaco, cruento del giorno, li amo

anch'io i vostri muri pallidamente
fioriti, i vostri sonnolenti acquari
televisivi dove i lampadari
nuotano come polpi, non c'è niente

che mi escluda tranne la serratura
chiusa che esclude voi dalla paura.

1998

I film porno mi annoiano.
Ma andare insieme in uno di quei cinema
dove si fa di tutto
tranne guardarli, dove tutti vagano
come anime in pena
tra fila e fila in cerca di qualcuno,
uomo o donna, pagante o a pagamento,
da portarsi nei cessi,
ah questo no che non mi annoierebbe!
Quante volte, mio puro e altero amore,
sei stata a tua insaputa nel girone,

There are evenings when I'd like to look out from
the windows on the roads I pass through, be
all of the scattered shadows that I see
keeping a vigil, or so I imagine them,

in their dim-lit sanctuaries. On the way
I murmur to myself, we share a dream,
to annul until tomorrow the dark dream
that turns all bloody in the light of day,

I love them too, your pale walls patterned by
flowers, the floating chandeliers that pass
across the somnolent aquarium glass
of your television screens like octopi,

and there is nothing keeping me out here
but the fastened locks you use to keep out fear.

MICHAEL PALMA

Porn flicks bore me.
But going together to one of those theaters
where people do everything
except watch them, where everyone wanders
like tormented souls
among the rows in search of someone,
man or woman, who'll pay or be paid
to join them in the john—
now that, no, that wouldn't bore me at all . . .
How many times, my pure, proud love,
have you unknowingly made your rounds,

quante volte mi sono mescolato
alla torma inquieta dei dannati
per spiare noi due coi loro occhi,
per vederci come loro s'inventano
che siamo, che ti tocco, che respiri . . .

2002

how many times have I merged
with the troubled throng of the damned
to watch the two of us with their eyes,
to see us the way they imagine us
to be, me touching you, you breathing . . .

GEOFFREY BROCK

DA APRIRE

I

Dietro la porta nulla, dietro la tenda,
l'impronta impressa sulla parete, sotto,
l'auto, la finestra, si ferma, dietro la tenda,
un vento che la scuote, sul soffitto nero
una macchia più oscura, impronta della mano,
alzandosi si è appoggiato, nulla, premendo,
un fazzoletto di seta, il lampadario oscilla,
un nodo, la luce, macchia d'inchiostro,
sul pavimento, sopra la tenda, la paglietta che raschia,
sul pavimento gocce di sudore, alzandosi,
la macchia non scompare, dietro la tenda,
la seta nera del fazzoletto, luccica sul soffitto,
la mano si appoggia, il fuoco nella mano,
sulla poltrona un nodo di seta, luccica,
ferita, ora il sangue sulla parete,
la seta del fazzoletto agita una mano.

III

Perché la tenda scuote, si è alzato,
il vento, nello spiraglio la luce, il buio,
dietro la tenda c'è, la notte, il giorno,
nei canali le barche, in gruppo, i quieti canali
navigano, cariche di sabbia, sotto i ponti,

Antonio Porta

1935–1989

FROM TO OPEN

1

Nothing behind the door, behind the curtain,
the fingerprint stuck on the wall, under it,
the car, the window, it stops, behind the curtain,
a wind that shakes it, a more obscure
stain on the black ceiling, a handprint,
he leaned on rising, nothing, pressing,
a silk handkerchief, the lamp swings,
a knot, the light, ink-spot,
on the floor, above the curtain, the scouring pad,
on the floor drops of sweat, rising,
the stain won't rub out, behind the curtain,
the black silk of the handkerchief, shines on the ceiling,
the hand comes to rest, the fire in the hand,
a silk knot on the armchair, it shines,
wounded, now the blood on the wall,
the handkerchief's silk waves a hand.

3

Because the curtain flutters, it rises,
the wind, the light in the fissure, the dark,
behind the curtain there is, the night, the day,
boats in the canals, in bunches, the smooth canals,
they sail, loaded with sand, under the bridges,

è mattina, il ferro dei passi, remi e motori,
i passi sulla sabbia, il vento sulla sabbia,
le tende sollevano i lembi, perché è notte,
giorno di vento, di pioggia sul mare,
dietro la porta sul mare, la tenda si riempie di sabbia,
di calze, di pioggia, appese, sporche di sangue.

VII

Il corpo sullo scoglio, l'occhio cieco, il sole,
il muro, dormiva, il capo sul libro, la notte sul mare,
dietro la finestra gli uccelli, il sole nella tenda,
l'occhio più oscuro, il taglio nel ventre, sotto l'impronta,
dietro la tenda, la fine, aprire, nel muro,
un foro, ventre disseccato, la porta chiusa,
la porta si apre, si chiude, ventre premuto,
che apre, muro, notte, porta.

1964

RAPPORTI UMANI: XII

Camminare diviene intollerabile, è passato
un altro anno, con i piedi incollati ai pavimenti,
prima o dopo, con le gambe ridotte all'osso,
miele dei muscoli, più che un'antica verità,
rinchiuso nella stanza, non ti sa dire, e poi non c'è.

Sulle strade di ghiaccio, pattinando, con la sciarpa
verde e un berretto scuro, per un complesso di colpe,
breve felicità, non s'incontrano mai, così t'infurii,
gratti il muro con l'unghia e te la spezzi, disteso
sulla panchina, anitre imbalsamate galleggiano sul lago,
«mi raccontava una storia»—«sí, ma soltanto la fine».

1964

it's morning, the iron steps, oars and motors,
the steps on the sand, the wind on the sand,
the curtains float their edges, because it's night,
day of wind, of rain on the sea,
the sea behind the door, the curtain fills with sand,
with stockings, with rain, hanging, stained with blood.

7

The body on the rock, the blind eye, the sun,
the wall, was sleeping, head on the book, the night on the sea,
behind the window the birds, the sun in the curtain,
the eye even darker, the cut in the belly, under the fingerprint,
behind the curtain, the end, to open, in the wall,
a hole, belly dissected, the door shut,
the door opens, it shuts, belly compressed,
that opens, wall, night, door.

PAUL VANGELISTI

HUMAN RELATIONS: XII

Walking becomes unbearable. I've spent
another year with my feet glued to the floor,
sooner or later, my legs shrunk to bone,
the honey of flesh more than an old expression,
shut up in this room, how to tell you this, then nothing.

Out on the icy street, skating along, in a green
scarf and dark beret, for various wrongs,
brief happiness, they never meet, so you get angry,
you scrape the walls with your nail and break it off, stretched out
on the bench, stuffed ducks floating on the lake,
"You were telling me a story"—"Only the ending."

MILLER WILLIAMS

DA AUTOCOSCIENZA

DI UN SERVO

1 (PRODURRE)

Ecco: sono già morto
cioè non produco più
sto al di qua della finestra
e guardo quello che succede fuori
ne questo stato mi piace
cancellato ogni rapporto
come quando producevo
quindi non v'è differenza
e vi invito a scoprire dove sta l'errore
poiche la vita non è
simile alla morte

4 (MORTE COME VITA)

allora io esco e l'altro muove il capo
io muovo il capo
e l'altro alza le braccia e io
alzo le braccia si siede e io
mi siedo cosl di continuo
e l'altro come gli altri
e poi tutti insieme ci alziamo e ci sediamo
le braccia le mani gli occhi
muove le labbra le muoviamo anche noi

ancora vivo un servo come
da morto vive il padrone poiche
i padroni si riconoscono
dalla morte e i servi nella vita
da questa vita ne nasce altra ancora
i padroni distribuiscono niente
e macchie di sangue

FROM SELF-CONSCIOUSNESS

OF A SERVANT

1 (TO PRODUCE)

There: I'm already dead
that is I don't produce anymore
I stay on this side of the window
and watch what's happening outside
nor do I like my situation
every connection canceled
like when I was producing
so there's no difference
and I invite you to find where the error lies
because life is not
similar to death

4 (DEATH AS LIFE)

so I go out and another moves his head
I move my head
and the other lifts his arms and I
lift my arms he sits and I
sit like this continuously
and the other like the others
and then all together we get up and we sit down
the arms the hands the eyes
he moves the lips we move them too

still alive a servant as
the boss lives dead because
bosses are recognized
in death and servants in life
from this life another is born again
the bosses distribute nothing
and blood stains

Antonio Porta 511

poiché da quella morte io provengo
dunque sono servo per vivere dunque
consapevoli di questo vedrete
come la morte i padroni
scancelleranno se stessi: il corpo
sembra continuare mentre l'anima
è morta!

9 (VISITA ALLA NECROPOLI DI NORCHIA)

uomo/morte	uomo/terra
vita/morte	uomo/tomba
tomba/albero	polvere/tomba
roccia/tomba	cavallo/tomba
uomo/vita	spade/vita
difese/vita	lotte/vita
acqua/vita	roccia/uomo
uomo/triangolo	uomo/scava
uomo/foglia	batte/uomo
tomba/uccello	uomo/preda
preda/morte	preda/vita
vivo/uomo	uomo/morte
uomo /cavallo	uomo/uccello
fuori/dentro	tu/io
l'altro/io	tutto/tu
io/tutto	occhio/tomba
suono/tomba	lingua/tomba
lingua/vede	romba/vita
cerchio/morte	amo/morte
vita/amo	polvere/uccello
vola/morte	preme/terra
striscio/vita	ardo/morte
sudo/vita	chiamo/tomba

because from that death I proceed
so I am a servant to live so
they are aware of this you'll see
how like death the bosses
cancel themselves out: the body
appears to continue while the soul
is dead!

9 (VISIT TO THE NECROPOLIS OF NORCHIA)

man/death
life/death
tomb/tree
rock/tomb
man/life
defenses/life
water/life
man/triangle
man/leaf
tomb/bird
quarry/death
live/man
man/horse
outside/inside
the other/me
me/everything
sound/tomb
rain/tomb
tongue/sees
circle/death
life/I love
flies/death
I crawl/life
I sweat/life

man/earth
man/tomb
dust/tomb
horse/tomb
swords/life
struggle/life
rock/man
man/digs
beats/man
man/quarry
quarry/life
man/death
man/bird
you/me
everything/you
eye/tomb
tongue/tomb
tongue/rain
roars/life
I love/death
dust/bird
crushes/earth
I rage/death
I call/tomb

```
tomba/vita          tetto/morte
buca/morte          buca/vola
stringo/tomba       tengo/vita
buca/vuoto          tomba/senza
```

(Agosto 1971–Gennaio 1972)

1 9 7 4

non penso a te, mia cara, non penso al lavoro
(come dovrei, come devo, per garantirmi
per garantirti . . .)
penso al legno dei miei zoccoli
a come è cresciuto, come l'hanno tagliato, levigato
così conforta i miei piedi nudi, troppo delicati, no
non sto diventando matto, vedo
quello che vivo, per mezzo delle cose, ne vedo
ne vivo, temo, troppe e il metro, lo sguardo
si allunga all'infinito, ho paura che sia
una fune per appendermi, dondolarmi
dentro un buco del cielo, uno strappo
ma tu lo sai
preferisco vivere, perfino guardarmi guardare,
adesso esco, sta suonando l'ora d'aria
e il danzatore disegnato sul piatto
muove i primi passi . . .

Orvieto, 28–31.12.1981

1 9 8 2

```
tomb/life          roof/death
hole/death         hole/flies
I squeeze/tomb     I keep/life
hole/empty         tomb/without
```

August 1971–January 1972

PAUL VANGELISTI

I'm not thinking of you, my dear, nor about work
(though I should, or must, to provide
for us both . . .)
I'm thinking about my clogs
how the wood grew, was cut, sanded
to comfort my bare, all-too-delicate feet, no
I'm not losing my mind, it's through objects
that I see my life, objects I see
thrive on, fear, they're too many—a tape measure
and my sights stretch out to infinity, I'm afraid
it's a rope to hang or swing from
through a hole in the sky, and cut loose
but you know
I prefer living, even watching myself keep watch
I'm going out now, it's time for a walk in the yard
as the dancer decorating an unearthed dish
comes to life . . .

Orvieto, December 28–31, 1981

ANTHONY MOLINO

FURIERI

Quando fu certo che gli indizi di esistere non bastano
e niente serve alla vita quanto un testimone,
provvide il cielo che ogni uomo avesse
un logografo al seguito. Ma le storie cantarono
subito e solamente di acrobati divini
perché, mortali o no, tutti i forieri
sono sempre uguali. A noi, rimase l'ombra.

1995

GIUGNO DI SICILIA (NOTO, 1998)

In questo buco caldo come l'alito di Dio
ora e controra persistono ubiqui nelle piazze uomini
e cani neri, prove di razze salate, di meticciato
lungo, uomini intenti a logica e a millenni
di leggende che non perdono terra neppure
se fanno notte fonda su concetti o su arguzie metafisiche.
Cosí femmine, madri e le cure loro rimangono
accidenti, puri sospetti della ragione. Il sole
insulta tutto, sbatte i salti dell'onda, scalfisce i denti
scolpisce palme esclamative e magre mentre
i fichi che crepano aborrati sulle rocce e le rocche

Lucio Mariani

1936–

QUARTERMASTERS

When it was clear that clues of being aren't enough
and nothing benefits life more than a witness,
the heavens decreed that every man
should have his own logographer. But what got sung
were only and always tales of divine acrobats
since, mortal or not, quartermasters are all the same.
We, we were left with shadows.

ANTHONY MOLINO

SICILY IN JUNE (NOTO, 1998)

In this hole hot as the breath of God
at wake-time and nap-time everywhere in the piazzas, men
and black dogs endure, signs of seasoned races, of long
crossbreeding, men bent on logic and on millennia
of legends which give no ground, not even
if they cast abstractions and metaphysical nuance into deepest night.
So women, mothers, and their own cares remain
accidents for them, mere hunches of the rational mind. The sun
assaults everything, slams the wave's surge, scrapes teeth,
carves the thin, exclamatory palm trees while
figs which burst straying down cliffs and fortresses

stillano sudori lenti e opachi dalla grana di carne.
Le zagare tardive e i gelsomini schiacciati
contro crete barocche, bianchi a sporcare bianchi,
attaccano la gola con un miele rancido d'oriente.
Niente di sacro sulle chiese dai fianchi inanellati
nel marmo sporco, dalla facciata cava
a nessun rito servono capitelli di maschere, di pomi
e di ippogrifi grigi di lava né i putti stolti e belli
che portano l'acquasanta a spalla cavalcando delfini.
Per l'aria grave mormorano storie infinite
di fallanze veniali, tacciono le ragioni della vita
non quelle della morte.

2 0 0 1

ooze slow, thick sweat as fat as meat.
Late orange and jasmine blossoms crushed
against baroque clays, white to stain white,
attack the throat with a rancid eastern honey.
Nothing's sacred on these churches with curlicued
flanks of dirty marble, with sunken façades.
These capitals of masks, fruit, and gray lava hippogriffs
serve no rite, nor do the foolish pretty cherubs
shouldering holy water astride dolphins.
In dense air, they whisper infinite tales
of venial sins, hushing the reasons for life,
not the reasons for death.

ROSANNA WARREN

UNA FINESTRA APERTA

una finestra aperta
il collo un poco denudato
la notte penzola
con le sue vele nere
dall'alto dei soffitti
una mezza lunetta di vetro
taglia l'orizzonte a meta
ho posato il libro
ho spento la lampada
aspetto un lupo
dai grandi occhi di agnello

1 9 9 1

NEL PALMO DELLA MANO DESTRA

nel palmo della mano destra
tengo un uomo senza testa
e la sua automobile azzurrina,
nel palmo della sinistra
tengo una pozza d'acqua
con ciuffi di sambuco e canne gialle.

Dacia Maraini

1936–

A WINDOW IS OPEN

a window is open
my neck is bare

night hangs its black
sails from the ceiling

a little glass half-moon
cuts through the horizon

I have put down my book
I have turned out the light

I wait for a wolf
with the big eyes of a lamb

MARTHA COLLINS

IN THE PALM OF MY RIGHT HAND

in the palm of my right hand
I hold a man without a head
and his sky-blue car

in the palm of my left hand
I hold a small pool of water fringed
with elderberry bushes and yellow reeds

se chiudo le due mani a preghiera
metterò l'uomo senza testa
e la sua automobile azzurrina
dentro la pozza d'acqua
dalle sambuche alte
e le canne gialle

1991

•

when I press my hands together
I put the headless man
and his sky-blue car

into the small pool
with the tall elderberry bushes
and yellow reeds

MARTHA COLLINS

LA FORMA

La forma non ha imperfezioni
non è partecipazione né parte:
si compie. La forma che guardi
ci conosce, si contrappone
alla disgregazione: già scontata
prima della fine.

1 9 6 9

TERZO MODO

Il terzo modo per
distinguere A con-
siste nel rapporto tra
A e se stessi. A
si identifica, non si ha
alternativa, da
qui il monoteismo.

1 9 6 9

Annalisa Cima

1941–

FORM

Form has no imperfections
is neither participation nor part:
it comes true. The form you consider
knows us, opposes
disgregation: already expiated
before the end.

MARIANNE MOORE

THIRD WAY

The third way to
distinguish A con-
sists of the connection between
A and oneself. A
identifies itself, there is
no alternative, hence
monotheism.

MARIANNE MOORE

A LUI

Per persuadermi al tuo amore
vieni da me a sciogliere
            questo nodo d'angoscia.

Tu solo puoi.
Tu fitto d'ali di laridi.

Guarda
siamo alti sul ramo
al sole del mattino.

E lasciamo perle sul cammino
dolci gocce
            dell'inganno.

1984

TO HIM

Convince me of your love
come to me to loosen
        this knot of anguish.

Only you can.
You dense with gulls' wings.

Look
we are high on the branch
in the morning sun.

And we're leaving pearls on the road,
sweet drops
        of illusion.

JONATHAN GALASSI

IL PRIMO MIO AMORE

Il primo mio amore il primo mio amore
erano due.
Perché lui aveva un gemello
e io amavo anche quello.
Il primo mio amore erano due uguali
ma uno più allegro dell'altro
e l'altro più serio a guardarmi
vicina al fratello.
Alla finestra di sera stavo sempre con quello
ma il primo mio amore il primo mio amore
erano due: lui e suo fratello gemello.

1981

A NOVE MESI

A nove mesi la frattura
la sostituzione il cambio di madre.
Oggi ogni volto ogni affetto
le sembrano copie. Cerca l'originale
in ogni cassetto affannosamente.

1981

Vivian Lamarque

1946–

MY FIRST LOVE

My first love my first love
were two.
Because he had a twin brother
and I loved him too.
My first love were two who looked the same
though one was happier than the other
to see me near his brother.
I was always with that one by the window
when evening came.
But my first love my first love were two:
one and the same.

GEOFFREY BROCK

AT NINE MONTHS

At nine months the fracture
the substitution the change of mother.
Today every face every affection
looks like a copy to her.
She looks for the original
frantically in every drawer.

MOIRA EGAN AND DAMIANO ABENI

A VACANZA CONCLUSA

A vacanza conclusa dal treno vedere
chi ancora sulla spiaggia gioca si bagna
la loro vacanza non è ancora finita:
sarà così sarà così lasciare la vita?

1996

AT VACATION'S END

At vacation's end from the train see
who still plays and bathes on the beach
their vacation isn't over yet
will it be like this will it be like this
to leave this life?

PETER COVINO

(STUPEFAZIONE)

a che aspirano formiche sempre in moto
in fila o sparse, a un obiettivo fisse

mentre l'ape solfeggia sul geranio
e il ragno fa l'acrobata sui fili . . .

che si chiede la mosca sullo specchio,
la forma è più complessa del ronzio . . .

l'aria qui d'intorno sembra ferma
e invece spela, sputa sulla faccia

e porta a Delfi l'inutile pesto
cioè il pensiero degli imponderabili

1991

Eugenio De Signoribus

1947–

(STUPEFACTION)

what leads the ants, in single file or scattered
to move unceasingly toward their goal

while the bee doh-ray-mi's on the geranium
and the spider does gymnastics on its threads . . .

what does the fly ask itself on the mirror,
its form more complicated than its buzzing . . .

'round here the air seems motionless,
but its cold nips, spits in the face

carries the useless tread of feet to Delphi,
that is, the unthinkable thought

CHRISTOPHER WHYTE

(ALTRE VOCI)

si può ignorare il coro contemporaneo
e ascoltare l'inverno sotterraneo

non c'è sonno nei morti continuamente
essi parlano, prendono la nostra voce

l'eco gira sulle vene acquose, fuma,
e la lingua è visitata dalla neve . . .

1 9 9 6

DA PRINCIPIO DEL GIORNO

(CONFIDENZE CON
L'ESTRANEO, PARTI . . .)
non hai luogo o non sai o tardi solo
è per saperlo o per vederci chiaro
ora che il giorno tutto ira è in volo
coi fumi cerebrali . . .

di qui non sei, qui non certo non hai base,
sei uno che non passa, che non erge
o che non altro . . . , o che alla sua pelle
sta come un senzacasa . . .

■ ■ ■

rmitta le parole che sse ffónne
perché 'nzaì da sole o so 'ferite . . .
rmànnele arrète, cciàcchete le dite
comme quanne 'na bbille vu nnasconne . . .

(OTHER VOICES)

you can ignore the chorus of now
and listen to the winter underground

the dead do not sleep always
they speak, they take our voice

the echo wanders watery veins, it steams,
and covers our tongue with snow . . .

V. JOSHUA ADAMS

FROM BEGINNING OF THE DAY

(INTIMACIES WITH THE
STRANGER, FRAGMENTS . . .)
you have no place or don't know or it's just
late to find out to get things straight
now the entirely angry day has taken
flight with the brainy fumes . . .

you're not from here, for sure this is not your base,
you're one who doesn't pass, doesn't arise
who anything but . . . or who in his skin
is homeless, so to speak . . .

■ ■ ■

pit aside the wurds that sink
acause they're skaithed or cannae gang alane . . .
sen them backweys, bite yer fingers
like whan ye're keen tae hain yer ire . . .

ma se rfiati anghe se 'ns'affile
rmandàndele co' lu prime vestite
è comme mannà n'atra faza vite
'ngire dentre a tte e pe' curtile . . .

■　■　■

il sorgere, no, negare non devi
al te che più nella casa è riposto
esposto a sé, impietoso . . .

no, al tuo piede di là non rinunciare,
trascinerà il suo passo ansioso
la volontà dell'altro . . .

anche nel varco è il nutrimento . . .
nell'incontro con chi nel caso opposto
sta uguale a te

2000

suppose ye mou them, even impreceesely,
happing them wi whitivir comes tae haun,
it's jist the same as senning furth anithir
fause life stravaigin ben ye an withoot . . .

                 ■ ■ ■

no, you must not deny arising
to the you that is most hidden at home
exposed to itself, ruthless . . .

no, do not abandon the foot that's there,
the will for another
will drag its anxious step along . . .

even in the breach there's nourishment . . .
in meeting who, with an opposite fate
is just like you

CHRISTOPHER WHYTE

Eugenio De Signoribus 537

Chissà perché quest'ansa attira
Gli invertiti come me?
Parola troppo cruda? La ritrovo
In una poesia dei sedicianni
Riferita ad altri,
Poesia descrittiva, oggettiva:
Dietro un muretto due invertiti smaniano.
È un verso mio di quando
Crescevo.

2000

Se non sai che significhi in inglese *to maroon*
Pensa ad un nero schiavo che fugge
È lui *a maroon*
E per una di quelle conversioni
Semantiche che fanno il bello delle lingue
Marronare qualcuno
Significa al contrario attivamente abbandonarlo
Specie su un'isola. Deserta.
Il verbo risale come è ovvio al settecento
E l'esempio classico e altrettanto ovvio
Cita Jan Svilt, *homosexual sailor marooned*.
Il verbo è regolare.

2002

Franco Buffoni

1948–

Who knows why this haven attracts
Inverts like me?
Too harsh a word? I found it
In a sixteen-year-old's poem
Applied to other people,
A descriptive, objective poem:
Behind a wall two inverts carried on.
It's a verse of mine from when
I was still growing.

MICHAEL PALMA

If you don't know what it means in English to maroon
Think of a runaway black slave
He's a maroon
And through one of those semantic
Conversions that are the jewel of languages
To maroon someone
Means on the contrary actively to abandon him
Especially on an island. A desert island.
The verb as is clear goes back to the eighteenth century
And the classic example which is equally clear
Cites Jan Svilt, *homosexual sailor marooned.*
The verb is regular.

MICHAEL PALMA

Se mangiano carne
Le tartarughine
Diventano cattive
Diventano carnivore,
Le vedi che scattano
Dal fondo del giardino
Se gliela metti lì
Sulla piastrella invece della
Fettina di banana
Della lattughina . . .

2 0 0 5

Da Marte dio crudo della guerra
La voglia di legare il cadavere al carro
E di trascinarlo ogni mattina,
Da Mercurio l'idea di piantarla
E di farselo pagare.
Perché tutto prima o poi diventa musical
Carta da gioco figurina,
Hitler e il Feroce Saladino
Dracula l'impalatore
E senza più coscienza di dolore:
Non c'è voce nelle pietre
Né parola che diventi carne o sangue.
(All'asta battuta da Bolaffi
Curioso il timbro a cuore o a C
Apposto a Firenze in ricezione
Sulle due lettere dal campo alla famiglia
Dello studente volontario a Curtatone.)

2 0 0 5

If they eat meat
The tiny turtles
They get nasty
They become carnivores.
You see them dash
From down in the garden
If you put it there
On the tile instead of
The little slice of banana
The shred of lamb's lettuce . . .

MOIRA EGAN AND DAMIANO ABENI

From Mars cruel god of war
The desire to tie the corpse to the chariot
And drag it around each morning,
From Mercury the idea to put a stop to that
And buy the body back.
Because everything sooner or later becomes a musical
Or a collectible card or figurine
Hitler or the Fierce Saladin
Dracula the Impaler
All stripped of any awareness of suffering:
There is no voice in stones
No word that turns to flesh or blood.
(At that auction held at Bolaffi,
Those intriguing heart-shaped or "C" postmarks
Stamped after their arrival in Florence
On two letters sent from the field to the family
Of a student volunteer at Curtatone.)

GEOFFREY BROCK

Qualcuno mi ha detto
che certo le mie poesie
non cambieranno il mondo.

Io risponde che certo sì
le mie poesie
non cambieranno il mondo.

1 9 7 4

I marocchini con i tappeti
sembrano santi e invece
sono mercanti.

1 9 7 4

Anche quando sembra che la giornata
sia passata come un'ala di rondine,
come una manciata di polvere
gettata e che non è possibile
raccogliere e la descrizione
il racconto non trovano necessità

Patrizia Cavalli

1949–

I was told
there's no way
my poems will change the world.

Yes I say
my poems will
in no way change the world.

BARRY CALLAGHAN AND
FRANCESCA VALENTE

The Moroccans with their carpets
seem like saints
but they're salesmen.

KENNETH KOCH

Even when it seems that the day
has passed like a swallow's wing,
like a handful of tossed
dust that can never be
regathered and no description
no story is needed

né ascolto, c'è sempre una parola
una paroletta da dire
magari per dire
che non c'è niente da dire.

1 9 7 4

Adesso che il tempo sembra tutto mio
e nessuno mi chiama per il pranzo e per la cena,
adesso che posso rimanere a guardare
come si scioglie una nuvola e come si scolora,
come cammina un gatto per il tetto
nel lusso immenso di una esplorazione, adesso
che ogni giorno mi aspetta
la sconfinata lunghezza di una notte
dove non c'è richiamo e non c'è più ragione
di spogliarsi in fretta per riposare dentro
l'accecante dolcezza di un corpo che mi aspetta,
adesso che il mattino non ha mai principio
e silenzioso mi lascia ai miei progetti
a tutte le cadenze della voce, adesso
vorrei improvvisamente la prigione.

1 9 8 1

Indietro, in piedi, da lontano,
di passaggio, tassametro in attesa
la guardavo, i capelli guardavo,
e che vedevo? Mio teatro ostinato,
rifiuto del sipario, sempre aperto teatro,
meglio andarsene a spettacolo iniziato.

1 9 9 9

or heard, there is always a word
a small word one can say
if only to say
there's nothing to say.

GEOFFREY BROCK

Now that time seems all mine
and no one calls me for lunch or dinner,
now that I can stay to watch
how a cloud loosens and loses its color,
how a cat walks on the roof
in the immense luxury of a prowl, now
that what waits for me every day
is the unlimited length of a night
where there is no call and no longer a reason
to undress in a hurry to rest inside
the blinding sweetness of a body that waits for me,
now that the morning no longer has a beginning
and silently leaves me to my plans,
to all the cadences of my voice, now
suddenly I would like prison.

JUDITH BAUMEL

From behind, standing, from a distance,
in passing, the taxi-meter running,
I would watch her, I would watch her hair,
and what would I see? My stubborn theater,
curtain won't fall, my always-open theater . . .
Best to leave as soon as the show begins.

GEOFFREY BROCK

Pigra divinità e pigra sorte
cosa non faccio per incoraggiarvi,
quante occasioni con fatica vi offro
solo perché possiate rivelarvi!
A voi mi espongo e faccio vuoto il campo
e non per me, non è nel mio interesse,
solo per farvi esistere mi rendo
facile visibile bersaglio. Vi do
anche un vantaggio, a voi l'ultima mossa,
io non rispondo, a voi quell'imprevisto
ultimo tocco, rivelazione
di potenza e grazia: ci fosse un merito
sarebbe solo vostro. Perché io non voglio
essere fabbrica della fortuna
mia, vile virtù operaia che
mi annoia. Avevo altre ambizioni, sognavo
altre giustizie, altre armonie: ripulse
superiori, predilezioni oscure,
d'immeritati amori regalìe.

2006

Eravamo tutti perdonati.
Perchè l'aria ci assorbiva
nella sua temperatura. La testa
piegata di lato, la guancia che tocca
la spalla e quasi l'accarezza. Liscio
il respiro, sollevato volante.
Il cuore pattinava controvento.
Oh varietà! Oh insieme!
Ogni strada è felice

Lazy gods and lazy fortune,
what I wouldn't do to encourage you,
how many chances do I tirelessly give you
so that you may reveal yourself!
I expose myself to you and clear the field
but not for me, it's not for my sake,
it's just in order to make you exist
that I turn into a visible, easy target. And I give you
an advantage: the last move is yours,
I don't take my turn, yours is that unexpected
final move, a revelation
of power and grace: whatever credit is due
will be yours. Because I don't want to be
the maker of my fortune,
that laborer's low virtue
bores me. I had other ambitions, I dreamed
of other justices, other harmonies: high
rejections, obscure predilections,
gifts of loves I don't deserve.

SUSAN STEWART AND
BRUNELLA ANTOMARINI

We were all forgiven.
Because the air absorbed us
in its climate. The head
cocked to the side, a cheek touching
a shoulder and almost caressing it. The breath
was smooth, lifted up in flight.
The heart skating against the wind.
O variety! O togetherness!
Each street is happy

se una pioggetta tiepida
intimidisce la luce
e la costringe a spargersi senza predizioni.
Più che perdono. Eravamo accolti.

2 0 0 6

Bene, vediamo un po' come fiorisci,
come ti apri, di che colore hai i petali,
quanti pistilli hai, che trucchi usi
per spargere il tuo polline e ripeterti,
se hai fioritura languida o violenta,
che portamento prendi, dove inclini,
se nel morire infradici o insecchisci,
avanti su, io guardo, tu fiorisci.

2 0 0 6

if a mild drizzle
overwhelms the light
and makes it scatter
any which way.
More than forgiven. We were welcome.

SUSAN STEWART AND
BRUNELLA ANTOMARINI

So, let's see how you flower,
how you open, the color of your petals,
how many pistils you have, what tricks you use
to scatter pollen and replicate yourself,
whether your blossoming is languid or violent,
which posture you take, where you lean,
if when dying you dry up or go sour:
come on now, I look, you flower.

MOIRA EGAN AND DAMIANO ABENI

UN'INDICAZIONE

È bello essere uno
del posto.

È bello quando in giro
si accostano
per chiederti la strada.

E se poi non la sai,
purché il discorso
non cada
vorresti improvvisare,
inventarla.

Ma un altro passa, sente di cosa si parla,
s'intromette, si volta
già dalla parte giusta, chiude gli occhi,
stende una mano.

E tu, che prima eri tanto di fretta,
ascolti raccontare di vialoni,
bivi, rotonde.

Rimani lì zitto, invisibile,
come uno spirito che deve
venire al mondo
e cerca qualcuno, qualcosa
che ce lo metta.

2002

Umberto Fiori

1949–

GIVING DIRECTIONS

It's good to be a person
from the locality.

It's good when you're out
and they come up
to ask you the way.

And if you don't know it,
to prevent the conversation
from flagging,
you would like to make up something,
invent the way.

But someone else comes by, hears what you're talking about,
butts in, turning already
towards the right way, shutting his eyes,
and stretching out an arm.

And you, who were before in such a hurry,
listen to the tale of avenues,
junctions and roundabouts.

You're stuck there speechless, invisible
like a soul that has to
come into the world
and is looking for someone, or something,
to get it an entrance there.

ALISTAIR ELLIOT

MUSEO

Guarda come riposa,
come regna il coltello
nella vetrina
senza la mano del soldato.

Come rimane uguale, la statua.
Dalla fronte bombata, dalle ombre
di questa guancia di legno,
senti com'è lontano
il modello.

Come vorrei anch'io
spegnermi nella luce
della cosa che resta,
essere stato.

2 0 0 2

AL CIRCO

In mezzo al cerchio illuminato, ritto
sui polpacci di zucchero filato,
appende le ciglia al cielo
il Clown Bianco; grattugia l'ukulele,
apre la bocca a cuore, fa un sospiro:
comincia la serenata.

È il momento. Dall'ombra
scoppia un barrito
laido, slabbrato. Scalcia come un cerbiatto,

MUSEUM

See how the knife rests,
how it reigns there
in its glass case,
free from the soldier's hand.

And how unchanging the statue is.
Feel how far—from this bulging brow,
from the shadows
of this wooden cheek—
the model is.

How I too would like
to go out in the light
of the thing that remains,
having been.

GEOFFREY BROCK

AT THE CIRCUS

At the center of the lit circle, rising
from cotton-candy calf muscles,
the White Clown ushers his
eyebrows skyward. He grates his ukulele,
opens a heart-shaped mouth, inhales—
his serenade begins.

Now's the time. From the shadows,
a blast like a trumpeting elephant:
obscene, ragged. The Auguste capers like a fawn,

scappa, ciabatta in giro l'Augusto
col suo trombone. L'oro della coulisse
va e torna dall'infinito.

Tutto sa di pantera,
di piscio, di mentine. Lo sguardo fisso
alla rissa tra i lacrimoni immobili
e le scarpacce che ridono,
il bambino diventa
sempre più serio, sempre più severo.

2 0 0 2

darts away, pads around
with his trombone. The gold of the slide
slips into and out of the infinite.

Everything smells of panther
and piss and mint. His gaze fixed
on the clash between the welled tears
and the awful laughing shoes,
the little boy grows
ever more grave, ever more severe.

GEOFFREY BROCK

SOLTANTO

Soltanto questo crescere
indifferente allo sguardo e pieno
di ciò che ha visto
era possibile: se ci sono
due barche
non contava il loro punto d'incontro, ma la bellezza
del cammino dentro l'acqua: solo così,
solo adesso, non spiegare.
Ed è atroce
ma bisogna dire di no alla sua fronte che
piange e non capisce, e ama
come per millenni si è amato, promettendo
in una terrazza buia, accarezzandosi
tra le foglie minacciose.

1 9 7 6

Ora c'è la disadorna
e si compiono gli anni, a manciate,
con ingegno di forbici e
una boria che accosta
al gas la bocca

Milo de Angelis

1951–

ONLY

Only this growing
indifferent to the glance and full
of what was seen
was possible: if there are
two boats
it isn't their meeting point that mattered, but the beauty
of the journey in the water: only this way,
only now, don't explain.
And it's cruel
but you must say no to his face that
weeps and doesn't understand, and loves
as people have loved for millennia, vowing
to a dark balcony, stroking themselves
among the threatening leaves.

LAWRENCE VENUTI

Now she is unadorned
and the years come to pass, in handfuls,
with the wit of shears and
an arrogance that draws
to the gas the mouth

dura fino alla sua spina
dove crede
oppure i morti arrancano verso un campo
che ha la testa cava
e le miriadi
si gettano nel battesimo
per un soffio.

1976

RITROVO UNA SINTASSI

Ritrovo una sintassi nei secoli già studiati
allontanando sia l'oriente sia le nubi.
È forte plasmare il sogno con ciò che l'idea abbraccia.
Nessuno violerà un sogno ereditato.

Ecco gelarsi, nel torace, le corse infantili
e alte che esso spinse. A volte so fermare
gli occhi sui cartelli stradali, sulla
forza d'urto precisa, che restituisce
a quel teatro la sua paura di morire.

1976

Milano era asfalto, asfalto liquefatto. Nel deserto
di un giardino avvenne la carezza, la penombra
addolcita che invase le foglie, ora senza giudizio,
spazio assoluto di una lacrima. Un istante
in equilibrio tra due nomi avanzò verso di noi,
si fece luminoso, si posò respirando sul petto,
sulla grande presenza sconosciuta. Morire fu quello

persistent down to the spine
where it believes
or else the dead trudge toward a field
with a hollow head
and the myriads
hurl themselves into the baptism
for a breath.

LAWRENCE VENUTI

I RECOVER A SYNTAX

I recover a syntax in centuries already studied
dismissing both the east and the clouds.
Molding the dream with what the idea embraces is hard.
No one will violate an inherited dream.

Here the loud, childlike races urged by it
freeze in the chest. Sometimes I can fix
my eyes on the street signs, on the
precise force of impact, which restores
to that theater its fear of death.

LAWRENCE VENUTI

Milan was asphalt, liquid asphalt. In the desert
of a garden, there was a caress, the melting
penumbra invading the leaves, the hour without censure,
a tear's absolute space. An instant,
balanced between two names, came toward us,
luminous, settling, breathing, on the chest
of the great unknown presence. To die was that

sbriciolarsi delle linee, noi lì e il gesto ovunque,
noi dispersi nelle supreme tensioni dell'estate,
noi tra le ossa e l'essenza della terra.

2005

In te si radunano tutte le morti, tutti
i vetri spezzati, le pagine secche, gli squilibri
del pensiero, si radunano in te, colpevole
di tutte le morti, incompiuta e colpevole,
nella veglia di tutte le madri, nella tua
immobile. Si radunano lì, nelle tue
deboli mani. Sono morte le mele di questo mercato,
queste poesie tornano nella loro grammatica,
nella stanza d'albergo, nella baracca
di ciò che non si unisce, anime senza sosta,
labbra invecchiate, scorza strappata al tronco.
Sono morte. Si radunano lì. Hanno sbagliato,
hanno sbagliato l'operazione.

2005

Il luogo era immobile, la parola scura. Era quello
il luogo stabilito. Addio memoria di notti
lucenti, addio grande sorriso il luogo era lì.
Respirare fu un buio di persiane, uno stare primitivo.
Silenzio e deserto si scambiavano volto e noi
parlavamo a una lampada. Il luogo era quello. I tram
passavano radi. Venere ritornava nella sua baracca.
Dalla gola guerriera si staccano episodi. Non abbiamo
detto più niente. Il luogo era quello. Era lì
che stavi morendo.

2005

crumbling of lines, we were there and the gesture was everywhere,
we were scattered in the high tensions of summer,
we were caught between the bones and the essence of the earth.

SUSAN STEWART AND PATRIZIO CECCAGNOLI

In you all deaths gather, all
the broken glasses, the sere pages, the derangements
of thought, they gather in you, guilty
of all deaths, incomplete and guilty,
in the wake of every mother, in your wake,
motionless. They gather there, in your
weak hands. The apples of this market are death,
these poems retreat into their grammar,
in the hotel room, in the hut
of what does not join, souls without rest,
aged lips, bark ripped from the trunk.
They are dead. They gather there. They failed,
the operation failed, they failed.

SUSAN STEWART AND PATRIZIO CECCAGNOLI

The place was motionless, the word obscure. That was
the place we agreed on. Goodbye, memory of the sparkling
nights, goodbye, big smile, the place was there.
To breathe was a darkness shutters had made, a primitive state.
Silence and desert were switching positions and we
were talking to a lamp. The place was that one. The trolleys
rarely passed. Venus was returning to her hut.
Out of the warrior throat, episodes broke free. We didn't
say anything more. The place was that one. It was there
that you were dying.

SUSAN STEWART AND PATRIZIO CECCAGNOLI

E tu le ricordi le cene, le sere, lunghe
del jazz, il sole ultimo, caldo nella stanza,
traverso le serrande del crepuscolo, ai muri
battuti dall'arancio, ed al profumo degli intingoli . . .

Fummo mai di nessuno, nel più nostro
folle amore di noi stessi, e nell'altro
consunto, appassionato spasmo d'ideale
e il cartoncino di stagnola, di paradiso artificiale,

e le bevute, tirando di Joyce e di Brecht . . .
E questo mondo ottuso, che si voleva cambiare,
ora che soli e accompagnati, in ore querule
per caso ci s'incontra, vagando, prima d'un temporale . . .

                    1 9 8 9

Perché ci fanno sentire colpevoli le cose,
anche un aspirapolvere, un cesto colmo
di panni già lavati, da stirare, l'accorgersi
di vivere senza cura di esse, e soprattutto

senza un amore che non sia rimorso
per il nostro essere cosí pigri e viziati,
per il nostro mancare a chi ci amò in esse,
ancora, a chi ama con amore di madre . . .

Gianni D'Elia

1953–

You remember them, the dinners, the long jazz-
filled evenings, the last sun in the warm room
filtered through the twilight shutters, orange
beating on the walls, the fragrant sauces . . .

Nobody ever had a claim upon us,
mad with self love, with no room left for other
agonizing, passionate ideals—
the tinfoil parcel, a false paradise,

drinking and getting high on Joyce and Brecht . . .
The stupid, stubborn world we would have changed,
while now, alone, in company, in peevish
hours we meet by chance, as a storm brews . . .

CHRISTOPHER WHYTE AND MARCO FAZZINI

Because things make us feel we are to blame,
even a vacuum cleaner or a basket
piled with washing waiting to be ironed,
the fact that we ignore them, especially

that all the love we have is our remorse
at being so spoiled and lazy, at still failing
to live up to whoever loved us through them,
and loves us still, the way a mother loves . . .

Perché in una sí trattenuta gratitudine,
è ancora con ansia filiale che vogliamo
un desiderio sterile in canto seriale,
ed in compianto rituale il nostro malessere . . .

1 9 8 9

ALTRE ISTRUZIONI

«L'impoetico: raccontalo a lampi.
Nomina le nuove impercepite
cose del mondo in cui ora siamo
immersi. E siano i versi

attenti al comune, alla prosa
che servi. E all'arso
cicalío delle stampanti, poi che canto
è forza di memoria e sentimento

e oggi nient'altro che il frammento
sembra ci sia dato per istanti,
tu pure tentalo, se puoi, come tanti
durando un poco oltre quel vento . . .»

1 9 9 6

Because, while holding back our gratitude,
we still with filial anxiety
turn barren longing to sequential song
and our unease to ritual lament . . .

CHRISTOPHER WHYTE AND MARCO FAZZINI

FURTHER INSTRUCTIONS

"The impoetic: tell it to the lightning.
Name the imperceived new
things of the world in which we're now
immersed. And let the verse

be sensitive to prose, the commonness
you serve. And to the arid
chatter of the press, for singing
is duress of memory and sentiment

and today nothing but the fragment
seems to be given in the flash,
try it, if you can, as others have,
lasting a little longer beyond that wind . . ."

CARLA BILLITTERI

A me creduta esangue, non veduta,
un'oncia di coraggio, una manciata
di ragione scovata e già perduta,
lo dica qui dei vati la brigata,

di astrologi e indovini, il ciel li aiuta,
a che punto, lo dica di volata,
io sono con la vita (a mia insaputa)
e con la morte . . . a che punto agguantata

e goduta, di che godente . . . O notte,
che su di me t'inarchi e mi tormenti,
mi sono inutili i pensieri . . . Notte

sifone del mio sangue e alba di lenti
lenti piaceri, disperdi le rotte
d'amore, sveleniscile ai tuoi venti.

1 9 8 9

Signore caro tu vedi il mio stato,
vedi che ho l'avvenire nel passato,
e questo rotto scoppiato e crepato.
Vita non sono mia ma del peccato.

Patrizia Valduga

1953–

Let them tell the one they failed to see,
thought bloodless, now I've found and lost an ounce
of courage, a mere smattering of sense,
let the brigade of seers, soothsayers,

astrologers (God help them!) tell me here
and now the stage I've reached (unwittingly)
with life, with death, to what extent I've been
caught up with, how far taken pleasure of

and what it is that pleasures me . . . Oh night,
arched over me, tormenting me, I have
no use for thoughts . . . Oh night siphoning off

my blood, oh dawn of much protracted joys,
scatter and confound the routes of love
and give their poisons issue in your winds.

CHRISTOPHER WHYTE AND MARCO FAZZINI

You see, kind lord, the state I am reduced
to, see my future's in the past, a past
that's broken, fissured, detonated. I
don't own my life. Rather, I'm owned by sin.

O notte senza oggetti dal tuo lato,
dove non corre tempo, io ho cercato
una gioia lontana dal mercato
del giorno che m'imbara, disensato.

O ombra del morire, se in agguato
alla memoria chiami il tempo andato,
lo chiami come un sogno già sognato,

su un amore zoppo è sempre andato,
né medica la morte, se è malato,
se vive come un morto sotterrato.

1 9 8 9

DA REQUIEM

Oh no, non lui, Signore, prendi me,
che sto morendo più di lui, Signore,
liberalo dal male e prendi me!
prendi me, per giustizia, me, Signore,
per la vita morente dentro me,
per la vita che vive in lui . . . Signore,
sii giusto, prendi me, donna da niente,
e vissuta così, morentemente . . .

1 9 9 4

Oh night deprived of objects, at your side,
where time's flow is arrested, I have sought
a joy sequestered from the marketplace
of senseless day which turns me to a corpse.

Oh shade of dying, if in ambushing
memory you summon up time past,
you're summoning a dream already dreamed

about a love that always went on crutches,
a love whose malady death cannot cure,
for it lives like a dead man underground.

CHRISTOPHER WHYTE

AND MARCO FAZZINI

FROM REQUIEM

Oh no, not him, my Lord, take me—
I'm dying more than he is, Lord,
free him from sickness and take me!
Take me, it's only just, my Lord,
for life is dying out in me,
for life still lives in him . . . Oh Lord,
be just, take me: take worthless me,
who've lived my whole life dyingly . . .

GEOFFREY BROCK

DA CENTO QUARTINE

8

Ora lo sai: ho bisogno di parole.
Devi imparare a amarmi a modo mio.
È la mente malata che lo vuole:
parla, ti prego! parla, Cristoddio!

1 7

Fa' presto, immobilizzami le braccia,
crocefiggimi, inchiodami al tuo letto;
consolami, accarezzami la faccia;
scopami quando meno me l'aspetto.

4 5

Da nervi vene valvole ventricoli
da tendini da nervi e cartilagini
papille nervi costole clavicole . . .
in spasmi da ogni poro mi esce l'anima.

4 7

«Allora che l'hai fatta? sei venuta?
e come sei venuta? Dimmi.» Prego?
«Se ti è piaciuto molto sei perduta.»
Non lo posso negare e non lo nego.

7 1

Perché anche il piacere è come un peso
e la mente che è qui mi va anche via?
Su, spiegamelo tu. «Per chi mi hai preso?
per un docente di filosofia?»

FROM ONE HUNDRED QUATRAINS

8

By now you know: I need the words.
You'll learn to give me what I seek.
It's my sick mind, it feeds on words.
I'm begging you, for God's sake: speak!

1 7

Hurry, pin my wrists in place,
nail me to your bed like Christ . . .
comfort me, caress my face . . .
fuck me when I expect it least.

4 5

From nerves veins valves ventricles
from tendons cartilage nerves ducts
from follicles nerves ribs clavicles . . .
from every pore my soul erupts.

4 7

You liked that? you actually came?
but how? Explain to me. But why?
If you got off on that, you're doomed.
A charge I can't and don't deny.

7 1

Why is even pleasure a kind of chore?
Why is what sense I have left leaving me?
Come on, explain. *Who do you take me for,*
your personal doctor of philosophy?

«Vuoi che tutto finisca e niente duri?
che ognuno vada a fare i fatti suoi?
stacco il telefono, chiudo gli scuri:
e che la notte ricominci! Vuoi?»

1997

DA QUARTINE:

SECONDA CENTURIA

107

Io sono sempre stata come sono
anche quando non ero come sono
e no saprà nessuno come sono
perché non sono solo come sono.

122

Lui o un altro che differenza fa
se poi ho da sentirmi sempre sola?
Sola con la mia moribilità . . .
se esistesse questa bella parola . . .

2001

You want it all to end, nothing to last?
Go separate ways, each to his own?
I'll close the shutters, I'll unplug the phone—
let night start over! You want that?

GEOFFREY BROCK

FROM QUATRAINS:

SECOND HUNDRED

1 0 7

I have always been the way I am
even when I wasn't the way I am
and none can ever know the way I am
because I am not merely the way I am.

1 2 2

Him or someone else, what's it to me
if every time I'm lonely afterward?
Alone here with my moribility . . .
if there only were such a lovely word . . .

GEOFFREY BROCK

Per trovare la ragione di un verbo
perché ancora davvero non è tempo
e non sappiamo se accorrere o fuggire.

Fai sera come fosse dicembre
sulle casse innalzate sul cuneo del trasloco
dai forma al buio
mentre il cibo s'infiamma alla parete.

Queste sono le notti di pace occidentale
nei loro raggi vola l'angustia delle biografie
gli acini scuri dei ritratti, i cartigli dei nomi.

Ci difende di lato un'altra quiete
come un peso marino nella iuta
piegato a lungo, con disperazione.

1999

ABBANDONO

Il mio amore è un osso. Sporge sul mondo dal mio petto.
È una delle punte di cancello che circondano i parchi tenebrosi.

Il vento gli arde vicino, la pioggia lo bagna.
È un dettaglio di spina che sibila al freddo dei cespugli.

2003

Antonella Anedda

1955–

To unearth the reason for a verb
because the truth is it's not time yet
and we don't know whether to rush forward or take flight.

Make it evening, say an evening in December,
the tea-chests levered up on chocks for removal.
Give form to the darkness
whilst the cooking flares against the wall.

These are the nights of Western peace
and flying in their rays are the cramped biographies,
the berry-dark portraits, the scrolls of names.

A different quietness shields us on one side
like a marine weight wrapped in jute
and folded carefully, with desperation.

JAMIE MCKENDRICK

ABANDONMENT

My love is a bone. It leans out of my chest into the world.
It's one of the gateposts that fence the dusky parks.

The wind is burning next to it, the rain is giving it a bath.
It is a detail from a thorn that whistles to the cold of the brambles.

SUSAN STEWART AND GIAN MARIA ANNOVI

FIGLIA (A MIA FIGLIA)

Mi piace la sua fierezza quando combatte contro di me
e grida «non e giusto». E i suoi occhi a fessura
come le persiane nelle città di mare.
La sua vita piena di falò—visibili e invisibili—
fuochi che ardono a ogni anno che avanza
per farla vivere ancora e ancora in un miracolo di fumo.
È questo stare al caldo, credo, a darle il senso del perdono
quel suo baciarmi la spalla all'improvviso, se la sgrido.
Forse ricorda i ferri da cui è nata
e il cui segno mi attraversa la pelle senza orrore.
È uscita dalla pancia mentre io dormivo. Ci unisce la pace
l'assenza di urla, il mio pudore.
Siamo una tela di Giovanni Bellini: una vergine e un coniglio gentile.

2 0 0 3

VENDETTA (DÀ GIOIA SOLO SE LETTA A RITMO SPEZZATO, FERMANDOSI A OGNI PUNTO, SCHIUDENDO LEGGERMENTE LE LABBRA AI DUE PUNTI)

Che: peccato morire amore mio. Dire: «non ti amo più»
così nel vuoto. Che: vergogna la voce spazientita la fretta.
La distanza tra il primo sussurro innamorato e questo timbro
nuovo. Che poca vergogna ho. di averti ucciso e messo qui.
sotto la stessa distesa che hai creato.
La: distesa. È: una tela. È: bianca. È: un lenzuolo.
È: una terra su cui è caduta la neve.

FOR MY DAUGHTER

I love her fierceness when she fights me,
shouting "Not fair!" Her eyes slitting
like shutters in cities by the sea.
Her life is rife with bonfires—seen and unseen—
fires that burn through the turning years
bringing her to life again, and again, in a miracle of smoke.
This heat gives her a sense of forgiveness—or so I imagine—
she kisses my back, capriciously, when I scold her.
Maybe she recalls the scalpel by which she was born.
Easy, the mark of its slash in my skin.
She rose from my belly as I slept. We're bound together
by peace, no shrieks of pain, and my modesty.
We're a canvas by Giovanni Bellini: a virgin and a sweet rabbit.

SARAH ARVIO

VENDETTA (GIVES JOY ONLY IF READ IN A BROKEN RHYTHM, PAUSING AT A PERIOD, PARTING THE LIPS AT A COLON)

This: sad for my love to die. Saying: I don't love you anymore,
thus, in the void. This: a shame, the vexed voice, the hurry.
The distance between the first loving whisper and this new sound.
How little shame I feel. to have killed you and put you there.
beneath the vastness that you made.
The: vast. Is: a cloth. Is: white. Is: a sheet.
Is: land where snow fell.

Sst. starai là da solo. Non più sopra. ma. sotto. come si addice
ai morti, come si addice ai semi. e. ai gigli prima de spuntare.
Sentirai come dei griffi in corsa: sono gli uccelli i topi le mie
stesse mani ossute che adoravi la mia lingua che ha sete.
Brr. amore. che. pena ho di vederti reso più piccolo dal gelo così
privo di doni in questa tomba dove non posso piangerti
ma solo scavare fino alla terra fino al suo ferro
al fuoco che ora la stringe e che mi onora.

2 0 0 3

Shh . . . you will be alone there. No longer above. no. below. as is
natural for the dead, for seeds, for lilies not yet sprouted.
You will feel a sort of scratching on your body. birds mice
my bony hands you loved, my tongue and its thirst.
Brrr . . . love. how. sad. to see you shrunken by the cold
stripped of your gifts in this grave where I can't grieve
for you. can only dig down into the earth the iron core
the fire that rings the core and honors me.

SARAH ARVIO

Antonella Anedda 579

C'è silenzio tra una pagina e l'altra.
La lunga distesa della terra fino al bosco
dove l'ombra raccolta
si sottrae al giorno,
dove le notti spuntano
separate e preziose
come frutta sui rami.
In questo delirio
luminoso e geografico
io non so ancora
se essere il paese che attraverso
o il viaggio che vi compio.

1 9 8 0

Ho spesso immaginato che gli sguardi
sopravvivano all'atto del vedere
come fossero aste,
tragitti misurati, lance
in una battaglia.
Allora penso che dentro una stanza
appena abbandonata
simili tratti debbano restare
qualche tempo sospesi ed incrociati
nell'equilibrio del loro disegno
intatti e sovrapposti come i legni
dello shangai.

1 9 8 7

Valerio Magrelli

1 9 5 7 –

There's silence between one page and another.
The long stretch of the land up to the woods
where gathered
shadows escape the day
and nights show through
discrete and precious
like fruit on branches.
In this luminous
and geographic frenzy
I am still unsure
whether to be the landscape I am crossing
or the journey I am making there.

JONATHAN GALASSI

I have often imagined that glances
survive the act of seeing
as if they were poles,
measuring rods, lances
thrown in a battle.
Then I think that in a room
one has just left
those same lines must stay behind
sometimes suspended there and crisscrossed
in the equilibrium of their design
untouched and overlaid like the wooden pieces
in a game of pick-up-sticks.

DANA GIOIA

Amo i gesti imprecisi,
uno che inciampa, l'altro
che fa urtare il bicchiere,
quello che non ricorda,
chi è distratto, la sentinella
che non sa arrestare il battito
breve delle palpebre,
mi stanno a cuore
perché vedo in loro il tremore,
il tintinnio familiare
del meccanismo rotto.
L'oggetto intatto tace, non ha voce
ma solo movimento. Qui invece
ha ceduto il congegno,
il gioco delle parti,
un pezzo si separa,
si annuncia.
Dentro qualcosa balla.

1987

Che la materia provochi il contagio
se toccata nelle sue fibre ultime
recisa come il vitello dalla madre
come il maiale dal proprio cuore
stridendo nel vedere le sue membra strappate;

Che tale schianto generi
la stessa energia che divampa
quando la società si lacera, sacro velo del tempio
e la testa del re cade spiccata dal corpo dello stato
affinché il taumaturgo diventi la ferita;

I love uncertain gestures:
someone who stumbles, someone else
who bangs his glass,
who can't remember,
gets distracted, or the sentinel
who can't stop the slight flickering
of his lashes—
they matter to me
because in them I see the wobbling,
the familiar rattle
of the ruptured mechanism.
The whole object makes no sound,
has no voice; it only moves.
But here the apparatus,
the play of parts, has given way,
a piece breaks off,
declares itself.
Inside, something dances.

JONATHAN GALASSI

That matter engenders contagion
if interfered with in its deepest fibres
cut out from its mother like a veal calf
like the pig from its own heart
screaming at the sight of its torn entrails;

That this destruction generates
the same energy that blazes out
when society turns on itself, the temple's veil torn
and the king's head axed from the body of the state
until the faith healer becomes the wound;

Valerio Magrelli

Che l'abbraccio del focolare sia radiazione
rogo della natura che si disgrega
inerme davanti al sorriso degli astanti
per offrire un lievissimo aumento
della temperatura ambientale;

Che la forma di ogni produzione
implichi effrazione, scissione, un addio
e la storia sia l'atto del combùrere
e la Terra una tenera catasta di legname
messa a asciugare al sole,

è incredibile, no?

1992

L'IMBALLATORE

Cos'è la traduzione? Su un vassoio
la testa pallida e fiammante d'un poeta.
—V. NABOKOV

L'imballatore chino
che mi svuota la stanza
fa il mio stesso lavoro.
Anch'io faccio cambiare casa
alle parole, alle parole
che non sono mie,
e metto mano a ciò
che non conosco senza capire
cosa sto spostando.
Sto spostando me stesso
traducendo il passato in un presente
che viaggia sigillato

That the hearth's embrace is radiation
nature's pyre which unravels
helplessly before the smiling company
so as to effect the slightest increase
of the surrounding temperature;

That the form of every production implies
breaking and entry, fission, a final leavetaking
and that history is the act of combustion
and the Earth a tender stockpile of firewood
left out to dry in the sun,

is hard to credit, is it not?

JAMIE MCKENDRICK

THE MOVER

What is translation? On a platter
a poet's pale and glaring head.
—VLADIMIR NABOKOV

The bent man
emptying my room
does the same work I do.
I too help words
change houses, words
that aren't mine,
and handle something
unfamiliar without knowing
what it is I'm moving.
I am moving myself
translating the past into a present
that stays sealed in transit

racchiuso dentro pagine
o dentro casse con la scritta
«Fragile» di cui ignoro l'interno.
È questo il futuro, la spola, il traslato,
il tempo manovale e citeriore,
trasferimento e tropo,
la ditta di trasloco.

1 9 9 2

CODICE A BARRE

Onoriamo l'altissimo vessillo
che sventola sul regno della cosa
l'anima crittografica del prezzo
rosa del nome e nome della rosa
mazzo di steli, fascio
di tendini e di vene
—polso
per auscultare
il battito del soldo.

1 9 9 9

DAL NOSTRO INVIATO A:

TROIS-RIVIÈRES, QUÉBEC, CAPITALE

MONDIALE DELLA CELLULOSA

Questo odore di pesce e di zolfo,
quest'aria dove come fuochi fatui
guizzano zolfanelli
e pesciolini celesti,

packaged in pages
or crates marked
"fragile," whose contents I don't know.
This is the future, the shuttle, the shift,
manual, otherwhere Time,
transfer and trope,
the moving company.

ANTHONY MOLINO

BAR CODE

Let us honour the topmost banner
fluttering over the kingdom of commodities—
the encoded soul of price
rose of the name and name of the rose,
bundle of stems, fasces
of tendons and veins—
wrist on which
to auscultate
the pulse of money.

JAMIE MCKENDRICK

FROM OUR CORRESPONDENT IN:

TROIS-RIVIÈRES, QUÉBEC,

CELLULOSE CAPITAL OF THE WORLD

This smell of fish and sulfur,
this air where matches
and little celestial fish
flicker like will-o'-the-wisps,

non ha a che fare con reti
né con fiamme,
bensì con una lenta metamorfosi
del legno, con tronchi
macerati che diventano zuppa
e pappa e magma e fibre: la carta.
Sento il mondo corrompersi, disfarsi
e Dafne proseguire la sua corsa
per diventare, dopo fronda,
pagina.

1 9 9 9

DAL NOSTRO INVIATO A:

DRESDA, PIAZZA DEL TEATRO

Non troppo a lungo,
sull'acciottolato.
La statua equestre, venga
via, raffigura il re.
Sì, il traduttore di Dante,
ora muoviamoci.
Bello il teatro, bello,
però andiamo
perché questo è pavé contaminato
(un incidente nucleare accanto
alla cava) e noi qui siamo già
larve su lastra, lèmuri,
turisti ragiologici, ampolline,
vetro che soffia un soffio di elettroni.

1 9 9 9

has nothing to do with nets
or flames,
but with the slow metamorphosis
of wood, with macerated
logs that turn into thick soup
and pap and magma and pith: paper.
I feel the world going corrupt, undoing itself
and Daphne fleeing down her path
only to become a leafy branch, and then
a page.

RICCARDO DURANTI AND

ANAMARÍA CROWE SERRANO

FROM OUR CORRESPONDENT IN:

THEATRE SQUARE, DRESDEN

Don't let's hang about
on the cobblestones.
The equestrian statue—keep
going—represents the king.
Yes, the Dante translator.
Now let's move on.
Lovely theatre, first-rate, but
no point in dawdling
because this paving is contaminated
(a nuclear accident
near the quarry) and here we are
already like ghosts on this x-ray plate, like ghouls,
radiological tourists, little glass vessels
blown with a breeze of electrons.

JAMIE MCKENDRICK

QUASI UN'ALLEGORIA

In questi giorni gallinelle d'acqua
si tuffano a pescare. Se riemergono
più in là, è con l'alborella
d'argento dentro la bocca. I pocchi cigni
candidamente stolti che le incrociano
nuotano al largo alteri, come se
non ne sapessero nulla. Però fingono
dall'alto di inutili, lunghissimi colli.

(La notte li senti sbattere le ali, cadenzare
lo sforzo quando cercano, ma con quale fatica,
di prendere il volo)

1999

IL SACCHEGGIO

Non c'erano allarmi, sentinelle: come avrebbero potuto esserci? Anche le
porte erano spalancate, e se potessimo tornare indietro certo faremmo lo
stesso. Indifesi, non preferibile? Inermi?

Ora seguiamo questi sconosciuti, che ci conducono con loro senza
amarci, senza curiosità o comprensione, solo abbastanza convinti del nos-
tro valore, e forse decisi a ricavare da noi qualche vantaggio. Passeremo di
mano in mano, sui mercati della grande pianura. Saremo sempre più muti,

Fabio Pusterla

1957–

ALMOST AN ALLEGORY

These are the days when gallinules
dive down for fish. When they resurface
farther on, it's with silver bleaks
caught in their bills. The few frankly
silly swans that cross their paths
swim haughtily away, as if they know
nothing of all that. But they are posing,
up there above their useless, endless necks.

(At night you hear them beat their wings,
giving a rhythm to their efforts, so laborious,
to take flight)

GEOFFREY BROCK

PLUNDERED

There were no alarms, no sentries: how could there have been? The doors
were even standing open, and if we could do it again we wouldn't change
a thing. Defenseless—isn't it better that way? Unarmed?

Now we follow these strangers, who lead us along without loving us,
without curiosity or comprehension, merely sufficiently convinced of our
value, and perhaps intent on profiting from us. We will be passed from
hand to hand in the markets of the great prairie. We will grow ever qui-

sempre più condannati a rinchiuderci nella nostra cieca solitudine di oggetti.

Sotto l'azione di innumerevoli stracci, lasceremo che vada cancellata ogni minuscola traccia della nostra origine.

1 9 9 9

STELLA, METEORA,

QUALCOSA DI FILANTE

Quello che esce da un palazzo con il casco integrale
e va saltando verso un pomeriggio d'asfalto
e di vento sul collo, impaziente, e pregusta
l'odore di miscela e motore a due tempi
o forse d'erba appena tagliata, i chilometri brevi

che sfrecceranno senza impegno, pure immagini
di volti e corpi in fuga, le finestre
come schermi o intraviste nostalgie, dimenticabili
tristezze: una luce lo accompagna. Andare via,
soltanto andare, smarrirsi, diventare
stella, meteora, qualcosa di filante.

Periferia del nulla, e in ogni casa
la stessa vampa azzurra, e chiari segni
di speranze deluse e resistenze
nettamente bruciate.
Cani al guinzaglio, vecchi, parchi giochi.
«Lo sa che qui una volta pascolavano
forse quaranta bestie?», dice uno
picchiando col piede il tartan del campetto.

È questo il pomeriggio: un fulgore diffuso,
l'inatteso saluto di chi incroci. E certi sguardi

eter, ever more condemned to wrap ourselves in the blind solitude of ob-
jects.

Beneath the touch of countless rags, we will let the slightest traces of
our origin be erased.

GEOFFREY BROCK

STAR, METEOR, SOME
SHOOTING THING

That one coming out of a building with a crash helmet,
jumping towards an afternoon of tar
and wind against his neck, impatient, savoring
the scent of the two-stroke motor oil
or perhaps of fresh-cut grass, the swift kilometers

that will zip by free of care, pure images
of fleeting faces and bodies, windows
like screens or glimpsed nostalgias, forgettable
sorrows: a light accompanies him. To leave,
just leave, get lost, become
star, meteor, some shooting thing.

Suburbs of nothingness, and in every house
the same blue flame, and clear signs
of frustrated hopes and struggles
that have been utterly crushed.
Dogs on leashes, old folks, playgrounds.
"Do you know that once upon a time some forty head
of cattle used to graze here?" says one,
tapping his foot on the polyurethane surface of the small field.

This is the afternoon: a diffused dazzle,
the unexpected greeting of those you pass by.

complici, che dicono grazie.
Che dicono siamo qui, malgrado tutto.

L'anguria, per esempio, che un gruppo di turchi
ci ha offerto gentilmente era buonissima.

1 9 9 9

CANZONETTA DELL'UNIVERSO

IN ESPANSIONE

La repulsione cosmica
non è una brutta cosa, dottor Newton.
È come uno squarcio di luce nella realtà.

Sapere che una forza
oggi soltanto supposta
spinge tutto alla fuga, alla partenza;
e che ogni corpo
o nube di pulviscolo o galassia
vuole andar via, e tenta di farlo come può;
pensare un'energia che vuole opporsi
anche alla gravità: non è un motivo di gioia?
Di quell'ordine antico,
dell'antica unità,
resta un ronzio di fondo nello spazio, un borborigmo
d'oggetti quasi stellari, nane bianche
intristite, teogonie; ma già universi
chiamano, e se anche le mele o le bombe
continuano a cadere inesorabili,
forse non tutto è perduto. Leggerezze
relative, desideri, qualche forma di felicità.

2 0 0 4

And some knowing looks, that say thank you.
That say we are here, in spite of it all.

The watermelon, for example, that a group of Turks
kindly offered us, was delicious.

CHAD DAVIDSON AND

MARELLA FELTRIN-MORRIS

CANZONETTA ON THE

EXPANDING UNIVERSE

Cosmic repulsion
is not a bad thing, Doctor Newton.
It's like a gash of light in reality.

Knowing that a force
we can today only surmise
urges everything to escape, to depart;
and that each body
or cloud of dust or galaxy
wants to leave, and tries to do so as it can;
to imagine an energy that seeks to resist
even gravity: isn't that a reason to rejoice?
Of that ancient order,
that ancient unity,
only a background buzz remains in space, a grumbling sound
of objects nearly stellar, saddened white
dwarves, theogonies; but already universes
are calling, and even though apples or bombs
continue to fall inexorably,
perhaps not all is lost. Relative
lightnesses, desire, some form of happiness.

CHAD DAVIDSON AND

MARELLA FELTRIN-MORRIS

MAL TARDATO REMO

àlzati, apri la porta, e dopo chiudila,
riaprila, e ancora chiudila, ma quante
volte, ma quante ancora, e quanto grande
il numero degli attimi, dei nudi
minuti, ore che spoglie, a caso, inutili
andarono, chiudendo, aprendo, vennero
affrante, o solite, contale, muti
calcoli, di chi aprí, di chi trattenne
un istante la porta, e poi finisce,
e poi finisce che non apri piú,
non chiudi piú, e poi finisce che tu
stai lí, fermo, alla porta, e poi finisce

1995

Gabriele Frasca

1957–

ILL-BELATED OAR

get up, open and close the door, and now
reopen it, close it once more, how many
times, and how many after that, and how
large the sum of instants, of naked minutes,
of bare, haphazard, useless hours that fled,
opening, closing, that wore themselves out,
becoming commonplace, count them, the mute
math of one who opened, of one who held
the door a while, and then, then it ends up
that you're no longer opening the door,
or closing it, it ends up that you're there,
standing still, at the door, and it ends up

GEOFFREY BROCK

ABOUT THE POETS

Antonella Anedda (Rome 1955–), of Sardinian extraction, received her university degree in art history. Her many books of poetry include *Residenze invernali* (Winter Residences, 1992), *Il catalogo della gioia* (The Catalog of Joy, 2002), and *Dal balcone del corpo* (From the Body's Balcony, 2007). She has also published several books of prose, including *La luce delle cose* (The Light of Things, 2000), and her translations include works by Ovid, Jamie McKendrick, and Anne Carson. She teaches at the University of Lugano.

Raffaello Baldini (Santarcangelo di Romagna 1924–Milan 2005) published his first collection of poetry, *É solitèri* (Solitaire, 1976), when he was in his fifties and went on to publish five others, including *Furistír* (Outsider, 1988), which won the Viareggio Prize, and *Ad nòta* (At Night, 1995), which won the Bagutta Prize. He is best known for his often funny, often moving monologues, written (usually in blank verse) in his native Romagnolo. But to call him one of Italy's best dialect poets of the latter twentieth century may obscure the fact that he was, more simply, one of Italy's best poets.

Giacomo Balla (Turin 1871–Rome 1958), son of a chemist, studied music as a child before turning to visual art after his father's death. He made his debut at the Venice Biennale in 1899 and a decade later was one of the signatories to the Futurist Manifesto. Several of his paintings, including *Lampada ad arco* (Streetlight, 1911) and *Dinamismo di un cane al guinzaglio* (Dynamism of a Dog on a Leash, 1912), are among the most recognizable images of Futurist art. He also participated in the *"parole in libertà"* (words set free) experiments and designed Futurist furniture and clothing.

Giorgio Bassani (Bologna 1916–Rome 2000), known primarily for his fiction, was born to a wealthy Jewish family from Ferrara. One of the established writers against which the avant-garde Gruppo 63 would define themselves, he received the Strega Prize in 1956 for his story collection *Cinque storie Ferrarese* (Five Ferrara Stories) and the Viareggio Prize for his 1962 novel, *Il giardino dei Finzi-Contini* (The Garden of the Finzi-Continis), which was later made into an Oscar-winning film by Vittorio de Sica. Bassani's collected poems, *In rima e senza* (Rhymed and Not, 1982), received the Bagutta Prize.

Attilio Bertolucci (Parma 1911–Rome 2000) published seven volumes of poetry over a span of nearly seventy years, beginning with *Sirio* (Sirius, 1929). His finest works are widely thought to be *Viaggio d'inverno* (Winter Journey, 1971) and *La camera da letto* (The Bedroom, 1984–1988), a two-volume verse novel for which he won his second Viareggio Prize. He is sometimes considered, along with poets such as Sandro Penna and Giorgio Caproni, as part of what Pasolini called the "Sabian line"—an anti-Hermetic strain of modern Italian poetry. He was the father of Bernardo and Giuseppe Bertolucci, both successful filmmakers.

Carlo Betocchi (Turin 1899–Bordighera 1986) led a double life, working for decades as a surveyor and engineer while reading and writing poetry and helping to found the influential Catholic literary journal *Il Frontespizio*, a hotbed of Florentine Hermeticism. Despite his ties to that journal, the Hermetic label seems ill-suited to his work. His books include *Realtà vince il sogno* (Reality Beats Dreams, 1932), *L'estate di San Martino* (St. Martin's Summer, 1961), and *Tutte le poesie* (Complete Poems, 1984), which received the Librex Montale Prize. His work often evokes a Franciscan vision of a natural world steeped in the divine.

Franco Buffoni (Gallarate 1948–) teaches comparative literature at the University of Cassino. His many collections of poems include *Suora carmelitana* (Carmelite Sister, 1997), *Il profilo del Rosa* (The Outline of Monte Rosa, 1999), and *Guerra* (War, 2005), and his prose works include an autobiographical novel, *Piú luce, padre: Dialogo su Dio, la guerra e l'omosessualità* (More Light, Father: A Dialogue on God, War, and Homosexuality, 2006). He edits a journal, *Testo a fronte* (Facing Page), on the theory and practice of poetic translation, and his own translations include an anthology of English Romantic poetry.

Dino Campana (Marradi 1885–Scandicci 1932), Italy's *poète maudit*, suffered from mental illness, as did his mother. In both their cases, one symptom seems to have been a compulsion to wander, and the single book for which he is known, *Canti orfici* (Orphic Songs, 1914), is a visionary account of his physical and spiritual journeys. When Ardengo Soffici lost the manuscript (rediscovered in 1971 among his effects), Campana rewrote and self-published the now-classic version. In 1918, after a failed affair with the writer Sibilla Aleramo, he was committed to a psychiatric hospital near Florence, where he lived until his death.

Giorgio Caproni (Livorno 1912–Rome 1990) grew up in Genoa, which figures prominently in his work. He is sometimes considered, with Sandro Penna and Attilio Bertolucci, as part of the so-called Sabian line, an anti-Hermetic tendency in modern poetry. High points in a career that spanned fifty years include *Il passaggio d'Enea* (The Passage of Aeneas, 1956); *Il seme del piangere* (The Seed of Tears,

1959), which won the Viareggio Prize; and *Il franco cacciatore* (The Free Hunter, 1982), which won the Librex Montale Prize. He was also a great translator of French authors such as Proust, Baudelaire, and Céline.

Vincenzo Cardarelli (Corneto Tarquinia 1887–Rome 1959) was the pen name of Nazareno Caldarelli, who grew up motherless and received only an elementary school education. He was the leading spokesman for *La Ronda* (founded in 1919), an influential anti-avant-garde journal that advocated a return to Leopardian poetic ideals of clarity and eloquence. (About the only thing he had in common with Marinetti was his support for Mussolini.) He was also a master prose stylist and received the Bagutta Prize for *Il sole a picco* (The Sun on High, 1928) and the Strega Prize for *Villa Tarantola* (1948), both collections of autobiographical prose.

Bartolo Cattafi (Barcellona Pozzo di Gotto 1922–Milan 1979), born to a wealthy Sicilian family after his father's death, took a law degree in 1944 but never practiced. After the war he moved to Milan, where he spent two decades and became linked, despite his southern roots, with the Lombard line. In 1967 he returned to Sicily, where for several years he focused on painting. His collections include *Le mosche del meriggio* (The Flies of Midday, 1958), *Qualcosa di preciso* (Something Exact, 1961), and *L'aria secca del fuoco* (The Fire's Dry Air, 1972). He died of cancer at age fifty-six.

Patrizia Cavalli (Todi 1949–) has been called a "modern-day Sappho." Her first collection of poems was *Le mie poesie non cambieranno il mondo* (My Poems Will Not Change the World, 1974). More recent volumes include *L'io singolare proprio mio* (My Own Singular I, 1992) and *Sempre aperto teatro* (Always-Open Theater, 1999), for which she received the Viareggio Prize. She is known for her brief slices of daily (and nightly) life and for marrying elements of traditional prosody with fresh, colloquial language, stripped of poeticisms. Her translations include versions of *Othello*, *The Tempest*, and *A Midsummer Night's Dream*.

Annalisa Cima (Milan 1941–) is a writer and painter. Her books of poetry include *Terzo modo* (Third Way, 1969), *Immobilità* (Immobility, 1974), and *Quattro tempi* (Four Times, 1986). She has also written extensively about her long friendship with Montale, whose last poems, collected in *Diario postumo* (Posthumous Diary, 1996), were left in Cima's care on the condition that she not publish them until after his death.

Sergio Corazzini (Rome 1886–Rome 1907) was the exemplary poet of the so-called Crepuscular group. Like Pascoli, he focused on "small things," and much of his work is characterized by simple and sometimes sentimental language. He debuted with *Dolcezze* (Mildnesses, 1904) and published several volumes in quick succession. In the last of his five brief collections, *Libro per la sera della domenica* (Book for Sunday Evening, 1906), he became one of the earliest Italian poets to experiment with free verse. He had intense correspondences with poets including Aldo Palazzeschi and Corrado Govoni before dying at age twenty-one of tuberculosis.

Gabriele D'Annunzio (Pescara 1863–Gardone Riviera 1938) was one of the most gifted and influential writers of modern Italy, yet his political infamy often obscures his literary legacy. His best work includes the collections *Poema paradisiaco* (Paradise Poem, 1893) and *Alcione* (Halcyon, 1903), as well as an early trilogy of novels. In 1919, having reinvented himself as a war hero, he mustered a private army, seized a disputed city then called Fiume, which he felt belonged to Italy, and ruled it as self-proclaimed "Duce" for several months. Mussolini learned from him, feared his popularity, and later gave him a state funeral.

Milo De Angelis (Milan 1951–) made a precocious and widely heralded debut with *Somiglianze* (Resemblances, 1975), and his reputation has only risen since. A half dozen collections have followed, including *Terra del viso* (Land of the Face, 1985) and the elegiac *Tema dell'addio* (Theme of Farewell, 2005), which received the Viareggio Prize and is dedicated to his late wife, the poet Giovanna Sicari. His translations include works by Baudelaire, Blanchot, and Lucretius. He lives in Milan, a city that figures often in his poems, and teaches in a prison there.

Gianni D'Elia (Pesaro 1953–) is an independent writer and teacher. His many books of verse, most published by Einaudi, include *Trentennio: Versi scelti e inediti 1977–2007* (Thirty Years: Selected and Unpublished Poems, 1977–2007). He has also written extensively about Pasolini, whom he considers to have been in the "avant-garde of tradition," a phrase that aptly describes his own position. His translations include works by Gide and Baudelaire.

Alfredo de Palchi (Verona 1926–) has edited or co-edited (with his late wife, the poet Sonia Raiziss) *Chelsea* magazine since the early 1960s. His collections of poetry include *Sessioni con l'analista* (Sessions with My Analyst, 1967) and *Paradigma: Tutte le poesie 1947–2005* (Paradigm: Complete Poems, 2006). He now serves as trustee of the Sonia Raiziss Giop Charitable Foundation, which supports various magazines and literary prizes. He has lived in New York since coming to the United States in 1956.

Eugenio De Signoribus (Cupra Marittima 1947–) is the author of several collections of poetry, including *Istmi e chiuse* (Isthmuses and Locks, 1996), *Principio del giorno* (Beginning of the Day, 2001), and *Poesie: 1976–2007* (Poems, 2008), for which he received the Viareggio Prize. He edits *Istmi* (Isthmuses), a biannual journal of literature and art, and lives and teaches in the small Adriatic beach town where he was born.

Salvatore Di Giacomo (Naples 1860–Naples 1934), one of Italy's great dialect poets, wrote many enduringly popular poems, songs, and plays in his native Neapolitan. His collections of poetry range from *Sonetti* (Sonnets, 1884) to *Canzone e ariette nove* (New Songs and Airs, 1916), and his collections of short stories include *Pipa e boccale: Racconti fantastici* (Pipe and Jug: Fantastic Tales, 1893). One of his most important plays, *Assunta Spina* (1910), which he based on one of his stories, was made into a now-classic silent film in 1915 and has been adapted for film and TV several times since.

Luciano Erba (Milan 1922–Milan 2010) was one of six poets included in Luciano Anceschi's influential 1952 anthology *Linea lombarda* (Lombard line). A longtime professor of French and comparative literature at the Catholic University in Milan, his works include *Il nastro di Moebius* (The Moebius Strip, 1980), which won the Viareggio Prize; *Il tranviere metafisico* (The Metaphysical Tramdriver, 1987), which won the Bagutta Prize; and *L'ippopotamo* (The Hippopotamus, 1988), which won the Librex Montale Prize. His many translations include work by Thom Gunn, Francis Ponge, and Henri Michaux.

Farfa (Trieste 1879–San Remo 1964) was the *nome di arte* of Vittorio Osvaldo Tommasini, a Futurist painter, potter, and poet. His work was included in Marinetti's 1925 anthology, *I nuovi poeti futuristi* (The New Futurist Poets), and among his own books are *Noi miliardario della fantasia* (We, Imagination's Millionaire, 1933). In 1932, he was named the "national champion" of Futurist poetry. He died after being hit by—accounts differ—either a car or a motorcycle. His reputation was given a boost a few years later when he was included in Edoardo Sanguineti's major anthology of twentieth-century Italian poetry.

Fillia (Ravello 1904–Turin 1936) was the pseudonym (and mother's maiden name) of Luigi Colombo, a poet and visual artist who began publishing and exhibiting while still in his teens and soon became the leader of the Turin Futurists. He collaborated extensively with Marinetti, with whom he co-authored both the *Manifesto dell'arte sacra futurista* (Manifesto of Futurist Sacred Art, 1931) and *La cucina futurista* (Futurist Cuisine, 1932), the latter a classic of what might be called decadent Futurism. He also wrote, in the 1920s, a trilogy of novels on the evolution of Futurist man. He died of tuberculosis at age thirty-one.

Umberto Fiori (Sarzana 1949–) was a longtime vocalist and songwriter for the Italian progressive rock group Stormy Six. He is author, more recently, of several collections of poetry, including *Chiarimenti* (Clarifications, 1995), *La bella vista* (The Beautiful View, 2002), and *Voi* (You, 2009). He has also co-translated Robert Browning's *The Pied Piper of Hamelin* and Leonard Cohen's *Book of Longing*. He lives in Milan.

Franco Fortini (Florence 1917–Milan 1994) was born Franco Lattes to a Jewish father and a Catholic mother, but after the racial laws of 1938 traded his surname for his mother's maiden name. Drafted into the army in 1941, he deserted in 1943 and joined the partisans. His first book of poetry was *Foglio di via* (Deportation Order, 1946). Other collections include *Questo muro* (This Wall, 1973); *Paesaggio con serpente* (Landscape with Snake, 1985), which won the Librex Montale Prize; and *Composita solvantur* (Latin for "Let Compounds Be Dissolved," 1994). His many translations include many volumes by Brecht.

Gabriele Frasca (Naples 1957–) might be described as an experimental formalist. His four books, the titles of which form a minimalist quatrain, are *Rame* (1984), *Lime* (1995), *Rive* (2001), and *Prime* (2007). He has also published several books of fiction and several collections of essays, and his translations include a novel by Philip K. Dick and several volumes by Samuel Beckett. He teaches comparative literature at the University of Salerno.

Alfonso Gatto (Salerno 1909–Capalbio 1976) dropped out of the University of Naples and eked a living from odd jobs as he wrote his first book, *Isola* (Island, 1932), which showed Hermetic and Surrealist tendencies, as did his second, *Morto ai paesi* (Dead in the Towns, 1937). But his poetry, like Quasimodo's, became more *engagé* after his wartime experience, which included six months in a Fascist prison; he received the Viareggio Prize for *La storia delle vittime* (The History of the Victims, 1966). Also an occasional actor, he appeared in two Pasolini films. He was killed in a car crash.

Giovanni Giudici (Le Grazie di Portovenere 1924–La Spezia 2011) was the fourth of five children and the only one to survive infancy; his mother died with the fifth when he was three. A major representative of an anti-Hermetic strain of postwar Italian poetry, his many books, spanning half a century, include *La vita in versi* (Life in Verse, 1965); *Autobiologia* (Autobiology, 1969), which won the Viareggio Prize; *Salutz* (1986), which won the Librex Montale Prize; and his collected poems, *Poesie 1953–1990*, which received the Bagutta Prize. His translations include Pushkin's *Eugene Onegin* and Pound's "Hugh Selwyn Mauberley."

Alfredo Giuliani (Mombaroccio 1924–Rome 2007) was a poet and a deeply influential theoretician and editor. His anthology, *I novissimi* (The Newest Ones, 1961), was a foundational text for the Neo-avant-garde movement of the 1960s, and he was also an important contributor to the original meeting of what became known as Gruppo 63. His collections of poems include *Povera Juliet* (Poor Juliet, 1965), *Il tautofono* (The Tautophone, 1969), and *Chi l'avrebbe detto* (Who Would Have Said It, 1973). His many translations include works by James Joyce, T. S. Eliot, Alfred Jarry, and Dylan Thomas.

Corrado Govoni (Tàmara 1884–Lido dei Pini 1965), among the first Italians to experiment with free verse, began his career in the Crepuscular vein, with *Le fiale* (The Vials, 1903). A decade later, after collections such as *Poesie elettriche* (Electric Poems, 1911), he was a leading Futurist, though his inspiration remained unchanged: the natural world and the senses that perceive it. In the 1930s, he published two long poems lauding Mussolini; in 1946 he published an elegy for his son, a partisan killed in the Ardeatine Massacre, in which he called Mussolini "the monstrous executioner of the Italian people."

Guido Gozzano (Turin 1883–Turin 1916), the best of the so-called Crepuscularists, has been described as a poet of "sentimental irony." The tension between sentiment and irony is a modernizing force in his essential second collection, *I colloqui* (The Talks, 1911), especially in poems such as "Totò Merúmeni," which in many ways anticipates "The Love Song of J. Alfred Prufrock" by T. S. Eliot. His later work includes an unfinished long poem about butterflies and a prose narrative inspired by a year spent in India in the vain hope of improving his health. After a decade of illness, he died at age thirty-two of tuberculosis.

Margherita Guidacci (Florence 1921–Rome 1992), who wrote her thesis on Ungaretti at the University of Florence, is known for her religious themes. Her many collections of poetry include *La sabbia e l'Angelo* (The Sand and the Angel, 1946), written during World War II; *Neurosuite* (1970), written after long confinement in a psychiatric hospital; and *L'altare di Isenheim* (The Isenheim Altarpiece, 1980), written after her husband's death. Her many translations include works by John Donne, Emily Dickinson, Ezra Pound, and Elizabeth Bishop.

Vivian Lamarque (Tesero 1946–) was adopted at nine months, lost her new father at four years, and learned she had two mothers at ten. Her work is often characterized by phrasal doublings and childlike tones, and her collections include *Teresino* (1981), which won the Viareggio Prize for a first book, and *Poesie 1972–2002*. She is also the author of many children's books, and her translations from the French include works by Jean de la Fontaine, Jacques Prévert, and Charles Baudelaire. She lives in Milan.

Primo Levi (Turin 1919–Turin 1987), a chemist by training, became a concentration camp inmate in 1943. His first book, *Se questo è un uomo* (If This Is a Man,

1947), about his year in Auschwitz, is a classic of Holocaust literature. In 2006, his mixed-genre collection of short prose, *Il sistema periodico* (The Periodic Table, 1975), was named the best science book of all time by the Royal Institution of Great Britain. He died from a three-story fall down the stairwell of his apartment building in Turin. It was the same building in which he had been born.

Franco Loi (Genoa 1930–) moved with his family in 1937 to Milan, where he has lived ever since. A leading voice in postwar dialect poetry generally, he may turn out to have been the last major voice in the venerable but dying literature of the Milanese dialect. His numerous books include *Stròlegh* (1975), *Lünn* (Moons, 1982), and *Umber* (Shadow, 1992). His selected poems, *Aria de la memoria* (Air of Memory, 2005), received the Librex Montale Prize. He has also published several volumes of essays and one of short stories.

Mario Luzi (Florence 1914–Florence 2005) was a leading figure of Florentine Hermeticism during the early part of a publishing career that spanned seventy years. His many collections of poetry include *Un brindisi* (A Toast, 1946); *Al fuoco della controversia* (In the Fire of Controversy, 1978), which received the Viareggio Prize; and *Per il battesimo dei nostri frammenti* (For the Baptism of Our Fragments, 1985), which won the Librex Montale Prize. He was often nominated for the Nobel Prize, and received a lifetime appointment to the Italian Senate on his ninetieth birthday, a few months before his death.

Valerio Magrelli (Rome 1957–) made a precocious and highly praised debut with *Ora serrata retinae* (Latin for "Serrated Border of the Retina," 1980). Later collections include *Nature e venature* (Natures and Venations, 1987), which received the Viareggio Prize; *Didascalie per la lettura di un giornale* (Instructions for Reading a Newspaper, 1999); and *Disturbi del sistema binario* (Disturbances of the Binary System, 2006). He teaches French literature at the University of Cassino and has translated poets including Valéry, Mallarmé, and Verlaine. He played the "first dermatologist" in Nanni Moretti's brilliant film *Caro diario* (Dear Diary, 1993).

Dacia Maraini (1936–) is a novelist and playwright as well as a poet. In 1938, her parents—Fosco Maraini, an influential Florentine ethnographer and photographer, and Topazia Alliata, a Sicilian princess and painter—left Fascist Italy for Japan, where the family spent the last several years of the war in a concentration camp. Her more than fifty books include *L'eta del malessere* (*The Age of Malaise*, 1963), a novel that brought early acclaim; *Il bambino Alberto* (*Baby Albert*, 1986); an interview with her longtime companion Alberto Moravia about his childhood; and *Buio* (*Dark*, 1999), a story collection that received the Strega Prize.

Lucio Mariani (Rome 1936–) is the author of more than a dozen collections, including *Bestie segrete* (Secret Beasts, 1987), *Dispersi gli alleati* (Allies Missing, 1990), *Il torto della preda* (The Prey's Mistake, 1995), and *Qualche notizia del tempo* (Some News of Time, 2001). He lives in Rome.

F. T. Marinetti (Alexandria, Egypt, 1876–Bellagio 1944) was—like Ungaretti—an Italian born in Egypt and educated in French. His famous 1909 manifesto, published first in Italian and then, on the front page of *Le Figaro*, in French, marks both the beginning of Futurism as a movement and, arguably, its high point. (It also marks Marinetti as the godfather of Vorticism and nearly every other subsequent avant-garde movement.) Among his works are *Mafarka le futuriste* (Mafarka the Futurist, 1910), a novel; *Zang Tumb Tumb* (1912), "freeword" poems; and, with Fillia, *La cucina futurista* (Futurist Cuisine, 1932), a cookbook.

Pino Masnata (Stradella 1901–Stradella 1968) was, like Farfa and Fillia, a second-generation Futurist. A surgeon by day, he was named the "national champion" of Futurist poetry—succeeding Farfa—following the publication of his *Tavole parolibere* (Freeword Paintings, 1932), good examples of the later "*parole in libertà*" (words set free) style of visual poetry. His study of the genre, *Poesia visiva: storia e teoria con un percorso iconografico* (Visual Poetry: History and Theory, with an Iconographic Survey, 1984), was published posthumously. He was also a practitioner and proponent of a type of Futurist drama he dubbed "visionic theater."

Alda Merini (Milan 1931–Milan 2009) debuted early: by age twenty, her work had appeared in two important anthologies, and by thirty she had published four books of verse and one of prose. Her quick rise, however, was followed by two decades of silence as she struggled with mental illness. When she began writing again, nothing could stop her: in her last three decades she published, by some counts, more than a hundred collections. Popular and critically lauded, she received both the Librex Montale Prize and the Viareggio Prize. Her poetry often arises from the union of erotic and religious impulses.

Eugenio Montale (Genoa 1896–Milan 1981) was an autodidact who made his living as a journalist and critic. Widely regarded as the greatest Italian poet of his century, he published only three full-length collections, all enormously influential, in his first seventy-five years: *Ossi di seppia* (Cuttlefish Bones, 1925), *Le occasioni* (The Occasions, 1939), and *La bufera e altro* (The Storm and Other Things, 1956). Then, in a late flowering the merit of which is debated, he published another four in his final decade. He received a lifetime appointment to the Italian Senate in 1967 and the Nobel Prize in 1975.

Saturno Montanari (Voltana 1918–Albania[?] 1941) published two collections of poems in 1939, *Occhilucenti* (Brighteyes) and *Voci in tono minore* (Voices in a Minor Key), but is virtually unknown in Italy. After his death in the Greco-Italian war, for which he had volunteered, his father sent his poems to Ezra Pound, who translated five of them, thus elevating Montanari from oblivion to obscurity.

Giorgio Orelli (Airolo, Switzerland, 1921–) is a Swiss poet and critic often associated with the Lombard line. His many collections include *Nel cerchio familiare* (In the Family Circle, 1960), *Sinopie* (Sinopias, 1977), and *Il collo dell'anitra* (The Duck's Neck, 2001). His criticism includes *Il suono dei sospiri: Sul Petrarca volgare* (The Sound of Sighs: On the Vernacular Petrarch, 1990) as well as works on Montale and Foscolo, and his translations include the selected poems of Goethe. In 1988 he was awarded the Schiller Prize, Switzerland's highest literary honor.

Aldo Palazzeschi (Florence 1885–Rome 1974) was the pen name of Aldo Giurlani, who mocked the literary tradition and culture of his day and became a major influence, both as poet and novelist, on the Neo-avant-garde. Though his early poetry was Crepuscular, he soon moved toward Futurism and Absurdism, and his 1910 collection *L'incendario* (The Arsonist) was published by Marinetti's press. In 1914, however, he broke with Futurism over his opposition to the war. His many works of fiction include a Futurist "antinovel" called *Il Codice di Perelà* (Perelà's Code, 1911) and *Sorelle Materassi* (Materassi Sisters, 1934).

Giovanni Pascoli (San Mauro di Romagna 1855–Bologna 1912) survived a famously tragic childhood, including his father's unsolved murder, to become arguably the best Italian poet writing at the dawn of the twentieth century. While certainly not a Modernist, his almost imagistic focus on *"piccole cose"* (small things) and his scaling back of the era's often overblown rhetoric both contributed to the modernization of Italian poetry. His major collections, which he revised and expanded in the years following their first publication, are *Myricae* (Latin for "Tamarisks," 1891–1903), *Poemetti* (Longer Poems, 1897–1904), and *Canti di Castelvecchio* (Songs of Castelvecchio, 1903–1906).

Pier Paolo Pasolini (Bologna 1922–Ostia 1975) was a major writer and filmmaker. His poetry includes *La meglio gioventù* (The Best of Youth, 1954), written in the Friulian dialect; *Le cenere di Gramsci* (Gramsci's Ashes, 1957), his most famous poetic work; and *La religione del mio tempo* (The Religion of My Time, 1961). He also wrote and directed a dozen films, including *Mamma Roma* (1962), *Il vangelo secondo Matteo* (The Gospel According to Matthew, 1964), and *Salò o le 120 giornate di Sodoma* (Salò, or the 120 Days of Sodom, 1975). He was murdered—run over with his own car—under still-mysterious circumstances.

Cesare Pavese (Santo Stefano Belbo 1908–Turin 1950) was the author of *Lavorare stanca* (Work Is Tiring, 1936, expanded 1943), a book of realistic "poem stories" that, out of step with the Hermetic times, went largely unnoticed on publication. After translating fiction throughout the 1930s, he turned to writing it in the 1940s, publishing ten volumes in ten years. He killed himself with barbiturates at age forty-one, shortly after receiving the Strega Prize, Italy's highest literary honor. A popular chapbook of poems, *Verrà la morte e avrà i tuoi occhi* (Death Will Come and Will Have Your Eyes, 1951), appeared posthumously.

Sandro Penna (Perugia 1906–Rome 1977) was a lapidary modern-day Catullus: a major poet who wrote almost exclusively minor poems, often epigrammatic in manner and erotic in matter. Like Umberto Saba, his primary model and an early advocate, he was immune to poetic fashions such as Hermeticism, though like the Hermetics he eschewed the public world for the private one. His collections include *Una strana gioia di vivere* (A Strange Joy in Living, 1956), *Un po' di febbre* (A Slight Fever, 1973), and *Stranezze* (Oddities, 1976), for which he was awarded, a few days before his death, the Bagutta Prize.

Camillo Pennati (Milan 1931–) debuted with *Una preghiera per noi* (A Prayer for Us) in 1957, and the following year he moved to London, where he spent more than a decade as chief librarian for the Italian Cultural Institute. His later collections include *L'ordine delle parole* (The Order of Words, 1964), *Erosagonie* (Erosagonies, 1973), and *Una distanza inseparabile* (An Inseparable Distance, 1998). His translations include work by Philip Larkin, Thom Gunn, and Ted Hughes. From 1973 to 1987 he was an editor at the Einaudi publishing house in Turin.

Antonio Porta (Vicenza 1935–Milan 1989) was the pen name of Leo Paolazzi, who became a central figure of the Neo-avant-garde thanks to his editorial involvement in the quarterly *Il Verri*, his inclusion in the 1961 anthology *I novissimi*, and his active role in Gruppo 63. His later work, like Montale's, took a diaristic turn. His many collections include *Aprire* (To Open, 1964), *Week-End* (1974), and *Invasioni* (Invasions, 1984), which was awarded the Viareggio Prize. His translations include Edgar Lee Masters's *Spoon River Anthology* and Amelia Rosselli's *Sleep*. He died of a heart attack at age fifty-three.

Antonia Pozzi (Milan 1912–Milan 1938), daughter of a high-powered lawyer and a countess, was part of a circle at the University of Milan that included Luciano Anceschi, Daria Menicanti, and her close friend Vittorio Sereni. An avid alpinist and talented photographer, she killed herself with barbiturates at age twenty-six in 1938—the year the Fascist racial laws went into effect—out of a "mortal despair" that she described as both personal and political. A collection of her poems, *Parole* (Words, 1939, expanded in several later editions), appeared posthumously, as did her thesis on Flaubert.

Fabio Pusterla (Mendrisio, Switzerland, 1957–) is a Swiss poet, critic, and translator. His numerous collections of verse include *Le cose senza storia* (Things Without History, 1994), *Folla sommersa* (Sunken Crowd, 2004), and *Le terre emerse: Poesie scelte 1985–2008* (Dry Land: Selected Poems, 2009). His translations include several volumes by the Francophone Swiss poet Philippe Jaccottet, and his awards include the Gottfried Keller Prize. He lives in Lugano, where he teaches at the Liceo Cantonale.

Salvatore Quasimodo (Modica 1901–Napoli 1968) exemplified the lyrical Hermeticism of the 1930s in his early collections *Acque e terre* (Waters and Lands, 1930) and *Oboe sommerso* (Sunken Oboe, 1932), but in his increasingly discursive postwar volumes, such as *Giorno dopo giorno* (Day After Day, 1947) and *Il falso e vero verde* (The False and True Green, 1953), he sought more direct engagement with his readers and his society. Among his most highly regarded works are his translations from the late 1930s, a pivotal point in his career, of Greek lyric poets. He received the Nobel Prize in 1959.

Giovanni Raboni (Milan 1932–Parma 2004) gave up a legal career for a journalistic and literary one. His many collections include *Le case della Vetra* (Vetra's Houses, 1966), *Ogni terzo pensiero* (Every Third Thought, 1993), and *Barlumi di storia* (Glimmers of History, 2002), and his work received many of Italy's highest honors, including the Viareggio Prize, the Bagutta Prize, and the Librex Montale Prize. Also a prolific translator from the French, he rendered the whole of *À la recherche du temps perdu* into Italian. Influenced by his wife, the poet Patrizia Valduga, his later work became increasingly formal.

Clemente Rèbora (Milan 1885–Stresa 1957) was a child of the Risorgimento; his father fought alongside Garibaldi and raised Clemente according to secular, Mazzinian ideals. He left medical school to pursue literary studies, publishing his first collection of poems, *Frammenti lirici* (Lyric Fragments), in 1913. After spending 1916–1919 in military hospitals as the result of a head injury and shell shock, he published *Canti anonimi* (Anonymous Songs) in 1922. In the late 1920s, a spiritual crisis led to his conversion to Catholicism, and in 1936 he became a Rosminian priest. His subsequent poetry, most of which appeared posthumously, is overtly religious.

Nelo Risi (Milan 1920–) trained in medicine before becoming a poet and filmmaker. His work appeared in the original *Linea lombarda* anthology, and his many collections include *Di certe cose che dette in versi suonano meglio che in prosa* (Regarding Certain Things That Sound Better Said in Poetry Than in Prose, 1970), which received the Viareggio Prize, and *Poesie scelte 1943–1975* (Selected Poems, 1977), edited by Giovanni Raboni. His translations include work by Pierre Jean Jouve, Jules Laforgue, and Constantine Cavafy, and among his dozen films is *Una stagione dell'inferno* (A Season in Hell, 1971), about Rimbaud and Verlaine.

Amelia Rosselli (Paris, France, 1930–Rome 1996) was the daughter of an English Quaker activist and an Italian Resistance hero (Carlo Rosselli) who was assassinated when she was seven. After his death, she was raised in England and America before returning to Italy and being moved by the death of her best friend, Rocco Scotellaro, to write poetry in Italian. One of the few women associated with Gruppo 63, her collections include *Variazioni belliche* (War Variations, 1964), *Documento* (Document, 1976), and *Sleep* (1992, in English). She killed herself by jumping from her fifth-floor apartment on the deathday of Sylvia Plath, whose poetry she translated.

Umberto Saba (Trieste 1883–Gorizia 1957), born Umberto Poli, collected his early poems in 1921 in *Il canzoniere* (The Songbook), which he expanded and reissued, as Whitman did *Leaves of Grass*, throughout his life. He also wrote a prose companion volume, *Storia e cronistoria del Canzoniere* (History and Chronicle of the Songbook, 1948), and a novel, *Ernesto* (published posthumously). He ran a bookshop, Libreria antica e moderna, for two decades before the 1938 Racial Laws forced him to sell it and flee Trieste. His 1946 Viareggio Prize marked the beginning of his belated recognition as one of Italy's great poets.

Edoardo Sanguineti (Genoa 1930–Genoa 2010) was a leading poet and theorist of the Neo-avant-garde, part of both the *Novissimi* anthology and Gruppo 63. His verse, known for its wit, its long discursive lines, and its linguistic (and often multilingual) play, is gathered in *Mikrokosmos: Poesie 1951–2004*. He was also a prolific translator (from Latin, Greek, French, and English) and the editor of an influential two-volume anthology, *Poesia italiana del Novecento* (Italian Poetry of the Twentieth Century, 1969). A lifelong leftist, he served in the Italian Parliament from 1979 to 1983. His awards include the Bagutta Prize and the Librex Montale Prize.

Camillo Sbarbaro (Santa Margherita Ligure 1888–Savona 1967) grew up (like Montale, who dedicated a section of his first book to Sbarbaro) on the Ligurian coast. He's best known for the plainspoken autobiographical poems of *Pianissimo* (Very Softly, 1914) and the chiseled prose poems of *Trucioli* (Shavings, 1920, expanded

1948). He also translated many major works from several languages, primarily French. His true passion, however, was lichenology: he discovered 127 new species, many of which bear his name, and his herbaria now reside in museums and universities. His monograph on lichen appeared days after his death.

Leonardo Sciascia (Racalmuto 1921–Palermo 1989), one of Italy's best postwar writers, began his career as a poet with *Favole della dittatura* (Fables of the Dictatorship, 1950) and *La Sicilia, il suo cuore* (Sicily, Its Heart, 1952), but is famous for novels such as *Il giorno della civetta* (The Day of the Owl, 1961), *A ciascuno il suo* (To Each His Own, 1966), and *Porte aperte* (Open Doors, 1987), made into a 1990 film. He also served in Italy's parliament and helped investigate Aldo Moro's kidnapping and assassination, about which he wrote *L'affaire Moro* (The Moro Affair, 1978, expanded 1983).

Rocco Scotellaro (Tricarico 1923–Portici 1953), son of a cobbler, may be the purest representative of Neorealism in this anthology. A socialist, he was elected mayor of his hometown at age twenty-three, but his attempts at land reform were thwarted and he resigned. He died of heart failure at thirty, while researching agrarian economics near Naples. All his books appeared posthumously, including an unfinished sociological study, *Contadini del Sud* (Southern Peasants, 1954), and a volume of verse, *È fatto giorno* (Day Has Broken, 1954), which received the Viareggio Prize. Grief over his death spurred his friend Amelia Rosselli to begin writing poetry in Italian.

Vittorio Sereni (Luino 1913–Milan 1983), a major poet of the Lombard line, was drafted into the army in 1941, captured by the Allies in 1943, and spent the rest of the war in North African POW camps, where he wrote his lauded second collection, *Diario d'Algeria* (Algerian Diary, 1947). In the year before his death he received both the Bagutta Prize for his selected translations, *Il musicante di Saint-Merry* (The Musician of Saint-Merry, 1981), and the Viareggio Prize for the last of his many collections of poetry, *Stella variabile* (Variable Star, 1981). He was literary director of the publisher Mondadori for nearly thirty years.

Leonardo Sinisgalli (Montemurro 1908–Rome 1981), from a famously poor region, took a degree in engineering, worked as an art director for Olivetti and Pirelli, but is best known as a poet. His many collections include *Vidi le muse* (I Saw the Muses, 1943), *L'età della luna* (The Age of the Moon, 1952), and *Mosche in bottiglia* (Bottled Flies, 1975). His prose works include *Furor mathematicus* (Mathematical Passion, 1944), a personal study of the scientific culture of his time. As an undergraduate, he turned down an invitation from Enrico Fermi to join the Institute of Physics at the University of Rome.

Ardengo Soffici (Rignano sull'Arno 1879–Forte dei Marmi 1964) spent a crucial seven years as a young man in Paris, exhibiting his paintings with the likes of Picasso and Braque. Returning to his native Tuscany, he co-founded, in 1913, the avant-garde journal *Lacerba* (model for Wyndham Lewis's *BLAST*) and became one of the most innovative poets linked with Futurism. His later, more conservative work pales beside his 1915 volume *Bïf§zf+18: Simultaneità e Chimismi lirici* (Bïf§zf+18: Simultaneity and Lyric Chemisms). It was Soffici who famously lost the first manuscript of *Canti Orfici*, forcing Dino Campana to rewrite it.

Maria Luisa Spaziani (Turin 1924–) entered the literary world as an undergraduate, founding a journal in which she published new work by major writers. Her thesis on Proust began a lifelong relationship with French literature; she translated prolifically (Ronsard, Flaubert, Yourcenar, et al.) and taught French language and literature for decades. Her own work, by turns epigrammatic and narrative, includes *Le acque del sabato* (Sabbath Waters, 1954), her first book; *Geometria del disordine* (Geometry of Disorder, 1981), recipient of the Viareggio Prize; and *Giovanna d'Arco* (Joan of Arc, 1990), a novel in verse. She was the real-life inspiration for Montale's "Volpe."

Trilussa (Rome 1871–Rome 1950) is the anagrammatic pen name of Carlo Alberto Salustri, an enormously popular (and populist) poet who wrote in Romanesco, the dialect of Rome. He grew up poor and precocious, publishing his first collection at fifteen. A sociopolitical, often Aesopian, satirist, his many volumes include *Favole romanesche* (Romanesco Fables, 1900), *Ommini e bestie* (Men and Beasts, 1908), and *Lupi e agnelli* (Wolves and Lambs). He died on the deathday of G. G. Belli, the great Romanesco poet of the nineteenth century, just twenty days after receiving a lifetime (or "deathtime," as he called it) appointment to the Italian Senate.

Giuseppe Ungaretti (Alexandria, Egypt, 1888–Milan 1970), of Tuscan stock, was educated in French on the edge of the Sahara. After two years in Paris befriending Apollinaire and others, he joined the Italian army; his pioneering free-verse debut, *Il porto sepolto* (The Buried Port, 1916), was written in the trenches. After the war, he flirted with Dadaism, supported Fascism, and became a leading figure of Hermeticism. His later, more traditional work includes *La terra promessa* (The Promised Land, 1950) and *Il taccuino del vecchio* (The Old Man's Notebook, 1960). He is, with Saba and Montale, one of Italy's great modern poets.

Patrizia Valduga (Castelfranco Veneto 1953–) spent three years in medical school in Padua before transferring to the University of Venice to study literature. A profoundly physical metaphysical poet, she writes frankly about sex, love,

God, and pain in strictly rhymed and metered verse. She debuted with *Medicamenta* (1982); more recent collections include *Cento quartine* (A Hundred Quatrains, 1997), *Requiem* (2002), and *Lezioni d'amore* (Love Lessons, 2004). She founded the monthly journal *Poesia* in 1988, and her many translations include works by Shakespeare, Donne, Molière, and Mallarmé. Widow of the poet Giovanni Raboni, she lives in Milan.

Diego Valeri (Piove di Sacco 1887–Rome 1976), a scholar and translator of French literature, was an intensely musical poet, influenced by Pascoli and the Symbolists. Like many, he lost work by refusing to support Fascism, and he spent part of World War II in a Swiss refugee camp (with, among others, Nelo Risi). His collections include *Taccuino Svizzero* (Swiss Notebook, 1947); *Poesie* (1967), which won the Viareggio Prize; and *Calle del vento* (Path of the Wind, 1975). His translations include works by Flaubert, Stendhal, and La Fontaine. In 1969 he was made an officer of the French Legion of Honor.

Andrea Zanzotto (Pieve di Soligo 1921–Conegliano 2011), though not a part of Gruppo 63, was one of the most interesting experimentalists of the last century. A student of the traditionalist Diego Valeri at Padua, he debuted with *Dietro il paessaggio* (Behind the Landscape, 1951). Later volumes include *Il Galateo in bosco* (The Book of Woodland Manners, 1979), which received the Viareggio Prize; *La beltà* (Beauty, 1968), widely considered his masterpiece; and *Poesie e prose scelte* (Selected Poetry and Prose, 2000), which received the Bagutta Prize. In addition to his poetry in standard Italian, he has done important work in his native Veneto dialect.

ABOUT THE TRANSLATORS

Damiano Abeni (1956–) is an Italian epidemiologist who since 1973 has been translating American poets such as Ashbery, Bidart, Bishop, Ferlinghetti, Ginsberg, Strand, Simic, C. K. Williams, and others. With Mark Strand, he edited *West of Your Cities* (2003), a bilingual anthology of contemporary American poetry.

V. Joshua Adams (1978–) is a doctoral candidate in comparative literature at the University of Chicago. He edited *Chicago Review* from 2008 to 2010, and his translations of Italian poetry have appeared in *Circumference* and *Aufgabe*.

Beverly Allen (1945–) is the author of *Rape Warfare: The Hidden Genocide in Bosnia-Herzegovina and Croatia* (1996) and *Andrea Zanzotto: The Language of Beauty's Apprentice* (1988); and she is the editor of *The Defiant Muse: Italian Feminist Poems from the Middle Ages to the Present* (1986) and *Pier Paolo Pasolini: The Poetics of Heresy* (1982).

Al Alvarez (1929–), a Londoner, is author of *New & Selected Poems* (2002), *The Writer's Voice* (2004), and several nonfiction books that are classics in their fields: *The Savage God* (1971), on suicide; *The Biggest Game in Town* (1983), on poker; and *Feeding the Rat* (1988), on mountaineering.

Gian Maria Annovi (1978–), a doctoral candidate in Italian at Columbia, is the author of four collections of poetry and one of essays, and he has translated poets such as Anne Carson, Michael Palmer, and Bruce Andrews into Italian. He writes on art for the Italian newspaper *Il Manifesto*.

Brunella Antomarini (1952–) teaches aesthetics at John Cabot University in Rome. Her books include *Pensare con l'errore* (Thinking with Error, 2007), and her translations include Paul Vangelisti's *La vita semplice* (The Simple Life, 2009). She also edits *InVerse*, a yearly anthology of Italian poetry in English translation.

William Arrowsmith (1924–1992) was an influential classicist and translator, renowned for his versions of ancients, including Petronius, Euripides, and Aristophanes, and moderns, including Montale and Pavese. He was a founder of *The Hudson Review* and general editor of Oxford's thirty-three-volume Greek Tragedy in New Translations series.

Sarah Arvio (1954–) is author of two books of poetry, *Visits from the Seventh* (2002) and *Sono: cantos* (2006). She has lived in Caracas, Paris, Rome, Mexico, and New York. For years a translator for the United Nations in New York and Switzerland, she now also teaches poetry at Princeton.

Gabrielle Barfoot (1949–) co-edited several volumes with G. Singh, including *Modern Italian Poetry* (2003), a bilingual anthology published in India, and *Il Novecento inglese e italiano* (The English and Italian Twentieth Century, 1998), a collection of comparative essays. Born in Belfast, she teaches English at the University of Trieste.

Patrick Barron (1968–), originally from Montana, spent most of the 1990s in Ireland and Italy, and now lives in Boston, where he teaches at the University of Massachusetts. His poems, essays, and translations of Andrea Zanzotto and others have appeared in publications including *Poetry East, Two Lines, The Worcester Review*, and *Ditch*.

Douglas Basford (1973–), the recipient of two Der-Hovanessian Translation Awards and a translation residency at the Santa Fe Art Institute, teaches at SUNY-Buffalo and co-edits the online poetry journal *Unsplendid*. His translations have appeared in *Poetry, Subtropics, Two Lines*, and elsewhere.

Judith Baumel (1956–) is the author of three books of poetry: *The Weight of Numbers* (1988), which won the Walt Whitman Award; *Now* (1996); and *The Kangaroo Girl* (2011). A graduate of the Writing Seminars at Johns Hopkins, she teaches at Adelphi University and lives in the Bronx, where she was born.

Samuel Beckett (1906–1989) studied French, Italian, and English at Trinity College, Dublin. His best work—the absurdist plays *Waiting for Godot* (1953) and *Endgame* (1957); the poioumenon trilogy of novels, *Molloy* (1951), *Malone Dies* (1951), and *The Unnamable* (1953)—was originally written in French. He received the Nobel Prize in 1969.

Nicholas Benson (1966–) was born in West Germany to an American diplomat and grew up in Turkey, Yugoslavia, and elsewhere. His translations include Aldo Palazzeschi's *The Arsonist*, for which he received an NEA award, and Attilio Bertolucci's *Winter Journey* (2005). He holds a PhD in Italian Studies from New York University.

Adria Bernardi (1957–) is the author of two novels, *Openwork* (2007) and *The Day Laid on the Altar* (1999), and a book of short stories, *In the Gathering Woods* (2000). She received the Raiziss/de Palchi Translation Fellowship for her translations of Raffaello Baldini, published as *Small Talk* (2009). She lives in Nashville.

Carla Billitteri (1961–) is the author of the critical study *Language and the Renewal of Society in Walt Whitman, Laura (Riding) Jackson and Charles Olson* (2009), and translator of *I Am a Furious Little Bee* (2008), a chapbook of Alda Merini's aphorisms. A member of the editorial collective of the National Poetry Foundation, she teaches English at the University of Maine.

Willard Bohn (1939–) explores the intersections of modern poetry and modern art in books including *Modern Visual Poetry* (2001), *The Rise of Surrealism* (2002), *Apollinaire and the International Avant-Garde* (1997), and *Italian Futurist Poetry* (2005). He is Distinguished Professor Emeritus of French and Comparative Literature at Illinois State University.

Luigi Bonaffini (1947–), the founder and editor of *Journal of Italian Translation*, was born in Isernia and teaches at Brooklyn College. He has edited five trilingual anthologies of dialect poetry and translated books by Dino Campana, Mario Luzi, Vittorio Sereni, Pier Paolo Pasolini, Attilio Bertolucci, and many others.

Vittoria Bradshaw (1925–2003), born near Venice, studied languages and translation in Heidelberg and Geneva. In 1957 she married an American painter and moved to California. She edited and translated *From Pure Silence to Impure Dialogue* (1971), a large anthology of postwar Italian poetry and related prose.

Geoffrey Brock (1964–), born in Atlanta, is author of *Weighing Light: Poems* (2005). His translations include Cesare Pavese's *Disaffections: Complete Poems 1930–1950* (2002), and his awards include two NEA fellowships and a Guggenheim Fellowship. He teaches at the University of Arkansas.

Van K. Brock (1932–) is the author of several books, including *The Hard Essential Landscape* (1979), *Unspeakable Strangers* (1995), and *Lightered: New and Selected Poems* (2005). He founded Anhinga Press and *The Southeast Review*, taught creative writing for thirty years at Florida State, and now lives in Arkansas.

Barry Callaghan (1937–), a Torontonian, is the author of more than a dozen volumes of poetry and prose and translator of many others. He is a professor emeritus at York University, where he taught for thirty-five years, and he still edits *Exile: A Literary Quarterly*, which he founded in 1972.

Emanuel Carnevali (1897–1942) fled Italy at sixteen for New York, where he learned English and traveled in Modernist circles. He was hired by Harriet Monroe at *Poetry* shortly before contracting encephalitis lethargica, which forced his return to Italy. He is the author of *Tales of a Hurried Man* (1925).

Cyrus Cassells (1957–) is the author of *The Mud Actor* (1982), *Soul Make a Path Through Shouting* (1994), *Beautiful Signor* (1997), and *More Than Peace and Cypresses* (2004). His fifth book, *The Crossed-Out Swastika*, and a translation, *Still Life with Children: Selected Poems of Francesc Parcerisas*, are forthcoming in 2012.

Patrizio Ceccagnoli (1975–), born in Perugia, is a doctoral candidate in Italian at Columbia University, specializing in nineteenth- and twentieth-century literature with an emphasis on Modernism. He is currently working with Susan Stewart on a volume of translations of Milo De Angelis's last two books.

Wayne Chambliss (1973–) lives in Portland, Oregon. His translations of Italian and Russian poetry have appeared in *Words Without Borders, Fence, jubilat, Octopus Magazine, Fascicle, Drunken Boat, Verse Daily, The Germ*, and other periodicals, and were anthologized previously in *New European Poets* (2008).

Fred Chappell (1936–) has written many books, including *Backsass: Poems* (2004) and *I Am One of You Forever* (1987), a novel. His awards include the Bollingen Prize for Poetry and the French Academy's Prix du Meilleur Livre Étranger, for his novel *Dagon* (1968). He taught for forty years at the University of North Carolina, Greensboro.

Frederick Mortimer Clapp (1879–1969), a New Yorker, was the author of eight volumes of verse and translator of various modern Italian poets. But he is best known as an art historian. His early work on Pontormo did much to resurrect that artist's reputation, and he was the Frick Collection's first director.

Martha Collins (1940–) is the author of *Blue Front* (2006) and *White Papers* (2012). She has also published four earlier collections of poems and two collections of co-translated Vietnamese poetry, as well as translations of Italian, Spanish, and German poems. She is editor-at-large for *FIELD* magazine.

Ned Condini (1940–), born in Turin, is the author of several books of fiction and poetry and translator of Giorgio Caproni's *The Earth's Wall* (2004), Carlo Betocchi's *Awakenings* (2008), and, most recently, *An Anthology of Modern Italian Poetry* (2009). In 1986 he received PEN's Renato Poggioli Translation Award.

Cid Corman (1924–2004), an extremely prolific poet and translator, edited the seminal journal *Origin* from 1951 until the mid-'80s. Born in Boston to Ukrainian parents, he lived in France and Italy before moving in 1958 to Kyoto, Japan, where he spent most of his later life.

Peter Covino (1963–) is the author of *Cut Off the Ears of Winter* (2005), winner of the PEN America/Osterweil Award, and the co-editor of *Essays on Italian-American Literature and Culture* (2011). A founding editor of *Barrow Street*, he teaches English and creative writing at the University of Rhode Island.

Patrick Creagh (1930–), born in London, is the author of several volumes of poetry and a leading translator of Italian literature. From 1966 to 1969 he organized the Poetry Readings of the Festival of Two Worlds at Spoleto, where he featured Pound, Neruda, Olsen, Berryman, Paz, Ungaretti, and others.

Anamaría Crowe Serrano is an Irish poet and translator. Her collections of poems include *Femispheres* (2008) and *one columbus leap* (2011), and her translations include (with Riccardo Duranti) Valerio Magrelli's *Instructions on How to Read a Newspaper* (2007). She teaches Spanish in Dublin.

Pádraig J. Daly (1943–) is the author of several volumes of poems, including *The Last Dreamers: New & Selected Poems* (1999), and translator of several volumes of Italian poetry, including Edoardo Sanguineti's *Libretto* (1999). Born in Dungarvan, Ireland, he is now an Augustinian priest in Dublin.

Chad Davidson (1970–) is the author of two collections of poetry, *Consolation Miracle* (2003), which received the Crab Orchard Prize, and *The Last Predicta* (2008). His poems, articles, and translations have appeared widely in journals, and he teaches literature and creative writing at the University of West Georgia.

Donald Davie (1922–1995) was a Yorkshire poet associated with the Movement. In his poetry and criticism he explored both the English tradition that descends from Thomas Hardy and the Modernist vein of poets such as Ezra Pound and Basil Bunting. His *Collected Poems* appeared in 1991.

Peter Davison (1928–2004) was an editor at the *Atlantic Monthly* and Houghton Mifflin and the author of many collections of poetry. His first, *The Breaking of the Day and Other Poems* (1976), won the Yale Younger Poets Prize in 1963, and his last, *Breathing Room* (2000), won the Massachusetts Book Award.

Alfredo de Palchi (Verona 1926–) immigrated to New York in 1956. His volumes of poetry include *Paradigma: tutte le poesie 1947–2005* (2006). He has been an editor at *Chelsea* for fifty years and is trustee of the Sonia Raiziss Giop Charitable Foundation, which promotes the translation of Italian poetry into English.

Mary di Michele (1949–) was born in Lanciano, Italy, and immigrated to Canada in 1955. A novelist and poet, her many volumes include *Tenor of Love* (2005), a novel about Enrico Caruso, and *The Flower of Youth* (2011), poems about Pier Paolo Pasolini. She teaches at Concordia University in Montreal.

W. S. Di Piero (1945–) is the author of numerous volumes of poetry, translation, and essays on culture and personal experience. A native of South Philadelphia, he now lives in San Francisco, contributes frequently to *The Threepenny Review*, and writes a regular column on art for the *San Diego Reader*.

Laurie Duggan (1949–), born in Melbourne, is the author of several volumes of poetry, including *Compared to What: Selected Poems 1971–2003* (2005). His awards include the Australian Literature Society Gold Medal and the Dinny O'Hearn Poetry Prize, both for *Mangroves* (2003). He now lives in England.

Riccardo Duranti (1949–) teaches English literature and translation at the University of Rome. He is the author of *L'affettuosa fantasia, poesie 1987–1997* (The Affectionate Fantasy, Poems 1987–1997) and the translator of the complete works of Raymond Carver into Italian.

John DuVal (1940–) has translated two volumes of Romanesco poetry—*Tales of*

Trilussa (1990) and Cesare Pascarella's *The Discovery of America* (1991)—and several from Old French. Winner of the Raiziss/de Palchi Book Prize and the Harold Morton Landon Translation Award, he teaches at the University of Arkansas.

Michael Egan (1939–1992), a Baltimorean, earned an MA from the Writing Seminars at Johns Hopkins, and his collections include *The Oldest Gesture* (1970) and *We Came Out Again to See the Stars* (1986). He died having finished half of an epic poem, *Leviathan*. He was Moira Egan's father.

Moira Egan (1962–) is the author of *Cleave* (2004), *La Seta della Cravatta/The Silk of the Tie* (2009), *Bar Napkin Sonnets* (2009), and *Spin* (2010), and translator, with Damiano Abeni, of a substantial selection of poems by John Ashbery into Italian. Born in Baltimore, she now lives in Rome.

Alistair Elliot (1932–), born in Liverpool, is a poet and translator. His original work includes *My Country: Collected Poems* (1989) and *The Real Poems* (2008), and his translations include *Italian Landscape Poems* (1993), *Roman Food Poems* (2003), and *French Love Poems* (1991). He received a Cholmondeley Award in 2000.

Marco Fazzini (1962–) has studied in Edinburgh, Durban, and Venice, where he now teaches at Ca' Foscari. His books include *Crossings: Essays on Contemporary Scottish Poetry and Hybridity* (2000). His translations into Italian include work by Philip Larkin, Hugh MacDiarmid, and Geoffrey Hill.

Ruth Feldman (1911–2003), an American who split time for much of her life between Boston and Rome, was a leading translator of Italian poetry, known for her renderings of Andrea Zanzotto, Primo Levi, Rocco Scotellaro, and others. Her honors include the John Florio Prize and the Italo Calvino Prize.

Marella Feltrin-Morris (1970–) teaches Italian at Ithaca College. Her translations include Domenico Losurdo's *Heidegger and the Ideology of War* (2001, co-translated with Jon Morris) and Paola Masino's 1945 novel *Birth and Death of the Housewife* (2009), as well as short stories and poems by various authors.

Lawrence Ferlinghetti (1919–) is an American poet and painter, best known as the author of *A Coney Island of the Mind* (1958) and as co-founder of City Lights Booksellers and Publishers. He was also the defendant in the 1957 "Howl" trial, a landmark First Amendment case. His first language was French.

Rina Ferrarelli (1939–), a poet, essayist, and translator, was born in Calabria and immigrated, at fifteen, to Pittsburgh, where she still lives. She translates poets who were shaped by the war into which she was born, such as Bartolo Cattafi (*Winter Fragments*, 2006) and Leonardo Sinisgalli (*I Saw the Muses*, 1997).

Robert Fitzgerald (1910–1985) was an American poet, translator, and critic. His renderings of Homer's and Virgil's epics are classics of twentieth-century translation. He was Boylston Professor of Rhetoric at Harvard from 1965 to 1981 and held, for the last few months of his life, the position now known as Poet Laureate.

R. W. Flint (1921–) is a critic, mainly of poetry, and a translator, mainly of prose. His articles have appeared in *The Nation, The New York Review of Books*, and *Parnassus*. His translations include Marinetti's *Selected Writings* (1971) and several novels by Cesare Pavese, including *The Moon and the Bonfires* (2002).

Andrew Frisardi (1968–) has translated two books of poetry: Giuseppe Ungaretti's *Selected Poems* (2003), which won the Raiziss/de Palchi Book Prize, and Franco Loi's *Air and Memory* (2008). His annotated edition of Dante's *Vita Nuova* is forthcoming from Northwestern. Born in Boston, he now lives in Orvieto.

Jonathan Galassi (1949–) is an American poet, translator, and editor. His translations include Montale's *Collected Poems: 1920–1954* (1998) and Leopardi's *Canti* (2010); his own collections include *North Street* (2000). A former poetry editor of *The Paris Review*, he is president and publisher of Farrar, Straus and Giroux.

Adam Giannelli (1978–) was a Henry Hoyns Fellow at the University of Virginia and lived for several years in Latin America. Editor of *High Lonesome: On the Poetry of Charles Wright* (2001), his poems and translations have appeared in journals including *Smartish Pace, FIELD*, and *American Literary Review*.

Estelle Gilson (1926–) has translated several volumes of prose from the Italian, including *The Stories and Recollections of Umberto Saba* (1993) and several novels by Massimo Bontempelli. Her translation honors include the Italo Calvino Award, the Renato Poggioli Award, and the Aldo and Jean Scaglione Award.

Allen Ginsberg (1926–1997) was the leading bard of the Beat Generation, best known for two long poems, "Howl" (1956), which was the subject of a landmark obscenity trial, and "Kaddish" (1961). In 1974 he founded, with Anne Waldman, the Jack Kerouac School of Disembodied Poetics at the Naropa Institute.

Dana Gioia (1950–) is the author of three collections of poems: *Daily Horoscope* (1986), *The Gods of Winter* (1991), and *Interrogations at Noon* (2001). His criticism includes *Can Poetry Matter?* (1991), and his translations include Montale's *Mottetti: Poems of Love* (1990). He was director of the NEA from 2003 to 2009.

David Goldstein (1972–) has published a poetry chapbook, *Been Raw Diction* (2006), as well as essays on Shakespeare, Robert Duncan, and Martha Stewart. He has degrees from Yale, Johns Hopkins, and Stanford, and he teaches Renaissance literature and creative writing at York University in Toronto.

Eamon Grennan (1941–), a Dublin native, has lived in the United States since the

1960s. His many collections include *So It Goes* (1995), *The Quick of It* (2005), and *Matter of Fact* (2008), and his translations include *Selected Poems of Giacomo Leopardi* (1997). He taught English at Vassar for thirty years.

Charles Guenther (1920–2008), from St. Louis, was a prolific poet and translator. His work is gathered in *Moving the Seasons: Selected Poems* (1994), *Hippopotamus: Selected Translations 1945–1985* (1986), and *Three Faces of Autumn* (2006), a six-hundred-page retrospective of his poetry, prose, and translations.

Robert Hahn (1938–), based in Boston, is the author of the collections of poetry *All Clear* (1996) and *No Messages* (2001). His essays and translations have appeared widely in journals including *Yale Review*, *Parnassus*, and *Literary Imagination*, and his awards include an NEA poetry fellowship.

Peter Hainsworth (1942–), whose interests range from Petrarch and Dante to Carlo Emilio Gadda and Andrea Zanzotto, is editor of *The Language of Literature in Renaissance Italy* (1988) and, with David Robey, of *The Oxford Companion to Italian Literature* (2002). He is Emeritus Fellow of Lady Margaret Hall, Oxford.

Michael Hamburger (1924–2007) was born to German-Jewish parents who moved to England in 1933. A leading translator of German writers such as Hölderlin, Celan, and W. G. Sebald, he appeared as the latter's doppelganger in Sebald's *Rings of Saturn* (1999). Hamburger's own *Collected Poems* appeared in 1995.

Kevin Hart (1954–) is a British-Australian poet, theologian, and philosopher who teaches at the University of Virginia. He is the author of many books, including *Flame Tree: Selected Poems* (2002) and *The Dark Gaze: Maurice Blanchot and the Sacred* (2004), and translator of *The Buried Harbour: Selected Poems of Giuseppe Ungaretti* (1990).

Seamus Heaney (1939–), a Northern Irish poet, received the Nobel Prize in 1995. His collections include *North* (1975); *The Spirit Level* (1996), which won the Whitbread Prize; and *District and Circle* (2006), which won the T. S. Eliot Prize. His *Beowulf: A New Translation* (1999) also received the Whitbread Prize.

Anthony Hecht (1923–2004), born in New York to German-Jewish parents, was among the liberators of the Flossenbürg concentration camp in 1945, and some of his best poems confront our worst horrors. (Yet he also co-invented the double dactyl.) His awards include the Pulitzer, Bollingen, and Librex Montale Prizes.

Geoffrey Hill (1932–), from Bromsgrove, England, is a famously difficult poet whose career has come, like Montale's, in two acts: chiseled, widely spaced early books such as *Mercian Hymns* (1971) and *Tenebrae* (1978), followed by an astonishing late flowering, with ten new books since 1997, most recently *Clavics* (2011).

Ted Hughes (1930–1998) was British Poet Laureate from 1984 till his death. His collections include *The Hawk in the Rain* (1957), his debut; *Crow* (1970), his master-piece; and *Birthday Letters* (1998), which posthumously broke his silence regarding his marriage to Sylvia Plath. It won the Whitbread, Forward, and T. S. Eliot prizes.

Peter Jay (1945–) is the author of *Shifting Frontiers* (1980), co-editor, with Caroline Lewis, of *Sappho Through English Poetry* (1996), and editor of *The Sea! The Sea!: An Anthology of Poems* (2005) and *The Greek Anthology* (1973). He is also the founder and editorial director of Anvil Press.

Stephanie H. Jed (1953–) is the author of *Chaste Thinking: The Rape of Lucretia and the Birth of Humanism* (1989) and translator, with Pasquale Verdicchio, of Alda Merini's *The Holy Land* (2002). She teaches comparative literature and directs the Italian Studies program at the University of California, San Diego.

George Kay (1924–), a Scottish poet, is best known for two translations: *The Penguin Book of Italian Verse* (1958), with its useful prose renderings in small type beneath, and the *Selected Poems of Eugenio Montale* (1969), which first brought Montale to a wide English-speaking audience.

Kenneth Koch (1925–2002), a leading poet of the New York School, spent six months in Italy in 1954. His volumes of verse included *Ko, or A Season on Earth* (1959), *The Art of Love* (1975), and *One Train* (1994), which won the Bollingen Prize. He taught at Columbia University for more than forty years.

Stanley Kunitz (1905–2006) was twice U.S. Poet Laureate. Over his seventy-five-year publishing career, he received the Pulitzer, the National Book Award, and the Bollingen Prize. A conscientious objector in World War II, he co-founded the Fine Arts Work Center in Provincetown and Poets House in Manhattan.

Lynne Lawner (1935–) is the translator of Antonio Gramsci's *Letters from Prison* (1973) and Maria Luisa Spaziani's *Painted Fire* (2009). Her other work includes *Lives of the Courtesans* (1987) and *Triangle Dream: Poems* (1969). Born in Ohio, she lived in Italy for many years and now lives in New York.

Paul Lawton (1924–), a Salopian, was for many years director of coordination for the World Health Organization. His translations include Franco Fortini's *Summer Is Not All: Selected Poems* (1992) and Giacomo Leopardi's *Canti* (1996), selected and introduced by Fortini.

Robert Lowell (1917–1977), born to a prominent Boston family, received the Pulitzer Prize at age thirty for *Lord Weary's Castle* (1947) and the National Book Award for *Life Studies* (1959), an early landmark of so-called confessional poetry. Other works included *Imitations* (1962) and *The Dolphin* (1974), for which he won another Pulitzer.

$\mathcal{T}$*homas* $\mathcal{L}$*ux* (1946–), born in Massachusetts, was awarded the Kingsley Tufts Prize for *Split Horizon* (1994); his most recent collection is *God Particles* (2008). The recipient of fellowships from the Guggenheim Foundation, the Mellon Foundation, and the NEA, he is currently Bourne Professor of Poetry at Georgia Tech.

$\mathcal{R}$*ob* $\mathcal{A}$. $\mathcal{M}$*ackenzie* (1964–), a Glaswegian, studied law and theology, and spent five years in Turin. Author of a chapbook, *The Clown of Natural Sorrow* (2005), and the full-length collection *The Opposite of Cabbage* (2009), he runs a poetry reading series in Edinburgh called Poetry at the Great Grog.

$\mathcal{A}$*llen* $\mathcal{M}$*andelbaum* (1926–2011) was a leading translator of Latin, Greek, and Italian. His versions of classics by Homer, Virgil, Ovid, and Dante are widely read, and his translations of modern Italian poets include the *Selected Writings of Salvatore Quasimodo* (1960) and the *Selected Poems of Giuseppe Ungaretti* (1975).

$\mathcal{M}$*ichela* $\mathcal{M}$*artini* (1974–), a Genoa native, now lectures and works as a freelance writer-translator in the United States. Her translations, in collaboration with the poet Robert Hahn, of poets such as Edoardo Sanguineti and Giorgio Caproni have appeared in journals including *Chicago Quarterly Review* and *Italian Poetry Review*.

$\mathcal{J}$. $\mathcal{D}$. $\mathcal{M}$*cClatchy* (1945–) is the author of six collections of poems, including *Hazmat* (2002) and *Mercury Dressing* (2009), several collections of essays, and many libretti. The recipient of fellowships from the Guggenheim Foundation and the NEA, he teaches at Yale and is the longtime editor of *The Yale Review*.

$\mathcal{J}$*amie* $\mathcal{M}$*cKendrick* (1955–), a Liverpudlian, is author of *The Marble Fly* (1997), winner of the Forward Prize, and *Sky Nails* (2010). Editor of *The Faber Book of 20th-Century Italian Poems* (2004), his translations include Giorgio Bassani's *The Garden of the Finzi-Continis* (2007) and Valerio Magrelli's *Vanishing Points* (2011).

$\mathcal{J}$*ames* $\mathcal{M}$*errill* (1926–1995), son of the co-founder of Merrill Lynch, won the National Book Award for *Nights and Days* (1966) and for *Mirabell: Books of Number* (1978), the Pulitzer for *Divine Comedies* (1976), and the National Book Critics Circle Award for his epic, *The Changing Light at Sandover* (1982).

$\mathcal{A}$*nthony* $\mathcal{M}$*olino* (1957–) is an anthropologist and psychoanalyst whose translations include Antonio Porta's *Kisses from Another Dream* (1987), Valerio Magrelli's *Nearsights* (1991) and *Contagion of Matter* (2000), and Lucio Mariani's *Echoes of Memory* (2003). He grew up in Philadelphia and now lives in Vasto, on the Adriatic.

$\mathcal{M}$*arianne* $\mathcal{M}$*oore* (1887–1972), tricorned syllabicist, was among the most original Modernist poets of the last century. Her *Collected Poems* (1951) received the Pulitzer, the National Book Award, and the Bollinger Prize. A passionate sports fan, she wrote the liner notes for Cassius Clay's spoken-word record, *I Am the Greatest* (1963).

Michael F. Moore (1955–) took his BFA at the Brera Academy in Milan and his PhD in Italian at New York University. His translations include novels by Erri De Luca, Sandro Veronesi, and a new version, forthcoming, of the nineteenth-century classic *The Betrothed.*

Paul Muldoon (1951–), born on a farm in Northern Ireland, moved to the United States in 1987. His many poetry collections include *Moy Sand and Gravel* (2002), for which he received the Pulitzer, Griffin, and T. S. Eliot prizes, and *Maggot* (2010). Poetry editor for *The New Yorker,* he teaches at Princeton.

Elizabeth R. Napier (1950–) is the author of *The Failure of Gothic: Problems of Disjunction in an Eighteenth-Century Literary Form* (1987) and translator of Wassily Kandinsky's *Sounds* (1981) and, with Barbara R. Studholme, Marinetti's *Selected Poems and Related Prose* (2002). She is professor of English at Middlebury College.

John Frederick Nims (1913–1999) was a Midwestern poet, author of collections including *Iron Pastoral* (1947) and *Zany in Denim* (1990), and editor of the popular poetry textbook *Western Wind* (1974). From 1978 to 1984 he was editor of *Poetry* magazine, whose annual translation prize is now named for him.

Catherine O'Brien (1944–) is the editor and translator of *Italian Women Poets of the Twentieth Century* (1996) and, with Alessandro Gentili, of *The Green Flame: Contemporary Italian Poetry with English Translations* (1987). She is professor emeritus of Italian at the National University of Ireland, Galway.

Desmond O'Grady (1935–) was born in Limerick, lived in Rome and Cairo, and received a PhD from Harvard. His many volumes of poems and translations include *The Road Taken: Poems 1956–1996* (1996) and *Trawling Tradition: Translations 1954–1994* (1994). He has taught at universities on four continents.

Jacqueline Osherow (1956–), the author of six poetry collections, has received fellowships from the Guggenheim Foundation, the NEA, and the Ingram Merrill Foundation, as well as the Witter Bynner Prize from the American Academy and Institute of Arts and Letters. She is Distinguished Professor of English at the University of Utah.

Michael Palma (1945–), born in the Bronx, is a prolific translator of Italian poetry. His volumes include Dante's *Inferno* (2002), Franco Buffoni's *The Shadow of Mount Rosa* (2002), and Guido Gozzano's *The Man I Pretend to Be* (1981), which received the Raiziss/de Palchi Book Prize. He lives in Vermont.

Don Paterson (1963–), a Dundonian poet and aphorist, has received the Forward and Whitbread prizes, the Geoffrey Faber Memorial Award, and the T. S. Eliot Prize, twice. He is poetry editor for Picador Macmillan and teaches at the University of St. Andrews, where he lives. He is also a jazz guitarist.

Roberta L. Payne (1945–) is the author of *The Influence of Dante on Medieval English Dream Visions* (1989) and translator of several books, including *A Selection of Modern Italian Poetry in Translation* (2004). She has degrees from Stanford, Harvard, and the University of Denver, where she taught for two decades.

V. Penelope Pelizzon (1967–) is the author of a collection of poems, *Nostos* (2000), which received the Poetry Society of America's Norma Farber First Book Award, and co-author, with Nancy M. West, of *Tabloid, Inc: Crimes, Newspapers, Narratives* (2010). She has lived in Italy, Syria, and Namibia.

Marcus Perryman (1956–), a freelance translator, was born in England but has lived much of his life in Italy. His translations include two Renaissance madrigal comedies by Adriano Banchieri and, with Peter Robinson, *The Selected Poetry and Prose of Vittorio Sereni* (2006). He also plays tournament chess.

Giovanni Pontiero (1932–1997), born in Glasgow to Italian immigrant parents, was the author of *Eleanora Duse: In Life and Art* (1986). Among the leading translators of twentieth-century Lusophone literature, he brought into English six novels by Clarice Lispector and five, including *Blindness* (1999), by José Saramago.

Ezra Pound (1885–1972), who spent most of his adult life in Italy, was the author of *The Cantos* (1964) and a leader of the Imagist and Vorticist movements and of Modernism generally. His pro-Fascist wartime radio broadcasts led to his arrest for treason and to twelve years in a psychiatric hospital. He died in Venice.

Sonia Raiziss (1909–1994), born in Germany, grew up in Philadelphia. The author of *Through a Glass Darkly* (1932), poems, and *Metaphysical Passion: Seven Modern American Poets and the Seventeenth-Century Tradition* (1952), she edited *Chelsea* from 1960 till her death. Her awards include a Guggenheim Fellowship.

Lucia Re (1953–), born in Rome, is the author of *Calvino and the Age of Neorealism: Fables of Estrangement* (1990), awarded the MLA's Marraro Prize for Italian studies, and translator, with Paul Vangelisti, of Amelia Rosselli's *War Variations* (2003), winner of the PEN USA Translation Award. She teaches Italian and women's studies at the University of California, Los Angeles.

Gayle Ridinger (1957–) is the translator of Camillo Sbarbaro's *Shavings: Selected Prose Poems 1914–1940* (2005) and *Italian Poetry 1950–1980* (1996). She is also the author of a novel, *The Shadow Wife* (2007), and a children's book, *The Star at the Bottom of the Sea* (2002). She has lived in Italy since 1981.

Blake Robinson (1932–2011), born in Worcester, Massachusetts, lived in Africa, Asia, and Europe. His translations include Sandro Penna's *Remember Me, God of Love* (1993), Alberto Savinio's *Paris Then* (2002), and Eugène Fromentin's *Between Sea and Sahara: An Algerian Journal* (1999).

Peter Robinson (1953–) grew up in Liverpool, spent seventeen years in Japan, and now teaches at Reading University. He is the author of many books of poetry, translator of Luciano Erba's *The Greener Meadow: Selected Poems* (2006), and co-translator, with Marcus Perryman, of *The Selected Poetry and Prose of Vittorio Sereni* (2006).

Peter Russell (1921–2003), Bristolian by birth, spent the last half of his life in Tuscany. His dozens of volumes of poetry include *The Elegies of Quintilius* (1975, enlarged in 1996) and *All for the Wolves: Selected Poems 1947–1975* (1984). He was also, apparently, the first English translator of Osip Mandelstam.

J. L. Salomon (1899–1985) was the author of a volume of poetry, *Unit and Universe* (1959), and translator of several books, including Carlo Betocchi's *Poems* (1964), Dino Campana's *Orphic Songs* (1968), Alfredo de Palchi's *Sessions with My Analyst* (1970), and Mario Luzi's *In the Dark Body of Metamorphosis* (1975).

Stephen Sartarelli (1954–) is the author of several volumes of poetry and many translations, including Umberto Saba's *Songbook* (1998), for which he received the Raiziss/de Palchi Book Prize. He has also translated a dozen (and counting) of Andrea Camilleri's popular Inspector Albano novels. Born in Ohio, he lives in France.

Cinzia Sartini-Blum (1956–) is the author of *The Other Modernism: F. T. Marinetti's Futurist Fiction of Power* (1996) and *Rewriting the Journey in Contemporary Italian Literature* (2008). She also co-edited and co-translated, with Lara Trubowitz, *Contemporary Italian Women Poets* (2001). She is a professor of Italian at the University of Iowa.

Jennifer Scappettone (1972–) is the author of *From Dame Quickly* (poems, 2009) and translator of *Locomotrix: Selected Poetry and Prose of Amelia Rosselli* (2012). She guest-edited *Aufgabe 7* (2008), a special issue devoted to Italian poetry, and was a 2010–2011 Rome Prize Fellow. She teaches at the University of Chicago.

E. J. Scovell (1907–1999), born in Sheffield, published several books of verse, including *Collected Poems* (1988), which contains her translations of Giovanni Pascoli, and *Selected Poems* (1991), a Poetry Book Society Recommendation. She received a Cholmondeley Award in 1989. Her husband was the great ecologist Charles Elton.

George Scrivani (1948–) translated Alberto Savinio's *The Departure of the Argonaut* (1986), Tano Festa's *18 Poems* (1992), and Sandro Penna's *Confused Dream* (1988), and he edited *The Collected Writings of Willem de Kooning* (1988). He was also editor of the Madras-based publisher of tiny volumes, Hanuman Books.

Olivia Sears (1964–) is the author of *self/cell* (2005) and *Photo/Synthesis* (2011), and founder of the San Francisco–based Center for the Art of Translation and of *Two Lines: World Writing in Translation*. She has a PhD in Italian from Stanford and lives in San Francisco.

Gail Segal (1952–) is a poet, author of *In Gravity's Pull* (2002), and filmmaker. She was co-producer of the Peabody-winning documentary *Arguing the World* (1988), and her own films include *Soapy* (2008), a short documentary about a barber. She teaches at the Tisch School of the Arts in New York.

Hal Steven Shows (1953–) is a Floridian musician, songwriter, and poet. His books include *Parasol: Poems 1977–2007* (2007), and his albums include *Changing the Weather* (1984) and *The Movie* (1986), as front man for Persian Gulf, and *Birthday Suit* (1989) and *Lifeboat* (1995), solo efforts. He lives in Tallahassee.

G. Singh (1929–2009), born in Jaipur, was the author and editor of dozens of books of poetry and criticism. He was the first to translate most of Montale's late work into English, and he co-translated Kabir into Italian with Ezra Pound (*Le poesie di Kabir*, 1966). From 1965 to 1992, he taught Italian at Queen's University, Belfast.

Lawrence R. Smith (1945–) is the author of *The Map of Who We Are* (1997) and *Annie's Soup Kitchen* (2003), novels; and *The Plain Talk of the Dead* (1988), poems. His translations include *The New Italian Poetry, 1945 to the Present* (1981) and Antonio Porta's novel *The King of the Storeroom* (1992).

William Jay Smith (1918–), from Louisiana, is the author of more than fifty books, including *The World Below the Window: Poems 1937–1997* (2002), *Collected Translations: Italian, French, Spanish, Portuguese* (1985), and *Army Brat: A Memoir* (1980). He was a Rhodes Scholar and the nineteenth U.S. Poet Laureate.

Kendrick Smithyman (1922–1995) is among New Zealand's major poets. His works include *Earthquake Weather* (1972) and his masterpiece, *Atua Wera* (1997), an epic finished shortly before his death. His *Campana to Montale: Versions from Italian* (2004) appeared posthumously, as did his massive *Collected Poems 1943–1995* (2004), published online.

W. D. Snodgrass (1926–2009) won the Pulitzer for his debut, *Heart's Needle* (1959), which influenced his teacher, Robert Lowell, and helped give rise to Confessionalism—a term he disliked. His later work includes *The Führer Bunker: The Complete Cycle* (1995) and *Selected Translations* (1998), winner of the Harold Morton Landon Award.

A. E. Stallings (1968–) is the author of *Archaic Smile* (1999), winner of the Richard

Wilbur Prize, and *Hapax* (2006), winner of the Poets' Prize, and translator—into rhymed fourteeners, like Chapman's *Iliad*—of Lucretius' *The Nature of Things* (2007). She studied classics in Athens, Georgia, and resides in Athens, Greece.

Felix Stefanile (1920–2009), born in New York to Italian immigrant parents, was the first recipient of the John Ciardi Lifetime Achievement Award, for Italian-American poets. Author of many books, his translations include *The Blue Moustache: Some Italian Futurist Poets* (1981) and *Umberto Saba: 31 Poems* (1978).

Susan Stewart (1952–) is the author of several collections, including *Columbarium* (2003), which received the National Book Critics Circle Award, and co-editor, with Robert Pogue Harrison, of *TriQuarterly 127: Contemporary Italian Poetry* (2007). The Annan Professor of English at Princeton, her awards include a Guggenheim Fellowship and a MacArthur Fellowship.

David Stivender (1933–1990) was the author of *Mascagni: An Autobiography Compiled, Edited and Translated from Original Sources* (1988)—a synthetic biography of the Veristic composer. A Milwaukeean, he was the first American-born chorus master of the Metropolitan Opera, a position he held from 1973 until his death.

Laura Stortoni (1942–), born in Sicily, raised in Milan, and educated internationally, is the translator of Maria Luisa Spaziani's *Sentry Towers* (1996) and, with Mary Prentice Lillie, *Women Poets of the Italian Renaissance* (1997) and *Gaspara Stampa: Selected Poems* (1994). She has translated several Beat poets into Italian.

Barbara R. Studholme (1952–) is co-translator, with Elizabeth R. Napier, of Marinetti's *Selected Poems and Related Prose* (2002). She is librarian at Tandem Friends School in Charlottesville, Virginia.

Brian Swann (1940–), Northumbrian by birth, has published many books in many genres, most recently *Born in the Blood: On the Translation of Native American Literatures* (2011). His co-translations with Ruth Feldman include Andrea Zanzotto's *Selected Poetry* (1975) and Primo Levi's *Collected Poems* (1992). He teaches at the Cooper Union.

Henry Taylor (1942–), a Virginian, received the Pulitzer for *The Flying Change* (1986), one of his many volumes of verse. His translations include Sophocles' *Electra* (1998) and, with Roberta Brooke, Euripides' *The Children of Herakles* (1981). He taught in Washington, D.C., for thirty-two years and now lives in Washington State.

Harry Thomas (1952–) is the translator of Joseph Brodsky's book-length poem, "Gorbunov and Gorchakov" (in *To Urania*, 1988), and editor of many volumes, including *Selected Poems of Thomas Hardy* (1993), *Talking with Poets* (2002), and *Montale in English* (2004). He lives in San Diego.

Diana Thow (1981–) grew up in California, earned an MFA in literary translation from the University of Iowa, and has published her translations of Italian poetry in *eXchanges, Carte Italiane, Mare Nostrum, 91st Meridian*, and elsewhere. She received a Fulbright for her work on Amelia Rosselli, and she lives in Berkeley.

Charles Tomlinson (1927–), from Stoke-on-Trent, is a major British poet strongly influenced by Americans. He is the author of *New Collected Poems* (2009) and *Metamorphoses: Poetry and Translation* (2003) and the editor of *The Oxford Book of Verse in English Translation* (1980). His many translations, from several languages, include Attilio Bertolucci's *Selected Poems* (1993).

Lara Trubowitz (1966–) is the author of *Civil Antisemitism, Modernism and British Culture, 1902–1939* (2012). She has co-edited, with Cinzia Sartini-Blum, *Contemporary Italian Women Poets: A Bilingual Anthology* (2001), and, with Phyllis Lassner, *Antisemitism and Philosemitism in the Twentieth and Twenty-first Centuries* (2008). She teaches English at the University of Iowa.

Francesca Valente (1943–), born in Vicenza, co-translated, with Lawrence Ferlinghetti, Pasolini's *Roman Poems* (1986), and co-edited, with Barry Callaghan, Patrizia Cavalli's *My Poems Will Not Change the World* (1998). She has been director of Italian Cultural Institutes in San Francisco, Toronto, Chicago, and Los Angeles.

Paul Vangelisti (1945–) is a poet, anthologist, and translator. In 2010 his translation of Adriano Spatola's *The Position of Things: Collected Poems, 1961–1992* (2008) won the Academy of American Poets Raiziss/de Palchi Book Prize. He chairs the MFA writing program at Otis College of Art and Design in Los Angeles.

Lawrence Venuti (1953–) is a translation theorist and historian. His books include *The Translator's Invisibility* (2008) and *Translation Changes Everything* (2012). Among his translations are Milo De Angelis's *Finite Intuition* (1995), Antonia Pozzi's *Breath* (2002), and Ernest Farrés's *Edward Hopper* (2009), which won the Robert Fagles Translation Prize.

Pasquale Verdicchio (1954–) is a Neapolitan poet, scholar, and translator of works including Giorgio Caproni's *The Wall of the Earth* (1992), Antonio Porta's *Passenger* (1996), and, with Stephanie Jed, Alda Merini's *The Holy Land* (2002). After years in Canada, he now teaches at the University of California, San Diego.

Rosanna Warren (1953–) is an American poet who has often lived in France and Italy. Her many books include *Fables of the Self: Studies in Lyric Poetry* (2008), *Departure: Poems* (2003), and *The Art of Translation: Voices from the Field* (1989). Her awards include Guggenheim and Cullman Center fellowships.

William Weaver (1923–) is the foremost translator of modern Italian literature into English. Best known for his versions of Umberto Eco and Italo Calvino, he has also translated Italo Svevo, Carlo Emilio Gadda, Giorgio Bassani, Luigi Pirandello, and many others. His honors include the now-defunct National Book Award for translation.

Christopher Whyte (1952–), a Glaswegian, writes poetry in Gaelic and fiction in English—and has translated Ungaretti into Gaelic and Pasolini and Penna into English. The author of *The Gay Decameron* (1999) and editor of *Modern Scottish Poetry* (2004), he lived in Rome from 1977 to 1985 and now lives in Budapest.

Richard Wilbur (1921–), U.S. Poet Laureate from 1987 to 1988, won the Pulitzer Prize for *Things of This World* (1956) and again for *New and Collected Poems* (1988). He is also a celebrated translator, most notably of Molière and other seventeenth-century French playwrights, and he was the primary lyricist for Leonard Bernstein's *Candide*.

Miller Williams (1930–) is the author of many books, including *Some Jazz a While: Collected Poems* (1999) and *Patterns of Poetry* (1986). He founded the University of Arkansas MFA program in translation and helped found the university's press. The father of the musician Lucinda Williams, he was Bill Clinton's inaugural poet in 1997.

Alan Williamson (1944–), born in Chicago, is the author of books including *Pity the Monsters: The Political Vision of Robert Lowell* (1974), *Eloquence and Mere Life: Essays on the Art of Poetry* (1995), and *The Pattern More Complicated: New and Selected Poems* (2004). He has taught at the University of California, Davis, since 1982.

Charles Wright (1935–), Tennessean by birth, is the author of many collections, including *Country Music* (1982), winner of the National Book Award, and *Black Zodiac* (1997), winner of the Pulitzer Prize. His translations include Montale's *The Storm and Other Poems* (1978) and Campana's *Orphic Songs* (1984). He has taught since 1983 at the University of Virginia.

Andrew Wylie (1947–), months after graduating from Harvard with a BA in French literature, guest-edited a special issue of the English poetry journal *Agenda* (Spring 1970) devoted to Giuseppe Ungaretti. He went on to become a cabdriver and, later, a prominent literary agent. He lives in New York.

David Young (1936–), born in Iowa, is the author of many books, most recently *Field of Light and Shadow: Selected and New Poems* (2010). His many translations include *The Poetry of Petrarch* (2004), *Du Fu: A Life in Poetry* (2008), and several volumes of Rilke. He taught at Oberlin from 1961 to 2003.

INDEX OF TITLES, FIRST LINES,
POETS, AND TRANSLATORS

O my family, my, 297

O sister of the shadow, 167

O sorella dell'ombra, 165, 167

O tu che sei sì triste ed hai presagi, 102

O you who are so sad and foresee horrors, 103

O'Brien, Catherine, 363, 365

Of course I saw the Muses, 271

Of the long and scorching days, 307

Ogni cosa, puoi dirlo, è assai più buia, 330

Ognuno sta solo sul cuor della terra, 222

O'Grady, Desmond, 291, 459

Oh come là nella corusca, 192

Oh how faint the twilight hubbub rising from, 193

Oh no, non lui, Signore, prendi me, 568

Oh no, not him, my Lord, take me, 569

One grievous day, 281

One spring day I saw, 213

One whole night, 157

Only this growing, 557

Onoriamo l'altissimo vessillo, 586

Ora c'è la disadorna, 556

Ora è la grande ombra d'autunno, 144

Ora lo sai: ho bisogno di parole, 570

Ore perdute invano, 486

Orelli, Giorgio, 382–87

Ormai la primula e il calore, 368

Ormai somiglio a una vite che vidi un dì con stupore. Cresceva su un, 150

Osherow, Jacqueline, 97

osservare quel treno sbuffante, 72

Ossigeno nelle mie tende, sei tu, a, 470

Out of a motionless infernal, 5

Over there by the river, the song of boys, 251

Oxygen in my tents, it's you, 471

Ozio dolce dell'ospedale!, 70

Padre, il mondo ti ha vinto giorno per giorno, 328

Padre, se anche tu non fossi il mio, 148

Palazzeschi, Aldo, 131–37

Palma, Michael, 19, 77, 85, 131, 139, 145, 349, 499, 501, 539

Pareva facile giuoco, 184

Parigi dorme. Un enorme silenzio, 458

Paris sleeps. An enormous silence, 459

Parla il cipresso equinoziale, oscuro, 310

Pascoli, Giovanni, 2–17

Pasolini, Pier Paolo, 388–409

Passa el tò cör tra j òmm, nissün le sa, 464

PERMISSIONS ACKNOWLEDGMENTS

*The editor gratefully acknowledges the following sources
for permission to reprint the poems in this anthology.*

ITALIAN-LANGUAGE CREDITS

Antonella Anedda, ["Per trovare la ragione di un verbo"] from *Notti de pace occidentale*. Copyright © 2001 by Antonella Anedda. "Vendetta," "Figlia (a mia figlia)," and "Abbandono" from *Il catalogo della gioia*. Copyright © 2003 by Antonella Anedda. All reprinted with the permission of the poet and Donzelli Editore S.r.L., Roma.

Rafaello Baldini, "La pinàida" and "Furistír" from *La nàiva*. Copyright © 1982 by Rafaello Baldini. "Capè" from *Furistír*. Copyright © 1988 by Rafaello Baldini. "L'igiene" and "Guèra" from *Ciacri*. Copyright © 2000 by Rafaello Baldini. All reprinted with the permission of Giulio Einaudi Editore.

Giorgio Bassani, "Variazione sul tema precedente" from *Storie dei poveri e altri versi* (Rome: Astrolabio, 1945). Copyright 1945 Giorgio Bassani. Reprinted with the permission of the heirs of Giorgio Bassani. "Saluto a Roma" from *L'alba ai vetri: Poesie 1942–1950*. Copyright © 1963 by Giorgio Bassani. Reprinted with the permission of Giulio Einaudi Editore. "Le leggi razziali" from *Epitaffio*. Copyright © 1974 by Giorgio Bassani. Reprinted with the permission of Arnoldo Mondadori Editore.

Attilio Bertolucci, "Al fratello," excerpt from "O salmista: Don Attilio," "A sua madre, che aveva nome Maria," "I papaveri," "Giardino pubblico," and "Ritratto di uomo malato," from *Le poesie*. Copyright 1951, © 1955, 1971, 1984 by Attilio Bertolucci. Reprinted with the permission of Garzanti Libri S.p.A.

Carlo Betocchi, "Dell'ombra" from *Realta vince il sogno*. Copyright 1943 by Carlo Betocchi. "D'estate" from *Poesie*. Copyright © 1955 by Carlo Betocchi. Both reprinted with the permission of Vallecchi S.p.A. Excerpt from "Diaretto invecchiando (VIII)" from *L'estate di San Martino*. Copyright © 1961 by Carlo Betocchi. Reprinted with the permission of Arnoldo Mondadori Editore.

Franco Buffoni, ["Chissà perché quest'ansa attira"] from *Il profilo del Rosa* (Milan: Mondadori, 2000), ["Se non sai che significhi in inglese"] from *Del maestro in bottega* (Rome: Edizioni Empirla, 2002), and ["Se mangiano carne"] and ["Da Marte dio crudo della guerra"] from *Guerra* (Milan: Mondadori, 2005). Reprinted with the permission of the poet.

Dino Campana, "Notturno teppista," "Donna genovese," and "O l'anima vivente delle cose" from *Inediti*. Copyright by Dino Campana. Reprinted with the permission of Vallecchi S.p.A.

Giorgio Caproni, "Il gibbone" from *Il congedo del viaggiatore cerimonioso*. Copyright © 1965 by Giorgio Caproni. "I coltelli," "Bibbia," "Dopo la notizia," and "Ritorno" from *Il muro della terra*. Copyright © 1975 by Giorgio Caproni. All reprinted with the permission of Garzanti Libri S.p.A.

Vincenzo Cardarelli, *Opere*, © 1981 Arnoldo Mondadori Editore S.p.A., Milan: "Autunno," "Alba."

Bartolo Cattafi, "Mio amore non credere" and "Da Nyhavn" from *Le mosche del meriggio*. Copyright © 1958 by Bartolo Cattafi. "Api" from *L'aria secca del fuoco*. Copyright © 1972 by Bartolo Cattafi. "Non si evade" from *L'allodola ottobrina*. Copyright © 1979 by Bartolo Cattafi. All reprinted with the permission of Arnoldo Mondadori Editore.

Patrizia Cavalli, ["Qualcuno mi ha detto"] and ["I marocchini con I tappeti"] from *Le mie poesie non cambieranno il mondo*. Copyright © 1974 by Patrizio Cavalli. ["Adesso che il tempo sembra tutto mio"] from *Il cielo*. Copyright © 1981 by Patrizia Cavalli. ["Indietro, in piedi, da lontano"] from *Sempre aperto teatro*. Copyright © 1999 by Patrizia Cavalli. ["Pigra divinità e pigra sorte"], ["Eravamo tutti perdonati"], and ["Bene, vediamo un po' come fiorisci"] from *Pigra divinità e pigra sorte*. Copyright © 2006 by Patrizia Cavalli. All reprinted with the permission of the poet.

Annalisa Cima, "La forma" and "Terzo modo" from *Terzo modo, poesie* (Milan: All'insegna del Pesce d'Oro, 1969). Reprinted by permission. "A lui" from *Ipotesi d'amore*, preface by Marisa Bulgheroni. Copyright © 1984 by Annalisa Cima. Reprinted with the permission of Garzanti Libri S.p.A.

Milo de Angelis, "Soltanto," ["Ora c'è la disadorna"], and "Ritrovo una sintassi" from *Somiglianze*. Copyright © 1976 by Milo de Angelis. Reprinted with the permission of Ugo Guanda Editore S.p.A. "Tema dell'addio," © 2005 Arnoldo Mondadori Editore S.p.A., Milan: nos. 2, 8, and 9.

Gianni d'Elia, ["E tu ricordi le cene . . ."] and ["Perché ci fanno sentire . . ."] from *Segreta*. Copyright © 1989 by Gianni d'Elia. "Altre istruzione" from *Congedo della vecchia Olivetti*. Copyright © 1996 by Gianni d'Elia. Reprinted with the permission of Giulio Einaudi Editore.

Alfredo de Palchi, ["La neve sfuria . . ."] and ["Seguo quelle che"] from *Paradigma: Tutte le poesie: 1947–2005*. Copyright © 1999, 2006 by Alfredo de Palchi. Reprinted with the permission of Xenos Books and Mimesis/Hebenon.

Eugenio De Signoribus, "(Stupefazione)" from *Altre educazioni*. Copyright © 1991 by Eugenio De Signoribus. Reprinted with the permission of Crocetti Editore. Excerpt from "Principio del giorno." Copyright © 2000 by Eugenio De Signoribus. Reprinted with the permission of Garzanti Libri S.p.A. "(Altre Voci)" from *Istme e chiuse*. Copyright © 1996 by Eugenio De Signoribus. Reprinted with the permission of Marsilio Editori S.p.A.

Luciano Erba, "Grafologia di un addio" and "Il tranviere metafisco" from *L'ippopotamo*. Copyright © 1989 by Luciano Erba. Reprinted with the permission of Giulio Einaudi Editore. *Poesie*, © 2002 Arnoldo Mondadori Editore S.p.A., Milan: "La grande Jeanne," "Vanitas varietatum," "Un'equazione di primo grado," "Terra e mare." "Gli anni quaranta" from *Il prato più verde*. Copyright © 1977 by Luciano Erba. Reprinted with the permission of Ugo Guanda Editore S.p.A.

Farfa (Vittorio Osvaldo Tommasini), "Se in me," "Le rondine," "Grande delizia," and "Gigi" from *Noi Miliardario della Fantasia*. Copyright 1933 by Vittorio Osvaldo Tommasini. Reprinted with the permission of La Prora, Milan.

Fillia (Luigi Colombo), "Lirismo geometrico" and "Notturno" from *Nuovi poeti futuristi*, edited by F. T. Marinetti. Reprinted by permission.

Umberto Fiori, "Un'indicazione," "Museo," and "Al circo" from *La bella vista*. Copyright ©
2002 by Umberto Fiori. Reprinted with the permission of Marcos y Marcos.

Franco Fortini, "Foglio di via" and "Lettera" from *Foglio di Via e altri versi*. Copyright © 1946
by Franco Fortini. Reprinted with the permission of Giulio Einaudi Editore. "Un'altra at-
tesa" and "Traducendo Brecht" from *Una volta per sempre*. Copyright © 1963 by Franco
Fortini. Reprinted with the permission of Arnoldo Mondadori Editore. "Agli dèi della mat-
tinata" and "La linea del fuoco" from *Questo muro*. Copyright © 1973 by Franco Fortini. Re-
printed with the permission of Arnoldo Mondadori Editore. "Sonetto dei sette cinesi" from
L'ospite ingrato. Copyright © 1985 by Franco Fortini. Reprinted with the permission of
Arnoldo Mondadori Editore. Nos. 1 and 2 from "Sette canzonette del golfo" from *Composita
solvantur*. Copyright © 1994 by Franco Fortini. Reprinted with the permission of Giulio
Einaudi Editore.

Gabriele Frasca, "Mal Tardato Remo" from *Lime*. Copyright © 1995 by Gabriele Frasca. Re-
printed with the permission of Giulio Einaudi Editore.

Alfonso Gatto, *Tutte le poesie*, © 2005 Arnoldo Mondadori Editore S.p.A., Milan: "Paesetto di
riviera," "Vento sulla Giudecca," "Per I Martiri di piazzale Loreto," "Anniversario."

Giovanni Giudici, *La vita in versi*, © 1965 Arnoldo Mondadori Editore S.p.A., Milan: "Epi-
gramma romano," "Mi chiedi cosa vuol dire," "Una sera come tante."

Alfredo Giuliani, "Resurrezione dopa la pioggia" and "Quando vidi il salice" from *I Novissimi:
Poesie per gli anni '60*. Copyright © 1961 by Alfredo Giuliani. Reprinted with the permis-
sion of Giulio Einaudi Editore.

Corrado Govoni, "La trombettina" from *Il quaderno dei sogni e delle stelle*. Copyright 1924 by
Corrado Govoni. Reprinted with the permission of Arnoldo Mondadori Editore.

Margherita Guidacci, nos. I, III, and V from "La sabbia e l'angelo" from *La Sabbia e l'Angelo*.
Copyright 1946 by Margherita Guidacci. Reprinted with the permission of Vallecchi S.p.A.
"La madre pazza" from *Neurosuite*. Copyright © 1970 by Margherita Guidacci. Reprinted
with the permission of Neri Pozza Editore S.p.A. "Sull'orlo della visione" from *Anelli del
tempo*. Copyright © 1993 by Margherita Guidacci. Reprinted with the permission of Città
di Vita.

Vivian Lamarque, "Il Primo Mio Amore" and "A Nove Mesi" from *Teresino*. Copyright © 1981
by Vivian Lamarque. Reprinted with permission. "A Vacanza Conclusa" from *Una quieta
polvere*. Copyright © 1996 by Vivian Lamarque. Reprinted with the permission of Arnoldo
Mondadori Editore.

Primo Levi, "Shemà" and "Alzarsi" from *Ad ora incerta*. Copyright © 1984 by Primo Levi. Re-
printed by permission.

Franco Loi, "Trâ, 'me 'na s'giaffa salti tri basèj" from *Stròlegh*. Copyright © 1975 by Franco Loi.
Reprinted with the permission of Giulio Einaudi Editore. "El sú, el dulur g'a 'n nòm . . ."
from *Amur del Temp*. Copyright © 1999 by Franco Loi. Reprinted with the permission of
Crocetti Editore. "Passa el tò cör tra j òmm, nissun le sa" from *Umber*. Copyright © 1992 by
Franco Loi. Reprinted with the permission of Piero Manni S.r.L.

Mario Luzi, "Avorio" from *Avvento notturno*. Copyright 1940 by Mario Luzi. "Notizie a Giusep-
pina dopo tanti anni" and "Nella casa di N, compagna d'infanzia" from *Primizie del deserto*
(Milan: Schwartz, 1952). Copyright 1952 by Mario Luzi. "La notte lava la mente" and "Nel-

l'imminenza dei quarant'anni" from *Onore del vero* (Venice: Neri Pozza, 1957). All reprinted with the permission of Giulio Einaudi Editore.

Valerio Magrelli, ["Ho spesso immaginato che gli sguardi"] and ["Amo I gesti imprecisi"] from *Nature e venature*. Copyright © 1987 by Valerio Magrelli. Reprinted with the permission of Arnoldo Mondadori Editore. "Dal nostro inviato a: Trois Rivières, Québec," "Codice a barre," and "Dal nostro inviato a: Dresda, piazza del Teatro" from *Didascalie per la lettura di un giornale*. Copyright © 1999 by Valerio Magrelli. ["Che la materia provochi il contagio"] and "L'imballatore" from *Esercizi di tiptologia*. Copyright © 1992 by Valerio Magrelli. All reprinted with the permission of Arnoldo Mondadori Editore. ["C'è silenzio tra una pagina e l'altra"] from *Ora serrata retinae*. Copyright © 1980 by Valerio Magrelli. Reprinted with the permission of Giangiacomo Feltrinelli Editore.

Dacia Maraini, "Una Finestra Aperta" and "Nel Palmo della Mano Destra" from *Viaggiando con passo di volpe: Poesie 1983–1991*. Copyright © 1991 by Dacia Maraini. Reprinted with the permission of Rizzoli International Publications.

Lucio Mariani, "Furieri" from *Il torto della preda: Versi scelti, 1974–1994*. Copyright © 1995 by Luciano Mariani. Reprinted with the permission of Crocetti Editore. "Giugno di Sicilia (Noto, 1998)" from *Qualche notizia del tempo*. Copyright © 2001 by Lucio Mariani. Reprinted with the permission of the author.

F. T. Marinetti, "Le soir, couchée dans son lit, Elle relisait la lettre de son artilleur su front." Reprinted with the permission of Marco Vigevani Agenzia Letteraria.

Pino Masnata, "Piccolo amore" and "L'ambizione" from *Tavole parolibere*. Copyright 1932 by Pino Masnata. Reprinted by permission.

Alda Merini, "Vicino al Giordano," ["Io ero un uccello"], and "Toeletta" from *La terra santa*. Copyright © 1984 by Alda Merini. Reprinted with the permission of Libri Scheiwiller. "Alda Merini" from *Vuoto d'amore*. Copyright © 1991 by Alda Merini. Reprinted with the permission of Giulio Einaudi Editore. "Apro la sigaretta" from *Ballate non pagate*. Copyright © 1995 by Alda Merini. Reprinted with the permission of Giulio Einaudi Editore. "13 aphorisms" from *Aforismi e magie*. Copyright © 1999 by Alda Merini. Reprinted with the permission of Rizzoli International Publications.

Eugenio Montale, *Tutte le poesie*, © 1967 Arnoldo Mondadori Editore S.p.A., Milan: "In limine," "I limoni," "Delta" from "Ossi di seppia," nos. 1, 2, 6, 7, 14, 19; "Xenia," nos. 1, 4, 5, 6, 9; "La bufera," "Nella serra," "Il sogno del prigioniero," "Nel parco," "L'anguilla," "Piccolo testamento." "Il balcone," "Verso Vienna," "Tempi di Bellosguardo (I)," "La casa dei doganieri," and nos. 1, 3, 6, 10, 14, 16, 20 from "Mottetti" from *Le occasioni*. Copyright © 1939 by Eugenio Montale. Reprinted with the permission of Giulio Einaudi Editore.

Saturno Montanari, "Autunno" and "Notte dietro le persiane" (1939). Reprinted by permission.

Giorgio Orelli, "Carnevale a Prato Leventina," "Nel cerchio familiare," and "Dove I ragazzi ammazzano il gennaio" from *Ora del tempo*. Copyright © 1962 by Giorgio Orelli. Reprinted with the permission of Arnoldo Mondadori Editore.

Pier Paolo Pasolini, "Il di da la me muart" from *La meglio gioventù*. Copyright 1954 by Pier Paolo Pasolini. Reprinted by permission. Nos. I and IV from "I ceneri di Gramsci" and no. I from "Il pianto della scavatrice" from *I Ceneri di Gramsci*. Copyright © 1957 by Pier Paolo Pasolini. Reprinted with the permission of Garzanti Libri S.p.A. Excerpt from "Vanno verso le Terme di Caracalla" and excerpt from "Vado anch'io verso le Terme di Caracalla" from *La religione del mio tempo*. Copyright © 1961 by Pier Paolo Pasolini. Reprinted with the permission of Garzanti Libri S.p.A.

Cesare Pavese, "Grappa a settembre," "Creazione," ["Verrà la morte"], "Disciplina," "Tolleranza," and nos. 4 and 5 from "La terra e la morte" from *Le poesie*. Copyright © 1998 by Cesare Pavese. Reprinted with the permission of Arnoldo Mondadori Editore.

Sandro Penna, ["La vita . . . è ricordarsi di un risveglio"], ["Se dietro la finestra illuminata"], "Sera nel giardino," "Il Nuotatore," "Interno," ["È pur dolce il ritrovarsi"], ["La veneta piazzetta"], and ["Il cielo è vuoto"] from *Poesie*. Copyright 1938 by Sandro Penna. ["Deserto è il fiume"], ["Il treno tarderà di almeno un'ora"], and ["Lumi del cimitero"] from *Poesie*. Copyright © 1955 by Sandro Penna. Penna, ["È l'ora"], ["O non ti dare arie"], and ["Passando sopra un ponte"] from *Poesie*. Copyright © 1956 by Sandro Penna. ["Io vado verso il fiume su un cavallo"] and "Letteratura" from *Poesie*. Copyright © 1976 by Sandro Penna. All reprinted with the permission of Garzanti Libri S.p.A. ["Ecco il fanciullo"] from *Poesie*. Copyright © 1955 by Sandro Penna. Reprinted with the permission of Garzanti Libri S.p.A.

Camillo Pennati, "Gabbiano" from *Gabbiano e altri versi / On Edge*. Copyright © 1990 by Camillo Pennati. Reprinted with the permission of Edizioni L'Arzana associazione culturale.

Antonio Porta, nos. 1, 3, and 7 from "Aprire" and excerpt [11 lines] from "Rapporti umani: XII" from *Aprire*. Copyright © 1964 by Antonio Porta. Reprinted with the permission of Libri Scheiwiller. Nos. 1, 4, and 9 from "Autocoscienza di un servo" from *Week End*. Copyright © 1974 by Antonio Porta. Reprinted with the permission of Cooperativa Scrittori Editrice. "Orvieto." Reprinted with permission.

Antonia Pozzi, "Pudore" and "Confidare" from *Parole*. Copyright 1933 by Antonia Pozzi. Reprinted with the permission of Arnoldo Mondadori Editore.

Fabio Pusterla, "Quasi un'allegoria," "Stella, meteora, qualcosa di filante" and "Il saccheggio" from *Pietra sangue* (Marcos y Marcos Publishers, 1999). "Canzonetta dell'universo in espansione" from *Folla sommersa* (Milan: Marcos y Marcos Publishers, 1999)." All reprinted with the permission of the author.

Salvatore Quasimodo, *Tutte le poesie*, © 1967 Arnoldo Mondadori Editore S.p.A., Milan: "Ed è subito sera," "Vento a Tindari," "Oboe sommerso," "Uomo del mio tempa," "Terra," "Antico inverno," "Strada di Agrigentum," "L'alto veliero," "Già vola il fiore magro," "Alle fronde dei salici," "Epitaffo per Bice Donetti."

Giovanni Raboni, "Cinema di pomeriggio" from *Le case della Vetra*. Copyright © 1966 by Giovanni Raboni. ["Eroi dispere . . ."] and ["Ci sono sere che vorrei"] from *Quare tristis*. Copyright © 1998 by Giovanni Raboni. "Compleanno di Mia Figlia, 1966" from *Cadenza d'inganno*. Copyright © 1975 by Giovanni Raboni. ["I film porno mi annoiano . . ."] from *Barlumi di storia*. Copyright © 2002 by Giovanni Raboni. All reprinted with the permission of Arnoldo Mondadori Editore.

Nelo Risi, "I meli I meli I meli," "Ambizioni," and "Torrido" from *Polso teso*. Copyright © 1956 by Nelo Risi. "Legittima speranza" from *Minime massime*. Copyright © 1962 by Nelo Risi. "La neve nell'armadio" from *Dentro la sostanza*. Copyright © 1965 by Nelo Risi. All reprinted with the permission of ALI—Agenzia Letteraria Internazionale.

Amelia Rosselli, "Dopo il dono di Dio" and "Per la tua pelle olivastra" from *Variazioni belliche*.

Giuseppe Ungaretti, *Vita di un uomo: Tutte le poesie*, © 1969 Arnoldo Mondadori Editore S.p.A., Milan: "Non gridate più," "Levante eterno," "Agonia," "In memoria," "Veglia," "Allegria di naufragi," "Mattina," "Un'altra note," "Soldati," "La pieta (1)," "La morte meditate: Canto primo," "Senza più peso," "Variazioni sul nulla," "Vanità."

Patrizia Valduga, ["A me creduta esangue, non veduta . . ."] and ["Signore caro tu vedi il mio stato . . ."] from *Medicamenta e altri medicamenta*. Copyright © 1989 by Patrizia Verduga. Nos. 8, 17, 45, 47, 71, and 100 from *Cento quartine*. Copyright © 1997 by Patrizia Verduga. Nos. 107 and 122 from *Quartine: Seconda centuria*. Copyright © 2001 by Patrizia Verduga. "Requiem" from *Requiem*. Copyright © 2002 by Patrizia Verduga. All reprinted with the permission of ALI—Agenzia Letteraria Internazionale.

Diego Valeri, "Vicenza 1915" from *Poesie*. Copyright © 1962 by Diego Valeri. "Riva di pena, canale d'oblio . . ." from *Poesie Vecchie e Nuove*. Copyright © 1930 by Diego Valeri. All reprinted with the permission of Arnoldo Mondadori Editore.

Andrea Zanzotto, "Quanto a lungo" and "Ormai" from *Dietro il paesaggio*. Copyright © 1951 by Andrea Zanzotto. "La perfezione della neve" and "Al mondo" from *La beltà*. Copyright © 1968 by Andrea Zanzotto. "Subnarcosi" from *Pasque*. Copyright © 1973 by Andrea Zanzotto. "Esistere psichicamente" from *Vocativo*. Copyright © 1957 by Andrea Zanzotto. "Così siamo" from *IX Ecloghe*. Copyright © 1962 by Andrea Zanzotto. Nos. I, IX, and Postscript from "Ipersonetto" from *Il galateo in bosco*. Copyright © 1978 by Andrea Zanzotto. All reprinted with the permission of ALI—Agenzia Letteraria Internazionale.

ENGLISH-LANGUAGE CREDITS

Unless otherwise specified, the English translations
are reprinted with the permission of the translators

Antonella Anedda, ["To unearth the reason for a verb"], translated by Jamie McKendrick. "Abandonment," translated by Susan Stewart and Gian Maria Annovi, from *Triquarterly 127: Contemporary Italian Poetry* (May 2007). Translation copyright © 2007 by Susan Stewart and Gian Maria Annovi. "For My Daughter" from *Poetry* (2007), and "Vendetta," translated by Sarah Arvio.

Rafaello Baldini, "The Pine Grove," "Outsider," "Picking," "Hygiene," and "War," translated by Adria Bernardi, from *Small Talk*, translated by Adria Bernardi (Stony Brook, New York: Gradiva Publications, 2009).

Giacomo Balla, "Noisist Onomatopoeia Printing Press," translated by Geoffrey Brock.

Giorgio Bassani, "Salute to Rome," translated by Peter Robinson, from *The Great Friend and Other Translated Poems* by Peter Robinson (Tonbridge, U.K.: Worple Press, 2002). "The Racial Laws," translated by Jamie McKendrick, from *Poetry* (April 2007). "Idyll," translated by Donald Davie, from Donald Davie, *Collected Poems*. Copyright © 1990 by Donald Davie. Reprinted with the permission of the University of Chicago Press.

Attilio Bertolucci, "To My Brother" and excerpt from "O Psalmist: Don Attilio" from *Selected Poems*, translated by Charles Tomlinson. Copyright © 1994 by Charles Tomlinson. Reprinted with the permission of Bloodaxe Books Ltd. "To His Mother, Whose Name Was

Maria," translated by Cyrus Cassells, from *Poetry* (July/August 2010). Copyright © 2010 by Cyrus Cassells. "Poppies," translated by Geoffrey Brock, from *Poetry* (December 2010). "Public Garden" and "Portrait of a Sick Man," translated by Nicholas Benson, from *Winter Journey* (Parlor Press, 2005).

Carlo Betocchi, "The Shadow," "Summer," and excerpt from "Little Diary of Getting Old (VIII)," translated by Geoffrey Brock, from *Poetry* (March 2010).

Franco Buffoni, ["Who knows why this haven attracts"] and ["If you don't know what it means . . ."], translated by Michael Palma, from *The Shadow of Mount Rosa*, translated by Michael Palma (Gradiva Publications, 2001). ["If they eat meat"], translated by Moira Egan and Damiano Abeni. ["From Mars cruel god of war"], translated by Geoffrey Brock, from *Poetry* (December 2007).

Dino Campana, excerpt from "The Night" and "Genoa Woman," translated by Charles Wright, from *Orphic Songs*. Copyright © 1984 by Oberlin College Press. "Nocturne," translated by Charles Wright. "The Chimera," translated by Luigi Bonaffini. "Campana, Nailed to a Boulder," translated by Thomas Lux from *Sunday: Poems*. Copyright © 1979 by Thomas Lux. Reprinted with the permission of Houghton Mifflin Harcourt Publishing Company. All rights reserved. "Autumn Garden," translated by John Frederick Nims, from John Frederick Nims, *Sappho to Valéry: Poems in Translation*. Copyright © 1971 by John Frederick Nims. Reprinted with the permission of Rutgers University Press.

Giorgio Caproni, "The Gibbon" from *An Anthology of Modern Italian Poetry* (Modern Language Association, 2009). "Bible" from *The Earth's Wall: Selected Poems 1932–1986*, translated by Ned Condini. Copyright © 2004, 2009 by Ned Condini. "The Knives" from *The Wall of the Earth (1964–1975)*, translated by Pasquale Verdicchio (Montreal: Guernica Editions, 1992). Copyright © 1992 by Pasquale Verdicchio. "After the News," translated by Peter Robinson, from *The Great Friend and Other Translated Poems* by Peter Robinson (Tonbridge, U.K.: Worple Press, 2002). "Return," translated by David Goldstein.

Vincenzo Cardarelli, "Autumn," translated by William Weaver, from *Adam: International Review* (London: Aug. 1946). "Dawn," translated by Allen Mandelbaum, from *The Atlantic Monthly* (December 1957).

Bartolo Cattafi, "My Love, Don't Believe," translated by Dana Gioia, from *Poetry* (October 1989). Copyright © 1989 by Dana Gioia. "From Nyhavn," translated by Ruth Feldman and Brian Swann, from *The Dry Air of the Fire: Selected Poems*, by Bartolo Cattafi (Translation Press, 1981). "Bees," translated by Rina Ferrarelli, from *Winter Fragments: Selected Poems 1945–1979* by Bartolo Cattafi (New York: Chelsea Editions, 2006). "No Escape," translated by Geoffrey Brock.

Patrizia Cavalli, ["I was told"], translated by Barry Callaghan and Francesca Valente, from *My Poems Will Not Change the World: Selected Poems, 1974–1992* (Exile Editions, 1998). ["Now that time seems all mine"], translated by Judith Baumel, from *My Poems Will Not Change the World: Selected Poems 1974–1992* (Exile Editions, 1998). ["From behind, standing, from a distance"], translated by Geoffrey Brock, from *Poetry* (Dec. 2007). ["Even when it seems that the day"], translated by Geoffrey Brock. ["Lazy gods and lazy fortune"] and ["We were all forgiven"], translated by Susan Stewart and Brunella Antomarini, from *Triquarterly 127: Contemporary Italian Poetry* (May 2007). Copyright © 2007 by Susan Stewart and Brunella

Antomarini. All rights reserved. ["So, let's see how you flower"], translated by Moira Egan and Damiano Abeni. ["The Moroccans with their carpets"], translated by Kenneth Koch. Reprinted with the permission of the Estate of Kenneth Koch.

Annalisa Cima, "Form" and "Third Way," translated by Marianne Moore, from *Poesie/Poems*, preface by Vanni Scheiwiller, translations by Jonathan Galassi, Christine Gugolz, Allen Mandelbaum, Marianne Moore, Walter de Rachewiltz, Demetrio Vittorini. All'insegna del Pesce d'Oro, Milan 1999. Reprinted with the permission of the Literary Estate of Marianne Moore, David M. Moore, Esq., Administrator. All rights reserved. "To Him," translated by Jonathan Galassi.

Sergio Corazzini, excerpt from "Desolation of the Poor Sentimental Poet," translated by Michael Palma, from *Saturday Evening: Selected Poems of Sergio Corazzini* (Gradiva Publications, 1997).

Gabriele D'Annunzio, "Rain in the Pine Grove," translated by Jonathan Galassi. "The Mouth of the Arno," translated by Alistair Elliot, from *Italian Landscape Poems* (Northumberland, U.K.: Bloodaxe Books, 1993). Copyright © 1993 by Alistair Elliot. "The Shepherds," translated by Geoffrey Brock, from *Unsplendid 3.3: A Special Translation Issue* (Winter 2011).

Milo de Angelis, "Only," translated by Lawrence Venuti. ["Now she is unadorned"] and "I Recover a Syntax" from *Finite Intuition: Selected Poetry and Prose*, translated by Lawrence Venuti (Los Angeles: Sun and Moon Press, 1995). Copyright © 1995 by Lawrence Venuti. 2 ["Milan was asphalt, liquid asphalt. In the desert"], 8 ["In you all deaths gather, all"], and 9 [The place was motionless, the word obscure. That was "] from "Theme of Farewell," translated by Susan Stewart and Patrizio Ceccagnoli. Copyright © 2012 by The University of Chicago. All rights reserved.

Gianni d'Elia, ["You remember them, the dinners . . ."] and ["Because things make us feel . . ."], translated by Christopher Whyte and Marco Fazzini, from *Lines Review* 130 (September 1994). "Further Instructions," translated by Carla Billitteri, from *Boundary* 2 (Spring 1999).

Alfredo de Palchi, "The snow rages and under its serum," translated by I. L. Saloman, from *Sessions with My Analyst* (October House, 1970). "I look at the woman," translated by Alethea Gail Segal, from *Addictive Aversions*. Copyright © 1999 by I. L. Salomon and Alethea Gail Segal. Reprinted with the permission of the author, Xenos Books, and Alethea Gail Segal.

Eugenio De Signoribus, "(stupefaction)," and excerpt from "Principle of the Day," translated by Christopher Whyte, from Marco Fazzini, ed., *Resisting Alterities: Wilson Harris and Other Avatars of Otherness* (Amsterdam and New York, Rodopi, 2004), translated by Christopher Whyte. "(other voices)," translated by V. Joshua Adams. Copyright © 2011 by V. Joshua Adams.

Salvatore di Giacomo, "March," translated by Michael Palma, from *Dialect Poetry of Southern Italy: Texts and Criticism*, edited by Luigi Bonaffini (Legas, 1997).

Luciano Erba, "A Graphology of Goodbye," translated by W. S. Di Piero. "La Grande Jeanne" and "Vanitas Varietatum," translated by Charles Wright, from *Poetry* (October 1989). "Equation of 1 Degree," translated by Lynne Lawner, from *Translations by American Poets*, Jean Garrigue, ed. (Ohio University Press, 1970). Copyright © 2011 by Lynne Lawner. Reprinted by permission of Georges Borchardt, Inc., on behalf of Lynne Lawner. Erba, "Land and Sea," translated by Robert Fitzgerald, from *Poetry* (August 1959). Reprinted with the permission of the Estate of Robert Fitzgerald. "My Forties" and "The Metaphysical Tram-driver" from *The Greener Meadow: Selected Poems,* translated by Peter Robinson. Copyright © 2007 by Peter Robinson.

Farfa (Vittorio Osvaldo Tommasini), "2 in 1," "The Swallows," "What Fun," and "Gigi," translated by Fred Chappell, from *C: Poems* (Baton Rouge: Louisiana State University Press, 1993).

Fillia (Luigi Colombo), "Geometric Lyricism" and "Nocturne" from *Italian Futurist Poetry,* edited and translated by Willard Bohn. Copyright © 2005 by the University of Toronto Press. Reprinted with permission of the publisher.

Umberto Fiori, "Giving Directions," translated by Alistair Elliot. "At the Circus" and "Museum" from *Poetry* (December 2007) translated by Geoffrey Brock.

Franco Fortini, "Deportation Order" from *The New Italian Poetry: 1945 to the Present,* edited and translated by Lawrence R. Smith (Berkeley: University of California Press, 1981). Copyright © 1981 by The Regents of the University of California. "Letter," translated by Van K. Brock. "Another Wait," translated by W. S. Di Piero. "The Line of Fire," translated by Michael Hamburger, from *Poems* (Todmorden, Lancashire: Arc Publications, 1978). "Sonnet of the Seven Chinese," translated by Lawrence R. Smith. Nos. 1 and 2 from "Seven Gulf Ditties," translated by Geoffrey Brock, from *Poetry* (December 2007). "Translating Brecht" and "To the Gods of the Morning," translated by Paul Lawton, from *Summer Is Not All: Selected Poems,* translated by Paul Lawton. Copyright © 1992 by Paul Lawton. Reprinted by permission of Carcanet Press, Ltd.

Gabriele Frasca, "ill-belated oar," translated by Geoffrey Brock, from *Unsplendid 3.3: A Special Translation Issue* (December 2011).

Alfonso Gatto, "Seaside Village," translated by Hal Shows. "Wind over Giudecca" from *A Selection of Modern Italian Poetry in Translation,* edited and translated by Roberta L. Payne. Copyright © 2004 by Roberta L. Payne. "For the Martyrs of Loreto Square" from *Campana to Montale: Versions from Italian,* translated by Kendrick Smithyman. Copyright © 2010 by Kendrick Smithyman. Reprinted with the permission of Edizioni Joker. "Anniversary," translated by Giovanni Pontiero, from *World Authors 1970–1975,* John Wakeman, ed. (Wilson, 1980). Reprinted with the permission of the Estate of Giovanni Pontiero.

Giovanni Giudici, "Roman Epigram" and "You Ask Me What It Means" from *The New Italian Poetry: 1945 to the Present,* edited and translated by Lawrence R. Smith (Berkeley: University of California Press, 1981). Copyright © 1981 by The Regents of the University of California. "An Evening Like So Many Others," translated by Charles Wright, from *Poetry* (October 1989). Copyright © 1989.

Alfredo Giuliani, "Resurrection After the Rain" and "When I Saw the Willow," translated by Michael F. Moore, from *I Novissimi: Poetry for the Sixties* (Los Angeles: Sun and Moon Press, 1995).

Corrado Govoni, "The Villages" from W. D. Snodgrass, *Selected Translations.* Copyright © 1998 by W. D. Snodgrass. Reprinted with the permission of The Permissions Company, Inc., on behalf of BOA Editions, Ltd., www.boaeditions.org. "Self-Portrait," translated by Geoffrey Brock. "The Little Trumpet," translated by Felix Stefanile, from *The Blue Moustache: Some Futurist Poets* (The Elizabeth Press, 1980). Reprinted with the permission of the Estate of Felix Stefanile.

Guido Gozzano, "A Wintry Scene" and "The Colloquies: 3," translated by Michael Palma, from *The Man I Pretend to Be: "The Colloquies" and Selected Poems of Guido Gozzano*. Copyright © 1981 by Princeton University Press. "Totò Merúmeni," translated by Geoffrey Brock, from *Two Lines: A Journal of Translation* (2006). "The Loveliest," translated by Geoffrey Brock, from *Italian Translation Review* 1, no. 1.

Margherita Guidacci, no. I from "The Sand and the Angel" and "The Mad Mother" from *Landscape with Ruins: Selected Poetry of Margherita Guidacci*, translated by Ruth Feldman. Copyright © 1992 by Wayne State University Press. Reprinted with the permission of Wayne State University Press. No. III from "The Sand and the Angel," translated by Cid Corman, from *Origin*, 2nd Series (April 1963). Reprinted with the permission of Bob Arnold, Literary Executor for the Estate of Cid Corman. No. V from "The Sand and the Angel" and "On the Edge of Vision," translated by Catherine O'Brien, from *In the Eastern Sky: Selected Poems of Margherita Guidacci* (Dedalus, 1993).

Vivian Lamarque, "My First Love," translated by Geoffrey Brock. "At Nine Months," translated by Moira Egan and Damiano Abeni. "At Vacation's End," translated by Peter Covino from *New European Poets*, Kevin Prufer and Wayne Miller, eds. (St. Paul, Minn.: Graywolf, 2008).

Primo Levi, "Shemà," translated by A. Alvarez from *The Faber Book of Modern European Poetry* (London: Faber & Faber, 1992). Copyright © 1992 by Al Alvarez. "Reveille" from *Collected Poems*, translated by Ruth Feldman and Brian Swann. Copyright © 1992 by Ruth Feldman and Brian Swann.

Franco Loi, "Hurled, like a slap I leap three stairs," "I know that suffering has a name, its chain," and "Your unknown heart among the people goes" from *Air and Memory* (Denver: Counterpath Press, 2007), translated by Andrew Frisardi. Copyright © 2007 by Andrew Frisardi.

Mario Luzi, "Ivory," translated by I. L. Salomon, from *In the Dark Body of Metamorphosis and Other Poems*. Copyright © 1975 by I. L. Salomon. Used by permission of W. W. Norton & Company, Inc. ["Out of Danger?"] and "Auctor," translated by Stephen Sartarelli. "Tidings for Giuseppina," translated by G. Singh and Gabrielle Barfoot, from *Modern Italian Poetry: A Bilingual Anthology* (New Delhi: Sampark, 2003). "In the House of a Girl I Knew in Childhood" and "Night Cleanses the Mind," translated by Geoffrey Brock. "On Approaching Forty," translated by Dana Gioia, from *Poetry* (October 1989). Copyright © 1989 by Dana Gioia.

Valerio Magrelli, ["I have often imagined that glances"], translated by Dana Gioia, from *New Italian Poets*, edited by Dana Gioia and Michael Palma (Story Line Press, 1991). Copyright © 1990 by Dana Gioia. "From Our Correspondent in: Trois Rivières, Québec," translated by Riccardo Duranti and Anamaría Crowe Serrano, from *Instructions on How to Read a Newspaper* (Chelsea Editions, 2007). "The Mover" from *The Contagion of Matter: New and Selected Poems*, translated by Anthony Molino (Teaneck, N.J.: Holmes and Meier, 2001). Copyright © 2001 by Anthony Molino. ["There's a silence between one page and another"] and ["I love uncertain gestures"], translated by Jonathan Galassi, from *Poetry* (October 1989). ["That matter engenders contagion"], "Bar Code," and "From Our Correspondent in: Theatre Square, Dresden" from *Vanishing Points: Poems*, translated by Jamie McKendrick. Copyright © 2010 by Jamie McKendrick. Reprinted by permission of Farrar, Straus and Giroux, LLC.

Dacia Maraini, "a window is open," translated by Martha Collins, from *The Poetry Miscellany*. "in the palm of my right hand," translated by Martha Collins, from *Snail's Pace Review*.

Lucio Mariani, "Quartermasters" from *Echoes of Memory: Selected Poems of Lucio Mariani*, translated by Anthony Molino. Translation copyright © 2003 by Anthony Molino. Reprinted with the permission of Wesleyan University Press. "Sicily in June," translated by Rosanna Warren. Reprinted with the permission of the author and translator.

F. T. Marinetti, excerpt from "The Founding and Manifesto of Futurism," translated by R. W. Flint, from *Selected Writings*, translated by R.W. Flint. Copyright © 1972 by R.W. Flint. Reprinted by permission of Farrar, Straus and Giroux, LLC. Excerpt from "Technical Manifesto of Futurist Literature" and "At Night, Lying in Bed, She Rereads the Letter from Her Gunner at the Front" from *Selected Poems and Related Prose*, translated by Elizabeth R. Napier and Barbara R. Studholme. Copyright © 2002 by Elizabeth R. Napier and Barbara R. Studholme. Reprinted with the permission of Yale University Press.

Alda Merini, "Near the Jordan" and "Toilette" from *The Holy Land*, translated by Stephanie Jed and Pasquale Verdicchio (Toronto: Guernica Editions, 2002). Copyright © 2002 by Stephanie Jed, Pasquale Verdicchio, and Guernica Editions Ltd. ["As for me, I used to be a bird"] and "Alda Merini" from *Love Lessons: Selected Poems of Alda Merini*, translated by Susan Stewart. Copyright © 2009 by Susan Stewart and Princeton University Press. "I Open the Cigarette," translated by Cinzia Sartini Blum and Lara Trubowitz, from *Contemporary Italian Women Poets* (New York: Italica Press, 2001). Seven aphorisms ["I am a furious," "To mistake shit," "Every man is a friend," "I never speak," "The gun," "Every tibia loves its fibula," and "Alda Merini"], translated by Carla Billittiei, from Alda Merini, *I Am a Furious Little Bee*, translated by Carla Billittieri (Oakland, Calif.: Hooke Press, 2008). Four aphorisms ["As I am Catholic," "I've had," "I am completely," and "No one can know."], translated by Douglas Basford, from *Poetry* (December 2007). Two aphorisms ["I'm not afraid of death" and "Sin"], translated by Douglas Basford.

Eugenio Montale, "In limine" and nos. 1 and 7 from *Cuttlefish Bones*, translated by William Arrowsmith. Copyright © 1993 by William Arrowsmith. Used by permission of W. W. Norton & Company, Inc. "The Lemons" and no. 6 ["Bring me the sunflower, let me plant it"] from "Cuttlefish Bones," "Arsenio," "In the Greenhouse," "The Prisoner's Dream," no. 10 ["Why wait? The squirrel beats his torch-tail"] from "Motets," translated by Jonathan Galassi, from *Collected Poems 1920–1954*, translated by Jonathan Galassi. Copyright © 1998 by Jonathan Galassi. Reprinted by permission of Farrar, Straus and Giroux, LLC. No. 2 from "Cuttlefish Bones," translated by David Young, from *Selected Poems*, translated by Jonathan Galassi, Charles Wright, and David Young. Copyright © 2004 by Oberlin College Press. Used by permission of Oberlin College Press. No. 14 from "Cuttlefish Bones," no. 20 [". . . but so be it. A note from a cornet"] from "Motets," and "The Balcony," translated by Geoffrey Brock. No. 19 from "Cuttlefish Bones," translated by Jamie McKendrick. "Delta," translated by Samuel Beckett. Originally in *This Quarter* 2, no. 4 (April–May–June 1930). Reprinted by permission of Georges Borchardt, Inc., on behalf of the Estate of Samuel Beckett. "En Route to Vienna," translated by Eamon Grennan, from *Montale in English* (New York: Other Press, 2005). No. 1 ["You know this: I must lose you again and cannot"] from *Mottetti, Poems of Love: The Motets of Eugenio Montale*, translated by Dana Gioia (St. Paul, Minn.: Graywolf Press, 1990). Copyright © 1990 by Dana Gioia. No. 3 ["Frost on the panes, the sick"] from "Motets" and "The Coastguard Station," translated by William Arrowsmith, from *The Occasions*. Used by permission of W. W. Norton & Company, Inc. No. 6 ["The hope of even seeing you again"] from "Motets," translated by George Kay, from *Poesie/Poems*, translated by George Kay. Reprinted with the permission of Edinburgh University Press. No. 14 ["Is it salt or hail that rages? It lacerates"] from "Motets," translated by Charles Wright, from *Eugenio Montale: Selected Poems*. Copyright © 1965 by New Directions Publishing Corp. Reprinted by permission of the translator and New Directions Publishing Corp. No. 16 ["The flower that rehearses"] from "Motets," translated by J. D. McClatchy, from *Stars Principal* (New York: Macmillan Publishing Company, 1986). "Bellosguardo," translated by Robert Lowell, from *Collected Poems*, edited by Frank Bidart. Copyright © 2003 by Harriet Lowell and Sheridan Lowell. Reprinted by permission of Farrar, Straus and Giroux, LLC. "The Storm," translated by Geoffrey Hill, from *Without Title*. Reprinted by permission of Yale University Press and Penguin Books Ltd. "In the Park," translated by James Merrill, from *Eugenio Montale: Selected Poems*. Copyright © 1965 by New Directions Publishing Corp. Reprinted by permission of New Directions Publishing Corp. "The Eel," translated by Paul Muldoon, from *Moy, Sand and Gravel*. Copyright © 2002 by Paul Muldoon. Reprinted by permission of Farrar, Straus and Giroux, LLC, and Faber & Faber, Ltd. "Little Testament," translated by Charles Wright. No. 1 from "Xenia I," translated by Jonathan Galassi. Nos. 4 and 9 from "Xenia I," translated by Harry Thomas, from *Montale in English* (New York: Other Press, 2005). No. 5 from "Xenia I," translated by Geoffrey Brock. No. 6 from "Xenia I," translated by William Arrowsmith, from *Satura*. Copyright © 1998 by William Arrowsmith. Used by permission of W. W. Norton & Company, Inc.

Saturno Montanari, "Autunno" and "Notte dietro le persiane," translated by Ezra Pound, from *Ezra Pound: Translations*. Copyright © 1963 by Ezra Pound. Reprinted by permission of New Directions Publishing Corp. and Faber & Faber, Ltd.

Giorgio Orelli, "Carnival at Prato Leventina" and "In the Family Circle," translated by Lynne Lawner, from *Chelsea* (2003). Copyright © 2003 by Lynne Lawner. Reprinted by permission of Georges Borchardt Inc., on behalf of Lynne Lawner. "Where the Children Kill," translated by Lawrence Venuti.

Aldo Palazzeschi, "Who Am I?," translated by Michael Palma. Excerpt from "So Let Me Have My Fun," translated by Felix Stefanile, from *The Blue Moustache: Some Futurist Poets* (The Elizabeth Press, 1980). Reprinted with the permission of the Estate of Felix Stefanile. "November," translated by Frederick Mortimer Clapp, from from *Voices: A Quarterly of Poetry* (Winter 1947). Reprinted by permission.

Giovanni Pascoli, "Oenotrus," translated by A. E. Stallings. "November," from *Able Muse* (Winter 2008), "Back Then!," and "Night Blooming Jasmine" from *Unsplendid 3.3: A Special Translation Issue* (Winter 2011), translated by Geoffrey Brock. "Last Dream," translated by Geoffrey Brock, from *Poetry* (December 2010). "In the Fog," translated by Geoffrey Brock, from *Poetry* (April 2006). "Wisdom" from *Italian Landscape Poems*, translated by Alistair Elliot (Northumberland, U.K.: Bloodaxe Books, 1993). Copyright © 1993 by Alistair Elliott. Excerpt from "The Kite," translated by Seamus Heaney. "Mist," translated by E. J. Scovell, from *Collected Poems*. Reprinted with the permission of Carcanet Press, Ltd.

Pier Paolo Pasolini, nos. I ["It's not May that brings this impure air"] and IV ["The scandal of self-contradiction —of being"] from "Gramsci's Ashes," translated by Stephen Sartarelli, from *Selected Poems of Pier Paolo Pasolini* (University of Chicago, 2012). "The Lament of the Excavator," "Toward the Caracalla Baths," and "I Too Am" from *Roman Poems*, translated by Lawrence Ferlinghetti and Francesca Valente. Copyright © 2001 by Lawrence Ferlinghetti and Francesca Valente. Reprinted with the permission of City Lights Books. "The Day of My Death," translated by Mary di Michele, from *The Flower of Youth: Pier Paolo Pasolini Poems* (ECW Press, 2011).

Cesare Pavese, "Grappa in September," "Creation," and ["Death will come and will have your eyes"] from *Disaffections: Complete Poems 1930–1950*, translated by Geoffrey Brock. Copyright © 2002 by Geoffrey Brock. Reprinted with the permission of the translator and The Permissions Company, Inc., on behalf of Copper Canyon Press, www.coppercanyonpress.com. "Discipline" and "Tolerance," from *Hard Labor*, translated by William Arrowsmith. Copyright 1943 by Guilio Einaudi Editore, Turin. Translation copyright © 1976 by William Arrowsmith. Used by permission of Viking Penguin, a division of Penguin Group (USA) Inc. No. 4 ["Your face sculpted from stone"] from "Earth and Death," translated by Alan Williamson, from *American Poetry Review* (September/October 1997). No. 5 ["You do not know the hills"] from "Earth and Death," translated by Charles Wright.

Sandro Penna, ["Life . . . is remembering a sad"], ["If a boy sleeping behind"], "Evening in the Park," ["The river's deserted. And you know"], and ["The train will be at least an hour late"], translated by W. S. Di Piero, from *This Strange Joy: Selected Poems of Sandro Penna* (Columbus: The Ohio State University Press, 1982). "The Swimmer," translated by William Jay Smith, from *Poetry* (October/November 1989). "Interior," ["It's good to find yourself"], ["The small Venetian square"], and ["Evening again, and every sleepy youngster"], translated by Geoffrey Brock. ["The sky is empty. But in the black eyes"], translated by Moira Egan and Damiano Abeni. ["Graveyard lights, don't tell me"] and ["I'm off to the river on a horse"], translated by Blake Robinson, from *Remember Me, God of Love*. Copyright © 1993 by Blake Robinson. Reprinted with the permission of Carcanet Press, Ltd. ["Here is the boy, aquatic and happy"], translated by William Weaver, from *Twentieth-Century Italian Poetry: A Bilingual Anthology*, edited by R. L. Lind (Indianapolis: The Bobbs-Merrill Company, 1974). ["Spare me the air"], translated by George Scrivani, from *Confused Dream* (New York and Madras: Hanuman Books, 1988). ["Are you passing high upon"], translated by Henry Taylor, from *Poems from Italy*, edited by William Jay Smith (New York: Crowell, 1972). Copyright © 1972 by Henry Taylor. "Literature," translated by Adam Gianelli.

Camillo Pennati, "Gull," translated by Ted Hughes from *Selected Translations*. Copyright © 1987 by Ted Hughes. Reprinted by permission of Farrar, Straus and Giroux, LLC, and Faber & Faber Ltd.

Antonio Porta, Sections 1, 3, and 7 from "To Open," and sections 1, 4, and 9 from "Self-Consciousness of a Servant," translated by Paul Vangelisti, from *Invasions & Other Poems*, edited by Paul Vangelisti (San Francisco/Los Angeles: Invisible City Editions, 1986). "Human Relations: XII," translated by Miller Williams, from *Barataria Review* (Spring/Summer 1977). ["I'm not thinking of you . . ."], translated by Anthony Molino.

Antonia Pozzi, "Shyness," translated by Desmond O'Grady, from *Trawling Tradition: Translations 1954–1994* (Salzburg, 1994). "To Trust," translated by Lynne Lawner, from *The Pen-*

guin *Book of Women Poets*, Carol Cosman et al, eds. (Penguin Classics, 1979). Copyright ©
1999 by Lynne Lawner. Reprinted by permission of Georges Borchardt, Inc., on behalf of
Lynne Lawner.

Fabio Pusterla, "Star, Meteor, Some Shooting Thing," translated by Chad Davidson and Marella
Feltrin, from *New European Poets*, Kevin Prufer and Wayne Miller, eds. (St. Paul, Minn.:
Graywolf, 2008). "Canzonetta on the Expanding Universe," translated by Chad Davidson
and Marella Feltrin. "Plundered" from *Poetry* (December 2007) and "Almost an Allegory"
translated by Geoffrey Brock.

Salvatore Quasimodo, "Wind at Tindari," "Sunken Oboe," and "Man of My Time," translated
by Allen Mandelbaum, from *Selected Writings of Salvatore Quasimodo* (New York: Farrar,
Straus and Giroux, 1960). Reprinted by permission of the Estate of Allen Mandelbaum.
"The Land," translated by Peter Russell, from *Adam: International Review* (1961). "Ancient
Winter," translated by Jonathan Galassi. "March Wind," translated by Don Paterson, from
Rain. Copyright © 2009 by Don Paterson. Reprinted by permission of Farrar, Straus and
Giroux, LLC, and Faber & Faber, Ltd. "On the Willow Branches," translated by Rob A.
Mackenzie. Copyright © by Rob A. Mackenzie. "Epitaph for Bice Donetti," translated by
Adam Gianelli. "And Suddenly It's Evening," translated by Charles Guenther. Reprinted
with the permission of Estate of Charles Guenther. "The Agrigentum Road," translated by
Richard Wilbur, from Richard Wilbur, *Collected Poems, 1943–2004*. Copyright © 1961, 2004
by Richard Wilbur. Reprinted by permission of Houghton Mifflin Harcourt Publishing
Company. "The Tall Schooner," translated by Michael Egan. Originally in *Antaeus* 16 (Win-
ter 1975). Reprinted with the permission of the translator's estate and Red Ozier Press.

Giovanni Raboni, "Movie Theater in the Afternoon" and ["There are evenings . . ."]," trans-
lated by Michael Palma, from *Iambs and Trochees* (Spring 2004). "My Daughter's Birthday
1966," translated by David Stivender and J. D. McClatchy, from *Poetry* (October 1989), later
published in *The Vintage Book of Contemporary World Poetry*, edited by J. D. McClatchy
(Vintage, 1996). ["Missing heroes . . ."] and ["Porn flicks bore me . . ."], translated by
Geoffrey Brock.

Clemente Rèbora, "Image Tensed," translated by Geoffrey Brock from *Poetry* (December 2010).

Nelo Risi, "Apple Trees Apple Trees Apple Trees" from *The New Italian Poetry: 1945 to the Pres-
ent*, edited and translated by Lawrence R. Smith (Berkeley: University of California Press,
1981). Copyright © 1981 by The Regents of the University of California. "Ambitions," trans-
lated by Michael Palma, from *Gradiva* 23/24 (Spring/Fall 2003). "Heat," translated by Miller
Williams, from *Barataria Review* (Spring/Summer 1977). "Justified Hope," translated by
Vittoria Bradshaw, from *From Pure Silence to Impure Dialogue: A Survey of Postwar Italian
Poetry* (New York: Las Americas, 1971). "The Snow in the Wardrobe," translated by Van K.
Brock.

Amelia Rosselli, "After God's gift . . ." and "For your olive skin," translated by Lucia Re and
Paul Vangelisti, from *War Variations* (Los Angeles: Green Integer, 2005). "Oxygen in my
tents . . . ," translated by Diana Thow. Copyright © Diana Thow. "Snow" from *The New
Italian Poetry: 1945 to the Present*, edited and translated by Lawrence R. Smith (Berkeley:
University of California Press, 1981). Copyright © 1981 by The Regents of the University of
California. "General Strike 1969" and "To change the prose of the world . . . ," translated
by Jennifer Scappettone. Copyright © 2012 by The University of Chicago.

Umberto Saba, "To My Wife" and excerpt from "Three Poems to My Wet Nurse" from *Songbook: Selected Poems from the Canzoniere of Umberto Saba,* translated by Stephen Sartarelli. Copyright © 1998 by Stephen Sartarelli. "The Goat" and "Winter Noon," translated by Geoffrey Brock, from *New England Review* 25 (2004). "A Memory," translated by Geoffrey Brock, from *TriQuarterly* (Fall 2001). "Autobiography: 3," translated by Geoffrey Brock. "Ulysses," "February Evening," "The Broken Pane," and "Love," translated by Geoffrey Brock, from *The New Criterion* 16 (February 1998). "Trieste," translated by Jacqueline Osherow. "Woman," translated by V. Penelope Pelizzon. Excerpt from "Shortcuts" from *The Stories and Recollections of Umberto Saba,* translated by Estelle Gilson (New York: Sheep Meadow Press, 1993). Copyright © 1993 by Estelle Gilson.

Edoardo Sanguineti, nos. 4 ["he slept in you like a dry fibroma, like a thin tapeworm, a dream"] from "Erotopaegina," and 8 ["through Hebecrevon, Lessay, Portbail, St. Sauveur (beneath the rain"] from "Hell's Purgatory," translated by Charles Tomlinson, from *Poetry* (October 1989). Nos. III and XV from *Libretto,* translated by Pádraig J. Daly. Copyright © 1999 by Pádraig J. Daly. Reprinted with the permission of the Dedalus Press. No. 10 ["I'll spare you the put-downs and let-downs (and hassles and wrangles, and"] from "Codicil," translated by Robert Hahn and Michela Martin.

Camillo Sbarbaro, ["Father, even if you were not my own"] and "The Vine," translated by Geoffrey Brock. ["Pierangelo's wish . . ."], translated by Gayle Ridinger, from *Shavings: Selected Prose Poems 1914–1940* (Chelsea Editions, 2005).

Leonardo Sciascia, "The Dead" and "Alive as Never Before," translated by Geoffrey Brock.

Rocco Scotellaro, "To the Carter's Daughter," translated by William Weaver, from *Wake 12* (1953). "Waiting," from *The Dawn Is Always New: Selected Poetry of Rocco Scotellaro* (Princeton, 1980) translated by Ruth Feldman and Brian Swann. "Beggars" and "The Poetry and the Snare," translated by Cid Corman, from *Origin,* 2nd series (October 1962). Reprinted with the permission of Bob Arnold, Literary Executor of the Estate of Cid Corman.

Vittorio Sereni, excerpt from "Algerian Diary," "Saba," and "A Dream" from *The Selected Poetry and Prose of Vittorio Sereni,* edited and translated by Peter Robinson and Marcus Perryman. Copyright © 2006 by The University of Chicago. Reprinted with the permission of The University of Chicago Press. "Passing Through" and "Lines" translated by W. S. Di Piero. "It Must Be the Boredom" from *Variable Star,* translated by Luigi Bonaffini (Toronto: Guernica Editions, 1999). Copyright © 1999 by Luigi Bonaffini. "Second Fear," translated by William Jay Smith, from *Poetry* (October 1989).

Leonardo Sinisgalli, "The Friend I Betrayed" from *I Saw the Muses,* translated by Rina Ferrarelli (Toronto: Guernica Editions, 1997). Copyright © 1997 by Rina Ferrarelli. "Elegy," translated by Geoffrey Brock. "Via Velasca" and "Holy Saturday in Manfredonia," translated by W. S. Di Piero, from *Night of Shooting Stars* (Tavern Books, 2011). "Old Tears," translated by William Weaver, from *Modern European Poetry,* edited by Willis Barnstone (New York: Bantam Books, 1966). "I Saw the Muses," translated by Sonia Raiziss and Alfredo de Palchi, from *The Atlantic* (December 1958).

Ardengo Soffici, "Rainbow," translated by Olivia Sears. "Crossroads," translated by Geoffrey Brock. "Field Hospital 026," translated by Laurie Duggan, from Laurie Duggan, *Mangroves* (Queensland: University of Queensland Press, 2003). Copyright © 2003 by Laurie Duggan.

Maria Luisa Spaziani, "March in Rue Mouffetard," translated by Peter Robinson, from *Kawauchi Review* (March 2004). "The Convent in '45" translated by Beverly Allen, from *New Italian Poets*, Michael Palma and Dana Gioia, eds. (Story Line, 1991). "Paris Sleeps" from *Sentry Towers*, translated by Laura Stortoni (Berkeley, Calif.: Hesperia Press, 1996). Copyright © 1996 by Laura Stortoni. "Ultrasound" from Desmond O'Grady, *Trawling Tradition: Translations 1954–1994*. Copyright © 1994 by Desmond O'Grady. Reprinted with the permission of the translator and the University of Salzburg. ["The garden was thick . . ."], translated by Geoffrey Brock.

Trilussa (Carlo Salustri), "Ventriloquist," "The Cat and the Dog," and "Happiness" from *Tales of Trilussa*, translated by John DuVal. Copyright © 1990 by John DuVal. Reprinted with the permission of the translator and The Permissions Company, Inc., on behalf of University of Arkansas Press, www.uapress.com. "Lying in the Shade," translated by Peter Davison, from *The Poems of Peter Davison, 1957–1995*. Copyright © 1995 by Peter Davison. Used by permission of Alfred A. Knopf, a division of Random House, Inc.

Giuseppe Ungaretti, "Eternal," translated by Patrick Creagh, from *Selected Poems of Giuseppe Ungaretti* (London: Penguin, 1972). Translation copyright © 1972 by Patrick Creagh. Used by permission of Arnoldo Mondadori Editore. "Agony," translated by Kevin Hart, from *The Buried Harbor: Selected Poems of Giuseppe Ungaretti* (Canberra: Leros Press, 1990). "In Memory" and "Soldiers," translated by Andrew Wylie. "Vigil," translated by Sarah Arvio. "Morning," translated by Allen Mandelbaum, from *Selected Poems of Giuseppe Ungaretti* (Ithaca, N.Y.: Cornell University Press, 1975). Reprinted by permission of the Estate of Allen Mandelbaum. "Another Night," translated by Peter Jay. from *Agenda* (Spring 1970). "Joy of Shipwreck," translated by Cid Corman, from *Origin*, 5th series (Fall 1985). Reprinted with the permission of Bob Arnold, Literary Executor for the Estate of Cid Corman. "Vanity," translated by Charles Tomlinson from *Translations*. Reprinted with the permission of Oxford University Press, Ltd. Excerpt from "Pity," translated by Anthony Hecht, from *Translations by American Poets*, edited by Jean Garrigue (Ohio University Press, 1970). Reprinted with the permission of Helen Hecht. "Meditations on Death: I," translated by Stanley Kunitz, from *The Collected Poems*. Copyright © 2000 by Stanley Kunitz. Used by the permission of W. W. Norton & Company, Inc. "Weightless Now" from Richard Wilbur, *The Whale and Other Uncollected Translations*. Copyright © 1982 by Richard Wilbur. Reprinted with the permission of The Permissions Company, Inc., on behalf of BOA Editions, Ltd., www.boaeditions.org. "No More Yelling," translated by Allen Ginsberg, from *Agenda* 8, no. 2 (Spring 1970): 36. Copyright © 1970. Reprinted with the permission of the Allen Ginsberg Estate. "Variations on Nothing" from *Selected Poems*, translated by Andrew Frisardi. Copyright © 2009 by Andrew Frisardi. Reprinted by permission of Farrar, Straus and Giroux, LLC.

Patrizia Valduga, ["Let them tell the one . . ."] and ["You see, kind lord, the state . . .]," translated by Christopher Whyte and Marco Fazzini, from *Lines Review* 130 (September 1994). Nos. 8, 17, 45, 47, and 71 from "One Hundred Quatrains" and nos. 107 and 122 from "Quatrains: Second Hundred," translated by Geoffrey Brock, from *Poetry* (December 2007). No. 100 from "One Hundred Quatrains," translated by Geoffrey Brock. "My Father," translated by Geoffrey Brock, from *Unsplendid 3.3: A Special Translation Issue* (December 2011).